8/06 m

WASHOE COUNTY LIBRARY

3 1235 00603 4529

S0-ATD-271

DODGE
COLT
1971-1979 REAR WHEEL DRIVE
SHOP MANUAL

ALAN AHLSTRAND
Editor

JEFF ROBINSON
Publisher

WASHOE COUNTY LIBRARY
RENO, NEVADA

629.2872
DG64
1980

CLYMER PUBLICATIONS

World's largest publisher of books
devoted exclusively to automobiles and motorcycles

12860 MUSCATINE STREET • P.O. BOX 4520 • ARLETA, CALIFORNIA 91333-4520

Copyright ©1976, 1977, 1980 Clymer Publications

All rights reserved. No part of this publication may be reproduced, stored in a retrieval system or transmitted, in any form or by any means, electronic, mechanical, photocopying, recording or otherwise, without the written permission of Clymer Publications.

FIRST EDITION
First Printing January, 1976
Second Printing September, 1976

SECOND EDITION
Revised to include 1975-1977 models
First Printing June, 1977
Second Printing November, 1977
Third Printing July, 1978
Fourth Printing November, 1979

THIRD EDITION
Revised to include 1978-1979 models
First Printing September, 1980
Second Printing October, 1981
Third Printing Septmber, 1982
Fourth Printing October, 1983
Fifth Printing May, 1985
Sixth Printing June, 1986

Printed in U.S.A.

ISBN: 0-89287-162-8

3 1235 00603 4529   RN

CONTENTS

QUICK REFERENCE DATA

TIMING MARKS

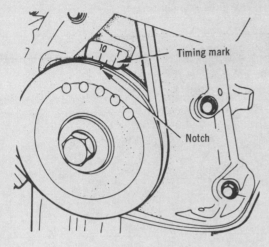

1971-1974 1600cc

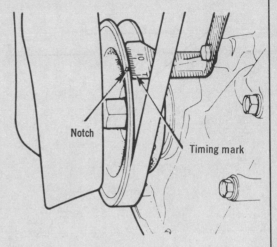

1971-1974 2000cc

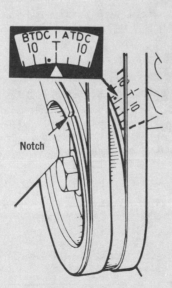

1975-1977 1600cc

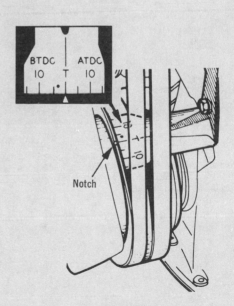

1975-1977 2000cc

Table 2   TUNE-UP SPECIFICATIONS

Ignition timing

Models through 1974	
1600cc	TDC @ 850 rpm (manual transmission & automatic transmission w/EGR)
2000cc	3° BTDC @ 850 rpm
1975 models	
1600cc and 2000cc	5° ATDC @ 950 rpm (manual transmission); 5° ATDC @ 850 rpm (automatic transmission)
1976 models	
1600cc	TDC @ 950 rpm (manual transmission); TDC @ 850 rpm (automatic transmission)
2000cc	3° BTDC @ 950 rpm (manual transmission); 3° BTDC @ 850 rpm (automatic transmission)
1977 models	
1600cc	5° BTDC @ 850 rpm (U.S. except California); 5° BTDC @ 950 rpm (California manual transmission models)
2000cc	5° BTDC @ 950 rpm; 5° BTDC @ 850 (49-state automatic transmission models)
1978 49-state models	
1600cc	5° BTDC ± 1° @ 650 ± 50 rpm (manual transmission except high altitude)
1600cc	5° BTDC ± 1° @ 700 ± 50 rpm (automatic transmission)
1600cc	10° BTDC ± 1° @ 650 ± 50 rpm (manual transmission, high altitude)
2000cc	5° BTDC ± 1° @ 650 ± 50 rpm (manual transmission); 5° BTDC ± 1° @ 700 ± 50 rpm (automatic transmission)
2600cc	7° BTDC ± 1° @ 850 ± 50 rpm (manual transmission); 7° BTDC ± 1° @ 850 ± 50 rpm (automatic transmission)
1978 California models	
1600cc	5° BTDC ± 1° @ 650 ± 50 rpm (manual transmission); 700 ± 50 rpm (automatic transmission)
2000cc	5° BTDC ± 1° @ 650 ± 50 rpm (manual transmission); 700 ± 50 rpm (automatic transmission)
2600cc	7° BTDC ± 1° @ 700 ± 50 rpm (manual transsision); 750 ± 50 rpm (automatic transmission)
1978 Canada models	
1600cc and 2000cc	5° BTDC ± 1° @ 850 ± 50 rpm (all models)
2600cc	7° BTDC ± 1° @ 850 ± 50 rpm (all models)
1979 U.S.A. models	
1600cc	5° BTDC ± 1° @ 650 ± 50 rpm (manual transmission); 700 ± 50 rpm (automatic transmission)
2600cc	7° BTDC ± 1° @ 850 ± 50 rpm (all models)
1979 Canada models	
1600cc and 2000cc	5° BTDC ± 1° @ 850 ± 50 rpm
2600cc	7° BTDC ± 1° @ 850 ± 50 rpm

(continued)

Valve clearance

Intake	0.006 in. (0.15 mm). hot engine; 0.003 in. (0.07 mm). cold engine
Exhaust	0.010 in. (0.25 mm). hot engine; 0.007 in. (0.17 mm). cold engine

Spark plug gap

Models through 1974	0.028-0.031 in. (0.71-0.78 mm)
1978-1979 U.S.A. models	0.039-0.043 in. (1.0-1.1 mm)
1978-1979 Canada models	0.028-0.031 in. (0.7-0.8 mm)

Distributor contact point gap   0.018-0.021 in. (0.45-0.55 mm)

Dwell

Models through 1977	49-55°
1978-1979 models	52° ± 3°

Firing order   1-3-4-2 (No. 1 at front of engine)

RECOMMENDED LUBRICANTS

Engine oil	
Type	Use only engine oil conforming to API classification "For Service SE" (Service Class E)
Viscosity	Above 32°F, 10W-40, 20W-40, 10W 30; as low as —10°F, 10W-30, 10W-40; consistently below 10°F, 5W-20, 5W-30
Manual transmission	Multipurpose gear oil conforming to API GL-5 (SAE 80)
Automatic transmission	Dexron ATF
Rear axle	Multipurpose gear oil conforming to API GL-5 (SAE 85W-90, SAE 90, above 10°F; SAE 80W-85, SAE 80, as low as —30°F; SAE 75W-85W, SAE 75, below —30°F
Steering gear	Multipurpose gear oil conforming to API GL-5
Brake fluid	Brake fluid conforming to DOT 3
Front wheel bearings, transmission control linkage, parking brake cable linkage, hood latch, door latches, and seat adjuster	Multipurpose grease NLG1, Grade No. 2 E.P.
Clutch cable, deck lid catch, door hinges, deck lid ringes, and hood hinges	Engine oil conforming to API classification "For Service SE" (Service Class E)

TIRE PRESSURE

	psi
Front	24
Rear	30

CLUTCH

Distance between pedal and toe board (top of silencer)	6.5-6.7 in.
Difference in height between clutch and brake pedals	0.4 in. or less
Pedal stroke	5.1 in. or less

BRAKES

Distance from top of pedal to toe board (top of silencer)	6.9-7.1 in. 6.5-6.7 in. (models with power brakes)
Brake pedal play	0.4-0.6 in.
Distance from brake pedal to toe board	1.6 in. or more
Parking brake extension lever-to-stopper clearance	0-0.04 in.
Parking brake lever free stroke	8-12 notches before brake is fully applied

TIGHTENING TORQUES

Description	1600cc (Ft.-lb.)	2000/2600cc (Ft.-lb.)
Front insulator to crossmember	22-29	22-29
Front insulator to engine bracket	10-14	10-14
Rear insulator to engine support bracket	4-7	10-14
Rear insulator to transmission	14-17	14-17
Engine support bracket to car body	7	7
Cylinder block to engine bracket	43.5-50.5	29-36
Cylinder head bolts (cold engine)	51-54	65-72
Cylinder head bolts (hot engine)	58-61	72-79
Camshaft bearing cap	14-15	13-14
Camshaft sprocket	43.5-57.5	36.5-43
Spark plugs	14.5-21.5	18-21.5
Rocker cover	4-5	4-5
Heater joint	14.5-28.5	14.5-28.5
Main bearing caps	36.5-39.5	54.5-61
Connecting rod caps	23.5-25	33-34.5
Flywheel (manual transmission)	94.5-101	94.5-101
Drive plate (automatic transmission)	83.5-90	83.5-90
Crank pulley	7.5-8.5	80-94
Crankshaft sprocket bolt	43.5-50.5	—
Oil pump sprocket	25-28.5	22-28.5
Timing belt tensioner nut	16-21.5	—
Oil pan	4.5-5.5	4.5-5.5
Oil pan drain plug	43.5-57.5	43.5-57.5
Oil filter	8-9	8-9
Oil pump cover	11-13	—
Oil pump	—	6-7
Intake/exhaust manifold	11-14	11-14
Front exhaust pipe-to-exhaust manifold connecting bolts	11-18	11-18
Counterbalance chamber cover	—	3-4
Counterbalance shaft bolt	—	22-28.5
Oil pressure switch and gauge	11-15.5	11-15.5
Front case	11-13	—
Jet valve	13.5-15.5	13.5-15.5
Oil screen	13.5-18	—

—NOTES—

DODGE
COLT
1971-1979 REAR WHEEL DRIVE
SHOP MANUAL

INTRODUCTION

This detailed, comprehensive manual covers 1971-1979 Dodge Colt automobiles. The expert text gives complete information on maintenance, repair, and overhaul. Hundreds of photos and drawings guide you through every step. The book includes all you need to know to keep your car running right.

Where repairs are practical for the owner/mechanic, complete procedures are given. Equally important, difficult jobs are pointed out. Such operations are usually more economically performed by a dealer or independent garage.

A shop manual is a reference. You want to be able to find information fast. As in all Clymer books, this one is designed with this in mind. All chapters are thumb tabbed. Important items are indexed at the rear of the book. Finally, all the most frequently used specifications and capacities are summarized on the *Quick Reference* pages at the front of the book.

Keep the book handy. Carry it in your glove box. It will help you to better understand your car, lower repair and maintenance costs, and generally improve your satisfaction with your vehicle.

CHAPTER ONE

GENERAL INFORMATION

The troubleshooting, tune-up, maintenance, and step-by-step repair procedures in this book are written for the owner and home mechanic. The text is accompanied by useful photos and diagrams to make the job as clear and correct as possible.

Troubleshooting, tune-up, maintenance, and repair are not difficult if you know what tools and equipment to use and what to do. Anyone not afraid to get their hands dirty, of average intelligence, and with some mechanical ability can perform most of the procedures in this book.

In some cases, a repair job may require tools or skills not reasonably expected of the home mechanic. These procedures are noted in each chapter and it is recommended that you take the job to your dealer, a competent mechanic, or machine shop.

MANUAL ORGANIZATION

This chapter provides general information and safety and service hints. Also included are lists of recommended shop and emergency tools as well as a brief description of troubleshooting and tune-up equipment.

Chapter Two provides methods and suggestions for quick and accurate diagnosis and repair of problems. Troubleshooting procedures discuss typical symptoms and logical methods to pinpoint the trouble.

Chapter Three explains all periodic lubrication and routine maintenance necessary to keep your vehicle running well. Chapter Three also includes recommended tune-up procedures, eliminating the need to constantly consult chapters on the various subassemblies.

Subsequent chapters cover specific systems such as the engine, transmission, and electrical systems. Each of these chapters provides disassembly, repair, and assembly procedures in a simple step-by-step format. If a repair requires special skills or tools, or is otherwise impractical for the home mechanic, it is so indicated. In these cases it is usually faster and less expensive to have the repairs made by a dealer or competent repair shop. Necessary specifications concerning a particular system are included at the end of the appropriate chapter.

When special tools are required to perform a procedure included in this manual, the tool is illustrated either in actual use or alone. It may be possible to rent or borrow these tools. The inventive mechanic may also be able to find a suitable substitute in his tool box, or to fabricate one.

The terms NOTE, CAUTION, and WARNING have specific meanings in this manual. A NOTE provides additional or explanatory information. A CAUTION is used to emphasize areas where equipment damage could result if proper precautions are not taken. A WARNING is used to stress those areas where personal injury or death could result from negligence, in addition to possible mechanical damage.

SERVICE HINTS

Observing the following practices will save time, effort, and frustration, as well as prevent possible injury.

Throughout this manual keep in mind two conventions. "Front" refers to the front of the vehicle. The front of any component, such as the transmission, is that end which faces toward the front of the vehicle. The "left" and "right" sides of the vehicle refer to the orientation of a person sitting in the vehicle facing forward. For example, the steering wheel is on the left side. These rules are simple, but even experienced mechanics occasionally become disoriented.

Most of the service procedures covered are straightforward and can be performed by anyone reasonably handy with tools. It is suggested, however, that you consider your own capabilities carefully before attempting any operation involving major disassembly of the engine.

Some operations, for example, require the use of a press. It would be wiser to have these performed by a shop equipped for such work, rather than to try to do the job yourself with makeshift equipment. Other procedures require precision measurements. Unless you have the skills and equipment required, it would be better to have a qualified repair shop make the measurements for you.

Repairs go much faster and easier if the parts that will be worked on are clean before you begin. There are special cleaners for washing the engine and related parts. Brush or spray on the cleaning solution, let it stand, then rinse it away with a garden hose. Clean all oily or greasy parts with cleaning solvent as you remove them.

WARNING
Never use gasoline as a cleaning agent. It presents an extreme fire hazard. Be sure to work in a well-ventilated area when using cleaning solvent. Keep a fire extinguisher, rated for gasoline fires, handy in any case.

Much of the labor charge for repairs made by dealers is for the removal and disassembly of other parts to reach the defective unit. It is frequently possible to perform the preliminary operations yourself and then take the defective unit in to the dealer for repair, at considerable savings.

Once you have decided to tackle the job yourself, make sure you locate the appropriate section in this manual, and read it entirely. Study the illustrations and text until you have a good idea of what is involved in completing the job satisfactorily. If special tools are required, make arrangements to get them before you start. Also, purchase any known defective parts prior to starting on the procedure. It is frustrating and time-consuming to get partially into a job and then be unable to complete it.

Simple wiring checks can be easily made at home, but knowledge of electronics is almost a necessity for performing tests with complicated electronic testing gear.

During disassembly of parts keep a few general cautions in mind. Force is rarely needed to get things apart. If parts are a tight fit, like a bearing in a case, there is usually a tool designed to separate them. Never use a screwdriver to pry apart parts with machined surfaces such as cylinder head and valve cover. You will mar the surfaces and end up with leaks.

Make diagrams wherever similar-appearing parts are found. You may think you can remember where everything came from — but mistakes are costly. There is also the possibility you may get sidetracked and not return to work for days or even weeks — in which interval, carefully laid out parts may have become disturbed.

Tag all similar internal parts for location, and mark all mating parts for position. Record number and thickness of any shims as they are removed. Small parts such as bolts can be identified by placing them in plastic sandwich bags that are sealed and labeled with masking tape.

Wiring should be tagged with masking tape and marked as each wire is removed. Again, do not rely on memory alone.

When working under the vehicle, do not trust a hydraulic or mechanical jack to hold the vehicle up by itself. Always use jackstands. See **Figure 1**.

Disconnect battery ground cable before working near electrical connections and before disconnecting wires. Never run the engine with the battery disconnected; the alternator could be seriously damaged.

Protect finished surfaces from physical damage or corrosion. Keep gasoline and brake fluid off painted surfaces.

Frozen or very tight bolts and screws can often be loosened by soaking with penetrating oil like Liquid Wrench or WD-40, then sharply striking the bolt head a few times with a hammer and punch (or screwdriver for screws). Avoid heat unless absolutely necessary, since it may melt, warp, or remove the temper from many parts.

Avoid flames or sparks when working near a charging battery or flammable liquids, such as brake fluid or gasoline.

No parts, except those assembled with a press fit, require unusual force during assembly. If a part is hard to remove or install, find out why before proceeding.

Cover all openings after removing parts to keep dirt, small tools, etc., from falling in.

When assembling two parts, start all fasteners, then tighten evenly.

The clutch plate, wiring connections, brake shoes, drums, pads, and discs should be kept clean and free of grease and oil.

When assembling parts, be sure all shims and washers are replaced exactly as they came out.

Whenever a rotating part butts against a stationary part, look for a shim or washer. Use new gaskets if there is any doubt about the condition of old ones. Generally, you should apply gasket cement to one mating surface only, so the parts may be easily disassembled in the future. A thin coat of oil on gaskets helps them seal effectively.

Heavy grease can be used to hold small parts in place if they tend to fall out during assembly. However, keep grease and oil away from electrical, clutch, and brake components.

High spots may be sanded off a piston with sandpaper, but emery cloth and oil do a much more professional job.

Carburetors are best cleaned by disassembling them and soaking the parts in a commercial carburetor cleaner. Never soak gaskets and rubber parts in these cleaners. Never use wire to clean out jets and air passages; they are easily damaged. Use compressed air to blow out the carburetor, but only if the float has been removed first.

Take your time and do the job right. Do not forget that a newly rebuilt engine must be broken in the same as a new one. Refer to your owner's manual for the proper break-in procedures.

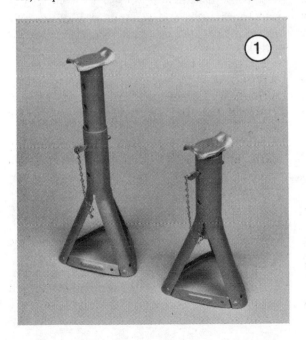

SAFETY FIRST

Professional mechanics can work for years and never sustain a serious injury. If you observe a few rules of common sense and safety, you can enjoy many safe hours servicing your vehicle. You could hurt yourself or damage the vehicle if you ignore these rules.

1. Never use gasoline as a cleaning solvent.

2. Never smoke or use a torch in the vicinity of flammable liquids such as cleaning solvent in open containers.

3. Never smoke or use a torch in an area where batteries are being charged. Highly explosive hydrogen gas is formed during the charging process.

4. Use the proper sized wrenches to avoid damage to nuts and injury to yourself.

5. When loosening a tight or stuck nut, be guided by what would happen if the wrench should slip. Protect yourself accordingly.

6. Keep your work area clean and uncluttered.

7. Wear safety goggles during all operations involving drilling, grinding, or use of a cold chisel.

8. Never use worn tools.

9. Keep a fire extinguisher handy and be sure it is rated for gasoline (Class B) and electrical (Class C) fires.

EXPENDABLE SUPPLIES

Certain expendable supplies are necessary. These include grease, oil, gasket cement, wiping rags, cleaning solvent, and distilled water.

Also, special locking compounds, silicone lubricants, and engine cleaners may be useful. Cleaning solvent is available at most service stations and distilled water for the battery is available at most supermarkets.

SHOP TOOLS

For proper servicing, you will need an assortment of ordinary hand tools (**Figure 2**).

As a minimum, these include:

a. Combination wrenches
b. Sockets
c. Plastic mallet
d. Small hammer
e. Snap ring pliers
f. Gas pliers
g. Phillips screwdrivers
h. Slot (common) screwdrivers
i. Feeler gauges
j. Spark plug gauge
k. Spark plug wrench

Special tools necessary are shown in the chapters covering the particular repair in which they are used.

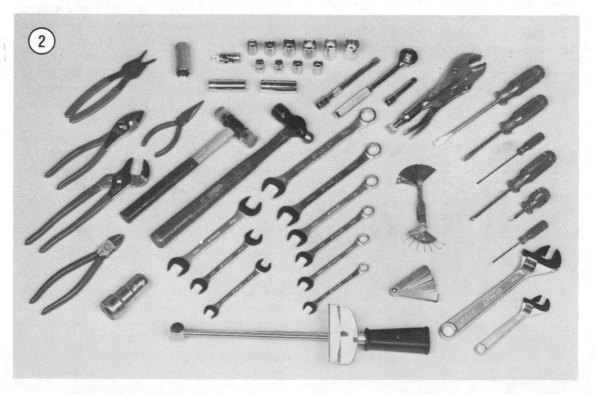

(2)

Engine tune-up and troubleshooting procedures require other special tools and equipment. These are described in detail in the following sections.

EMERGENCY TOOL KIT

A small emergency tool kit kept in the trunk is handy for road emergencies which otherwise could leave you stranded. The tools listed below and shown in **Figure 3** will let you handle most roadside repairs.

   a. Combination wrenches

   b. Crescent (adjustable) wrench

   c. Screwdrivers — common and Phillips

   d. Pliers — conventional (gas) and needle nose

   e. Vise Grips

   f. Hammer — plastic and metal

   g. Small container of waterless hand cleaner

   h. Rags for clean up

   i. Silver waterproof sealing tape (duct tape)

   j. Flashlight

   k. Emergency road flares — at least four

   l. Spare drive belts (water pump, alternator, etc.)

TROUBLESHOOTING AND TUNE-UP EQUIPMENT

Voltmeter, Ohmmeter, and Ammeter

For testing the ignition or electrical system, a good voltmeter is required. For automotive use, an instrument covering 0-20 volts is satisfac-

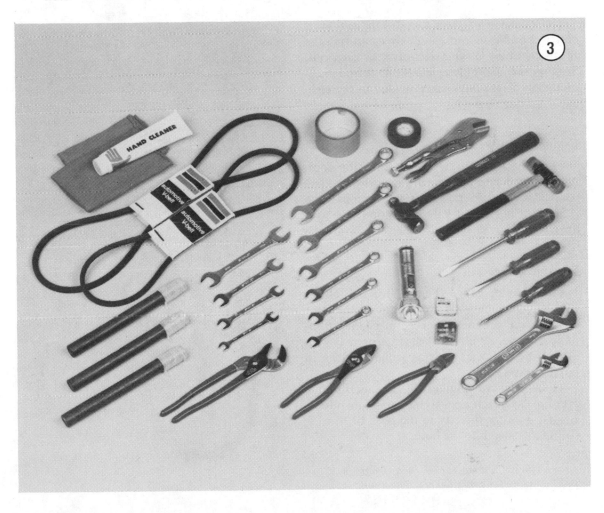

tory. One which also has a 0-2 volt scale is necessary for testing relays, points, or individual contacts where voltage drops are much smaller. Accuracy should be ± ½ volt.

An ohmmeter measures electrical resistance. This instrument is useful for checking continuity (open and short circuits), and testing fuses and lights.

The ammeter measures electrical current. Ammeters for automotive use should cover 0-50 amperes and 0-250 amperes. These are useful for checking battery charging and starting current.

Several inexpensive vom's (volt-ohm-milli-ammeter) combine all three instruments into one which fits easily in any tool box. See **Figure 4**. However, the ammeter ranges are usually too small for automotive work.

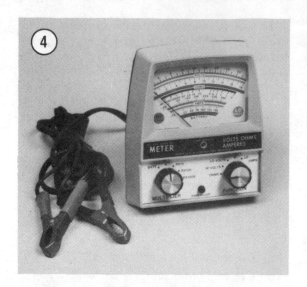

Hydrometer

The hydrometer gives a useful indication of battery condition and charge by measuring the specific gravity of the electrolyte in each cell. See **Figure 5**. Complete details on use and interpretation of readings are provided in the electrical chapter.

Compression Tester

The compression tester measures the compression pressure built up in each cylinder. The results, when properly interpreted, can indicate general cylinder and valve condition. See **Figure 6**.

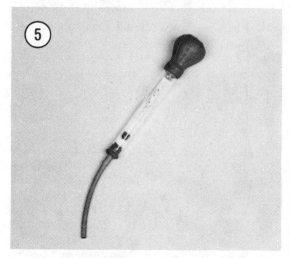

Vacuum Gauge

The vacuum gauge (**Figure 7**) is one of the easiest instruments to use, but one of the most difficult for the inexperienced mechanic to interpret. The results, when interpreted with other findings, can provide valuable clues to possible trouble.

To use the vacuum gauge, connect it to a vacuum hose that goes to the intake manifold. Attach it either directly to the hose or to a T-fitting installed into the hose.

NOTE: *Subtract one inch from the reading for every 1,000 ft. elevation.*

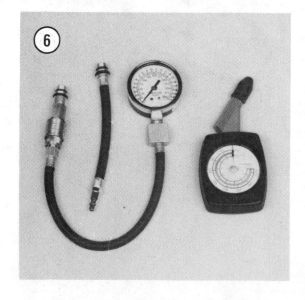

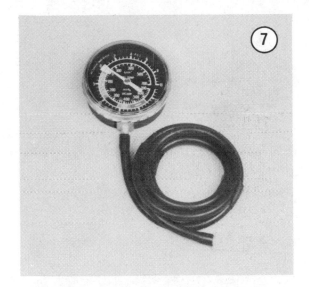

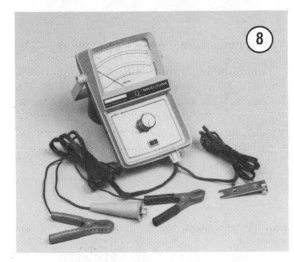

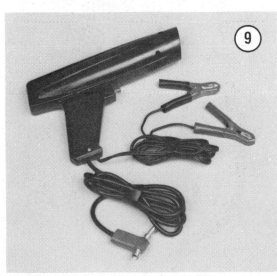

Fuel Pressure Gauge

This instrument is invaluable for evaluating fuel pump performance. Fuel system trouble-shooting procedures in this manual use a fuel pressure gauge. Usually a vacuum gauge and fuel pressure gauge are combined.

Dwell Meter (Contact Breaker Point Ignition Only)

A dwell meter measures the distance in degrees of cam rotation that the breaker points remain closed while the engine is running. Since this angle is determined by breaker point gap, dwell angle is an accurate indication of breaker point gap.

Many tachometers intended for tuning and testing incorporate a dwell meter as well. See **Figure 8**. Follow the manufacturer's instructions to measure dwell.

Tachometer

A tachometer is necessary for tuning. See **Figure 8**. Ignition timing and carburetor adjustments must be performed at the specified idle speed. The best instrument for this purpose is one with a low range of 0-1,000 or 0-2,000 rpm for setting idle, and a high range of 0-4,000 or more for setting ignition timing at 3,000 rpm. Extended range (0-6,000 or 0-8,000 rpm) instruments lack accuracy at lower speeds. The instrument should be capable of detecting changes of 25 rpm on the low range.

Strobe Timing Light

This instrument is necessary for tuning, as it permits very accurate ignition timing. The light flashes at precisely the same instant that No. 1 cylinder fires, at which time the timing marks on the engine should align. Refer to Chapter Three for exact location of the timing marks for your engine.

Suitable lights range from inexpensive neon bulb types ($2-3) to powerful xenon strobe lights ($20-40). See **Figure 9**. Neon timing lights are difficult to see and must be used in dimly lit areas. Xenon strobe timing lights can be used outside in bright sunlight. Both types work on this vehicle; use according to the manufacturer's instructions.

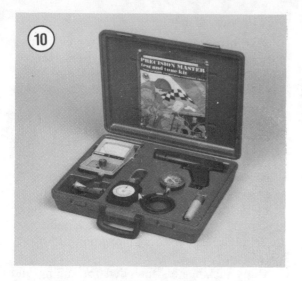

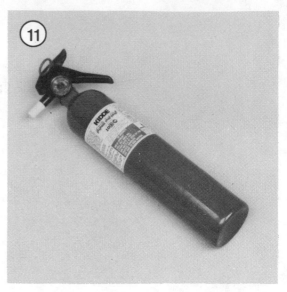

Tune-up Kits

Many manufacturer's offer kits that combine several useful instruments. Some come in a convenient carry case and are usally less expensive than purchasing one instrument at a time. **Figure 10** shows one of the kits that is available. The prices vary with the number of instruments included in the kit.

Fire Extinguisher

A fire extinguisher is a necessity when working on a vehicle. It should be rated for both *Class B* (flammable liquids—gasoline, oil, paint, etc.) and *Class C* (electrical—wiring, etc.) type fires. It should always be kept within reach. See **Figure 11**.

TROUBLESHOOTING

Troubleshooting can be a relatively simple matter if it is done logically. The first step in any troubleshooting procedure must be defining the symptoms as closely as possible. Subsequent steps involve testing and analyzing areas which could cause the symptoms. A haphazard approach may eventually find the trouble, but in terms of wasted time and unnecessary parts replacement, it can be very costly.

The troubleshooting procedures in this chapter analyze typical symptoms and show logical methods of isolation. These are not the only methods. There may be several approaches to a problem, but all methods must have one thing in common — a logical, systematic approach.

STARTING SYSTEM

The starting system consists of the starter motor and the starter solenoid. The ignition key controls the starter solenoid, which mechanically engages the starter with the engine flywheel, and supplies electrical current to turn the starter motor.

Starting system troubles are relatively easy to find. In most cases, the trouble is a loose or dirty electrical connection. **Figures 1 and 2** provide routines for finding the trouble.

CHARGING SYSTEM

The charging system consists of the alternator (or generator on older vehicles), voltage regulator, and battery. A drive belt driven by the engine crankshaft turns the alternator which produces electrical energy to charge the battery. As engine speed varies, the voltage from the alternator varies. A voltage regulator controls the charging current to the battery and maintains the voltage to the vehicle's electrical system at safe levels. A warning light or gauge on the instrument panel signals the driver when charging is not taking place. Refer to **Figure 3** for a typical charging system.

Complete troubleshooting of the charging system requires test equipment and skills which the average home mechanic does not possess. However, there are a few tests which can be done to pinpoint most troubles.

Charging system trouble may stem from a defective alternator (or generator), voltage regulator, battery, or drive belt. It may also be caused by something as simple as incorrect drive belt tension. The following are symptoms of typical problems you may encounter.

1. *Battery dies frequently, even though the warning lamp indicates no discharge* — This can be caused by a drive belt that is slightly too

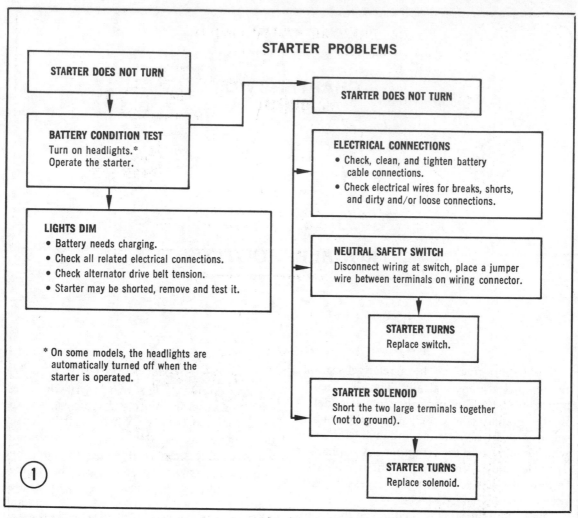

STARTER PROBLEMS

STARTER DOES NOT TURN

BATTERY CONDITION TEST
Turn on headlights.*
Operate the starter.

LIGHTS DIM
• Battery needs charging.
• Check all related electrical connections.
• Check alternator drive belt tension.
• Starter may be shorted, remove and test it.

* On some models, the headlights are
automatically turned off when the
starter is operated.

STARTER DOES NOT TURN

ELECTRICAL CONNECTIONS
• Check, clean, and tighten battery
  cable connections.
• Check electrical wires for breaks, shorts,
  and dirty and/or loose connections.

NEUTRAL SAFETY SWITCH
Disconnect wiring at switch, place a jumper
wire between terminals on wiring connector.

STARTER TURNS
Replace switch.

STARTER SOLENOID
Short the two large terminals together
(not to ground).

STARTER TURNS
Replace solenoid.

①

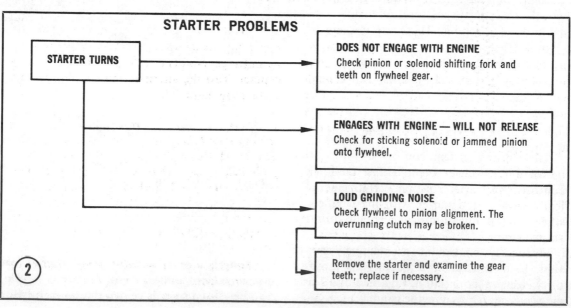

STARTER PROBLEMS

STARTER TURNS

DOES NOT ENGAGE WITH ENGINE
Check pinion or solenoid shifting fork and
teeth on flywheel gear.

ENGAGES WITH ENGINE — WILL NOT RELEASE
Check for sticking solenoid or jammed pinion
onto flywheel.

LOUD GRINDING NOISE
Check flywheel to pinion alignment. The
overrunning clutch may be broken.

Remove the starter and examine the gear
teeth; replace if necessary.

②

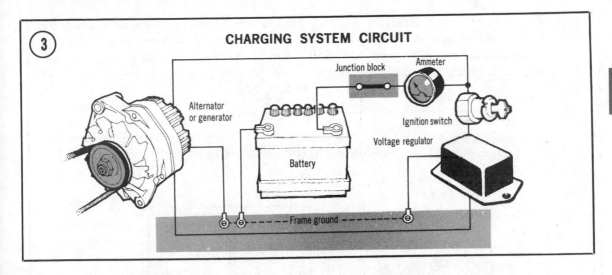

③ **CHARGING SYSTEM CIRCUIT**

Junction block

Ammeter

Alternator or generator

Ignition switch

Voltage regulator

Battery

Frame ground

2

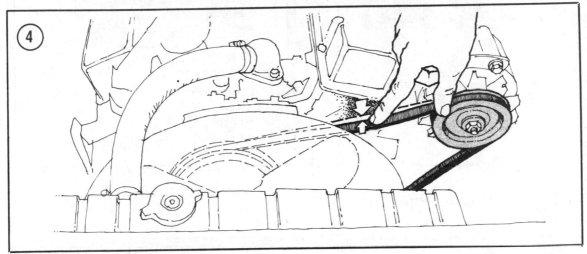

④

loose. Grasp the alternator (or generator) pulley and try to turn it. If the pulley can be turned without moving the belt, the drive belt is too loose. As a rule, keep the belt tight enough that it can be deflected about ½ in. under moderate thumb pressure between the pulleys (**Figure 4**). The battery may also be at fault; test the battery condition.

2. *Charging system warning lamp does not come on when ignition switch is turned on* — This may indicate a defective ignition switch, battery, voltage regulator, or lamp. First try to start the vehicle. If it doesn't start, check the ignition switch and battery. If the car starts, remove the warning lamp; test it for continuity with an ohmmeter or substitute a new lamp. If the lamp is good, locate the voltage regulator

and make sure it is properly grounded (try tightening the mounting screws). Also the alternator (or generator) brushes may not be making contact. Test the alternator (or generator) and voltage regulator.

3. *Alternator (or generator) warning lamp comes on and stays on* — This usually indicates that no charging is taking place. First check drive belt tension (**Figure 4**). Then check battery condition, and check all wiring connections in the charging system. If this does not locate the trouble, check the alternator (or generator) and voltage regulator.

4. *Charging system warning lamp flashes on and off intermittently* — This usually indicates the charging system is working intermittently.

Check the drive belt tension (**Figure 4**), and check all electrical connections in the charging system. Check the alternator (or generator). *On generators only*, check the condition of the commutator.

5. *Battery requires frequent additions of water, or lamps require frequent replacement* — The alternator (or generator) is probably overcharging the battery. The voltage regulator is probably at fault.

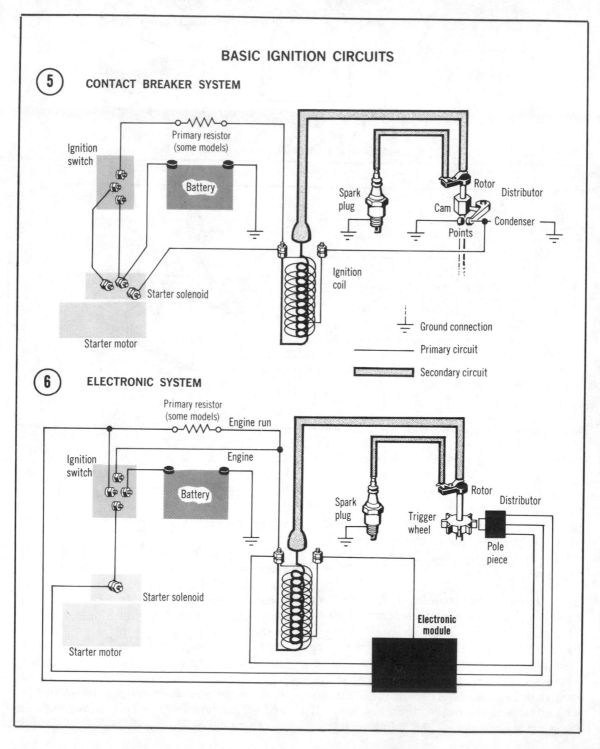

BASIC IGNITION CIRCUITS

⑤ CONTACT BREAKER SYSTEM

Ignition switch
Primary resistor (some models)
Battery
Spark plug
Cam
Rotor
Distributor
Points
Condenser
Ignition coil
Starter solenoid
Starter motor

Ground connection
Primary circuit
Secondary circuit

⑥ ELECTRONIC SYSTEM

Primary resistor (some models)
Engine run
Ignition switch
Engine
Battery
Spark plug
Trigger wheel
Rotor
Distributor
Pole piece
Starter solenoid
Starter motor
Electronic module

6. *Excessive noise from the alternator (or generator)* — Check for loose mounting brackets and bolts. The problem may also be worn bearings or the need of lubrication in some cases. If an alternator whines, a shorted diode may be indicated.

IGNITION SYSTEM

The ignition system may be either a conventional contact breaker type or an electronic ignition. See electrical chapter to determine which type you have. **Figures 5 and 6** show simplified diagrams of each type.

Most problems involving failure to start, poor performance, or rough running stem from trouble in the ignition system, particularly in contact breaker systems. Many novice troubleshooters get into trouble when they assume that these symptoms point to the fuel system instead of the ignition system.

Ignition system troubles may be roughly divided between those affecting only one cylinder and those affecting all cylinders. If the trouble affects only one cylinder, it can only be in the spark plug, spark plug wire, or portion of the distributor associated with that cylinder. If the trouble affects all cylinders (weak spark or no spark), then the trouble is in the ignition coil, rotor, distributor, or associated wiring.

The troubleshooting procedures outlined in **Figure 7** (breaker point ignition) or **Figure 8**

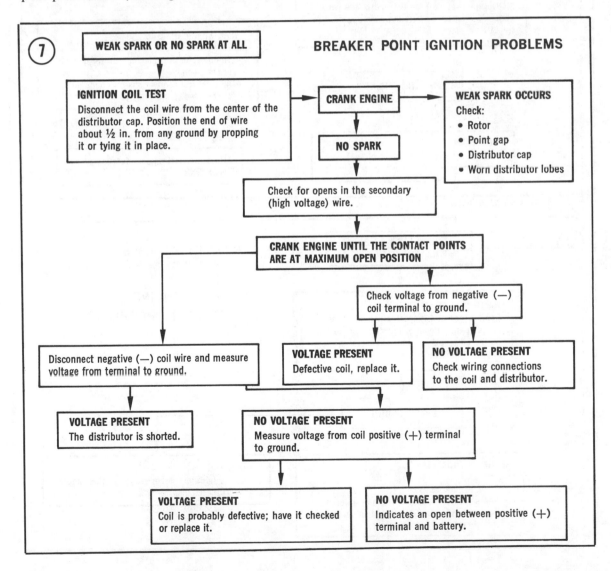

(electronic ignition) will help you isolate ignition problems fast. Of course, they assume that the battery is in good enough condition to crank the engine over at its normal rate.

ENGINE PERFORMANCE

A number of factors can make the engine difficult or impossible to start, or cause rough running, poor performance and so on. The majority of novice troubleshooters immediately suspect the carburetor or fuel injection system. In the majority of cases, though, the trouble exists in the ignition system.

The troubleshooting procedures outlined in **Figures 9 through 14** will help you solve the majority of engine starting troubles in a systematic manner.

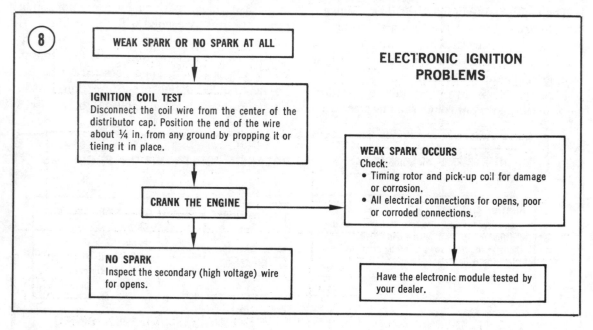

(8) WEAK SPARK OR NO SPARK AT ALL

ELECTRONIC IGNITION PROBLEMS

IGNITION COIL TEST
Disconnect the coil wire from the center of the distributor cap. Position the end of the wire about ¼ in. from any ground by propping it or tieing it in place.

CRANK THE ENGINE

WEAK SPARK OCCURS
Check:
• Timing rotor and pick-up coil for damage or corrosion.
• All electrical connections for opens, poor or corroded connections.

NO SPARK
Inspect the secondary (high voltage) wire for opens.

Have the electronic module tested by your dealer.

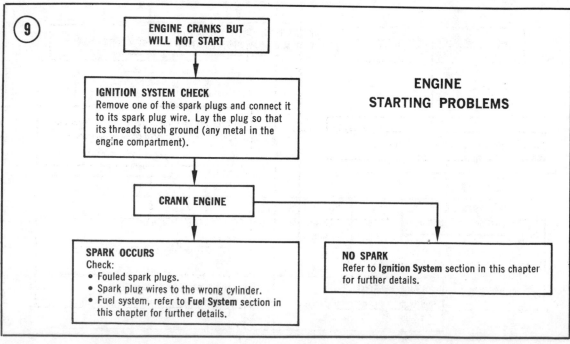

(9) ENGINE CRANKS BUT WILL NOT START

ENGINE STARTING PROBLEMS

IGNITION SYSTEM CHECK
Remove one of the spark plugs and connect it to its spark plug wire. Lay the plug so that its threads touch ground (any metal in the engine compartment).

CRANK ENGINE

SPARK OCCURS
Check:
• Fouled spark plugs.
• Spark plug wires to the wrong cylinder.
• Fuel system, refer to **Fuel System** section in this chapter for further details.

NO SPARK
Refer to **Ignition System** section in this chapter for further details.

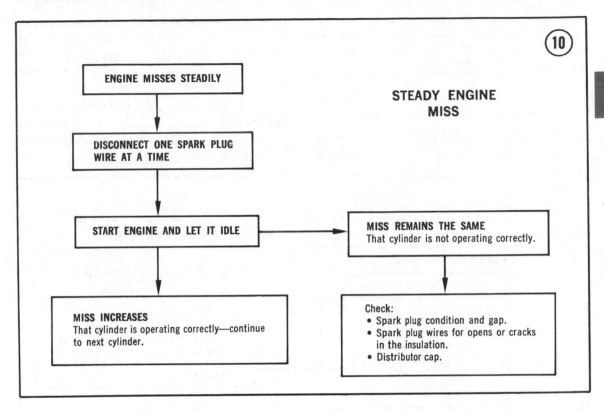

(10)

ENGINE MISSES STEADILY

STEADY ENGINE
MISS

DISCONNECT ONE SPARK PLUG
WIRE AT A TIME

START ENGINE AND LET IT IDLE → MISS REMAINS THE SAME
That cylinder is not operating correctly.

MISS INCREASES
That cylinder is operating correctly—continue
to next cylinder.

Check:
• Spark plug condition and gap.
• Spark plug wires for opens or cracks
  in the insulation.
• Distributor cap.

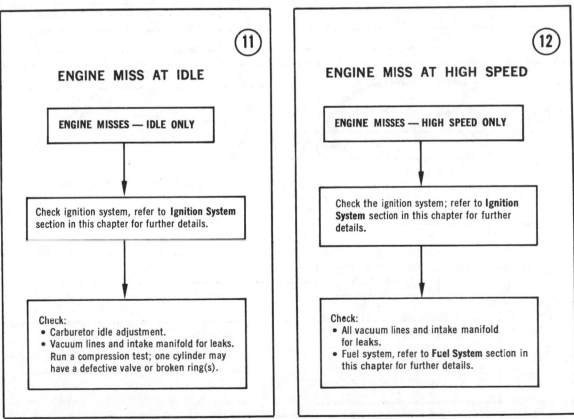

(11)

ENGINE MISS AT IDLE

ENGINE MISSES — IDLE ONLY

Check ignition system, refer to **Ignition System**
section in this chapter for further details.

Check:
• Carburetor idle adjustment.
• Vacuum lines and intake manifold for leaks.
  Run a compression test; one cylinder may
  have a defective valve or broken ring(s).

(12)

ENGINE MISS AT HIGH SPEED

ENGINE MISSES — HIGH SPEED ONLY

Check the ignition system; refer to **Ignition
System** section in this chapter for further
details.

Check:
• All vacuum lines and intake manifold
  for leaks.
• Fuel system, refer to **Fuel System** section in
  this chapter for further details.

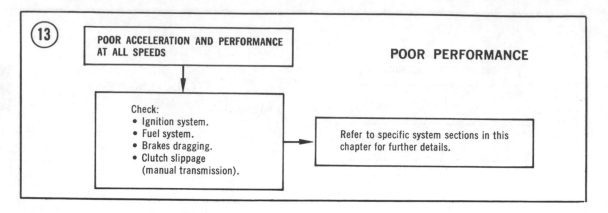

⑬ POOR ACCELERATION AND PERFORMANCE
AT ALL SPEEDS

POOR PERFORMANCE

Check:
• Ignition system.
• Fuel system.
• Brakes dragging.
• Clutch slippage
(manual transmission).

Refer to specific system sections in this
chapter for further details.

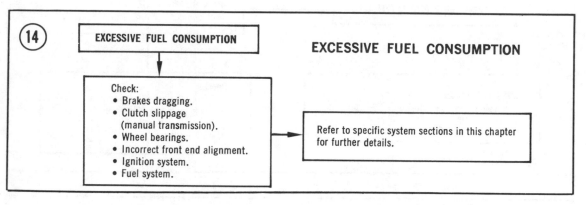

⑭ EXCESSIVE FUEL CONSUMPTION

EXCESSIVE FUEL CONSUMPTION

Check:
• Brakes dragging.
• Clutch slippage
(manual transmission).
• Wheel bearings.
• Incorrect front end alignment.
• Ignition system.
• Fuel system.

Refer to specific system sections in this chapter
for further details.

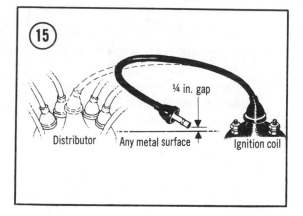

⑮ ¼ in. gap

Distributor   Any metal surface   Ignition coil

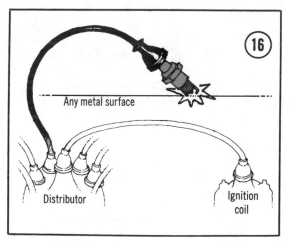

⑯

Any metal surface

Distributor   Ignition coil

Some tests of the ignition system require running the engine with a spark plug or ignition coil wire disconnected. The safest way to do this is to disconnect the wire with the engine stopped, then prop the end of the wire next to a metal surface as shown in **Figures 15 and 16**.

WARNING
Never disconnect a spark plug or ignition coil wire while the engine is running. The high voltage in an ignition system, particularly the newer high-energy electronic ignition systems could cause serious injury or even death.

Spark plug condition is an important indication of engine performance. Spark plugs in a properly operating engine will have slightly pitted electrodes, and a light tan insulator tip. **Figure 17** shows a normal plug, and a number of others which indicate trouble in their respective cylinders.

2

• Appearance—Firing tip has deposits of light gray to light tan.
• Can be cleaned, regapped and reused.

• Appearance—Dull, dry black with fluffy carbon deposits on the insulator tip, electrode and exposed shell.
• Caused by—Fuel/air mixture too rich, plug heat range too cold, weak ignition system, dirty air cleaner, faulty automatic choke or excessive idling.
• Can be cleaned, regapped and reused.

• Appearance—Wet black deposits on insulator and exposed shell.
• Caused by—Excessive oil entering the combustion chamber through worn rings, pistons, valve guides or bearings.
• Replace with new plugs (use a hotter plug if engine is not repaired).

• Appearance — Yellow insulator deposits (may sometimes be dark gray, black or tan in color) on the insulator tip.
• Caused by—Highly leaded gasoline.
• Replace with new plugs.

• Appearance—Yellow glazed deposits indicating melted lead deposits due to hard acceleration.
• Caused by—Highly leaded gasoline.
• Replace with new plugs.

• Appearance—Glazed yellow deposits with a slight brownish tint on the insulator tip and ground electrode.
• Replace with new plugs.

• Appearance — Brown colored hardened ash deposits on the insulator tip and ground electrode.
• Caused by—Fuel and/or oil additives.
• Replace with new plugs.

• Appearance — Severely worn or eroded electrodes.
• Caused by—Normal wear or unusual oil and/or fuel additives.
• Replace with new plugs.

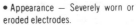

• Appearance — Melted ground electrode.
• Caused by—Overadvanced ignition timing, inoperative ignition advance mechanism, too low of a fuel octane rating, lean fuel/air mixture or carbon deposits in combustion chamber.

• Appearance—Melted center electrode.
• Caused by—Abnormal combustion due to overadvanced ignition timing or incorrect advance, too low of a fuel octane rating, lean fuel/air mixture, or carbon deposits in combustion chamber.
• Correct engine problem and replace with new plugs.

• Appearance—Melted center electrode and white blistered insulator tip.
• Caused by—Incorrect plug heat range selection.
• Replace with new plugs.

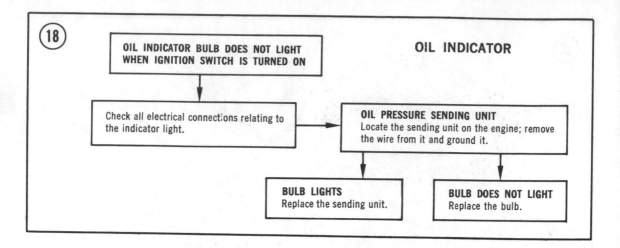

OIL INDICATOR

OIL INDICATOR BULB DOES NOT LIGHT WHEN IGNITION SWITCH IS TURNED ON

Check all electrical connections relating to the indicator light.

OIL PRESSURE SENDING UNIT
Locate the sending unit on the engine; remove the wire from it and ground it.

BULB LIGHTS
Replace the sending unit.

BULB DOES NOT LIGHT
Replace the bulb.

ENGINE OIL PRESSURE LIGHT

Proper oil pressure to the engine is vital. If oil pressure is insufficient, the engine can destroy itself in a comparatively short time.

The oil pressure warning circuit monitors oil pressure constantly. If pressure drops below a predetermined level, the light comes on.

Obviously, it is vital for the warning circuit to be working to signal low oil pressure. Each time you turn on the ignition, but before you start the car, the warning light should come on. If it doesn't, there is trouble in the warning circuit, not the oil pressure system. See **Figure 18** to troubleshoot the warning circuit.

Once the engine is running, the warning light should stay off. If the warning light comes on or acts erratically while the engine is running there is trouble with the engine oil pressure system. *Stop the engine immediately*. Refer to **Figure 19** for possible causes of the problem.

FUEL SYSTEM (CARBURETTED)

Fuel system problems must be isolated to the fuel pump (mechanical or electric), fuel lines, fuel filter, or carburetor. These procedures assume the ignition system is working properly and is correctly adjusted.

1. *Engine will not start* — First make sure that fuel is being delivered to the carburetor. Remove the air cleaner, look into the carburetor throat, and operate the accelerator

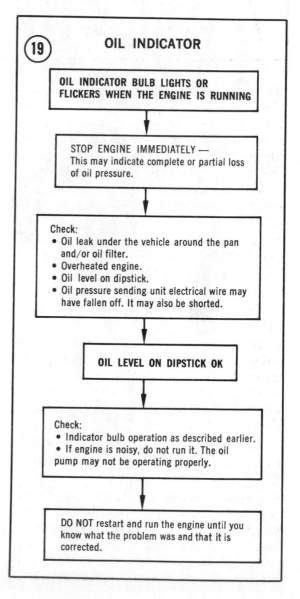

OIL INDICATOR

OIL INDICATOR BULB LIGHTS OR FLICKERS WHEN THE ENGINE IS RUNNING

STOP ENGINE IMMEDIATELY —
This may indicate complete or partial loss of oil pressure.

Check:
• Oil leak under the vehicle around the pan and/or oil filter.
• Overheated engine.
• Oil level on dipstick.
• Oil pressure sending unit electrical wire may have fallen off. It may also be shorted.

OIL LEVEL ON DIPSTICK OK

Check:
• Indicator bulb operation as described earlier.
• If engine is noisy, do not run it. The oil pump may not be operating properly.

DO NOT restart and run the engine until you know what the problem was and that it is corrected.

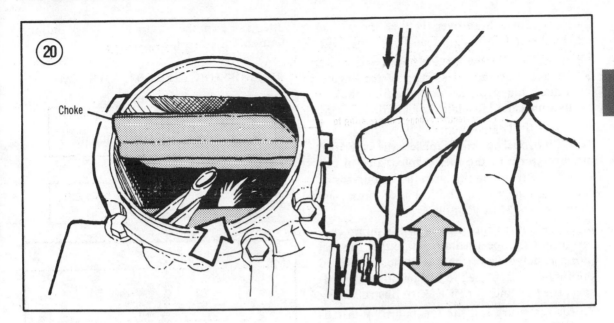

Choke

linkage several times. There should be a stream of fuel from the accelerator pump discharge tube each time the accelerator linkage is depressed (**Figure 20**). If not, check fuel pump delivery (described later), float valve, and float adjustment. If the engine will not start, check the automatic choke parts for sticking or damage. If necessary, rebuild or replace the carburetor.

2. *Engine runs at fast idle* — Check the choke setting. Check the idle speed, idle mixture, and decel valve (if equipped) adjustment.

3. *Rough idle or engine miss with frequent stalling* — Check idle mixture and idle speed adjustments.

4. *Engine "diesels" (continues to run) when ignition is switched off* — Check idle mixture (probably too rich), ignition timing, and idle speed (probably too fast). Check the throttle solenoid (if equipped) for proper operation. Check for overheated engine.

5. *Stumbling when accelerating from idle* — Check the idle speed and mixture adjustments. Check the accelerator pump.

6. *Engine misses at high speed or lacks power* — This indicates possible fuel starvation. Check fuel pump pressure and capacity as described in this chapter. Check float needle valves. Check for a clogged fuel filter or air cleaner.

7. *Black exhaust smoke* — This indicates a badly overrich mixture. Check idle mixture and idle speed adjustment. Check choke setting. Check for excessive fuel pump pressure, leaky floats, or worn needle valves.

8. *Excessive fuel consumption* — Check for overrich mixture. Make sure choke mechanism works properly. Check idle mixture and idle speed. Check for excessive fuel pump pressure, leaky floats, or worn float needle valves.

FUEL SYSTEM (FUEL INJECTED)

Troubleshooting a fuel injection system requires more thought, experience, and know-how than any other part of the vehicle. A logical approach and proper test equipment are essential in order to successfully find and fix these troubles.

It is best to leave fuel injection troubles to your dealer. In order to isolate a problem to the injection system make sure that the fuel pump is operating properly. Check its performance as described later in this section. Also make sure that fuel filter and air cleaner are not clogged.

FUEL PUMP TEST (MECHANICAL AND ELECTRIC)

1. Disconnect the fuel inlet line where it enters the carburetor or fuel injection system.

2. Fit a rubber hose over the fuel line so fuel can be directed into a graduated container with about one quart capacity. See **Figure 21**.

3. To avoid accidental starting of the engine, disconnect the secondary coil wire from the coil or disconnect and insulate the coil primary wire.

4. Crank the engine for about 30 seconds.

5. If the fuel pump supplies the specified amount (refer to the fuel chapter later in this book), the trouble may be in the carburetor or fuel injection system. The fuel injection system should be tested by your dealer.

6. If there is no fuel present or the pump cannot supply the specified amount, either the fuel pump is defective or there is an obstruction in the fuel line. Replace the fuel pump and/or inspect the fuel lines for air leaks or obstructions.

7. Also pressure test the fuel pump by installing a T-fitting in the fuel line between the fuel pump and the carburetor. Connect a fuel pressure gauge to the fitting with a short tube **(Figure 22)**.

8. Reconnect the coil wire, start the engine, and record the pressure. Refer to the fuel chapter later in this book for the correct pressure. If the pressure varies from that specified, the pump should be replaced.

9. Stop the engine. The pressure should drop off very slowly. If it drops off rapidly, the outlet valve in the pump is leaking and the pump should be replaced.

EMISSION CONTROL SYSTEMS

Major emission control systems used on nearly all U.S. models include the following:

a. Positive crankcase ventilation (PCV)

b. Thermostatic air cleaner

c. Air injection reaction (AIR)

d. Fuel evaporation control

e. Exhaust gas recirculation (EGR)

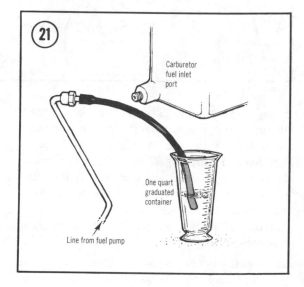

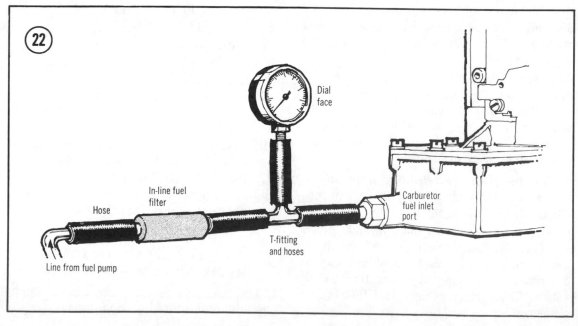

Emission control systems vary considerably from model to model. Individual models contain variations of the four systems described here. In addition, they may include other special systems. Use the index to find specific emission control components in other chapters.

Many of the systems and components are factory set and sealed. Without special expensive test equipment, it is impossible to adjust the systems to meet state and federal requirements.

Troubleshooting can also be difficult without special equipment. The procedures described below will help you find emission control parts which have failed, but repairs may have to be entrusted to a dealer or other properly equipped repair shop.

With the proper equipment, you can test the carbon monoxide and hydrocarbon levels.

Figure 23 provides some sources of trouble if the readings are not correct.

Positive Crankcase Ventilation

Fresh air drawn from the air cleaner housing scavenges emissions (e.g., piston blow-by) from the crankcase, then the intake manifold vacuum draws emissions into the intake manifold. They can then be reburned in the normal combustion process. **Figure 24** shows a typical system. **Figure 25** provides a testing procedure.

Thermostatic Air Cleaner

The thermostatically controlled air cleaner maintains incoming air to the engine at a predetermined level, usually about 100°F or higher. It mixes cold air with heated air from the exhaust manifold region. The air cleaner in-

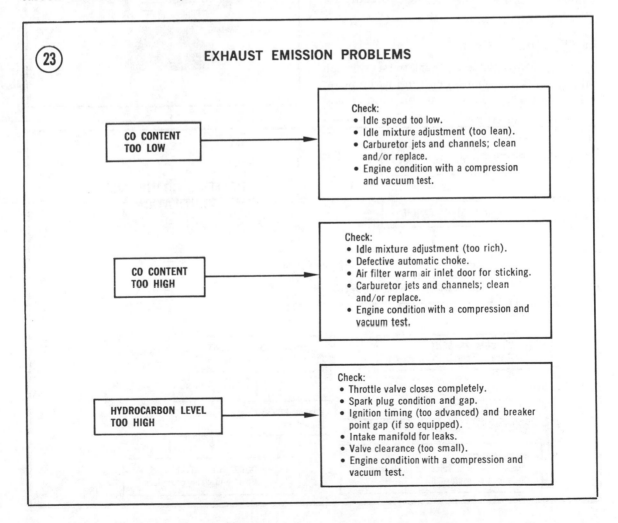

(23) **EXHAUST EMISSION PROBLEMS**

CO CONTENT TOO LOW

Check:
- Idle speed too low.
- Idle mixture adjustment (too lean).
- Carburetor jets and channels; clean and/or replace.
- Engine condition with a compression and vacuum test.

CO CONTENT TOO HIGH

Check:
- Idle mixture adjustment (too rich).
- Defective automatic choke.
- Air filter warm air inlet door for sticking.
- Carburetor jets and channels; clean and/or replace.
- Engine condition with a compression and vacuum test.

HYDROCARBON LEVEL TOO HIGH

Check:
- Throttle valve closes completely.
- Spark plug condition and gap.
- Ignition timing (too advanced) and breaker point gap (if so equipped).
- Intake manifold for leaks.
- Valve clearance (too small).
- Engine condition with a compression and vacuum test.

cludes a temperature sensor, vacuum motor, and a hinged door. See **Figure 26**.

The system is comparatively easy to test. See **Figure 27** for the procedure.

Air Injection Reaction System

The air injection reaction system reduces air pollution by oxidizing hydrocarbons and carbon monoxide as they leave the combustion chamber. See **Figure 28**.

The air injection pump, driven by the engine, compresses filtered air and injects it at the exhaust port of each cylinder. The fresh air mixes with the unburned gases in the exhaust and promotes further burning. A check valve prevents exhaust gases from entering and damaging the air pump if the pump becomes inoperative, e.g., from a fan belt failure.

Figure 29 explains the testing procedure for this system.

Fuel Evaporation Control

Fuel vapor from the fuel tank passes through the liquid/vapor separator to the carbon canister. See **Figure 30**. The carbon absorbs and

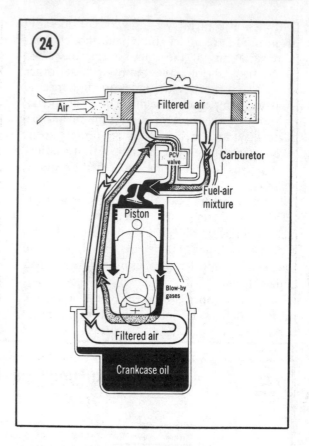

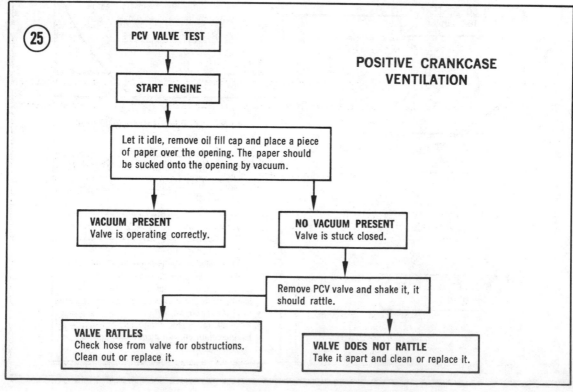

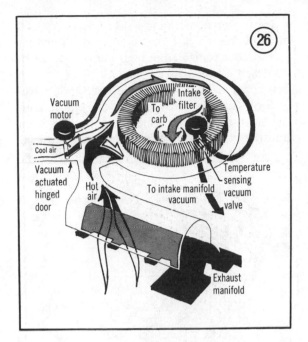

(26)

Vacuum motor

Intake filter

To carb

Cool air

Vacuum actuated hinged door

Hot air

Temperature sensing vacuum valve

To intake manifold vacuum

Exhaust manifold

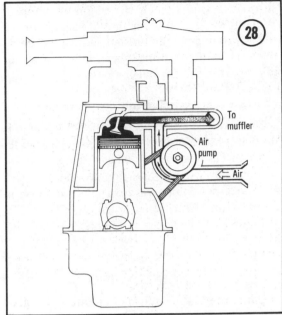

(28)

To muffler

Air pump

Air

2

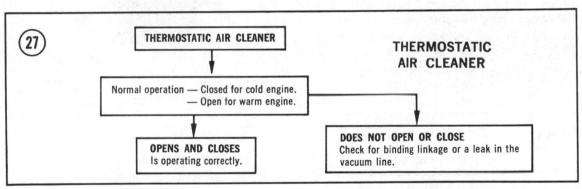

(27)

THERMOSTATIC AIR CLEANER

Normal operation — Closed for cold engine.
— Open for warm engine.

OPENS AND CLOSES
Is operating correctly.

DOES NOT OPEN OR CLOSE
Check for binding linkage or a leak in the vacuum line.

THERMOSTATIC AIR CLEANER

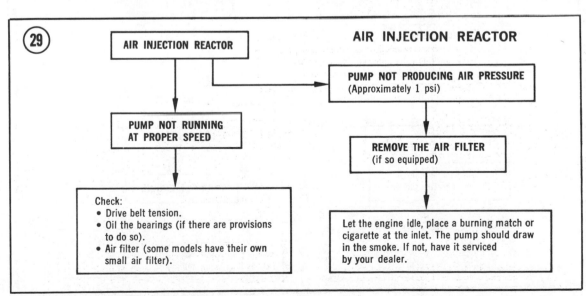

(29)

AIR INJECTION REACTOR

PUMP NOT RUNNING
AT PROPER SPEED

Check:
• Drive belt tension.
• Oil the bearings (if there are provisions to do so).
• Air filter (some models have their own small air filter).

PUMP NOT PRODUCING AIR PRESSURE
(Approximately 1 psi)

REMOVE THE AIR FILTER
(if so equipped)

Let the engine idle, place a burning match or cigarette at the inlet. The pump should draw in the smoke. If not, have it serviced by your dealer.

AIR INJECTION REACTOR

stores the vapor when the engine is stopped. When the engine runs, manifold vacuum draws the vapor from the canister. Instead of being released into the atmosphere, the fuel vapor takes part in the normal combustion process.

Exhaust Gas Recirculation

The exhaust gas recirculation (EGR) system is used to reduce the emission of nitrogen oxides (NOx). Relatively inert exhaust gases are introduced into the combustion process to slightly reduce peak temperatures. This reduction in temperature reduces the formation of NOx.

Figure 31 provides a simple test of this system.

ENGINE NOISES

Often the first evidence of an internal engine trouble is a strange noise. That knocking, clicking, or tapping which you never heard before may be warning you of impending trouble.

While engine noises can indicate problems, they are sometimes difficult to interpret correctly; inexperienced mechanics can be seriously misled by them.

Professional mechanics often use a special stethoscope which looks similar to a doctor's stethoscope for isolating engine noises. You can do nearly as well with a "sounding stick" which can be an ordinary piece of doweling or a section of small hose. By placing one end in contact with the area to which you want to listen and the other end near your ear, you can hear

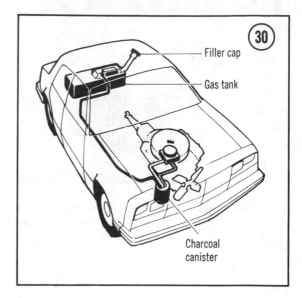

Filler cap

Gas tank

Charcoal canister

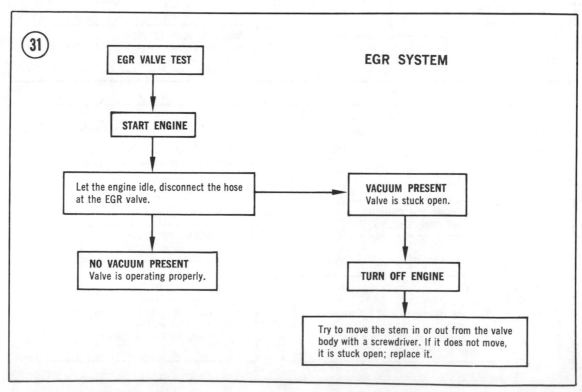

EGR VALVE TEST

EGR SYSTEM

START ENGINE

Let the engine idle, disconnect the hose at the EGR valve.

VACUUM PRESENT
Valve is stuck open.

NO VACUUM PRESENT
Valve is operating properly.

TURN OFF ENGINE

Try to move the stem in or out from the valve body with a screwdriver. If it does not move, it is stuck open; replace it.

sounds emanating from that area. The first time you do this, you may be horrified at the strange noises coming from even a normal engine. If you can, have an experienced friend or mechanic help you sort the noises out.

Clicking or Tapping Noises

Clicking or tapping noises usually come from the valve train, and indicate excessive valve clearance.

If your vehicle has adjustable valves, the procedure for adjusting the valve clearance is explained in Chapter Three. If your vehicle has hydraulic lifters, the clearance may not be adjustable. The noise may be coming from a collapsed lifter. These may be cleaned or replaced as described in the engine chapter.

A sticking valve may also sound like a valve with excessive clearance. In addition, excessive wear in valve train components can cause similar engine noises.

Knocking Noises

A heavy, dull knocking is usually caused by a worn main bearing. The noise is loudest when the engine is working hard, i.e., accelerating hard at low speed. You may be able to isolate the trouble to a single bearing by disconnecting

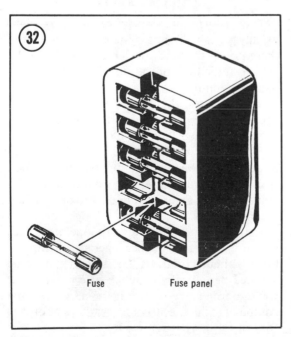

Fuse   Fuse panel

the spark plugs one at a time. When you reach the spark plug nearest the bearing, the knock will be reduced or disappear.

Worn connecting rod bearings may also produce a knock, but the sound is usually more "metallic." As with a main bearing, the noise is worse when accelerating. It may even increase further just as you go from accelerating to coasting. Disconnecting spark plugs will help isolate this knock as well.

A double knock or clicking usually indicates a worn piston pin. Disconnecting spark plugs will isolate this to a particular piston, however, the noise will *increase* when you reach the affected piston.

A loose flywheel and excessive crankshaft end play also produce knocking noises. While similar to main bearing noises, these are usually intermittent, not constant, and they do not change when spark plugs are disconnected.

Some mechanics confuse piston pin noise with piston slap. The double knock will distinguish the piston pin noise. Piston slap is identified by the fact that it is always louder when the engine is cold.

ELECTRICAL ACCESSORIES

Lights and Switches (Interior and Exterior)

1. *Bulb does not light* — Remove the bulb and check for a broken element. Also check the inside of the socket; make sure the contacts are clean and free of corrosion. If the bulb and socket are OK, check to see if a fuse has blown or a circuit breaker has tripped. The fuse panel (**Figure 32**) is usually located under the instrument panel. Replace the blown fuse or reset the circuit breaker. If the fuse blows or the breaker trips again, there is a short in that circuit. Check that circuit all the way to the battery. Look for worn wire insulation or burned wires.

If all the above are all right, check the switch controlling the bulb for continuity with an ohmmeter at the switch terminals. Check the switch contact terminals for loose or dirty electrical connections.

2. *Headlights work but will not switch from either high or low beam* — Check the beam selector switch for continuity with an ohmmeter

at the switch terminals. Check the switch contact terminals for loose or dirty electrical connections.

3. *Brake light switch inoperative* — On mechanically operated switches, usually mounted near the brake pedal arm, adjust the switch to achieve correct mechanical operation. Check the switch for continuity with an ohmmeter at the switch terminals. Check the switch contact terminals for loose or dirty electrical connections.

4. *Back-up lights do not operate* — Check light bulb as described earlier. Locate the switch, normally located near the shift lever. Adjust switch to achieve correct mechanical operation. Check the switch for continuity with an ohmmeter at the switch terminals. Bypass the switch with a jumper wire; if the lights work, replace the switch.

Directional Signals

1. *Directional signals do not operate* — If the indicator light on the instrument panel burns steadily instead of flashing, this usually indicates that one of the exterior lights is burned out. Check all lamps that normally flash. If all are all right, the flasher unit may be defective. Replace it with a good one.

2. *Directional signal indicator light on instrument panel does not light up* — Check the light bulbs as described earlier. Check all electrical connections and check the flasher unit.

3. *Directional signals will not self-cancel* — Check the self-cancelling mechanism located inside the steering column.

4. *Directional signals flash slowly* — Check the condition of the battery and the alternator (or generator) drive belt tension (**Figure 4**). Check the flasher unit and all related electrical connections.

Windshield Wipers

1. *Wipers do not operate* — Check for a blown fuse or circuit breaker that has tripped; replace or reset. Check all related terminals for loose or dirty electrical connections. Check continuity of the control switch with an ohmmeter at the switch terminals. Check the linkage and arms

for loose, broken, or binding parts. Straighten out or replace where necessary.

2. *Wiper motor hums but will not operate* — The motor may be shorted out internally; check and/or replace the motor. Also check for broken or binding linkage and arms.

3. *Wiper arms will not return to the stowed position when turned off* — The motor has a special internal switch for this purpose. Have it inspected by your dealer. Do not attempt this yourself.

Interior Heater

1. *Heater fan does not operate* — Check for a blown fuse or circuit breaker that has tripped. Check the switch for continuity with an ohmmeter at the switch terminals. Check the switch contact terminals for loose or dirty electrical connections.

2. *Heat output is insufficient* — Check the heater hose/engine coolant control valve usually located in the engine compartment; make sure it is in the open position. Ensure that the heater door(s) and cable(s) are operating correctly and are in the open position. Inspect the heat ducts; make sure that they are not crimped or blocked.

COOLING SYSTEM

The temperature gauge or warning light usually signals cooling system troubles before there is any damage. As long as you stop the vehicle at the first indication of trouble, serious damage is unlikely.

In most cases, the trouble will be obvious as soon as you open the hood. If there is coolant or steam leaking, look for a defective radiator, radiator hose, or heater hose. If there is no evidence of leakage, make sure that the fan belt is in good condition. If the trouble is not obvious, refer to **Figures 33 and 34** to help isolate the trouble.

Automotive cooling systems operate under pressure to permit higher operating temperatures without boil-over. The system should be checked periodically to make sure it can withstand normal pressure. **Figure 35** shows the equipment which nearly any service station has for testing the system pressure.

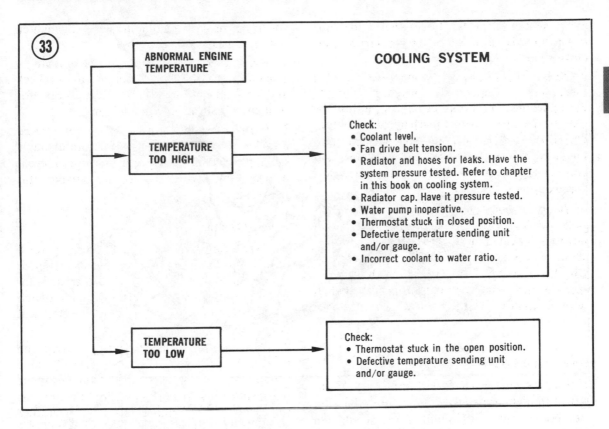

(33) **COOLING SYSTEM**

ABNORMAL ENGINE TEMPERATURE

TEMPERATURE TOO HIGH

Check:
• Coolant level.
• Fan drive belt tension.
• Radiator and hoses for leaks. Have the system pressure tested. Refer to chapter in this book on cooling system.
• Radiator cap. Have it pressure tested.
• Water pump inoperative.
• Thermostat stuck in closed position.
• Defective temperature sending unit and/or gauge.
• Incorrect coolant to water ratio.

TEMPERATURE TOO LOW

Check:
• Thermostat stuck in the open position.
• Defective temperature sending unit and/or gauge.

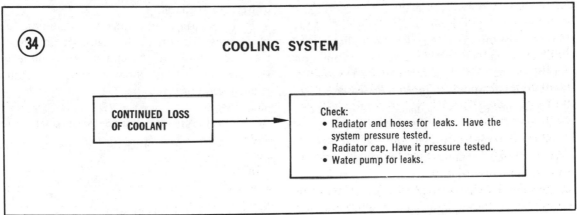

(34) **COOLING SYSTEM**

CONTINUED LOSS OF COOLANT

Check:
• Radiator and hoses for leaks. Have the system pressure tested.
• Radiator cap. Have it pressure tested.
• Water pump for leaks.

CLUTCH

All clutch troubles except adjustments require transmission removal to identify and cure the problem.

1. *Slippage* — This is most noticeable when accelerating in a high gear at relatively low speed. To check slippage, park the vehicle on a level surface with the handbrake set. Shift to 2nd gear and release the clutch as if driving off. If the clutch is good, the engine will slow and stall. If the clutch slips, continued engine speed will give it away.

Slippage results from insufficient clutch pedal free play, oil or grease on the clutch disc, worn pressure plate, or weak springs.

2. *Drag or failure to release* — This trouble usually causes difficult shifting and gear clash, especially when downshifting. The cause may be excessive clutch pedal free play, warped or bent pressure plate or clutch disc, broken or

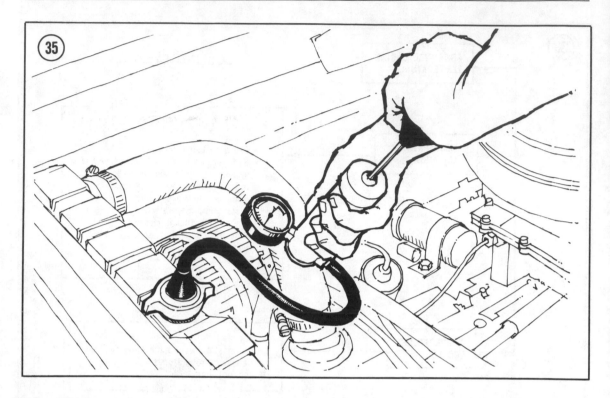

loose linings, or lack of lubrication in pilot bearing. Also check condition of transmission main shaft splines.

3. *Chatter or grabbing* — A number of things can cause this trouble. Check tightness of engine mounts and engine-to-transmission mounting bolts. Check for worn or misaligned pressure plate and misaligned release plate.

4. *Other noises* — Noise usually indicates a dry or defective release or pilot bearing. Check the bearings and replace if necessary. Also check all parts for misalignment and uneven wear.

MANUAL
TRANSMISSION/TRANSAXLE

Transmission and transaxle troubles are evident when one or more of the following symptoms appear:

   a. Difficulty changing gears

   b. Gears clash when downshifting

   c. Slipping out of gear

   d. Excessive noise in NEUTRAL

   e. Excessive noise in gear

   f. Oil leaks

Transmission and transaxle repairs are not recommended unless the many special tools required are available.

Transmission and transaxle troubles are sometimes difficult to distinguish from clutch troubles. Eliminate the clutch as a source of trouble before installing a new or rebuilt transmission or transaxle.

AUTOMATIC TRANSMISSION

Most automatic transmission repairs require considerable specialized knowledge and tools. It is impractical for the home mechanic to invest in the tools, since they cost more than a properly rebuilt transmission.

Check fluid level and condition frequently to help prevent future problems. If the fluid is orange or black in color or smells like varnish, it is an indication of some type of damage or failure within the transmission. Have the transmission serviced by your dealer or competent automatic transmission service facility.

BRAKES

Good brakes are vital to the safe operation of the vehicle. Performing the maintenance speci-

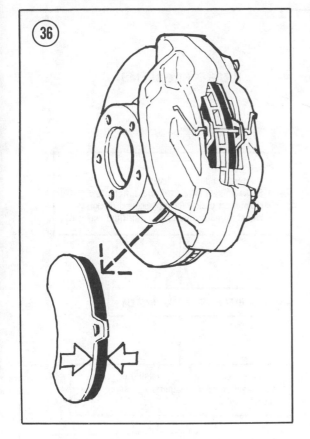

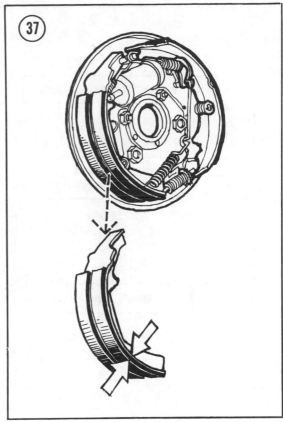

2

fied in Chapter Three will minimize problems with the brakes. Most importantly, check and maintain the level of fluid in the master cylinder, and check the thickness of the linings on the disc brake pads (**Figure 36**) or drum brake shoes (**Figure 37**).

If trouble develops, **Figures 38 through 40** will help you locate the problem. Refer to the brake chapter for actual repair procedures.

STEERING AND SUSPENSION

Trouble in the suspension or steering is evident when the following occur:

    a. Steering is hard

    b. Car pulls to one side

    c. Car wanders or front wheels wobble

    d. Steering has excessive play

    e. Tire wear is abnormal

Unusual steering, pulling, or wandering is usually caused by bent or otherwise misaligned suspension parts. This is difficult to check without proper alignment equipment. Refer to the suspension chapter in this book for repairs that you can perform and those that must be left to a dealer or suspension specialist.

If your trouble seems to be excessive play, check wheel bearing adjustment first. This is the most frequent cause. Then check ball-joints (refer to Suspension chapter). Finally, check tie rod end ball-joints by shaking each tie rod. Also check steering gear, or rack-and-pinion assembly to see that it is securely bolted down.

TIRE WEAR ANALYSIS

Abnormal tire wear should be analyzed to determine its causes. The most common causes are the following:

    a. Incorrect tire pressure

    b. Improper driving

    c. Overloading

    d. Bad road surfaces

    e. Incorrect wheel alignment

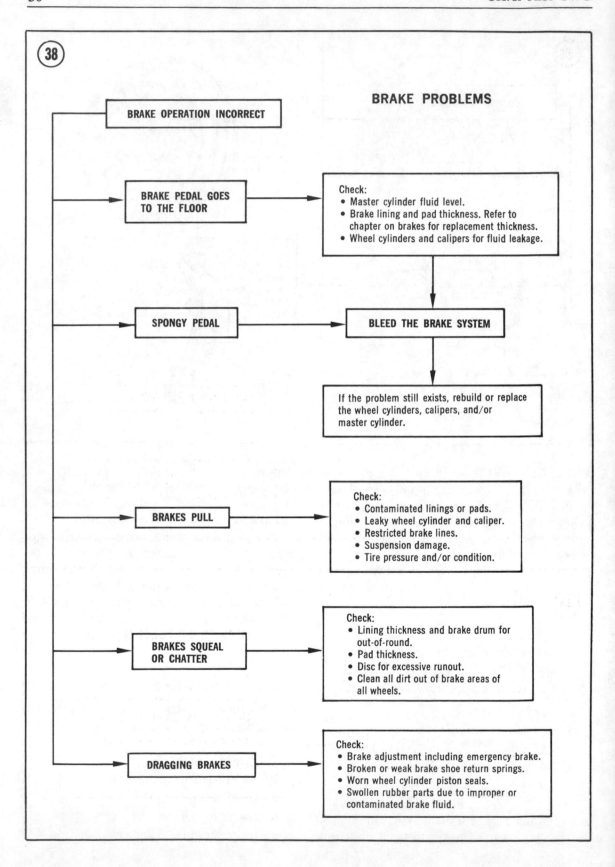

(38)

BRAKE PROBLEMS

BRAKE OPERATION INCORRECT

BRAKE PEDAL GOES TO THE FLOOR → Check:
• Master cylinder fluid level.
• Brake lining and pad thickness. Refer to chapter on brakes for replacement thickness.
• Wheel cylinders and calipers for fluid leakage.

SPONGY PEDAL → BLEED THE BRAKE SYSTEM

If the problem still exists, rebuild or replace the wheel cylinders, calipers, and/or master cylinder.

BRAKES PULL → Check:
• Contaminated linings or pads.
• Leaky wheel cylinder and caliper.
• Restricted brake lines.
• Suspension damage.
• Tire pressure and/or condition.

BRAKES SQUEAL OR CHATTER → Check:
• Lining thickness and brake drum for out-of-round.
• Pad thickness.
• Disc for excessive runout.
• Clean all dirt out of brake areas of all wheels.

DRAGGING BRAKES → Check:
• Brake adjustment including emergency brake.
• Broken or weak brake shoe return springs.
• Worn wheel cylinder piston seals.
• Swollen rubber parts due to improper or contaminated brake fluid.

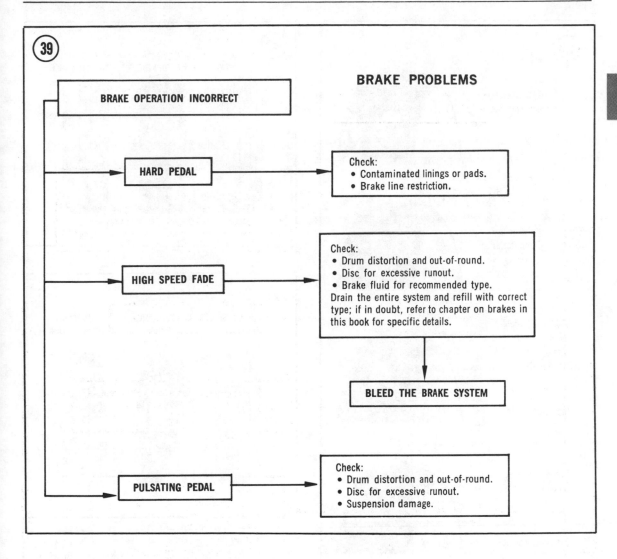

BRAKE PROBLEMS

BRAKE OPERATION INCORRECT

HARD PEDAL

Check:
• Contaminated linings or pads.
• Brake line restriction.

HIGH SPEED FADE

Check:
• Drum distortion and out-of-round.
• Disc for excessive runout.
• Brake fluid for recommended type.
Drain the entire system and refill with correct type; if in doubt, refer to chapter on brakes in this book for specific details.

BLEED THE BRAKE SYSTEM

PULSATING PEDAL

Check:
• Drum distortion and out-of-round.
• Disc for excessive runout.
• Suspension damage.

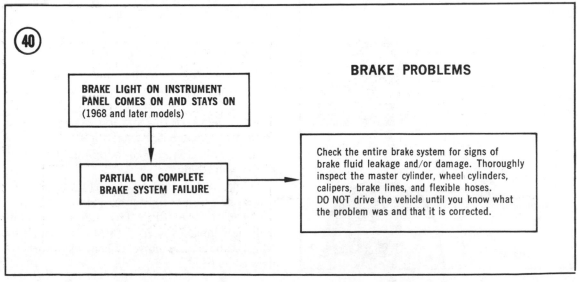

BRAKE PROBLEMS

BRAKE LIGHT ON INSTRUMENT PANEL COMES ON AND STAYS ON
(1968 and later models)

PARTIAL OR COMPLETE BRAKE SYSTEM FAILURE

Check the entire brake system for signs of brake fluid leakage and/or damage. Thoroughly inspect the master cylinder, wheel cylinders, calipers, brake lines, and flexible hoses.
DO NOT drive the vehicle until you know what the problem was and that it is corrected.

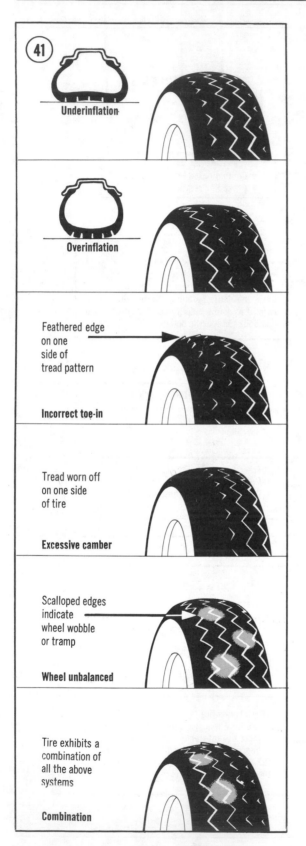

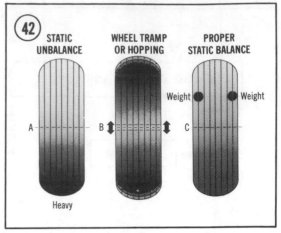

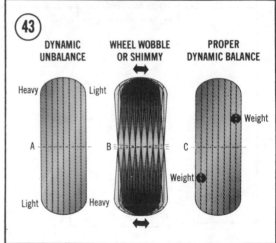

Figure 41 identifies wear patterns and indicates the most probable causes.

WHEEL BALANCING

All four wheels and tires must be in balance along two axes. To be in static balance (**Figure 42**), weight must be evenly distributed around the axis of rotation. (A) shows a statically unbalanced wheel; (B) shows the result — wheel tramp or hopping; (C) shows proper static balance.

To be in dynamic balance (**Figure 43**), the centerline of the weight must coincide with the centerline of the wheel. (A) shows a dynamically unbalanced wheel; (B) shows the result — wheel wobble or shimmy; (C) shows proper dynamic balance.

CHAPTER THREE

LUBRICATION, MAINTENANCE, AND TUNE-UP

A carefully followed program of lubrication and preventive maintenance will pay dividends in longer engine and vehicle life and fewer repair bills. Such a program is important, especially if the car is used in remote areas or on heavily travelled highways where breakdowns are not only inconvenient but dangerous. Breakdowns are much less likely to occur if the vehicle has been properly maintained.

GAS STOP CHECKS

Many of the following checks are made routinely by some service station attendants. You may want to do the tasks yourself. Even though the checks are simple, they are important. They also give an indication of the need for other maintenance.

Engine Oil Level

Engine oil level is checked by removing the dipstick, wiping it with a cloth or paper towel, replacing it until it seats firmly, then removing it again and reading the oil level on the lower end. Reinsert the dipstick after taking the reading. See **Figure 1**.

> NOTE: *Oil should be checked as the last step at a fuel stop. This will allow oil in the upper part of the engine to drain back into the crankcase.*

The oil level should be maintained between the dipstick marks. Do not overfill the engine. Too much oil can sometimes be as harmful to the engine as too little. Replenish as necessary with oil of the proper vicosity (see *Preventive Maintenance* section, *Engine Oil*, this chapter).

Besides checking the level, check the appearance of the oil on the dipstick. If it is very dark, it is dirty and should be changed. If it has a milky color, harmful water is present either from condensation or a head gasket leak. In either case, determine the cause and change the oil.

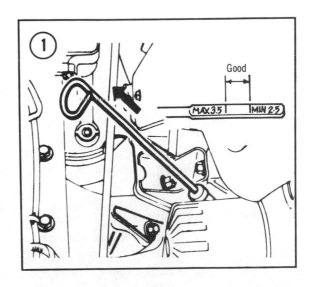

Drive Belts

Check the alternator V-belt and toothed camshaft belt for cracks and fraying. Check the alternator V-belt tension by pushing in on the belt halfway between the pulleys. There should be between $\frac{1}{4}$-$\frac{3}{8}$ in. (7-10 mm) deflection. If necessary, adjust belt tension as follows:

1. Loosen alternator mounting nut and bolt and move alternator with a pry bar to obtain proper belt tension (**Figure 2**).

2. Continue to hold the alternator with the pry bar and check belt tension. If correct, tighten mounting nut and bolt. Refer to **Figure 2**.

3. Check the toothed camshaft belt for proper tension. You should be able to turn the belt 90° from its normal position with your thumb and forefinger. If not, turn belt tensioner to the left until proper tension is achieved.

Coolant Level

Remove the radiator cap and check the radiator level only if there is evidence of leakage or overheating. Otherwise, check only at oil change intervals. The coolant level should be 2 inches below the top of the filler neck when the engine is cold. Add a 50/50 mixture of high quality ethylene glycol anti-freeze and water if coolant additions are necessary. Do not overfill.

> #### WARNING
> *Use care when removing radiator cap on a warm or hot engine. Hot water under pressure can boil out when pressure is released and cause severe scalding or burns. Loosen radiator cap to first notch and wait for pressure to escape before removing cap (Figure 3).*

Battery Electrolyte Level

Remove the vent plugs from the battery. If necessary, add distilled water until level contacts bottom of filler wells. Do not overfill, as this will result in loss of electrolyte and shorten battery life. See **Figure 4**.

Windshield Wipers/Washers

Check operation of wipers and condition and alignment of wiper blades. Check operation of washers and fill reservoir.

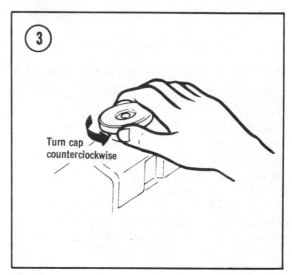

Turn cap
counterclockwise

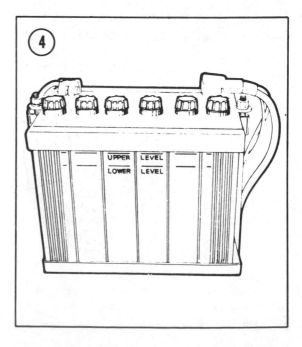

UPPER LEVEL
LOWER LEVEL

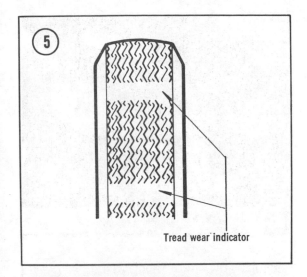

Tread wear indicator

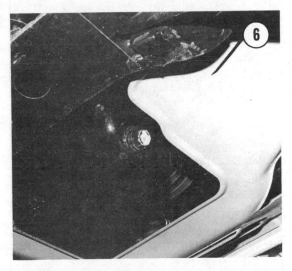

Tire Inspection

Check tires for abnormal wear. Check air pressure, preferably when tires are cold. Correct pressure is 24 psi front and 30 psi rear.

The original equipment tires incorporate built-in tread wear indicators. These indicators will appear as $\frac{1}{2}$ in. wide bands when tire tread depth is $\frac{1}{16}$ in. or less. When indicators appear in 2 or more adjacent grooves, tire replacement is recommended. See **Figure 5**.

PREVENTIVE MAINTENANCE

A conscientious, rigidly-followed lubrication and maintenance schedule pays off in vehicle reliability and high resale value.

Engine Oil

The engine oil should be changed every 4,000 miles (1971-1975 models) or 5,000 miles (1976 and later models). These intervals should be cut in half under any of the following conditions:

a. Driving in dusty areas
b. Trailer pulling
c. Extensive idling
d. Short trip operation in sub-freezing weather

Operation in a dust storm may require an immediate oil change.

With the engine at normal operating temperature, remove drain plug at bottom of oil pan (**Figure 6**) and allow oil to drain for at least 10 minutes. Check drain plug gasket and install plug. Remove oil filler cap and add oil labeled "For Service API/SE" with a viscosity of SAE 10W-40, 20W-40, 10W-30, or 20W-50 (above 32°F); SAE 10W-30, 10W-40, 10W-50, or 5W-40 (as low as 10°F); or SAE 5W-20, 5W-30, or 5W-40 (consistently below 10°F). Install oil filler cap, start engine, and check for leaks, Shut engine off and check oil level. Add more oil if necessary (but do not overfill). Refer to **Figure 1**.

Oil Filter

Replace the oil filter at every other oil change. Drain engine oil (refer to *Engine Oil* in preceding section), then replace filter by unscrewing it with a filter wrench (**Figure 7**).

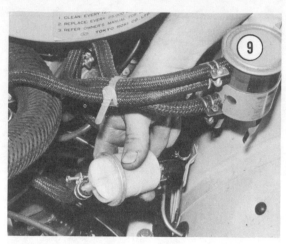

Wipe gasket area of base clean with a lint-free rag. Coat gasket with clean engine oil, then screw filter on by hand until gasket touches base. Tighten ½ turn more by hand (do not use a filter wrench). Fill engine with new oil, then check for leaks.

Air Filter

Clean the air filter element every engine tune-up by removing the air cleaner cover, lifting out the element, and tapping it lightly against a hard surface to dislodge any dirt.

> WARNING
> *Do not attempt to clean the paper element by washing it in solvent; tap lightly and use compressed air to blow away the dirt.*

Replace the filter element with a new one every other engine tune-up. See **Figure 8**.

Fuel Filter

Replace the carburetor fuel filter every other engine tune-up. Loosen the fuel line connections, discard the old filter, and install a new one. See **Figure 9**.

Vapor Separator and Filter

Replace the filter in the open end of the vapor separator at every engine tune-up on 1971-1975 models only.

Replace the entire vapor separator at every other engine tune-up (1971 models on), as follows:

1. Loosen the hose clamps and disconnect the fuel lines from the vapor separator nipples.

2. Loosen the vapor separator retaining clamp and slide the old vapor separator out and discard it.

3. Install a new vapor separator in position and tighten the retaining clamp.

4. Connect fuel lines as illustrated in **Figure 10**. Install and tighten the hose clamps.

5. Check all connections for fuel leaks.

Positive Crankcase Ventilation (PCV) System

Clean the PCV system every engine tune-up (check breather hoses for clogging). See **Figure 11**. Replace breather hoses every other engine tune-up.

Exhaust Gas Recirculation (EGR) System

Check and clean the EGR control valve and thermo valve every engine tune-up (**Figures 12 and 13**). Refer to Chapter Seven, *Exhaust Gas Recirculation* (EGR) section for removal, inspection, and installation procedures.

Manual Transmission

With transmission at normal operating temperature, remove filler plug (**Figure 14**). The oil level should just reach the bottom of the filler plug hole. If lubricant level is checked

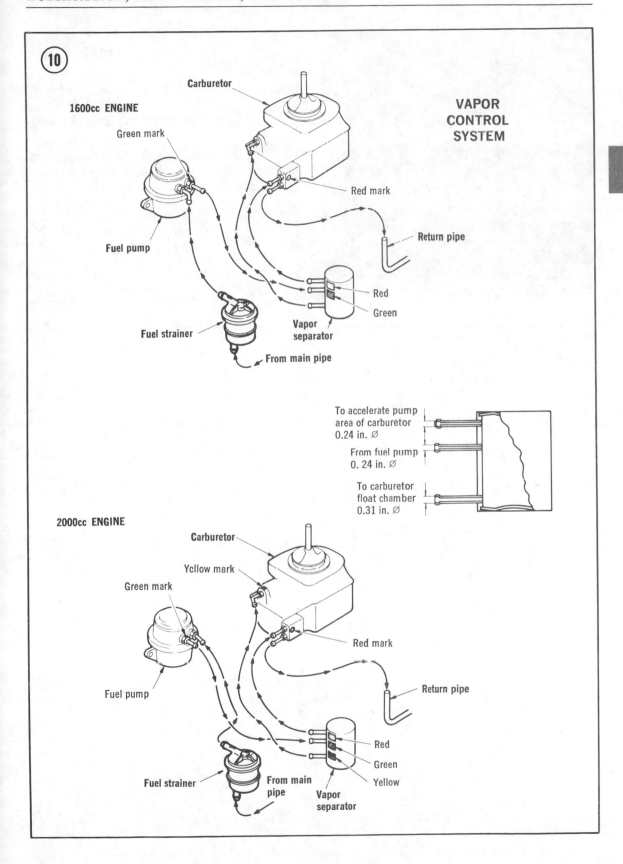

⑩

1600cc ENGINE

Carburetor

**VAPOR
CONTROL
SYSTEM**

3

Green mark

Red mark

Fuel pump

Return pipe

Red

Green

Fuel strainer

Vapor
separator

From main pipe

To accelerate pump
area of carburetor
0.24 in. ∅

From fuel pump
0. 24 in. ∅

To carburetor
float chamber
0.31 in. ∅

2000cc ENGINE

Carburetor

Yellow mark

Green mark

Red mark

Fuel pump

Return pipe

Red

Green

Yellow

Fuel strainer

From main
pipe

Vapor
separator

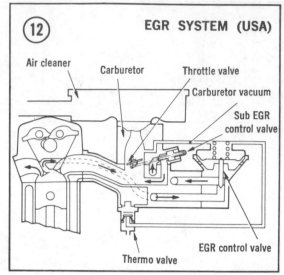

EGR SYSTEM (USA)

Air cleaner

Carburetor

Throttle valve

Carburetor vacuum

Sub EGR
control valve

EGR control valve

Thermo valve

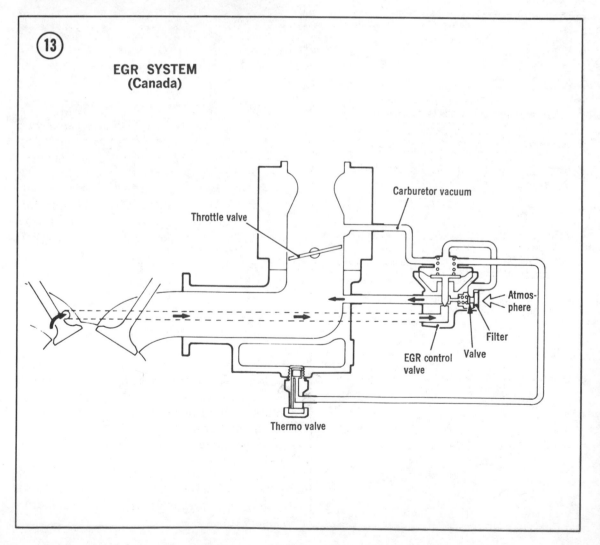

EGR SYSTEM
(Canada)

Carburetor vacuum

Throttle valve

Atmos-
phere

Filter

Valve

EGR control
valve

Thermo valve

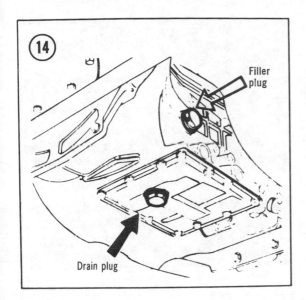

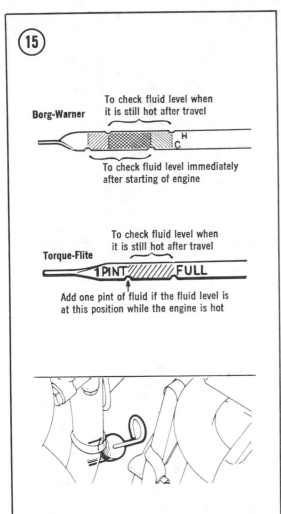

with the unit cold, level should be ½ in. below filler plug hole. If low, top up with SAE 80 Multipurpose Gear Oil conforming to API GL-5. Install filler plug and check for leaks.

Automatic Transmission

Check fluid level with transmission at normal operating temperature, car parked on level surface with gearshift lever in PARK, parking brake on, and engine idling. Remove dipstick, wipe clean, and reinsert it until it is fully seated. Remove dipstick and note reading (**Figure 15**). If level is below normal, add enough Dexron automatic transmission fluid to raise level to full mark.

CAUTION
Overfilling can cause foaming, which can result in overheating and/or over-flow from the transmission vent.

With normal usage, the fluid in the automatic transmission need not be changed. However, severe usage requires a fluid change and band adjustment every other engine tune-up. An authorized Chrysler Corporation dealer or service center is best equipped to handle this maintenance chore.

Lubricate the transmission control linkage connections every other oil change with multipurpose grease NLG1, Grade No. 2 E.P. (**Figure 16**).

Clutch Adjustment and Lubrication

Check clutch adjustment and lubricate clutch cable with SE grade engine oil every other oil change. Refer to Chapter Nine, *Clutch Control* section, for procedure.

Rear Axle

Remove rear axle filler plug and check lubricant level every oil change (**Figure 17**). The oil level should just reach the bottom of the filler plug hole. If necessary, top up with multipurpose gear oil API GL-5 SAE 85W-90 or SAE 90 (−10°F and above); SAE 80W-85 or SAE 80 (as low as −30°F); or SAE 75W-85W or SAE 75 (below −30°F).

Manual Steering

No lubrication of the steering or suspension is required except for the steering box which requires multipurpose gear oil API GL-5, SAE 90. Remove the filler plug (**Figure 18**) and bring oil level up to filler plug opening. Replace plug and check for leaks.

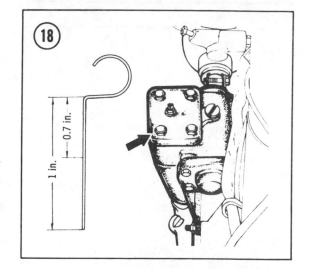

Power Steering

On cars with optional power steering, remove the oil pump reservoir cap and check fluid level with dipstick installed to the cap (**Figure 19**). Fluid level should be between MAX and MIN marks. If not, fill with DEXRON type automatic transmission fluid to the MAX level mark.

> NOTE: *Check hose connections for leakage and signs of deterioration every time you check the power steering fluid level.*

Suspension

Check all bushings and rubber parts for damage or looseness. Repair procedures for the front suspension, wheels, and steering can be found in Chapter Ten.

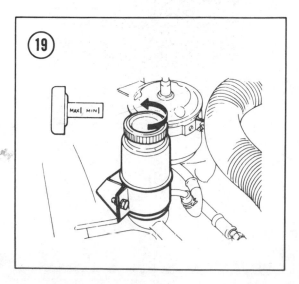

Shock Absorbers

Inspect shock absorbers whenever front wheel "tramp" (wheels bounce off ground) occurs while negotiating rough roads. Push down on each corner of the car with all of your

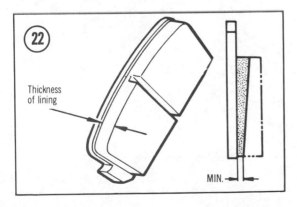

Thickness of lining

MIN.

weight, then release it. The car should rebound upward to its normal height and remain there without further "bobbing." If the car continues to oscillate, the shock absorbers need replacement. See Chapter Ten for removal and installation procedures. Refer to **Figure 20**.

Brakes

Inspect hydraulic system for leaks; crimped, cracked, or worn brake lines; and incorrect routing where binding could result.

Inspect the brakes while the road wheels are removed for tire rotation (every other oil change).

On disc brake models, check condition of pads and discs (**Figures 21 and 22**). Replace pads that are worn or contaminated with oil, grease, or brake fluid. Refer to **Table 1**. Have scored or corroded discs turned down by a qualified dealer or machine shop.

On drum brake models, remove drums and inspect linings. Replace brake shoes if linings are worn or contaminated with oil, grease, or brake fluid. Have drums turned down if necessary by a qualified dealer or machine shop. Check drums and shoes for blue-tinted areas indicating overheating. Replace any overheated parts.

All disc and drum brakes are self-adjusting.

Lubricate the parking brake cables and cable supports every other oil change with multipurpose grease NLG1, Grade 2, EP.

Adjust the parking brake every other oil change, as follows:

1. Release parking brake lever and adjust extension lever-to-backing plate clearance to

Table 1   BRAKE LINING SPECIFICATIONS

Model	Standard Value	Service Limit
Coupe and Sedan (Pin caliper type PS-15)	0.38 in. (9.7 mm)	0.08 in. (2.0 mm)
Station wagon (Sliding caliper F-type)	0.41 in. (10.5 mm)	0.04 in. (1.0 mm)

0-0.04 in. by screwing the adjusting nut on the cable (**Figure 23**).

2. Pull parking brake lever upward. The parking brake lever ratchet should not click more than 8-12 times. If it does, the rear brake automatic adjusters are malfunctioning.

Master Cylinder

Check fluid level in the master cylinder every oil change. Carefully wipe master cylinder lid and surrounding area clean with a lint-free cloth. Remove cover and add DOT-3 heavy-duty brake fluid until maximum reservoir level is reached. See **Figure 24**.

Change fluid every 12 months. Refer to *Brake Bleeding* section, Chapter Twelve, for procedure.

> WARNING
> *Always use DOT-3 heavy-duty brake fluid. The wrong type brake fluid could cause brake failure in an emergency. Avoid mixing different brands of brake fluid.*

Wheel Bearings

Repack the front wheel bearings every 25,000 miles (or when front disc brake pads are replaced) with multipurpose grease NLG1, Grade 2, EP. See **Figure 25**. Refer to Chapter Ten, *Wheel Bearing* section, for procedure.

Tire Rotation

To equalize tire wear, rotate tires every other oil change. See **Figure 26**. Adjust tire pressure to 24 psi front, 30 psi rear, after tire rotation. Check wheel lug nuts for tightness (50.8-58.0 ft.-lb. torque). Torque in sequence illustrated in **Figure 27**.

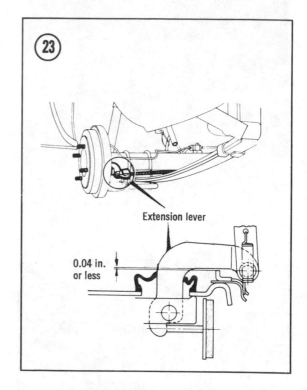

Extension lever

0.04 in. or less

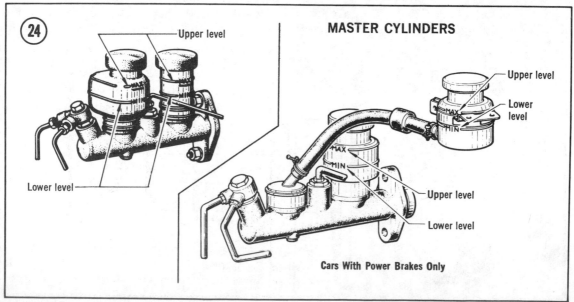

Upper level

Lower level

MASTER CYLINDERS

Upper level

Lower level

MAX

MIN

Upper level

Lower level

Cars With Power Brakes Only

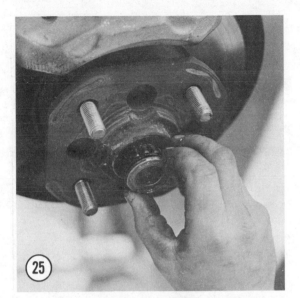

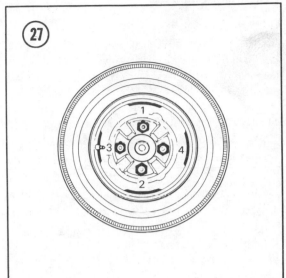

3

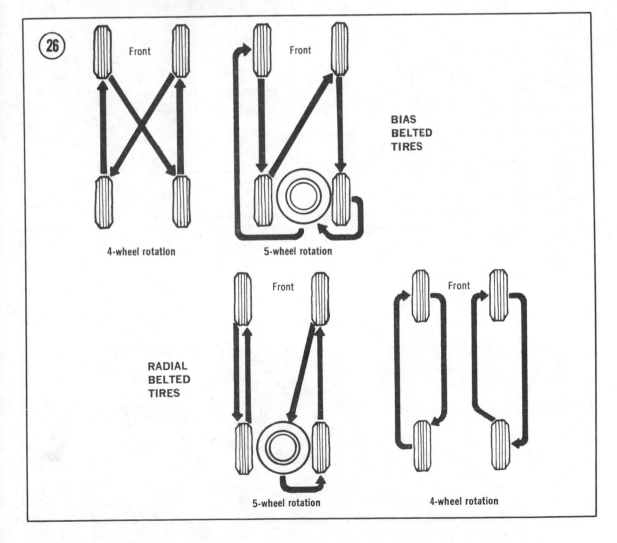

BIAS BELTED TIRES

4-wheel rotation

5-wheel rotation

RADIAL BELTED TIRES

5-wheel rotation

4-wheel rotation

Front

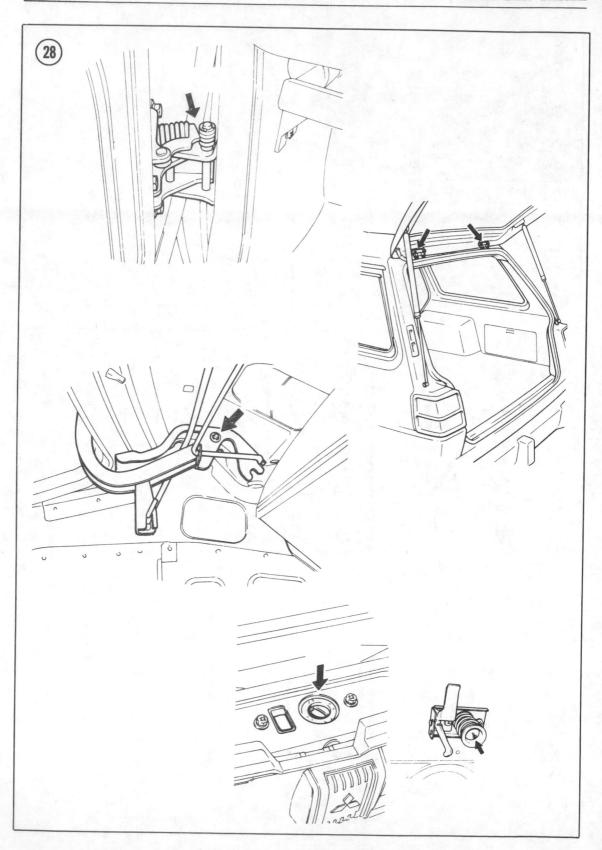

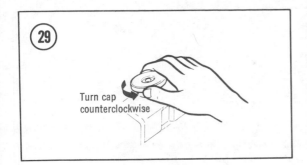

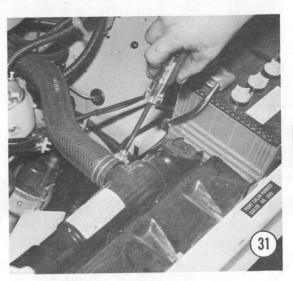

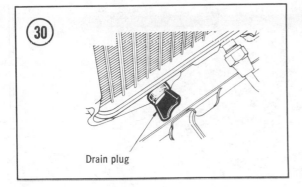

Drain plug

Body Lubrication

Lubricate hood, door, and deck lid locks, and striker seat adjuster at every oil change with multipurpose grease NLG1, Grade 2, EP. Lubricate hood, door, and deck lid hinges at every oil change with SE grade engine oil. Refer to **Figure 28**.

Exhaust System

Examine exhaust pipes, mufflers, and hangers at every other engine oil change for rust, holes, and other damage. Replace any damaged parts.

Radiator Coolant

Check the radiator level every engine oil change unless there is evidence of leakage or overheating. The coolant level should be 2 in. below the top of the filler neck when the engine is cold. Add a 50/50 mixture of high quality ethylene glycol anti-freeze and water if coolant additions are necessary. Do not overfill.

WARNING
Use care when removing radiator cap on a warm or hot engine. Hot water under pressure can boil out when pressure is released and cause severe scalding or burns. Loosen radiator cap to first notch and wait for pressure to escape before removing the cap. See Figure 29.

Drain and flush the cooling system every other engine tune-up as follows:

1. With engine at operating temperature, shut engine off and remove radiator cap. Refer to **Figure 29**.

2. Open radiator drain cock (**Figure 30**) and allow engine coolant to drain thoroughly. Close drain cock.

3. Fill cooling system with a 50/50 mixture of ethylene glycol anti-freeze and water.

4. Start engine and allow to idle. Check the water level in the radiator. Add the 50/50 mixture of anti-freeze and water until the radiator is filled to the proper level. Install radiator cap.

5. Check all hoses for correct installation and to be sure hose clamps are secure (**Figure 31**). Inspect hoses for cracks, deterioration, or extreme softness. Replace defective hoses.

6. Check entire cooling system for leaks.

NOTE: *If the cooling system is badly clogged, flush with a suitable commercial cleaner (refer to your local service station), following instructions on the container. Be sure to thoroughly flush the cooling system with fresh water after draining the cleaner. Then fill with fresh engine coolant as described in preceding steps.*

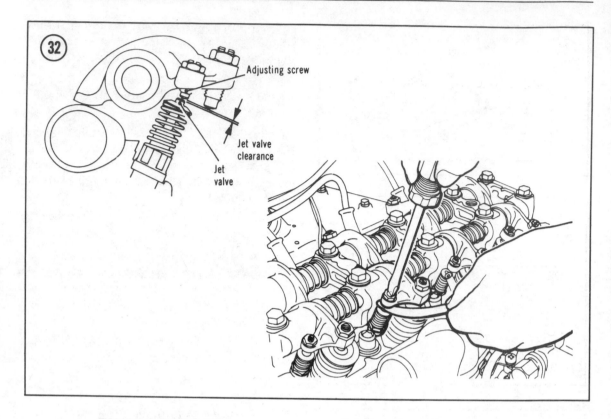

ENGINE TUNE-UP

The purpose of a tune-up is to restore power and performance lost over a gradual period of time due to normal wear.

Because of federal laws limiting exhaust emissions, it is important that the engine tune-up is done accurately. Economical, trouble-free operation can be assured if a complete tune-up is performed every 12,000 miles (1971-1975 models) or 15,000 miles (1976 models on).

Tune-ups generally consist of 3 distinct categories: compression, ignition, and carburetion. Carburetion adjustments should not be attempted until the compression and ignition phases have been completed. Carry out the tune-up in the exact sequence in this chapter for best results. See **Table 2** for tune-up specifications, end of chapter.

Tune-up Equipment Hook-up

A description of the various tools and specialized test instruments can be found in Chapter One. Always follow the manufacturer's recommendations for the use of test equipment. If such instructions are not available, the following can be used as a general guide:

a. *Voltmeter* — Connect the positive lead to the resistor side of the coil, and the negative lead to ground

b. *Timing light* — Connect the positive lead to the positive battery terminal; connect the trigger lead to the No. 1 spark plug; and connect the negative lead to ground

c. *Tachometer* — Connect the positive lead to the distributor side of the coil, and the negative lead to ground

d. *Dwell meter* — Connect the positive lead to the distributor side of the coil, and the negative lead to ground.

Jet Valve Adjustment
(1978 and Later Models)

NOTE: *Adjust the jet valve clearance prior to adjusting the intake valve clearance. Re adjust after retightening cylinder head bolts. Be sure to loosen adjusting screws prior to making jet valve clearance adjustment.*

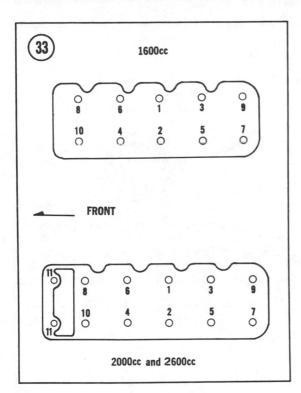

(33)

1600cc

8 6 1 3 9

10 4 2 5 7

← FRONT

11
8 6 1 3 9

10 4 2 5 7
11

2000cc and 2600cc

(34)

Table 3   TORQUE RECOMMENDATIONS

Cylinder head bolts[1]	
1600cc	51-54 ft.-lb. (69-73.5 N•m)
2000 & 2600cc	65-72 ft.-lb. (88.5-98 N•m)
Rocker cover[1] bolts	4-5 ft.-lb. (5-6.5 N•m)
1. Engine cold.	

Perform steps under *Valve Clearance Adjustment*, following, until the piston in the No. 4 cylinder comes to TDC. Then adjust jet valve as follows.

1. Back the intake valve adjusting screw out 2 or more turns.

2. Loosen jet valve adjusting screw locknut.

3. Turn the jet valve adjusting screw counterclockwise and insert 0.006 in. (0.15 mm) feeler gauge between the jet valve stem and adjusting screw (**Figure 32**).

4. Tighten adjusting screw until it touches the feeler gauge.

> NOTE: *The jet valve spring is weak in tensile strength. Therefore, take special precautions not to force the jet valve in. Be especially careful if the adjusting screw turns hard.*

5. Hold the rocker arm adjusting screw with a screwdriver so that it does not turn. Tighten the locknut.

Valve Clearance Adjustment

Noisy valves and valve lifters generally affect the driver's nerves more than they do engine performance. It is quite a simple problem to correct, however, so there is no point in enduring the din produced by clattering valve train components.

Before attempting to judge the valve noise level, warm the engine to operating temperature. Listen for valve noise while sitting in the driver's seat with the hood closed. Run the engine at idle and various higher speeds.

Adjust valve clearance (intake and exhaust) with the engine at normal operating temperature, as follows:

1. Shut the engine off and remove the valve cover. Torque the cylinder head bolts to specifications given in **Table 3**, with the engine still warm. See **Figure 33**.

2. At the top dead center of each cylinder, loosen rocker arm nuts. Adjust the valve clearance by turning the adjusting screw. Set valve clearance to 0.006 in. for the intake valve, 0.010 in. for the exhaust valve (engine still warm). Tighten the adjusting screw nuts. See **Figure 34**.

3

3. Install the breather and semicircular packing to the cylinder head after applying a sealant.

4. Install the rocker cover to the cylinder head through a rubber packing. Apply sealant to breather and semicircular packing surfaces. Torque rocker cover bolts down to 4-5 ft.-lb.

Compression Test

A compression test is performed to check for worn piston rings and/or valves. After adjusting the valves (see *Valve Clearance Adjustment*, preceding), check compression as follows:

1. Start engine and run until it reaches normal operating temperature. Shut engine off.

2. Remove spark plugs and washers from cylinder head (see *Spark Plug Inspection and Service*, following, for removal procedure).

3. Insert a compression gauge into the spark plug hole (**Figure 35**). Block the throttle valve open and have an assistant crank the engine over several revolutions to obtain the highest possible reading on the compression gauge. Write it down on a piece of paper.

4. Check compression on each cylinder. Repeat the compression check once more on each cylinder. Select the highest compression reading for each cylinder. The compression is considered normal if the lowest reading cylinder is more than 75% of the highest reading cylinder. **Table 4** may be used as a quick reference when checking cylinder compression pressures. It has been calculated so that the lowest reading number is 75% of the highest reading number.

Example: After checking the compression pressure in all cylinders it was found that the highest pressure obtained was 182 psi. The lowest pressure reading was 145 psi. By locating 182 psi in the maximum column, it is seen that the minimum allowable pressure is 136 psi. Since the lowest reading obtained was 145 psi, the compression is within satisfactory limits.

Spark Plug Inspection and Service

Spark plugs are available in various heat ranges hotter or colder than the plug originally installed at the factory.

Select plugs of a heat range designed for the loads and temperature conditions under which

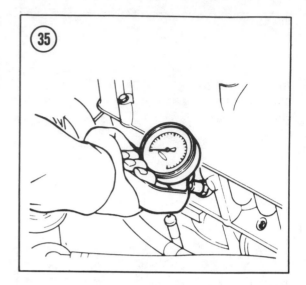

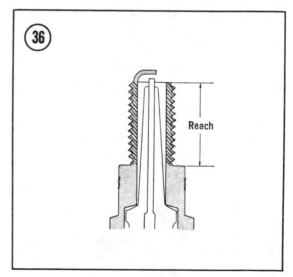

Reach

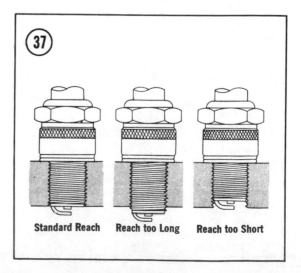

Standard Reach   Reach too Long   Reach too Short

the engine will be run. Use of incorrect heat ranges can cause seized pistons, scored cylinder walls, or damaged piston crowns.

In general, use a low-numbered plug for low speeds, low loads, and low temperatures. Use a higher-numbered plug for high speeds, high engine loads, and high temperatures.

NOTE: *Use the highest numbered plug that will not foul. In areas where seasonal temperature variations are great, the factory recommends a high-numbered plug for slower winter operation.*

The reach (length) of a plug is also important. A longer-than-normal plug could interfere with the piston, causing severe damage. Refer to **Figures 36 and 37**.

A quick test can be made to determine if the plug is correct for your usage. Accelerate hard and maintain a high, but lawful steady speed. Shut the throttle off, and kill the engine at the same time, allow the car to slow, out of gear. Do not allow the engine to slow the car. Remove the plug and check the condition of the electrode area. Spark plugs of the correct heat range, with the engine in a proper state of tune, will appear light tan. See **Figure 38**.

If the insulator is white or burned, the plug is too hot and should be replaced with a colder one. Also check the setting of the carburetor, for it may be too lean.

A too-cold plug will have sooty deposits ranging in color from dark brown to black. Replace with a hotter plug and check for too-rich carburetion.

If any one plug is found unsatisfactory, discard the set.

Changing spark plugs is generally a simple operation. Occasionally heat and corrosion can cause the plug to bind in the cylinder head making removal difficult. Do not use force; the head is easily damaged. Here is the proper way to replace a plug:

1. Blow out any debris which has collected in the spark plug wells (it could fall into the hole and cause damage).

2. Gently remove the spark plug leads by pulling up and out on the cap. Do not jerk the wires or pull on the wire itself.

3. Apply a penetrating oil (such as Liquid Wrench) to the base of the plug and allow it to work into the threads.

4. Back out the plugs with a socket that has a rubber insert designed to grip the insulator. Be careful not to drop the plugs where they could become lodged. See **Figure 39**.

NOTE: *Keep the plugs in order as they are removed; the condition of the spark plugs is an indication of engine condition and can warn of developing trouble that can be isolated by cylinder.*

5. Clean the seating area after removal, being careful that no dirt drops into the spark plug hole.

6. Using a round feeler gauge, check and adjust clearance between the electrodes (**Table 2**). Refer to **Figure 40**. Do not bend the inner electrode or damage to the insulator may result.

7. Apply a dab of graphite or drop of oil to the spark plug threads to simplify future removal.

Table 4 COMPRESSION PRESSURE LIMITS

Pressure (psi)		Pressure (psi)	
Maximum	Minimum	Maximum	Minimum
134	101	188	141
136	102	190	142
138	104	192	144
140	105	194	145
142	107	196	147
146	110	198	148
148	111	200	150
150	113	202	151
152	114	204	153
154	115	206	154
156	117	208	156
158	118	210	157
160	120	212	158
162	121	214	160
164	123	216	162
166	124	218	163
168	126	220	165
170	127	222	166
172	129	224	168
174	131	226	169
176	132	228	171
178	133	230	172
180	135	232	174
182	136	234	175
184	138	236	177
186	140	238	178

(38) **SPARK PLUG CONDITION**

NORMAL
- Identified by light tan or gray deposits on the firing tip.
- Can be cleaned.

GAP BRIDGED
- Identified by deposit buildup closing gap between electrodes.
- Caused by oil or carbon fouling. If deposits are not excessive, the plug can be cleaned.

OIL FOULED
- Identified by wet black deposits on the insulator shell bore electrodes.
- Caused by excessive oil entering combustion chamber through worn rings and pistons, excessive clearance between valve guides and stems, or worn or loose bearings. Can be cleaned. If engine is not repaired, use a hotter plug.

CARBON FOULED
- Identified by black, dry fluffy carbon deposits on insulator tips, exposed shell surfaces and electrodes.
- Caused by too cold a plug, weak ignition, dirty air cleaner, defective fuel pump, too rich a fuel mixture, improperly operating heat riser, or excessive idling. Can be cleaned.

LEAD FOULED
- Identified by dark gray, black, yellow, or tan deposits or a fused glazed coating on the insulator tip.
- Caused by highly leaded gasoline. Can be cleaned.

WORN
- Identified by severely eroded or worn electrodes.
- Caused by normal wear. Should be replaced.

FUSED SPOT DEPOSIT
- Identified by melted or spotty deposits resembling bubbles or blisters.
- Caused by sudden acceleration. Can be cleaned.

OVERHEATING
- Identified by a white or light gray insulator with small black or gray brown spots and with bluish-burnt appearance of electrodes.
- Caused by engine overheating, wrong type of fuel, loose spark plugs, too hot a plug, low fuel pump pressure, or incorrect ignition timing. Replace the plug.

PREIGNITION
- Identified by melted electrodes and possibly blistered insulator. Metallic deposits on insulator indicate engine damage.
- Caused by wrong type of fuel, incorrect ignition timing or advance, too hot a plug, burned valves, or engine overheating. Replace the plug.

8. Thread the plug into the spark plug holes finger-tight, then tighten ¼ turn more with a wrench. Further tightening will flatten the gasket and cause binding.

9. Connect spark plug wires to spark plugs (make sure you do not get the wires crossed). Push the plug wire connectors firmly onto the spark plug tips.

Distributor Cap and Rotor Check

Remove distributor retaining spring clips and remove distributor cap. Wipe away grease and dirt. Check cap and rotor for cracks, wear, or damage. Replace any part necessary. See **Figure 41**.

Contact Point Replacement

1. Remove distributor cap and rotor.

2. Remove the stop washer and separate the link from the breaker plate. Remove the 2 screws and then remove the vacuum controller as shown in **Figure 42** (1974 and earlier distributor illustrated).

3. Remove the breaker assembly (**Figure 43**).

4. Discard old points and install new points by reversing preceding steps. Adjust point gap (see *Contact Point Adjustment*, following).

Contact Point Adjustment

1. Rotate engine crankshaft until widest contact point gap is obtained (the heel of the contact arm is lifted to the highest position by the distributor cam).

2. Check the point gap with a feeler gauge. If the gap is not between 0.018 and 0.021 in. (0.45-0.55 mm), as shown in **Figure 44**, loosen the 2 lock screws and insert a screwdriver into the hole at (A) as shown in **Figure 45**. With the screwdriver blade in place in the cam base, twist the screwdriver to move the breaker arm support to adjust the breaker point gap. After the adjustment, securely tighten the 2 lock screws.

Distributor Lubrication

Apply a small amount of multipurpose grease to the cam oil felt, contact arm spindle, and control rod. See **Figure 46**.

Condenser

A faulty condenser will cause breaker points to fail early. Always replace the condenser when points are changed.

Spark Advance and Retard Mechanism Check

With the engine idling, check the timing with a timing light. See if the ignition timing advances when the distributor rubber plug is removed. See **Figure 47**. Then check to see if the ignition timing advances as the engine speed increases. If the spark neither advances or retards during these checks, readjust the timing and/or replace the vacuum control. Finally, see if the timing of the spark is advanced with increase in engine speed. After these checks, if the spark is neither advanced nor retarded, readjust ignition timing or replace vacuum control.

Ignition Timing (All Models Through 1974)

With the engine idling, check the ignition timing with a timing light. Loosen the 2 lock screws (refer to **Figure 46**), insert screwdriver blade into hole and adjust timing. Rotation of the screwdriver toward direction (A) makes the timing faster, toward direction (R), slower. If timing adjuster is varied one division, it changes timing 4 degrees. Refer to **Figures 48 and 49**.

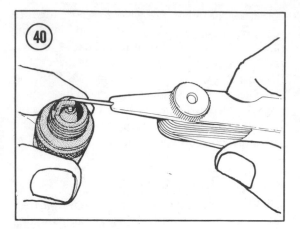

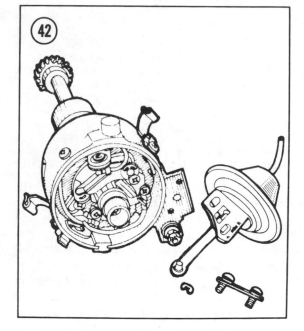

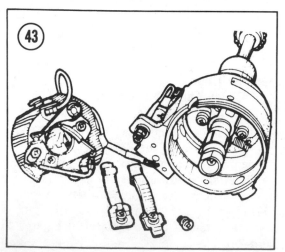

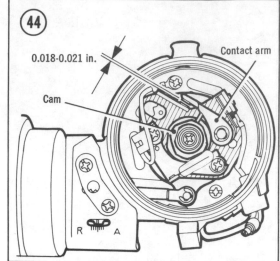

0.018-0.021 in.

Contact arm

Cam

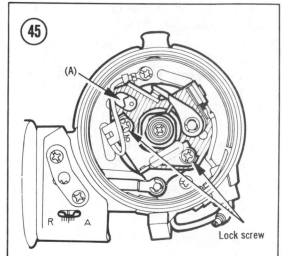

(A)

Lock screw

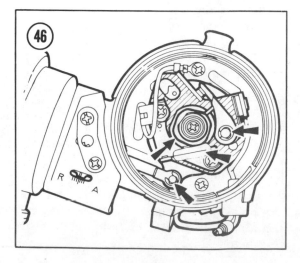

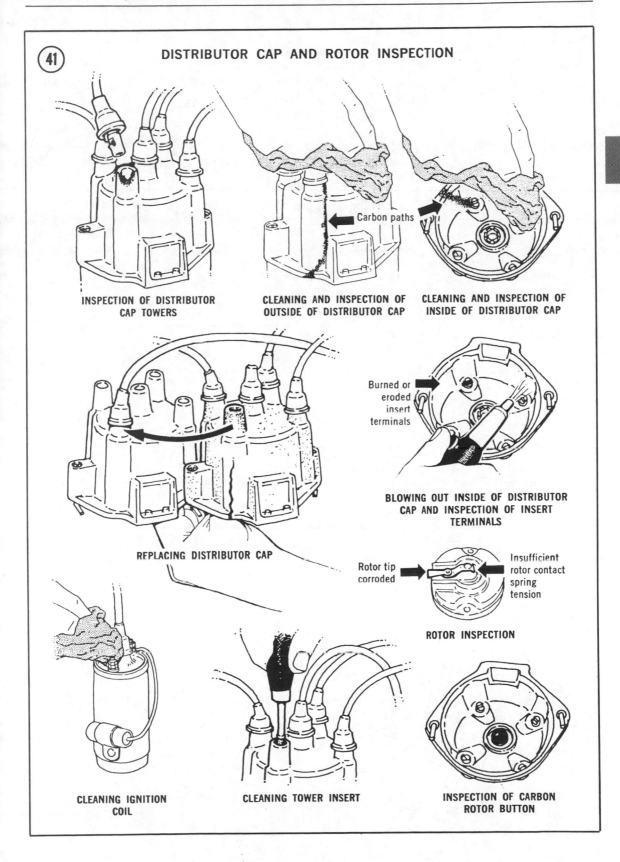

DISTRIBUTOR CAP AND ROTOR INSPECTION

INSPECTION OF DISTRIBUTOR
CAP TOWERS

CLEANING AND INSPECTION OF
OUTSIDE OF DISTRIBUTOR CAP

Carbon paths

CLEANING AND INSPECTION OF
INSIDE OF DISTRIBUTOR CAP

REPLACING DISTRIBUTOR CAP

Burned or
eroded
insert
terminals

BLOWING OUT INSIDE OF DISTRIBUTOR
CAP AND INSPECTION OF INSERT
TERMINALS

Rotor tip
corroded

Insufficient
rotor contact
spring
tension

ROTOR INSPECTION

CLEANING IGNITION
COIL

CLEANING TOWER INSERT

INSPECTION OF CARBON
ROTOR BUTTON

3

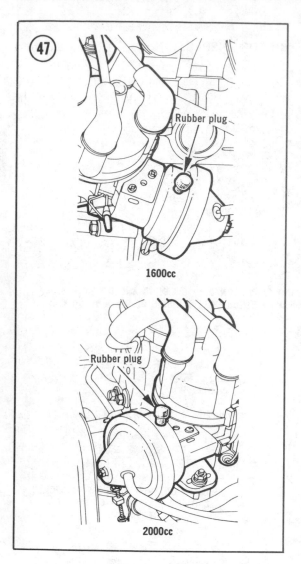

Rubber plug

1600cc

Rubber plug

2000cc

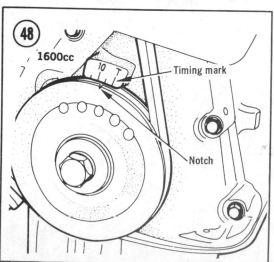

48

1600cc

10 T

Timing mark

Notch

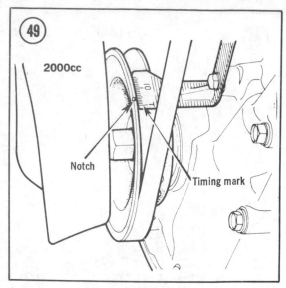

49

2000cc

Notch

Timing mark

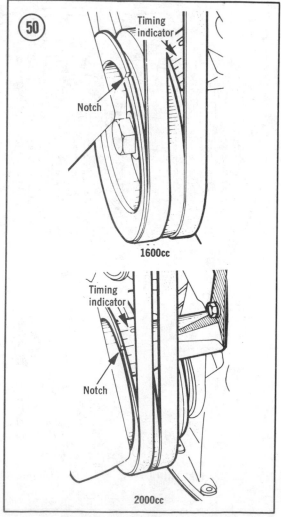

50

Timing indicator

Notch

1600cc

Timing indicator

Notch

2000cc

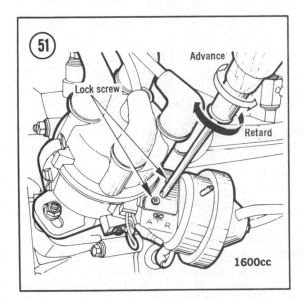

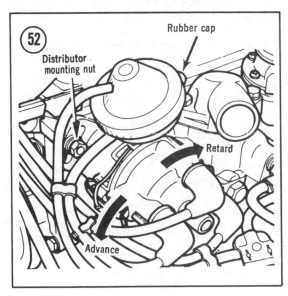

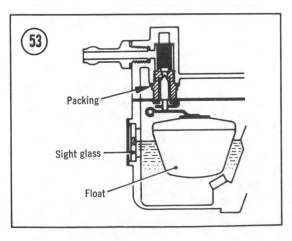

Ignition Timing (1975 Models on)

1. Set the No. 1 piston at TDC (top dead center) on compression stroke by aligning the crankshaft pulley notch with the "T" mark on the timing indicator (**Figure 50**). Rotate the crankshaft pulley to set the notch of the pulley to the basic ignition timing position (this varies with different engines, see **Table 2**).

2. Loosen distributor mounting nuts and turn distributor body so breaker points begin to open. Tighten distributor mounting nuts.

3. When so equipped, remove rubber plug from retard side of distributor vacuum control chamber (**Figure 47**). No manifold vacuum acts on the retard side and the ignition timing is not retarded.

4. On 1600cc engines without silent shaft, idle engine at its proper speed (**Table 2**). Loosen 2 lock screws with a Phillips screwdriver (**Figure 51**). Connect a timing light and make adjustments using the timing adjuster until the correct setting is reached (**Table 2**). Tighten the lock screws.

5. On silent shaft engines, idle engine at proper speed (**Table 2**) and loosen distributor mounting nut. (The 1600cc engine from 1977 on does not have the 2 lock screws that previous 1600cc engines have.) Turn the housing to adjust timing. Tighten mounting nut. Refer to **Figure 52**.

6. If so equipped, reinstall rubber cap on retard side of distributor vacuum control chamber as shown in **Figure 47**. Recheck timing after cap is installed.

> NOTE: *Effective with 1977 models, only the California cars use the retard system; cars for the remaining U.S. states have no retard system and no rubber cap.*

Carburetor Fuel Level Adjustment

The sight glass is fitted at the float chamber. Normal fuel level is within the center part ($\frac{1}{8}$ in. in diameter) on the sight glass. See **Figure 53**. Float level adjustment is accomplished by increasing or decreasing the number of needle valve packings. A sheet of needle valve packing is 0.039 in. thick. Adding or removing a sheet of packing will change the float level by 0.118 in.

Carburetor Idle Adjustment
(Through 1974 Models)

1. Race the engine up to 2,500 rpm 2 or 3 times after the engine has idled long enough to warm up to operating temperature.

2. Adjust the pilot screw (**Figure 54**) and the primary throttle stop screw (**Figure 55**) alternately until 800-900 rpm is obtained.

3. After adjustment, install the idle limiter (**Figure 56**) on the pilot screw.

Carburetor Idle Adjustment
(1975 Models)

1. Idle the engine until the coolant reaches normal operating temperature.

2. Remove air shutoff solenoid valve coupler on the air control valve (**Figure 57**).

3. See **Figure 58**. On manual transmission cars, adjust idle speed to approximately 900 rpm by means of throttle stop screw (B) and pilot screw (A). Be sure throttle stop screw does not touch throttle arm. On automatic transmission cars, adjust idle speed to approximately 800 rpm by means of throttle stop screw (C) and pilot screw (A).

4. Connect air shutoff solenoid valve coupler, then set engine speed to 900-1,000 rpm with screw (B) on manual transmission cars, and to 800-900 rpm with screw (C) on automatic transmission cars.

5. In automatic transmission cars, remove rubber plug from vacuum control chamber nipple to leave vacuum control chamber and vacuum hose open to atmosphere (**Figure 59**). Set idle speed at 800-900 rpm by adjusting throttle stop screw (B). Install rubber plug in nipple.

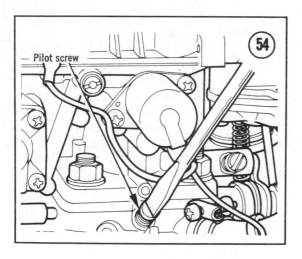

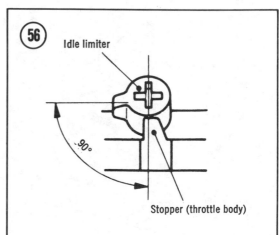

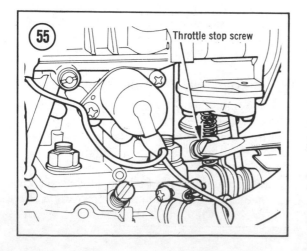

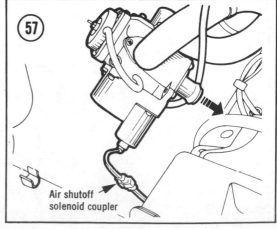

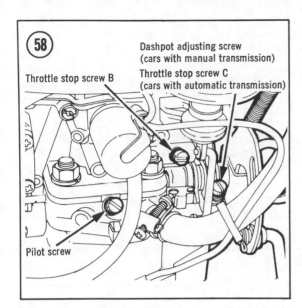

58

Throttle stop screw B

Dashpot adjusting screw
(cars with manual transmission)

Throttle stop screw C
(cars with automatic transmission)

Pilot screw

6. Increase engine speed to 2,500 rpm 2 or 3 times to be sure engine idle speed has been properly adjusted. After adjustment, install idle limiter on pilot screw (A) as shown in **Figure 60**.

**Carburetor Idle Adjustment
(1976 Models on)**

1. Idle the engine until the coolant reaches normal operating temperature.

2. Remove air hose between the reed valve and the air cleaner, at reed valve side, and plug air inlet of reed valve. See **Figure 61** or **Figure 62**.

3. Set engine speed about 50 rpm lower than that specified in **Table 2** by adjusting idle speed adjusting screw and idle mixture adjusting screw (**Figure 63**).

3

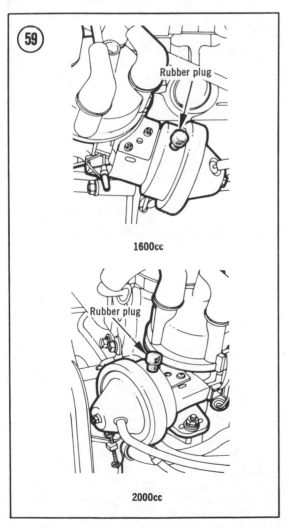

59

Rubber plug

1600cc

Rubber plug

2000cc

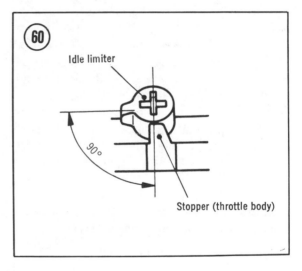

60

Idle limiter

90°

Stopper (throttle body)

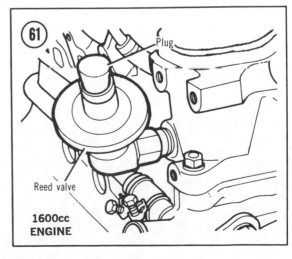

61

Plug

Reed valve

1600cc
ENGINE

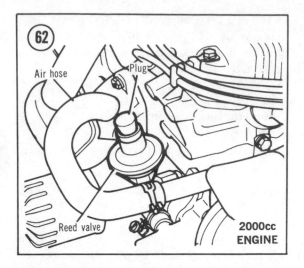

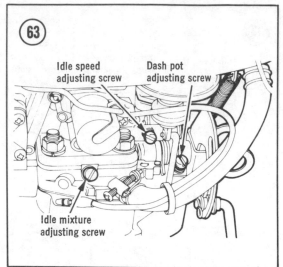

4. Slowly turn idle mixture adjusting screw
clockwise (refer to **Figure 63**) until engine
begins to idle poorly. Then turn idle mixture
adjusting screw counterclockwise slowly until
idle is smooth.

5. Fit air hose onto reed valve. Set engine speed
to the specified idle speed (see **Table 2**) by adjusting idle speed adjusting screw. Refer to
Figure 63.

6. Increase engine speed to 2,500 rpm 2 or 3
times to be sure that adjustments are correct.
Install idle mixture adjusting screw idle limiter
(**Figure 64**).

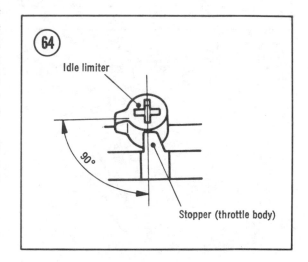

Dashpot Adjustment
(Manual Transmission Models Only)

1. Push up lower end of dashpot rod until it
stops. Check to see if engine is running at
1,500-2,000 rpm. See **Figure 65**.

2. When pushrod is quickly released, there
must be from 1.5-3.5 seconds before engine
speed drops to 900 rpm. If necessary, adjust
dashpot operating angle adjusting screw until
correct.

Carburetor High Altitude Compensator

On models equipped with a high altitude carburetor (for use at 4,000 ft. or above), a compensator knob is installed as shown in **Figure 66**. Set the knob to the ON position, readjust
the idle as outlined previously, and advance the
ignition timing from 5° BTDC to 10° BTDC by
rotating the distributor housing.

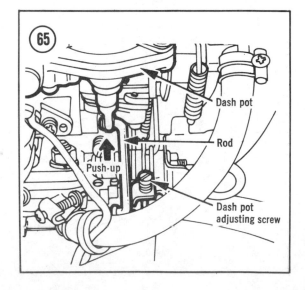

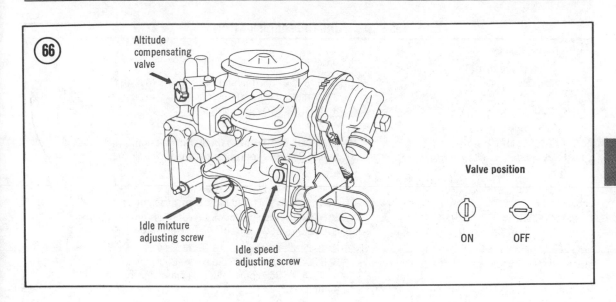

Table 2 is on the following page.

Table 2   TUNE-UP SPECIFICATIONS

Ignition timing

Models through 1974

   1600cc — TDC @ 850 rpm (manual transmission & automatic transmission w/EGR)

   2000cc — 3° BTDC @ 850 rpm

1975 models

   1600cc and
   2000cc — 5° ATDC @ 950 rpm (manual transmission);
5° ATDC @ 850 rpm (automatic transmission)

1976 models

   1600cc — TDC @ 950 rpm (manual transmission);
TDC @ 850 rpm (automatic transmission)

   2000cc — 3° BTDC @ 950 rpm (manual transmission);
3° BTDC @ 850 rpm (automatic transmision)

1977 models

   1600cc — 5° BTDC @ 850 rpm (U.S. except California);
5° BTDC @ 950 rpm (California manual transmission models)

   2000cc — 5° BTDC @ 950 rpm;
5° BTDC @ 850 (49-state automatic transmission models)

1978 49-state models

   1600cc — 5° BTDC ± 1° @ 650 ± 50 rpm (manual transmission except high altitude)

   1600cc — 5° BTDC ± 1° @ 700 ± 50 rpm (automatic transmission)

   1600cc — 10° BTDC ± 1° @ 650 ± 50 rpm (manual transmission, high altitude)

   2000cc — 5° BTDC ± 1° @ 650 ± 50 rpm (manual transmission);
5° BTDC ± 1° @ 700 ± 50 rpm (automatic transmission)

   2600cc — 7° BTDC ± 1° @ 850 ± 50 rpm (manual transmission);

   2600cc — 7° BTDC ± 1° @ 850 ± 50 rpm (automatic transmission)

1978 California models

   1600cc — 5° BTDC ± 1° @ 650 ± 50 rpm (manual transmission);
700 ± 50 rpm (automatic transmission)

   2000cc — 5° BTDC ± 1° @ 650 ± 50 rpm (manual transmission);
700 ± 50 rpm (automatic transmission)

   2600cc — 7° BTDC ± 1° @ 700 ± 50 rpm (manual transission);
750 ± 50 rpm (automatic transmission)

1978 Canada models

   1600cc and
   2000cc — 5° BTDC ± 1° @ 850 ± 50 rpm (all models)

   2600cc — 7° BTDC ± 1° @ 850 ± 50 rpm (all models)

1979 U.S.A. models

   1600cc — 5° BTDC ± 1° @ 650 ± 50 rpm (manual transmission);
700 ± 50 rpm (automatic transmission)

   2600cc — 7° BTDC ± 1° @ 850 ± 50 rpm (all models)

1979 Canada models

   1600cc and
   2000cc — 5° BTDC ± 1° @ 850 ± 50 rpm

   2600cc — 7° BTDC ± 1° @ 850 ± 50 rpm

(continued)

Table 2   TUNE-UP SPECIFICATIONS (continued)

Valve clearance	
Intake	0.006 in. (0.15 mm), hot engine; 0.003 in. (0.07 mm), cold engine
Exhaust	0.010 in. (0.25 mm), hot engine; 0.007 in. (0.17 mm), cold engine
Spark plug gap	
Models through 1977	0.028-0.031 in. (0.71-0.78 mm)
1978-1979 U.S.A. models	0.039-0.043 in. (1.0-1.1 mm)
1978-1979 Canada models	0.028-0.031 in. (0.7-0.8 mm)
Distributor contact point gap	0.018-0.021 in. (0.45-0.55 mm)
Dwell	
Models through 1977	49-55°
1978-1979 models	52° ± 3°
Firing order	1-3-4-2

3

CHAPTER FOUR

ENGINE

This chapter provides complete information on removing, overhauling, and installing the engine. Refer to **Figures 1 through 7** during these procedures. See **Table 1** (end of chapter) for general engine specifications.

The Silent Shaft engines incorporate 2 counter-balance shafts located at different heights on opposite sides of the crankshaft. The shafts rotate at 2 times crankshaft speed in opposite directions to cancel engine vibrations. (In the 2000/2600 cc engines, the left side shaft turns clockwise with the crankshaft; the right side turns in the opposite direction. In the 1600cc engines, the right side shaft turns clockwise with the crankshaft; the left side shaft turns in the opposite direction.)

General engine overhaul and teardown procedures are applicable to both types of engines. Refer to Chapter Three for maintenance and tune-up procedures for all engines.

ENGINE/TRANSMISSION REMOVAL

1. Remove under cover, then drain coolant from radiator and engine by opening drain plug located at bottom of radiator, and drain cock located at right rear of cylinder block.

2. Remove battery.

3. Remove ground strap. Disconnect ignition coil, vacuum control solenoid valve, fuel cutoff solenoid valve, generator, starting motor, transmission switch, backup light switch, water temperature gauge unit, and oil pressure switch wiring.

4. Remove air cleaner after disconnecting breather hose. Disconnect hot air duct and vacuum hose.

5. Disconnect accelerator rod.

6. Disconnect heater hose.

7. Disconnect hose between fuel pump return pipe and fuel strainer.

8. Disconnect exhaust pipe from exhaust manifold. Detach the muffler pipe bracket at the transmission.

9. Disconnect vacuum hose from purge control valve (through 1973 models) and remove purge air hose from between purge control valve and intake manifold.

10. Remove radiator cowl (only on the 1600cc model) and radiator. On cars with automatic transmission, remove oil cooler pipe when removing radiator.

11. Inside the car, remove console box. Detach control lever assembly from transmission.

12. Remove engine hood.

①

1600cc ENGINE
(Without Silent Shaft)

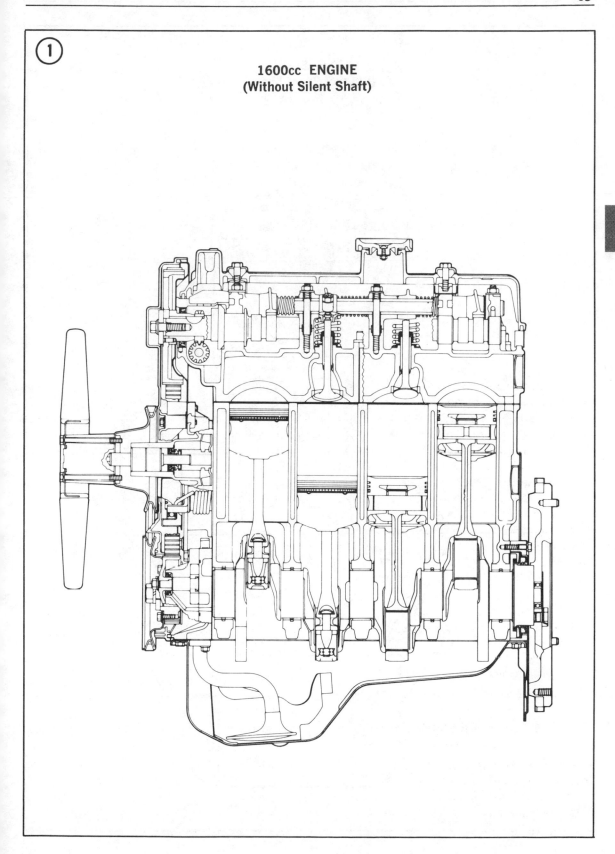

4

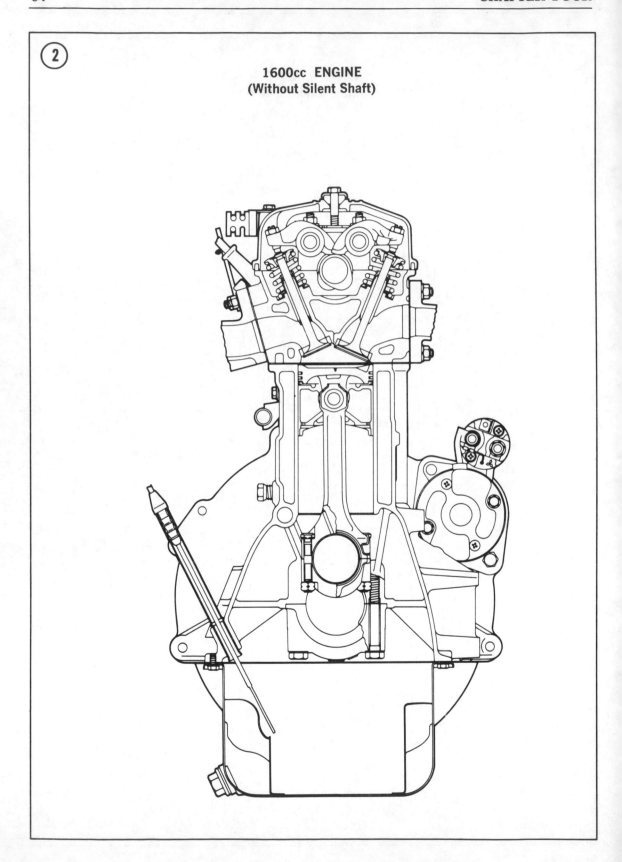

② 1600cc ENGINE
(Without Silent Shaft)

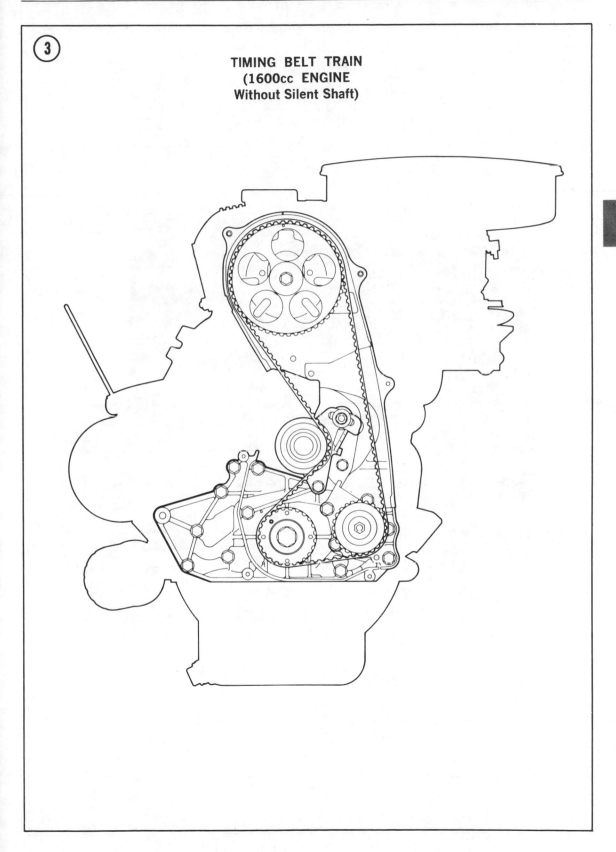

③ TIMING BELT TRAIN
(1600cc ENGINE
Without Silent Shaft)

4

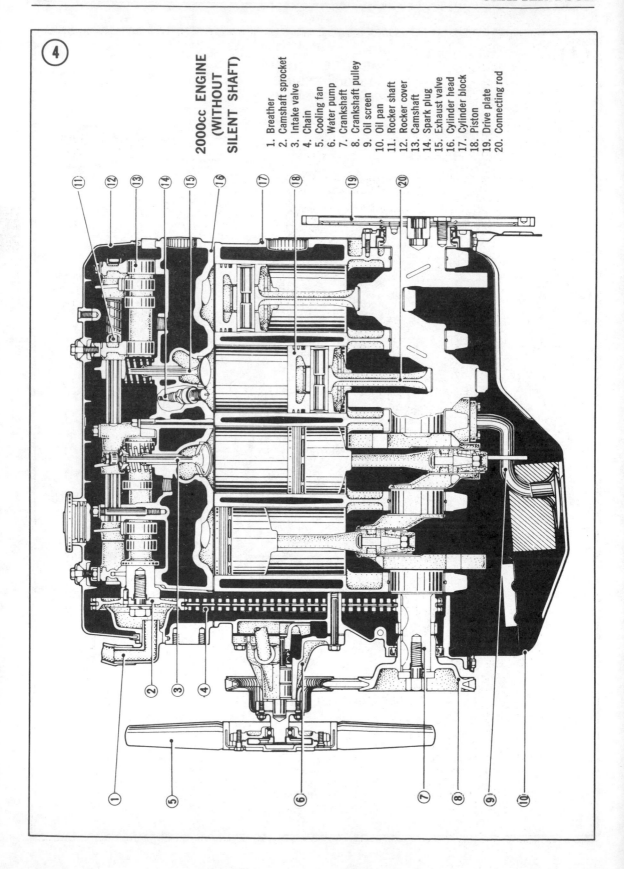

④

2000cc ENGINE (WITHOUT SILENT SHAFT)

1. Breather
2. Camshaft sprocket
3. Intake valve
4. Chain
5. Cooling fan
6. Water pump
7. Crankshaft
8. Crankshaft pulley
9. Oil screen
10. Oil pan
11. Rocker shaft
12. Rocker cover
13. Camshaft
14. Spark plug
15. Exhaust valve
16. Cylinder head
17. Cylinder block
18. Piston
19. Drive plate
20. Connecting rod

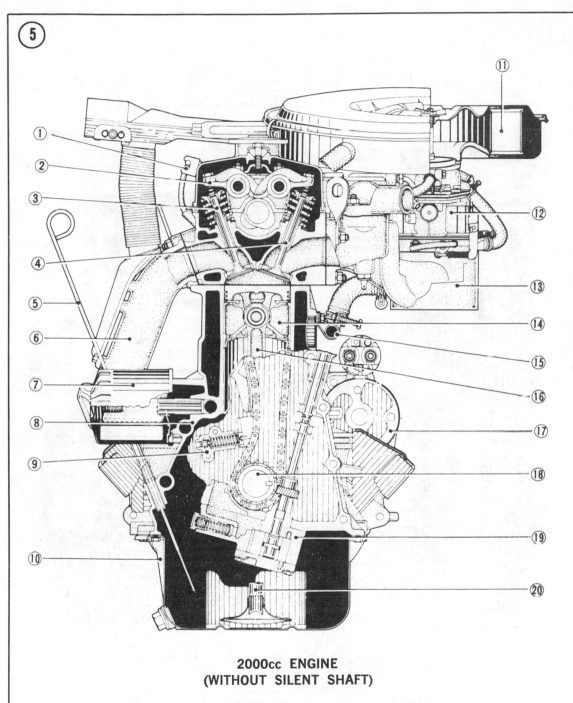

**2000cc ENGINE
(WITHOUT SILENT SHAFT)**

1. Spark plug cable
2. Rocker arm
3. Exhaust valve
4. Intake valve
5. Oil level gauge
6. Exhaust manifold
7. Oil filter
8. Cylinder block
9. Tensioner
10. Oil pan
11. Air cleaner
12. Carburetor
13. Intake manifold
14. Piston
15. Heater pipe
16. Connecting rod
17. Starter motor
18. Crankshaft
19. Oil pump
20. Oil screen

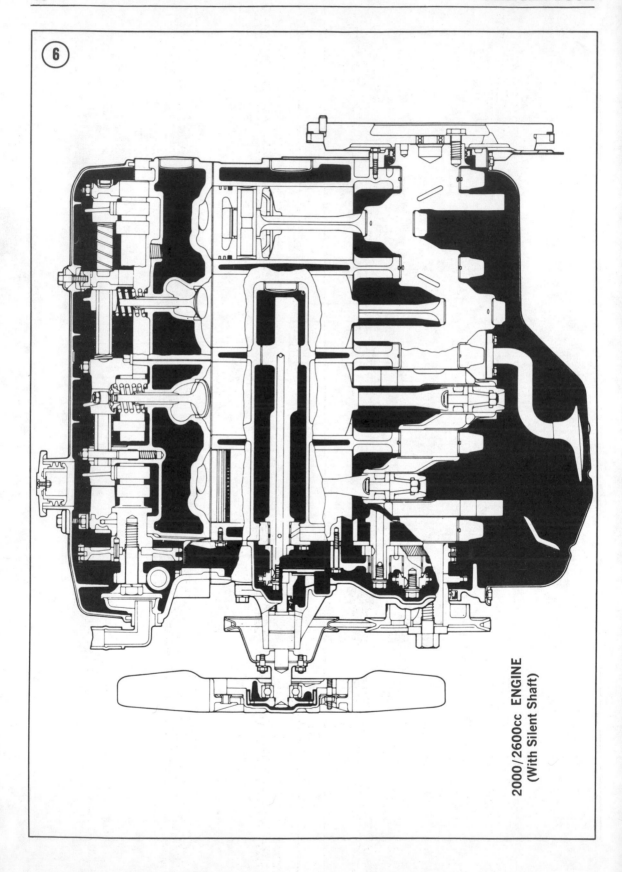

6

2000/2600cc ENGINE
(With Silent Shaft)

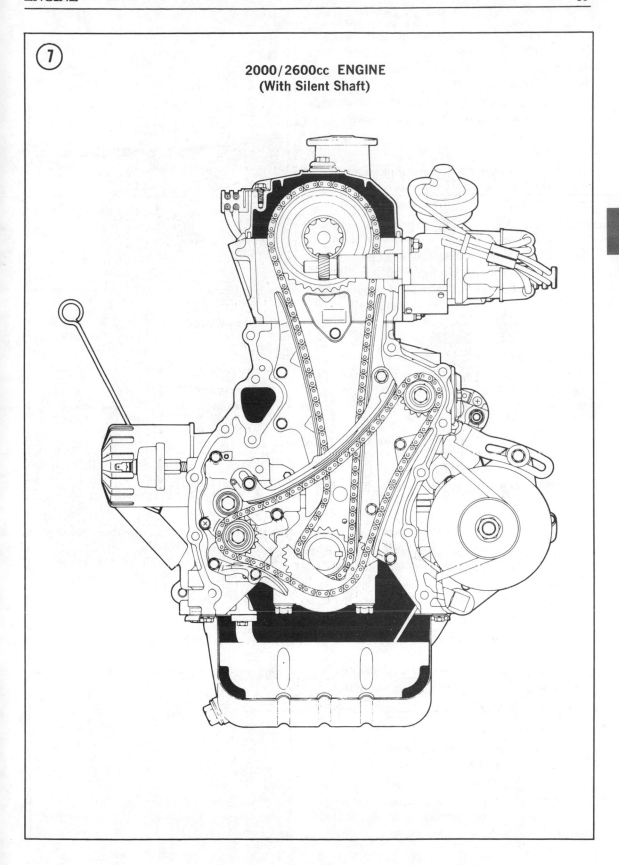

2000/2600cc ENGINE
(With Silent Shaft)

13. Disconnect speedometer cable and the wiring of the back-up lamp switch (and inhibitor switch on cars equipped with automatic transmission) from transmission.

14. Disconnect clutch shift lever from clutch cable. Disconnect cable from cable bracket.

15. Drain transmission fluid by removing the drain plug.

16. On cars equipped with dynamic dampers, remove dampers and locking bolts for attaching flange yoke at rear of drive shaft. Pull drive shaft out from the transmission.

17. On 1975 models on, equipped with Torque-Flite automatic transmission, remove tie rod.

18. See **Figure 8**. Support transmission on a jack. Remove front and rear insulator locking bolts and nuts. Take off rear engine support bracket.

19. Attach wire ropes to front and rear engine hangers. Lift engine/transmission unit with these wire ropes and a chain hoist. (Remove engine/transmission obliquely upward while moving it forward.)

> NOTE: *When engine/transmission unit cannot be removed because lower part of bell housing interferes with relay rod, raise rear of transmission slightly until bell housing is above relay rod. Then remove the unit.*

20. Check engine support insulators and pads for cracks or other damage. Replace any defective parts.

21. Check accelerator rod and cable.

22. Check heater, radiator, and fuel hoses for deterioration or damage. Replace where necessary.

23. Perform any engine overhaul procedure needed at this time, referring to individual sections in this chapter.

ENGINE/TRANSMISSION INSTALLATION

1. After engine overhaul or minor repair has been performed, the engine can be installed. Use rags at rear of cylinder head to prevent damage to toe board.

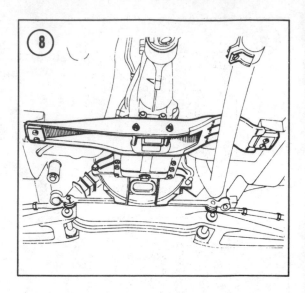

2. Lift engine/transmission higher than the mounting position. Install front insulators first, then rear insulators and related parts.

> CAUTION
> *Be careful not to twist rubber or smear it with gasoline when installing the insulator.*

3. When installing a front insulator rolling stopper, use care to provide sufficient clearance between the stopper and the side of the insulator. See **Figure 9**. On the 1600cc model, the distance indicated by (A) in the illustration should be 0.4 in. On the 2000/2600cc model, (B) should be 0.2 in.

4. When installing the rear engine support bracket to floor stringer of car body, tighten bolts to 7 ft.-lb. torque. Check to see if tongue of each lockwasher is properly aligned with a flat of the bolt head. If aligned, tighten bolt and bend tongue. After installation, make certain 3/4 in. or more clearance exists between engine support bracket (rear) and exhaust pipe.

> CAUTION
> *The location of the engine support bracket (rear) on the car body differs with the type of transmission used.*

5. Tighten bolts and nuts to standard torque indicated in **Table 2**, end of chapter.

6. Fill radiator with recommended quantity of cooling water and anti-freeze. Refer to Chapter Six.

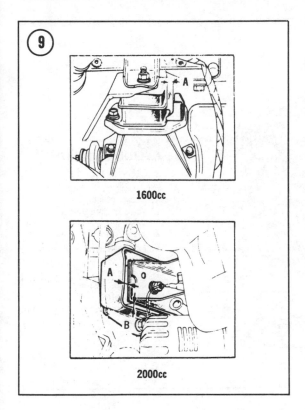

1600cc

2000cc

7. Fill crankcase with engine oil (refer to *Engine Lubrication System*, this chapter), and transmission case with transmission fluid (refer to Chapter Nine).

8. Adjust hood so there is a uniform clearance between car body and hood. (The height of the hood can be adjusted by means of the bumper screws.)

9. Adjust clutch pedal free travel (see Chapter Nine).

CYLINDER HEAD

The aluminum alloy cylinder head features hemispherical combustion chambers. Intake ports are arranged on the left, exhaust ports on the right. The air/fuel mixture is drawn into the cylinder and exhaust gases driven out from the cylinder in one direction. Valve arrangement is of the "V" type. The camshaft supports are formed integral with the top of the cylinder head, between the intake and exhaust valves. Camshaft bearing caps are tightened with stud bolts to the supports. These die-cast aluminum caps (front, rear, and center, No. 2 to No. 4) are located with dowel pins on the head. The

rear cap has an oil hole through which the oil coming from the cylinder block past the head is led to the rocker arm shaft. The caps are lubricated with the oil supplied through oil holes made in the rocker arm shaft, lubricating, in turn, the camshaft journals. See **Figure 10** for the sectional view of the cylinder head used on models through 1974. **Figure 11** shows the 1975-on cylinder head. The exhaust port on this head has been provided with a hole for installing an air injection pipe which supplies the secondary air. (In cars for Canada, the cylinder head is the same as 1974 models.)

NOTE: *While the cylinder head on 1975 models has been modified as described above, the servicing procedure is the same as for earlier models.*

Intake Manifold

The aluminum alloy intake manifold employs the independent branch type with efficient suction without suction interference. The cooling water from the cylinder head water jacket enters the manifold and then the radiator, through the thermostat. After heating the heat riser located on the lower side of the carburetor mounting, and passing through a bypass passage provided in the manifold, it returns to the water pump through the heater pipe.

On the 1600cc engine (1975-on) the location of the blow-by gas nipple and thermo valve in the intake manifold have been changed and a nipple for the control vacuum added. The intake manifold used in cars for Canada has no provision for the EGR valve installation. See **Figures 12 and 13**. The 2000cc engine (1975-on) is also changed from earlier models. The thermo valve location in the intake manifold has been changed and a nipple for the control vacuum added. See **Figures 14 and 15**. The intake manifold for Canadian cars (1975-on) has no provision for the installation of the EGR valve.

Exhaust Manifold

The cast iron exhaust manifold is of the dual exhaust type with 2 independent exhaust outlets, one for the No. 1 and No. 4 cylinders and one for the No. 2 and No. 3 cylinders.

4

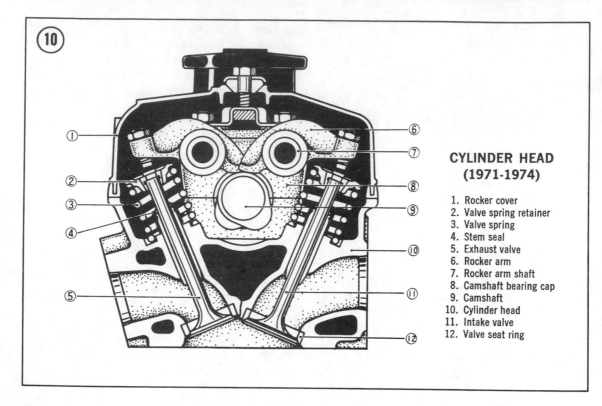

**CYLINDER HEAD
(1971-1974)**

1. Rocker cover
2. Valve spring retainer
3. Valve spring
4. Stem seal
5. Exhaust valve
6. Rocker arm
7. Rocker arm shaft
8. Camshaft bearing cap
9. Camshaft
10. Cylinder head
11. Intake valve
12. Valve seat ring

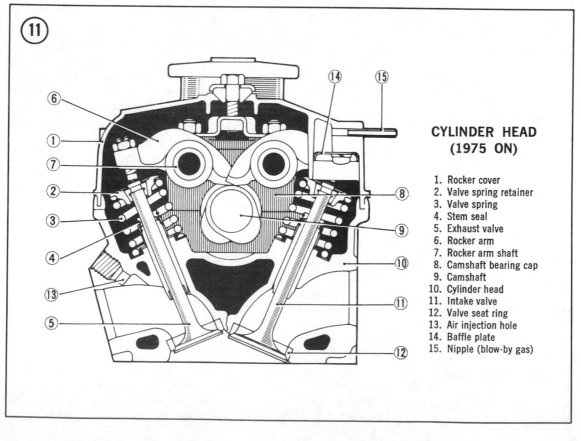

**CYLINDER HEAD
(1975 ON)**

1. Rocker cover
2. Valve spring retainer
3. Valve spring
4. Stem seal
5. Exhaust valve
6. Rocker arm
7. Rocker arm shaft
8. Camshaft bearing cap
9. Camshaft
10. Cylinder head
11. Intake valve
12. Valve seat ring
13. Air injection hole
14. Baffle plate
15. Nipple (blow-by gas)

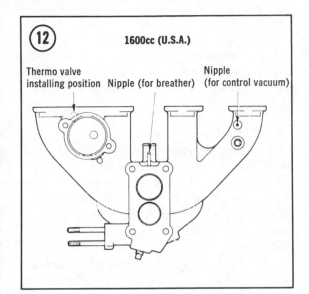

⑫ 1600cc (U.S.A.)

Thermo valve installing position Nipple (for breather) Nipple (for control vacuum)

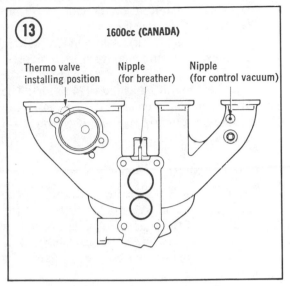

⑬ 1600cc (CANADA)

Thermo valve installing position Nipple (for breather) Nipple (for control vacuum)

4

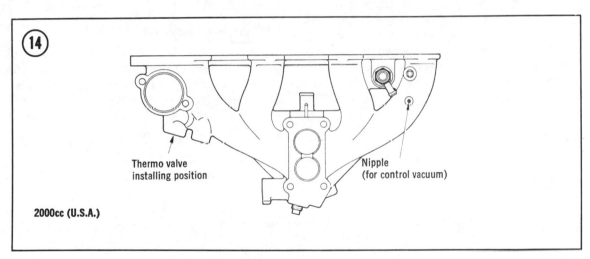

⑭

Thermo valve installing position

Nipple (for control vacuum)

2000cc (U.S.A.)

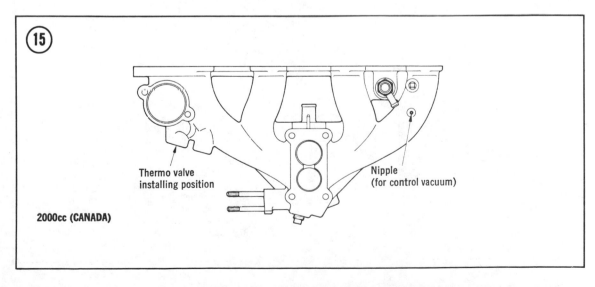

⑮

Thermo valve installing position

Nipple (for control vacuum)

2000cc (CANADA)

The exhaust manifold on the Colt (1975-on) for sale in California includes a thermal reactor (refer to Chapter Seven). All Colts for sale in the U.S. (except California) from 1975 on use a manifold reactor and are equipped with the same exhaust manifold as the 1974 model. The exhaust manifold on Canadian models from 1975 on is the same as that used on 1974 models.

Rocker Arm Shaft Assembly

Two rocker arm shafts are used; one for the exhaust valves (located on the right side of the camshaft), and the other for the intake valves (located on the left side of the camshaft). The intake and exhaust valves are actuated by rocker arms.

The rocker arm shafts are supported by 5 camshaft bearing caps. Rocker arms are cast iron and situated in line with the cam lobes. The arms have been flame-hardened and liquid-nitrated throughout their entire surfaces.

The camshaft and rocker arm shafts are lubricated with oil jetted from oil passages.

All the rocker pads have been induction-hardened.

Valves

Intake and exhaust valves are manufactured of heat resistant steel. The heads are welded to the stems and the valve faces are reinforced with Stellite for greater heat resistance.

Camshaft

The camshaft is an overhead type fitted between the exhaust and intake rocker arm shafts. The camshaft sprocket is driven by a timing chain. The camshaft is made of cast iron, supported by 5 journals with the cylinder head and caps. See **Figure 16**. Cam lobes are chill-hardened.

An offset cam using an induction-hardened lobe is employed to drive the fuel pump.

Cylinder Head Removal

1. Turn crankshaft until No. 1 piston is at TDC on compression stroke. If dowel pin at forward end of camshaft is in position shown in **Figure 17** when crankshaft pulley notch is aligned with timing mark "T" at front of timing chain-case, No. 1 piston is at TDC.

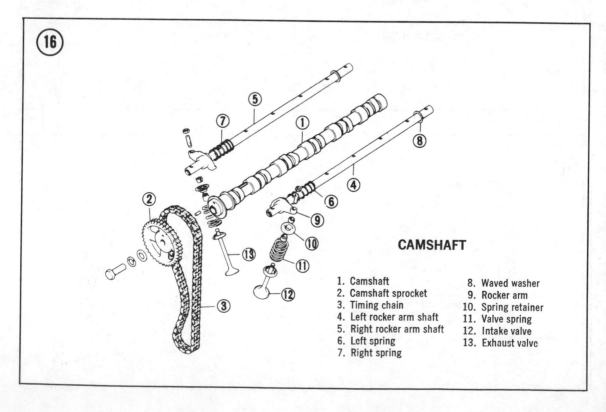

CAMSHAFT

1. Camshaft
2. Camshaft sprocket
3. Timing chain
4. Left rocker arm shaft
5. Right rocker arm shaft
6. Left spring
7. Right spring
8. Waved washer
9. Rocker arm
10. Spring retainer
11. Valve spring
12. Intake valve
13. Exhaust valve

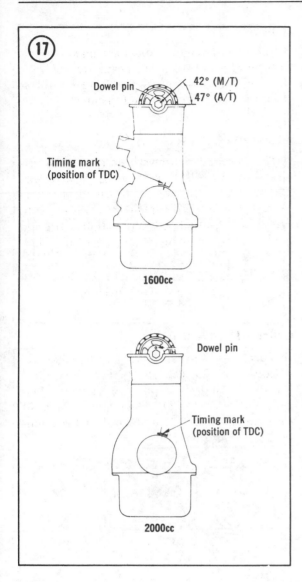

(17)

Dowel pin

42° (M/T)
47° (A/T)

Timing mark
(position of TDC)

1600cc

Dowel pin

Timing mark
(position of TDC)

2000cc

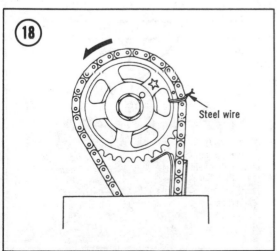

(18)

Steel wire

2. Use white paint to draw a mating mark on timing chain in line with mating mark on camshaft sprocket. On the 1600cc engine, the chain may be locked against rotation by means of a piece of steel wire as illustrated in **Figure 18**.

3. Remove camshaft sprocket.

4. Remove cylinder head bolts and nuts in proper sequence as illustrated in **Figure 19**. Head bolts should be loosened in several stages to prevent cylinder head from warping.

5. The cylinder head assembly is positioned by 2 dowel pins, front and rear, to the cylinder block. Be careful not to slide it or twist sprocket and chain when removing it.

Cylinder Head Installation

1. See **Figure 20**. Apply a sealer to the points illustrated by the 2 arrows. Install the cylinder head gasket with reference to a dowel pin on the top of the cylinder block.

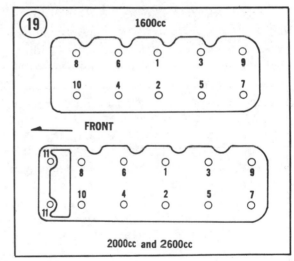

(19) 1600cc

8   6   1   3   9

10   4   2   5   7

FRONT

11

8   6   1   3   9

10   4   2   5   7

11

2000cc and 2600cc

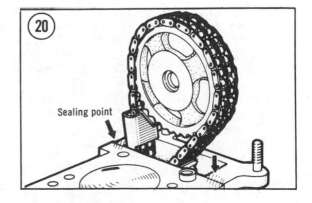

(20)

Sealing point

NOTE: *The joint surfaces of the top of the chaincase and cylinder block should be flat and smooth.*

2. Install the cylinder head on the cylinder block. Tighten head bolts and nuts in the sequence shown in **Figure 21**. Tighten bolts and nuts to the values indicated in **Table 3**. Dowel pins are provided at the front and rear of the top of the cylinder block. Do not slide the cylinder head when installing, and do not pry the sprocket and chain which are projecting.

3. Install camshaft sprocket on the camshaft, while pulling upward. Temporarily tighten the locking nut.

NOTE: *When it is hard to install the sprocket, slacken the timing chain by loosening tensioner holder to the left side of the chaincase. The sprocket installation can be done with ease. See* **Figure 22**.

4. Turn crankshaft about 90 degrees back.

5. Turn sprocket locking bolt to 36-43 ft.-lb.

6. Temporarily adjust valve clearance. Firing order is 1-3-4-2. Adjustment of valves is done with engine off. See **Figure 23** and proceed as follows:

a. At TDC of each cylinder, loosen rocker arm nuts. Turn adjusting screw to temporarily adjust valve clearance to 0.003 in. on intake side and 0.007 in. on exhaust side in cold engine by using a feeler gauge. Tighten the nuts to 7-9 ft.-lb.

b. After engine is assembled, run engine until the water temperature is approximately 176°F. Then readjust to 0.006 in.

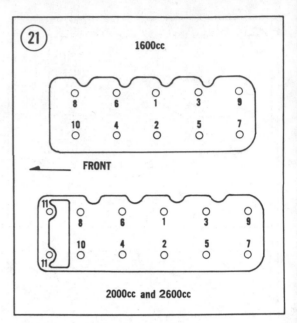

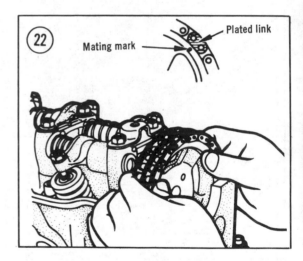

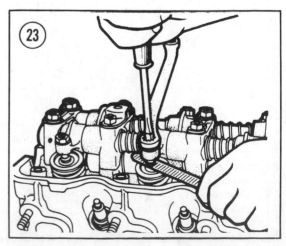

Table 3   HEAD BOLT TIGHTENING SEQUENCE

Part	Engine	Torque
Cylinder head bolts	1600	51 to 54 ft.-lb. (cold engine)
		58 to 61 ft.-lb. (hot engine)
	2000	65 to 72 ft.-lb. (cold engine)
		72 to 79 ft.-lb. (hot engine)
Cylinder head nuts (No. 11)	1600	7 to 9 ft.-lb.
Cylinder head bolts (No. 11)	2000	7 to 9 ft.-lb.

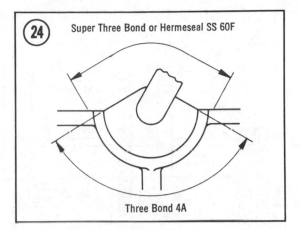

Three Bond 4A

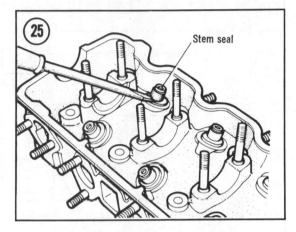

Stem seal

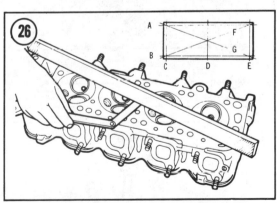

Table 4 HEAD DIMENSIONS

Description	Standard Dimension	Service Limit
Distortion	Less than 0.002 in.	
Machining and allowance overall thickness of head	3.4842 in.	—0.012 in. (1600 engine)
	3.5433 in.	—0.012 in. (2000 engine)

for intake, 0.010 in. for exhaust, on warm engine, using same procedure as described above.

> NOTE: *If cylinder head bolts are tightened after valve clearance adjustment, valve clearance will vary. Tighten head bolts before valve adjustment.*

7. Install breather and semicircular packing to cylinder head after applying sealant to points illustrated in **Figure 24**.

8. Install rocker cover to cylinder head through a rubber packing. Apply sealant to breather and packing surfaces. Torque cover bolts 4-5 ft.-lb.

Cylinder Head Disassembly

1. Remove spark plugs.

2. Remove camshaft bearing cap nuts.

3. Remove rocker arm shaft assembly, holding front and rear caps.

4. Divide rocker arm shaft assembly into the cap, rocker arm, springs (2), rocker arm shafts (2), and waved washer. Disassembled rocker arms should be kept in proper order after putting appropriate marks in the order of cylinders.

5. Remove camshaft.

6. Use a valve lifter to remove retainer lock. Remove spring retainer, valve spring, spring seat, and valve. These parts should also be kept in order for each cylinder.

7. Pry valve stem seals off with a screwdriver as illustrated in **Figure 25**. Do not reuse valve stem seals.

Cylinder Head Inspection

1. Remove dirt, oil and grease, carbon, etc., and check cylinder head for damage (water leakage, cracks etc.).

2. Use compressed air to blow oil holes clean.

3. Check the cylinder head for distortion by using a straightedge in the sequence of A, B, etc., as shown in **Figure 26**. If distortion exceeds limits indicated in **Table 4**, have it corrected at your dealer or a machine shop.

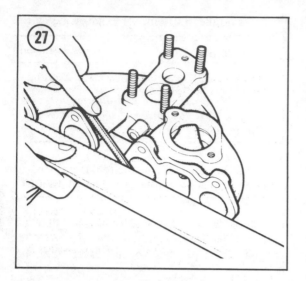

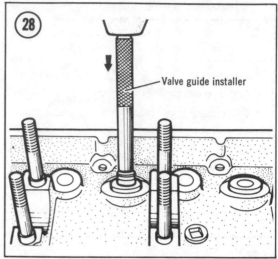

Intake/Exhaust Manifold Inspection

1. Check cylinder head mounting face of manifold for distortion as shown in **Figure 27**. The standard dimension is less than 0.006 in. The service limit is 0.0012 in.

2. Check each part for warping, cracks, etc.

Valve Guide Inspection

1. Check valve stem-to-guide clearance. The standard dimension for intake valve is 0.0010 to 0.0022 in., and the service limit is 0.004 in. The exhaust valve is 0.0020 to 0.0033 in. with a service limit of 0.006 in.

2. If valve guide clearance exceeds the limits given in Step 1, above, the valve guide should be replaced with the next oversize part. See **Table 5**.

Valve Guide Replacement

1. Valve guides have been shrink-fitted. Use a valve guide installer as shown in **Figure 28**. Press or hammer out each old valve guide toward cylinder block. This operation should be done with the cylinder head heated to approximately 480°F.

> WARNING
> *You can do this in your home oven. Be careful when handling the heads once they are hot.*

2. Ream each cylinder head guide hole to the specified size at normal temperature.

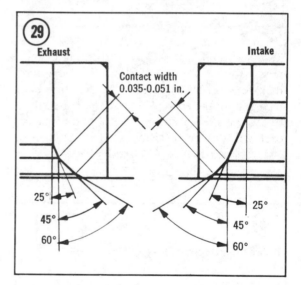

Table 5 VALVE GUIDE OVERSIZES

Size	Size Mark	Cylinder Head Hole Size
0.002 in. oversize	5	0.5138 to 0.5145 in.
0.010 in. oversize	25	0.5216 to 0.5224 in.
0.020 in. oversize	50	0.5315 to 0.5323 in.

Table 6 VALVE SEAT CUTTER RECOMMENDATIONS

		1600	2000
Exhaust valve seat cutter	45°	MD998157	MD998158
	65°	MD998165	←
	30°	MD998172	MD998173

Table 7 VALVE SEAT DIMENSIONS

Description	Standard Dimension
Valve seat contact width (both intake and exhaust)	0.035 to 0.051 in.
Valve seat angle (both intake and exhaust)	45°

Table 8 VALVE SPRING INSTALLED HEIGHT

Description	Engine	Standard Dimension	Service Limit
Installed height of spring A (both intake and exhaust)	1600	1.469 in.	+0.039 in.
Installed height of spring A (both intake and exhaust)	2000	1.590 in.	+0.039 in.

3. Insert guides quickly after heating cylinder head to approximately 480°F. Use a valve guide installer as shown in **Figure 28**. Press or hammer in both the exhaust and intake valve guides to the specified position. The special tool stops each guide at the specified position. Dimension (A) in **Figure 28** is 0.5394 to 0.5630 in.

4. Check the guide inside diameter after pressing in the valve guides. Ream the inside diameter if necessary.

Valve Seat Reconditioning

1. Check valve seat for improper contact with valve face, overheating, etc.

2. Check valve guides for wear. Replace worn guides (see preceding section).

3. Recondition valve seat with a seat grinder or cutter. The valve seat contact width should be of the specified size at the center of the valve face. See **Figure 29**.

4. See **Table 6**. Use special tool Valve Seat Cutter to correct exhaust valve seat.

5. Lap the valve and valve seat with lapping compound. See **Table 7**.

6. Check valve seat ring sinkage. If sinkage exceeds the service limits indicated in **Table 8**, replace the ring with next oversize part using the following procedure:

a. Measure installed height of spring between spring seat and retainer, with valve spring seat, retainer, and retainer lock installed. The amount of sinkage can be judged from the measured value. See **Figure 30**.

b. Remove valve seat ring that is worn over service limit (at room temperature) after thinning down ring with a cutter (A, **Figure 31**).

c. After removing seat ring machine, seat ring bore with a reamer or cutter to size indicated in **Table 9**.

d. Heat cylinder head to approximately 480°F. Press in oversize seat ring fit to the ring bore in cylinder head (at normal temperature). Correct valve seat surface after installing new valve seat.

Valve Reconditioning

1. See **Figure 32**. Check each valve for damage, wear, and warp. Replace badly worn or damaged valves; repair salvageable ones.

2. Correct pitted condition at point (A) on the stem tip, using an oil stone. This correction must be limited to a minimum.

3. Recondition valve face with a valve refacer. Replace valve if thickness (C) of the face has decreased to less than the service limit (see **Tables 10 and 11**).

Table 9   VALVE SEAT RING OVERSIZES

	Size	Size Mark	Seat Ring Height "H"	Cylinder Head Inner Diameter	Engine
Intake valve seat ring	0.012 in. oversize	30	0.2913 to 0.2992 in.	1.5472 to 1.5482 in.	(1600)
			0.311 to 0.3189 in.	1.7441 to 1.7451 in.	(2000)
	0.024 in. oversize	60	0.3031 to 0.311 in.	1.559 to 1.56 in.	(1600)
			0.3228 to 0.3307 in.	1.7559 to 1.7569 in.	(2000)
Exhaust valve seat ring	0.012 in. oversize	30	0.2913 to 0.2992 in.	1.3504 to 1.3514 in.	(1600)
			0.311 to 0.3189 in.	1.5079 to 1.5089 in.	(2000)
	0.024 in. oversize	60	0.3031 to 0.311 in.	1.3622 to 1.3632 in.	(1600)
			0.3228 to 0.3307 in.	1.5197 to 1.5207 in.	(2000)

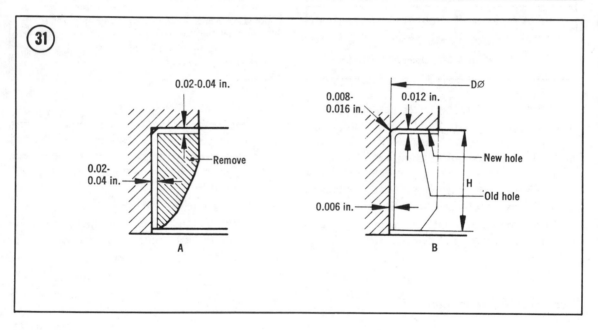

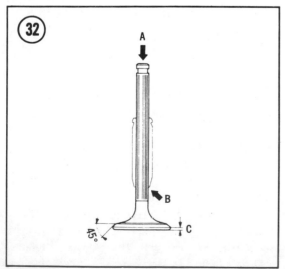

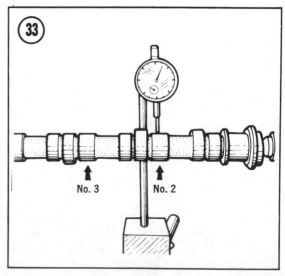

Table 10   VALVE LENGTH

Description	Standard Dimension	Repair Limit
Length of valve		
Intake		
1600	4.169 in.	—0.02 in.
2000	4.439 in.	—0.02 in.
Exhaust		
1600	4.035 in.	—0.02 in.
2000	4.396 in.	—0.02 in.

Table 11   VALVE DIMENSIONS

Description	Standard Dimension	Service Limit
Valve stem outer diameter		
Intake	0.315 in.	—0.004 in.
Exhaust	0.315 in.	—0.006 in.
Thickness (C)		
Intake		
1600	0.059 in.	0.04 in.
2000	0.0472 in.	0.028 in.
Exhaust		
1600	0.059 in.	0.04 in.
2000	0.0787 in.	0.059 in.

Table 12   VALVE SPRING DIMENSIONS

Description	Standard Dimension	Service Limit
Valve spring		
Free length		
1600	1.823 in.	—0.039 in.
2000	1.841 in.	—0.039 in.
Load		
1600	61.7 lb./1.469 in.	53 lb./1.469 in.
2000	62.6 lb./1.59 in.	55 lb./1.59 in.
Squareness	1.5° or less	3°

Table 13   CAMSHAFT END-PLAY

Description	Standard Dimension	Service Limit
Camshaft end-play		
1600	0.002 to 0.006 in.	0.012 in.
2000	0.0039 to 0.0079 in.	0.016 in.

Valve Spring Inspection

1. Check free length and tension of each valve spring as indicated in **Table 12**. Replace if service limit is exceeded.

2. Test squareness of each spring with a square. If spring is excessively out of square, replace it.

Camshaft/Camshaft Bearing Cap Inspection

1. Check camshaft for bend. If over 0.0008 in., correct or replace. See **Figure 33**. With the dial indicator set to No. 2 or No. 3 journal, turn camshaft once and read the total indicator reading. A half of the read value is the bend.

2. Check camshaft end-play (see **Figure 34**). If play exceeds service limit indicated in **Table 13**, replace camshaft or cylinder head assembly (whichever is worn more).

3. Check cam lobes and profile for cam height. See **Figure 35**. If lobe or profile is damaged or seriously worn, replace camshaft. See **Table 14**.

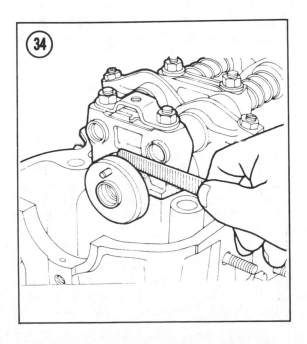

4. Check camshaft bearing caps for inner surface damage. If excessive damage is found, replace head assembly. Install cap to cylinder head and check clearance between cap inside diameter and camshaft journal outside diameter. See **Figures 36 and 37**. If clearance exceeds the standard dimension of 0.002 to 0.0035 in. (the service limit is 0.006 in.), or if camshaft journals are worn, replace camshaft. If cap is worn, replace head assembly. Measurements shall be taken at 2 points, front and rear, in the (A) and (B) direction.

5. Tighten camshaft bearing caps to 13-14 ft.-lb. torque.

Rocker Arms/Rocker Arm Shafts Inspection

1. Check rocker arm face for contact with cam lobe, and adjusting screw end for valve contact. If worn or damaged, replace. See **Figure 38**. A mildly worn rocker arm can be corrected with an oil stone.

2. If rocker arm to rocker arm shaft clearance exceeds the standard value of 0.0005 to 0.0017 in. (the service limit is 0.008 in.), replace rocker arm or shaft. See **Figure 39**.

3. Check rocker arm shafts for damage or wear.

Cylinder Head Reassembly

CAUTION
Clean each part before reassembly and apply clean, new engine oil to sliding and rotating parts.

1. Install spring seat and fit stem seal on valve guide by lightly hammering the special tool Valve Stem Seal Installer (MD998005) as shown in **Figure 40**. The seal is installed in the proper position by means of the special tool. Improper installation will adversely affect the lip inner diameter (ID) and eccentricity, resulting in "oil down." Do not twist during installation. Stem seals should not be used more than once. The stem seal pressed-in dimension should be 0.579 to 0.595 in. as indicated in dimension (A), **Figure 40**.

Table 14   CAM HEIGHT

Description	Standard Dimension	Service Limit
Cam height		
Intake		
1600	1.4377 in.	—0.020 in.
2000	1.6605 in.	—0.020 in.
Exhaust		
1600	1.4397 in.	—0.020 in.
2000	1.6630 in.	—0.020 in.

2. Apply clean engine oil to each valve. Insert valves into guides. Do not use force. Once installed, check to see if valve moves smoothly.

3. Install springs and spring retainers. Valve springs must be installed with enamel identification mark toward rocker arm.

4. Compress spring with a valve lifter and install retainer lock.

NOTE: *When compressing spring with valve lifter, check to see if valve stem seal is not pressed with bottom of the retainer. Install retainer lock. After installation of valves, check to be sure all retainer locks are properly installed.*

5. Install camshaft to cylinder head. Check to see if camshaft play is proper (0.002 to 0.006 in. on 1600cc engine; 0.0039 to 0.0079 in. on the 2000/2600cc engine).

6. To assemble the rocker arm shaft assembly, refer to **Figures 41 and 42**. Install the caps, rocker arms, springs, and wave washers onto both rocker arm shafts. The front bearing cap has an embossed mating mark on the front side (**Figure 43**), while an indented mark appears near the front end of the rocker arm shaft. When assembling, the shaft oil hole should face down and the mating marks match. There are 5 caps; front, rear, No. 2, No. 3, and No. 4. Each has an arrow mark indicating direction of installation. Install the caps with the arrow directed toward front of engine, in the arranged order. The rocker arms should be installed in proper order as previously arranged for respective cylinders. The right and left rocker arm

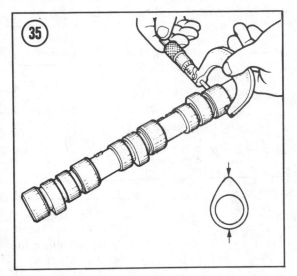

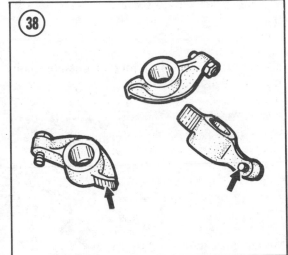

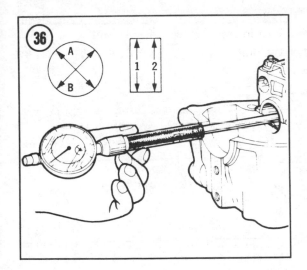

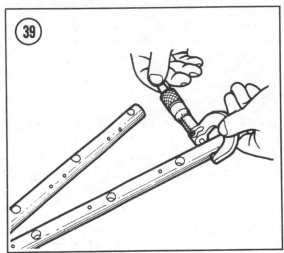

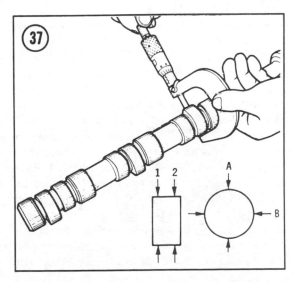

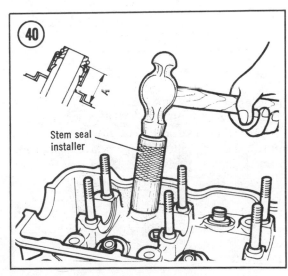

Stem seal
installer

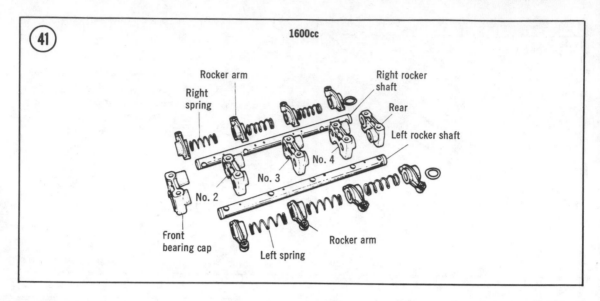

41   **1600cc**

Rocker arm

Right rocker shaft

Right spring

Rear

Left rocker shaft

No. 4

No. 3

No. 2

Front bearing cap

Left spring

Rocker arm

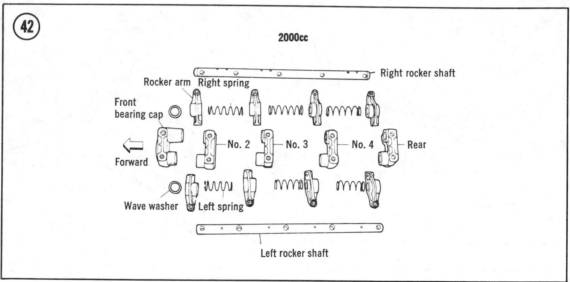

42   **2000cc**

Right rocker shaft

Rocker arm   Right spring

Front bearing cap

No. 2   No. 3   No. 4   Rear

Forward

Wave washer   Left spring

Left rocker shaft

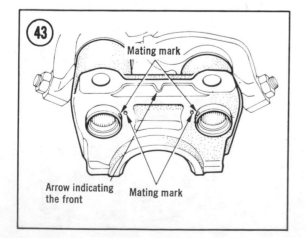

43

Mating mark

Arrow indicating the front

Mating mark

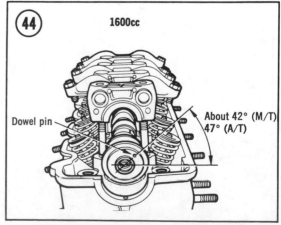

44   **1600cc**

Dowel pin

About 42° (M/T)
47° (A/T)

Table 15 ROCKER ARM SHAFT SPECIFICATIONS

Description	Right	Left
Rocker arm shaft oil hole	8 holes	4 holes
Spring free length		
1600	2.10 in.	2.57 in.
2000	3.24 in.	2.54 in.

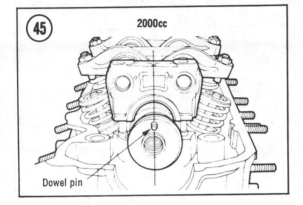

Dowel pin

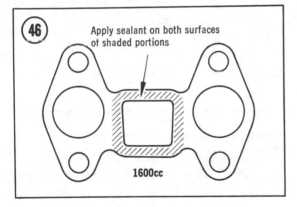

Apply sealant on both surfaces of shaded portions

1600cc

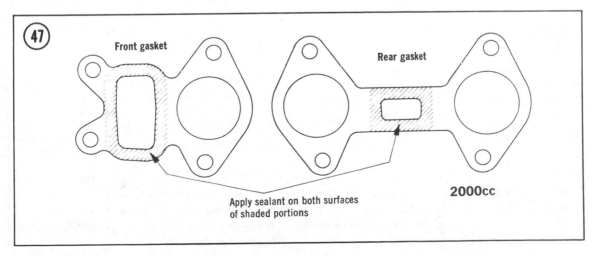

Front gasket

Rear gasket

Apply sealant on both surfaces of shaded portions

2000cc

shafts and springs are identified in **Table 15**. Install the wave washer with convex side toward front of engine.

7. Install assembled rocker arm shaft assembly to cylinder head. The camshaft should be positioned so dowel pin on front end is in position shown in **Figures 44 and 45**, as viewed from front. Remember to install bushing knocks of the caps. When installing caps on stud bolts, do not use force (or twisting motion). Tighten in 2 or 3 stages in order of No. 3, No. 2, No. 4, front, and rear. Tighten camshaft bearing caps to 13-14 ft.-lb. torque. (The front and No. 4 caps will be tightened together with rocker arm cover stay.)

8. Tighten spark plugs to 15-21 ft.-lb. after installing.

9. See **Figures 46 and 47**. Install intake manifold after applying sealer (Three-Bond 4A or equivalent) to gasket. Position gasket and manifold on cylinder head and tighten the manifold attaching nuts to 11-14 ft.-lb.

CYLINDER BLOCK COMPONENTS

The special alloy cast iron cylinder block is constructed in one piece. Five bearings carry the crankshaft. The 1600cc cylinder block is a Siamese type, the 2000/2600cc block a full water jacket type. See **Figure 48**.

The 1600cc cylinder block (1975-on) has the oil level gauge moved slightly rearward. The in-

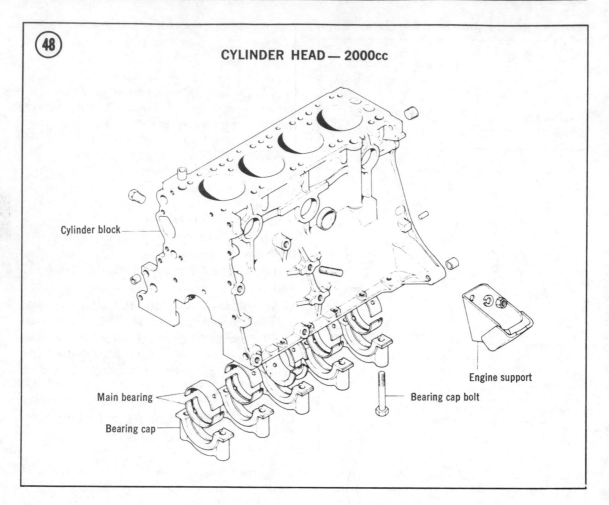

(48)

CYLINDER HEAD — 2000cc

Cylinder block

Engine support

Main bearing

Bearing cap bolt

Bearing cap

stalled angle has also been changed. See **Figure 49**. The cylinder block on the 2000/2600cc engine is the same as earlier models.

The timing indicator for 1975 and later models has an ATDC mark. See **Figures 50 and 51**.

Crankshaft

The carbon steel forged crankshaft turns in 5 copper sintered alloy metal bearings, overlayed and flashed for good run-in. Crankshaft thrust is taken by the center bearing. Four balance weights are formed integral with the crankshaft. See **Figure 52**.

Flywheel

The flywheel is a flat type designed for good heat dispersion and effective removal of worn material dust. The automatic transmission equipped car utilizes a drive plate.

Pistons, Piston Pins, and Piston Rings

The aluminum, solid pistons feature a tapered and elliptical skirt to obtain the best contact surface relative to the cylinder bore, and to prevent piston slap. See **Figure 53**. The piston pin is a hollow cold steel forging, the entire surface of which is carburized. The pin is a press fit in the connecting rod, fully floating relative to the piston. The pin is 0.039 in. offset from the piston center (toward the thrust side) to prevent piston slap. Piston rings are cast iron. Each piston uses 2 compression rings and one oil ring. The top and oil rings are hard chrome-plated.

Connecting Rods

The connecting rod is forged of carbon steel. The rod bearing is a copper sintered alloy metal lined with a back metal, overlayed and flashed for good run-in.

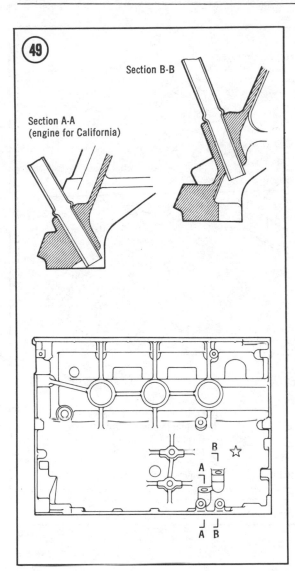

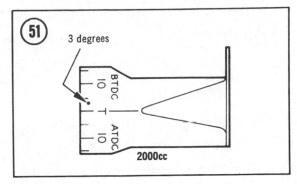

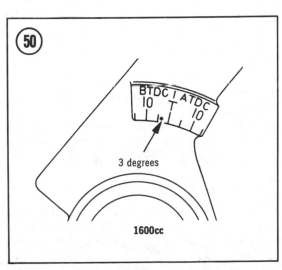

Timing Chain/Chain Case

The aluminum die-cast timing chain case is designed to fit the water pump, oil pump (1600cc model only), and distributor. The water pump, volute chamber, and oil pump housing (1600cc engine only) are integral with chain case. See **Figure 54**.

The camshaft drive chain is a duplex roller chain and is installed between crankshaft and camshaft sprockets in a single stage. To ensure quiet operation a tensioner lever is always pressed against the chain by means of a spring and hydraulic-type tensioner, preventing chain from fluttering.

Crankshaft Gear

The special aluminum bronze crankshaft gear drives the distributor gear (1600cc only) or oil pump gear (2000/2600cc only). On the 1600cc engine the oil pump is driven by the claw coupling with distributor shaft.

CYLINDER BLOCK OVERHAUL

Cylinder Block Disassembly

1. Using a one in. 12-point deep socket or open-end wrench, remove the oil pressure gauge.

2. Remove crankshaft pulley that has been previously loosened.

3. Remove the oil pan after the engine has been placed upside down.

4. Remove oil screen (on the 2000/2600cc engine remove oil pump also).

5. Remove tensioner holder on the right. Remove spring and plunger.

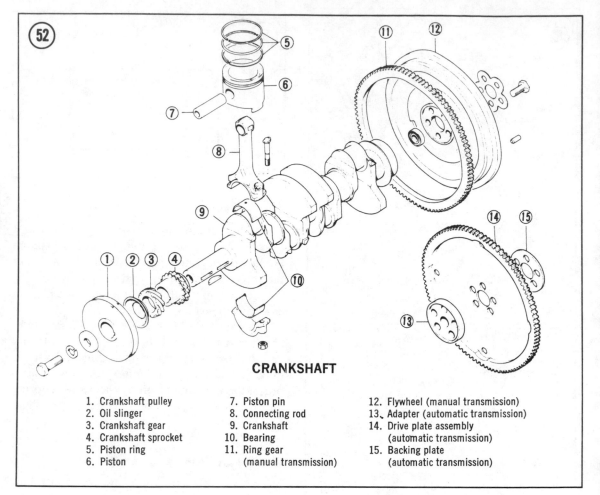

CRANKSHAFT

1. Crankshaft pulley
2. Oil slinger
3. Crankshaft gear
4. Crankshaft sprocket
5. Piston ring
6. Piston
7. Piston pin
8. Connecting rod
9. Crankshaft
10. Bearing
11. Ring gear
    (manual transmission)
12. Flywheel (manual transmission)
13. Adapter (automatic transmission)
14. Drive plate assembly
    (automatic transmission)
15. Backing plate
    (automatic transmission)

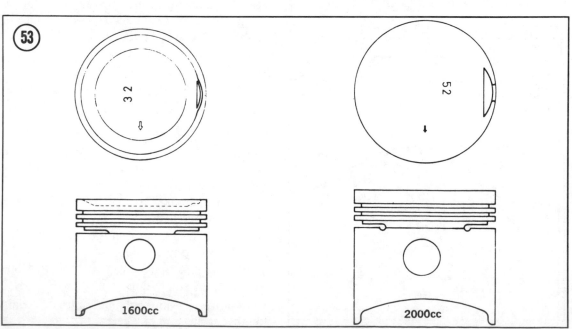

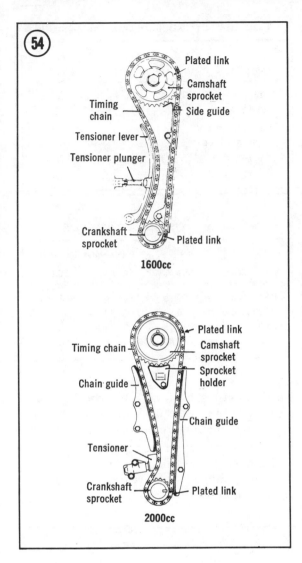

Plated link

Camshaft sprocket

Timing chain

Side guide

Tensioner lever

Tensioner plunger

Crankshaft sprocket

Plated link

1600cc

Plated link

Timing chain

Camshaft sprocket

Sprocket holder

Chain guide

Chain guide

Tensioner

Crankshaft sprocket

Plated link

2000cc

6. Remove timing chain case.

7. Remove oil slinger and crankshaft gear from crankshaft.

8. Remove camshaft sprocket and timing chain and at same time remove crankshaft sprocket.

9. Remove chain tensioner lever, side guide, and sprocket holder (2000/2600cc engine only).

10. Remove rear crankshaft oil seal case. The case can be split into 3 parts; oil seal, separator, and case.

11. Remove connecting rod caps. Push out each piston/rod assembly toward top of cylinder, using a soft piece of wood inserted between connecting rod and cap, so bearing surface is not damaged. Be careful that rod bearings are not mixed.

12. Disassemble piston/rod assembly in following order:

    a. Remove piston rings. Keep them with their respective piston.

    b. Insert pushrod of Piston Pin Setting Tool (special tool MD998006 for the 1600cc engine, MD998185 for the 2000/2600cc engine), into piston pin hole. See **Figure 55**.

    c. Set connecting rod/piston assembly to the piston pin setting tool body with lower surface of rod in firm contact with body support area. See **Figure 56**.

13. Remove crankshaft bearing cap along with lower bearing.

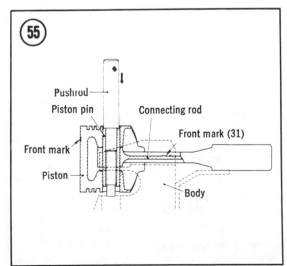

Pushrod

Piston pin

Connecting rod

Front mark (31)

Front mark

Piston

Body

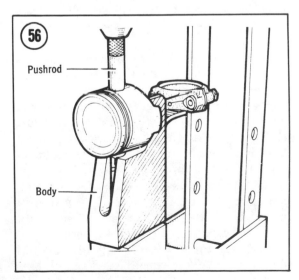

Pushrod

Body

14. Remove crankshaft and upper bearing. Except for the center main bearing, all the main bearings are identical. Be careful, however, that bearing halves are not confused.

Cylinder Block Inspection

1. Clean off dirt, oil and grease, and carbon.

2. Check block for water leakage, cracks, and flaws, etc.

3. Blow oil passages clear with compressed air.

4. Components should be properly arranged so as not to be confused with other parts.

5. Check cylinder block for distortion with a straightedge as illustrated in **Figure 57**. Follow the A, B, C, etc. sequence as illustrated. See **Table 16**. If the measured value exceeds the repair limit, correct block by grinding. (It is recommended that this operation be done by a qualified machine shop or your dealer.)

NOTE: *The upper surface of the timing chaincase should be corrected whenever the top of the cylinder block requires grinding.*

6. Measure cylinder bore size with a cylinder gauge at 3 levels. See **Figure 58** and **Table 17**. When wear or taper exceeds the repair limit rebore the cylinder and use an oversize piston. (All bores should be rebored to the same size when one cylinder requires reboring.)

7. When cylinder wear is slight, and when piston rings require only replacement, remove stepped wear of the top of the block by using a ridge reamer and hone. See **Figure 59**.

8. See **Table 18**. Oversize pistons come in 4 sizes. Pistons to be used should be determined on basis of the cylinder having largest bore size. Check the outer diameter (OD) of each piston at the skirt and across the thrust faces. See **Figure 60**. The piston OD should be checked at a point 0.079 in. above bottom of piston. The cylinder bore to be rebored can be obtained by calculating the measured value of the piston. Example: The measured value of the piston OD (piston that has been determined to be used), plus the clearance between the piston and cylinder wall equals 0.0008 to 0.0016 in., minus the honing margin equals 0.008 in. or less,

Table 16   CYLINDER BLOCK DIMENSIONS

Description	Standard Dimension	Service Limit
Distortion of cylinder block	0.002 in. or less	—
Overall height of cylinder block		
1600	11.228 in.	—0.008 in.
2000	12.441 in.	—0.008 in.

Table 18   PISTON SERVICE SIZE

		Piston Outer Diameter	
Size	Size Mark	1600	2000
0.010 in. oversize	0.25	3.0374 in.	3.3163 in.
0.020 in. oversize	0.50	3.0472 in.	3.3262 in.
0.030 in. oversize	0.75	3.0571 in.	3.3360 in.
0.039 in. oversize	1.00	3.0669 in.	3.3464 in.

equals a finished bore size after reboring of the measured value of the piston OD (piston that has been determined to be used) plus 0 to 0.0008 in.

9. The cylinder should be rebored to the finish size obtained by calculation. Be careful during the finish cutting (the margin is about 0.002). Do not cut too much at one time.

NOTE: *To prevent distortion due to temperature rise at the time of reboring, the reboring operation should be done in the sequence of 2-4-1-3 or 3-1-4-2.*

10. Hone the bore to the finish size. Hone to the extent that tool traces are removed. The honing angle is 30 to 45 degrees.

11. The clearance between the piston and the cylinder wall should be 0.0008 to 0.0016 in.

Piston, Piston Pins, and Piston Rings

1. Check each piston and piston ring for breakage or damage. When any ring requires replacement, all should be replaced.

2. Check piston pin to piston pin hole fit. Replace a piston and pin assembly that is defective.

Table 17   CYLINDER BORE SPECIFICATIONS

Description	Standard Dimension	Repair Limit	Service Limit
Cylinder bore size			
1600	3.0276 in.	+0.008 in.	+0.047 in.
2000	3.3071 in.	+0.008 in.	+0.047 in.
Taper	0.0004 in. or less	—	—
Variation in bore size among cylinders	0.0008 in. or less	—	—

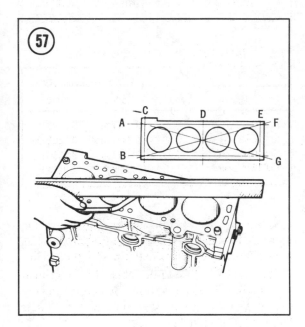

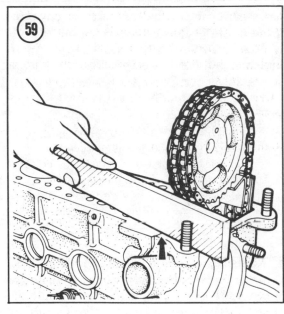

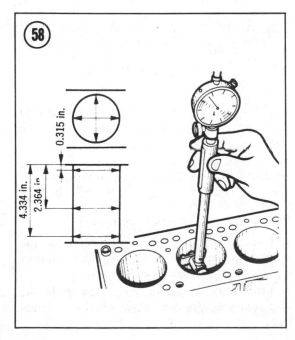

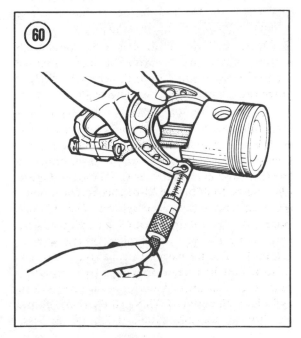

NOTE: *The piston pin should press easily into pin hole at normal temperature, by hand.*

3. Measure the piston side ring clearance (see **Table 19**). If over repair limit, insert a new ring in ring groove to measure side clearance. If clearance still exceeds repair limit, replace the piston and rings together. If less than repair limit, replace rings only. See **Figure 61**.

4. To measure piston ring end clearance insert a piston ring into cylinder bore. Correctly position ring at right angles to cylinder wall by gently pressing it down with a piston. Draw piston upward and out. Measure clearance with a feeler gauge. See **Figure 62**. If gap exceeds service limit (see **Table 20**) replace piston ring.

NOTE: *When replacing ring only (without correcting cylinder bore), check clearance at lower part of cylinder that is less worn. When replacing a ring, be sure to use a ring of the same size. See Table 21.*

Connecting Rods

1. Replace a connecting rod with damage on thrust faces (at either end), step wear, or rough surface of the inside diameter of the small end. When using a new connecting rod, cylinder number should be stamped on big end.

2. Check connecting rod for bend and twist using a connecting rod aligner. If bend exceeds the standard dimension of 0.001 in. or less (the service limit is 0.004 in.) replace the rod. Rod with slight bend can be corrected in a press. This operation should be done by a qualified machine shop.

3. Measure the ID of the connecting rod small end. Replace rods that do not meet the standard dimension of 0.7470 to 0.7474 in. (1600cc engine) or 0.8651 to 0.8655 in. (2000/2600cc engine).

4. See **Figure 63**. Install bearings to connecting rods, then install connecting rod assembly to each crankpin. Check rod side clearance. The standard dimension is 0.004 to 0.01 in., the service limit is 0.02 in. If clearance exceeds service limit, or is less than the standard dimension, replace connecting rod.

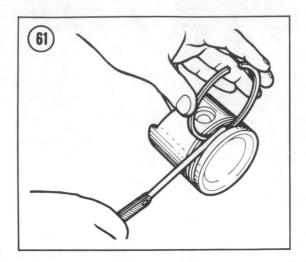

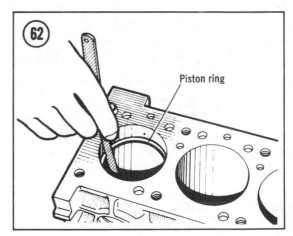

Piston ring

Crankshaft

1. Check crankshaft journals and pins for wear, damage, and clogged oil holes.

2. See **Figure 64**. Check crankshaft for bend by placing a dial indicator on center journal. Turn shaft once and read the total indicator reading. Half of the value is the bend. The standard dimension is 0.001 in. or less.

NOTE: *Crankshaft journals should not be reground until crankshaft bend has been corrected.*

3. Measure crankshaft journals and pins in (A) and (B) directions at 2 positions (see **Figure 65**), front and rear. If excessively out-of-round, tapered or worn over the repair limit indicated in **Table 22**, grind parts to next undersize. Replace part that has been worn over repair limit.

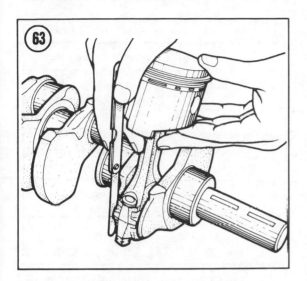

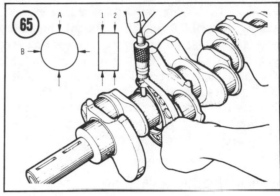

Table 19 PISTON RING SIDE CLEARANCE

Description	Standard Dimension	Service Limit
No. 1	0.0012 - 0.0028 in.	0.004 in.
No. 2	0.0008 - 0.0024 in.	0.004 in.
No. 3		
1600	0.0010 - 0.0030 in.	0.004 in.
2000	0.0008 - 0.0026 in.	0.004 in.

Table 20 PISTON RING END CLEARANCE

Engine	Standard Dimension	Service Limit
1600	0.006 - 0.014 in.	0.039 in.
2000	0.0118 - 0.0197 in.	0.039 in. (No. 1)
	0.0098 - 0.0177 in.	0.039 in. (No. 2 Oil ring)

Table 21 PISTON RING SERVICE SIZE

Size	Size Mark
Standard	None
0.010 in. oversize	25
0.020 in. oversize	50
0.030 in. oversize	75
0.039 in. oversize	100

Table 22 CRANKSHAFT SPECIFICATIONS

Description	Standard Dimension	Service Limit
Crankshaft journal outer diameter		
1600	2.2441 in.	—0.026 in.
2000	2.5984 in.	—0.035 in.
Craankshaft journal out-of-roundness and taper	0.0002 in. or less	
Crankpin outer diameter		
1600	1.7717 in.	—0.026 in.
2000	2.0886 in.	—0.035 in.
Crankpin out-of-roundness and taper	0.0004 in. or less	

NOTE: *Replace bearings with next undersize bearings when journals and pins have been corrected to the next undersize dimension. See Table 23.*

CAUTION
When grinding crankshaft to undersize, use care as to the size of (R) of each fillet of the journal and pin. See Figure 66 and Table 24.

4. With crankshaft bearing caps installed to the cylinder block, check thrust clearance by inserting feeler gauge between center bearing and crankshaft. See **Figure 67**. If clearance exceeds service limit of 0.01 in. (the standard dimension is 0.002 to 0.007 in.) replace center bearing. To check clearance tighten the caps lightly and tap the crankshaft back and forth with a wooden mallet. Measure the clearance. No center bearing of different size for adjustment is available. Tighten bearing cap bolt to 36 to 39 ft.-lb. (1600cc engine), or 54 to 61 ft.-lb. (2000/2600cc engine).

Main Bearings and Connecting Rod Bearings

1. Inspect bearings for seizure, improper contact, etc. Replace defective bearings.

2. Measure the OD of the crankshaft journal and the crank pin and ID of bearing. Clearance can be obtained by calculating difference between measured OD and ID. See **Table 25**.

NOTE: *Check the bearing ID at 2 places, front and rear, in the directions (A) and (B) as shown in Figure 68. Plastigage may be used to measure clearance. Cut a piece to same length as the width of the bearing. Place it parallel with the journal, off the oil holes. Install crankshaft, bearings, and caps. Tighten to the torques values indicated in Table 26. During this operation DO NOT turn crankshaft. Remove caps, measure width of Plastigage at widest part, using a scale printed on the gauge bag. See Figure 69.*

If clearance exceeds repair limit, bearing should be replaced or an undersized bearing used. When installing a new crankshaft use standard size bearings. Should the standard

Table 23 CRANKSHAFT UNDERSIZE

	Journal Outer Diameter	Pin Outer Diameter
0.01 in. undersize		
1600	2.2337 - 2.2342 in.	1.7612 - 1.7618 in.
2000	2.5880 - 2.5886 in.	2.0762 - 2.0768 in.
0.02 in. undersize		
1600	2.2238 - 2.2244 in.	1.7514 - 1.7520 in.
2000	2.5781 - 2.5787 in.	2.0663 - 2.0669 in.
0.03 in. undersize		
2000	2.5683 - 2.5089 in.	2.0565 - 2.0571 in.

Table 24 FILLET SPECIFICATIONS

Description	Standard Dimension
Fillet R	—0.098 R in.

Table 25 JOURNAL SPECIFICATIONS

Description	Standard Dimension	Repair Limit
Journal oil clearance		
1600	0.0006 - 0.0031 in.	0.005 in.
2000	0.0008 - 0.0028 in.	0.005 in.
Center journal		
2000	0.0010 - 0.0030 in.	0.005 in.
Pin oil clearance		
1600	0.0004 - 0.0028 in.	0.004 in.
2000	0.0006 - 0.0025 in.	0.004 in.

clearance not be obtained even after bearing replacement, the journal and pin should be ground to undersize and a bearing of the same size be installed.

Crankshaft Gear and Sprocket

Check the crankshaft gear for worn or missing teeth. Replace a defective gear. (The crankshaft gear may be reused by reversing its direction if its defect is slight.)

Timing Chain, Chain Tensioner, and Guide

1. Check chain tensioner rubber shoe for wear, and spring tensioner for weakness. See **Table 27** and **Figure 70**. Check chain guide for damage or wear.

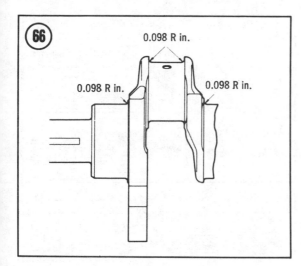

0.098 R in.

0.098 R in.   0.098 R in.

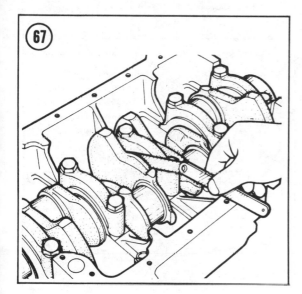

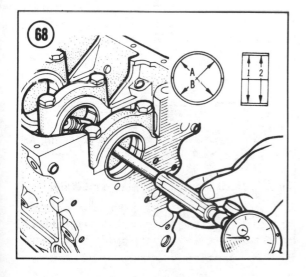

Table 26   BEARING CAP TORQUE VALUES

Part	Torque
Main bearing cap bolt	
1600	36 - 39 ft.-lb.
2000	54 - 61 ft.-lb.
Connecting rod cap nut	
1600	23 - 25 ft.-lb.
2000	33 - 35 ft.-lb.

Table 27   TENSIONER SPRING DIMENSIONS

Description	Standard Value	Service Limit
Tensioner spring		
Free length		
1600	2.181 in.	1.85 in.
2000	2.587 in.	2.20 in.
Load		
1600	27.8 lb./1.512 in.	22 lb./1.512 in.
2000	4.4 lb./1.453 in.	3.7 lb./1.453 in.

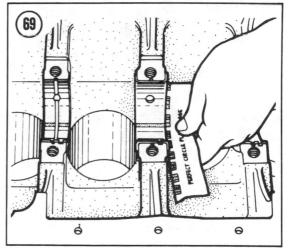

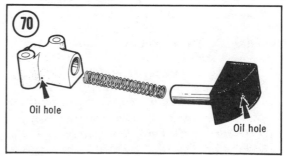

Oil hole

Oil hole

2. Replace seriously worn or cracked timing chain links.

Timing Chain Case

1. Replace timing chain case if damage or wear is found.

2. On the 2000/2600cc engine only, check the oil jet hole (0.047 in.) inside the case. The hole should be clear. See **Figure 71**.

Flywheel and Ring Gear

1. Replace excessively damaged or worn flywheel.

2. Check clutch disc contacting surface of flywheel for runout. The service limit is 0.008 in. The standard dimension is 0.005 in. or less. See **Figure 72**.

3. Check ring gear for wear or damage.

4. To replace ring gear, remove it by tapping it on the circumference of the flywheel. To install, heat to 500 to 536°F and shrink-fit it onto the flywheel.

> NOTE: *The ring gear cannot be removed if heated. It is sometimes possible to repair damaged ring gear teeth with a grinder. It is also a good way to shift the ring gear so that no damage will be done to the starting motor.*

Oil Seals

Check front and rear oil seals for wear or damage. Replace seal that is defective or suspect.

Oil Pan and Oil Screen

1. Check oil pan for cracks.

2. Check oil screen for damage and clogging. The O-ring of the screen should be replaced if necessary.

Cylinder Block Reassembly

> CAUTION
> *Apply oil to sliding and rotating parts prior to reassembly. Replace gaskets with new ones and apply sealant where specified. Torque all nuts and bolts to specifications.*

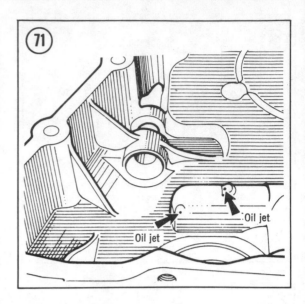

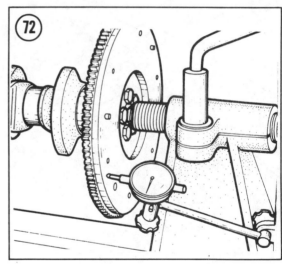

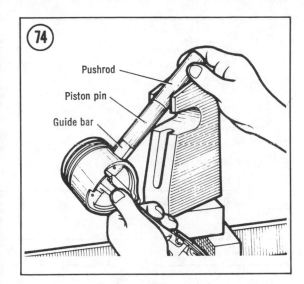

74

Pushrod

Piston pin

Guide bar

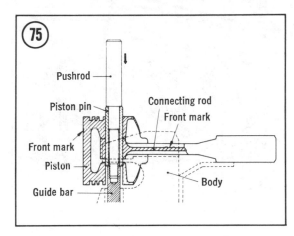

75

Pushrod

Piston pin

Connecting rod

Front mark

Front mark

Piston

Guide bar

Body

76

1. Place cylinder block on engine support or suitable substitute, upside down.

2. Install upper main bearing halves to cylinder block. Install the crankshaft.

> NOTE: *When reusing main bearings, remember to install them referring to marks written at time of disassembly. Install with attention to oil holes and dowel holes so that bearings will not float.*

3. Install bearing caps. Tighten cap bolts to 36 to 39 ft.-lb. (1600cc engine) or 54 to 61 ft.-lb. (2000/2600cc engine) in sequence: center, No. 2, No. 4, front and rear caps. Caps should be installed with arrow marks toward front of engine. Pay special attention to cap numbers. Tighten cap bolts evenly in 2 or 3 stages. See **Figure 73**.

4. Crankshaft should rotate lightly if clearance between center main bearing thrust flange and connecting rod big-end bearing is proper (0.002 to 0.007 in.).

5. Install piston, piston pin, connecting rod, and piston rings as follows:

a. Set piston pin between pushrod and guide bar of Piston Pin Setting Tool (special tool MD998006 for the 1600cc engine, MD998185 for 2000/2600cc engine). See **Figure 74**. Apply oil to outer surface of piston pin and small end bore of connecting rod.

b. See **Figure 75**. Set rod and piston with front mark facing up. Insert piston pin assembly.

c. Insert guide bar in slot provided in front of the support of the Piston Pin Setting Tool, with flat side of guide bar aligned with inner wall of slot. At same time, set piston/connecting rod assembly so rear side of connecting rod (small end) rests on support. Turn piston pin assembly a half turn.

d. Press pin into pin hole with 1,102 to 3,306 lb. pressure (1600cc engine) or 1,654 to 3,859 lb. pressure (2000/2600cc engine) at normal temperature, applied through pushrod to pin end by a press (**Figure 76**). Press until top end of guide bar bottoms the tool base.

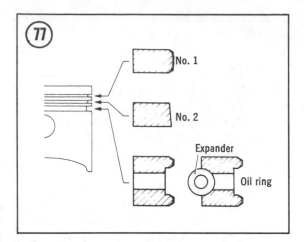

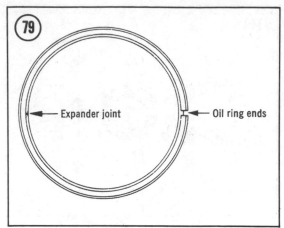

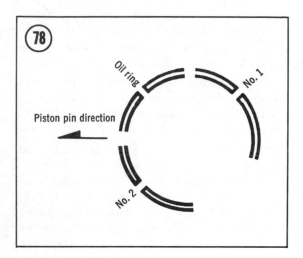

NOTE: *If more than the specified pressure is required to press pin into pin hole, turn pushrod 1/2 turn and dismount the piston connecting rod assembly from the support.*

e. After pressing in pin be sure connecting rod slides lightly and moves freely.

f. Install rings with the size mark and manufacturer's mark stamped at ends facing up, in proper order. See **Figure 77**. Piston rings should be spaced at 3 equal spacings. Do not install rings with ends in line with piston pin bosses and thrust direction. See **Figure 78** for proper position.

g. On the 2000/2600cc engine the oil ring should be installed so its ends are on the opposite side of expander joint (see **Figure 79**).

6. Turn engine sideways. Insert piston/connecting rod assembly into cylinder, using a piston ring band. The mating mark should agree with the cylinder number, and the front mark on piston head should be toward front of engine.

NOTE: *Use vinyl pipes on bolt caps in order to avoid damaging cylinder bore and crankpin.*

7. Tighten connecting rod cap bolts to 23 to 25 ft.-lb. (1600cc engine) or 33 to 35 ft.-lb. (2000/2600cc engine). See **Figure 80**.

8. Check the connecting rod big-end side clearance. It should be 0.004 to 0.010 in.

9. Install crankshaft rear oil seal case. Drive in the oil seal from inside the case, where the case, oil seal, and separator are separate, using the larger-diameter side of the Oil Seal Installer Plate (special tool MD998011 for 1600cc engine

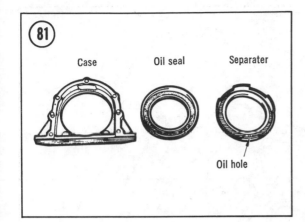

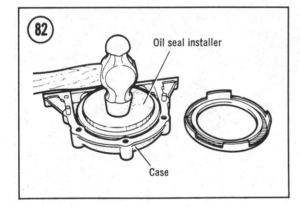

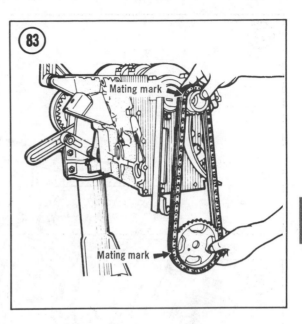

only). Install separator. The seal should be installed so that the oil seal plate fits in the inner contact surface of the seal case. See **Figures 81 and 82**. On the 2000/2600cc engine the oil seal may be pressed into the case by hand. The separator should be installed with oil hole pointing down toward bottom of case.

> NOTE: *Apply engine oil to oil seal lips at time of installation.*

10. Rotate crankshaft to TDC on No. 1 piston.

11. Place cylinder block upside down. Install timing chain guide, sprocket holder (2000/2600cc engine only), and tensioner.

> NOTE: *On the 1600cc engine, the chain guide must be installed so that the jet will be directed toward chain and sprocket meshing point.*

12. With mating marks (punch) of crankshaft sprocket and the camshaft sprocket aligned with the chrome-plated links of the chain, install sprockets onto crankshaft with chain fitted

in guide groove and against tensioner lever. See **Figure 83**. The chain and sprockets will be in a "suspended" state due to absence of supporters.

13. Install key, then install crankshaft gear and oil slinger. The gear should be installed with the "F" mark (1600cc engine), "C" or "A" mark (2000/2600cc engine) on end directed toward front of engine. The slinger must be installed with concave side pointing toward front of engine.

14. Install gasket. Install timing chaincase to cylinder block.

15. On the 1600cc engine insert tensioner lever plunger and spring through hole in the right-hand side of chain case. Tighten the holder to 29 to 36 ft.-lb., using a $\frac{5}{16}$ in. hex (Allen) wrench bit socket.

> NOTE: *The tensioner lever supports and stretches the camshaft sprocket and chain. Therefore, make sure mating marks match. When tightening holder, use care not to turn the packing together.*

16. On the 2000/2600cc engine install oil pump assembly beneath timing chaincase. Install the oil screen.

17. Install oil pan and gasket. (The gasket should be coated with a sealant on oil pan side. Also the block-to-chain case and block-to-rear

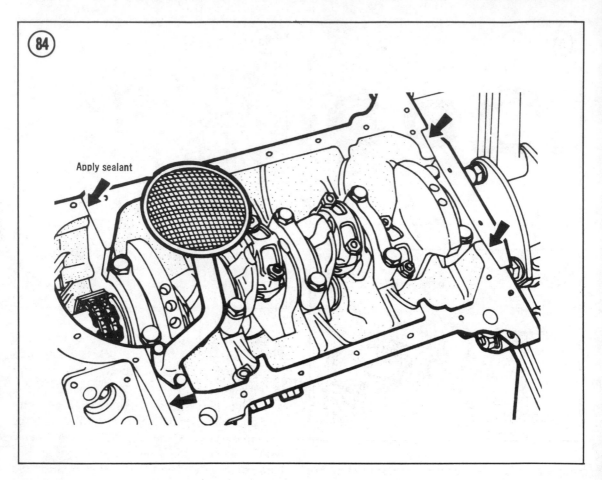

Apply sealant

oil seal case joint faces should be coated.) See **Figure 84**.

18. Tighten oil pan bolts to 4.3 to 5.8 ft.-lb. in criss-cross fashion starting with the one located farthest from the center in the predetermined sequence.

19. Install and temporarily tighten crankshaft pulley. Be careful not to lock crank against rotation.

20. Install oil pressure switch.

21. Turn engine upright. *Do not* turn crank before cylinder head assembly is installed and camshaft sprocket is fixed on camshaft. Cover top of chaincase with rags so case will not be damaged by bolts or other foreign objects falling into it.

22. Install the flywheel. Tighten mounting bolts to 83 to 90 ft.-lb. Lock each bolt by bending a tongued washer. On engine equipped with automatic transmission install an adapter, drive plate, and backing plate. Tighten bolts to 83 to

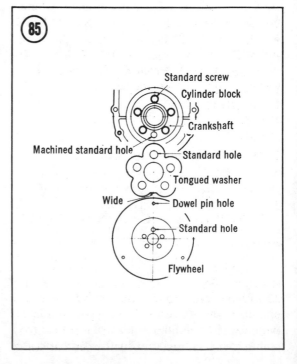

Standard screw
Cylinder block
Crankshaft
Machined standard hole
Standard hole
Tongued washer
Wide
Dowel pin hole
Standard hole
Flywheel

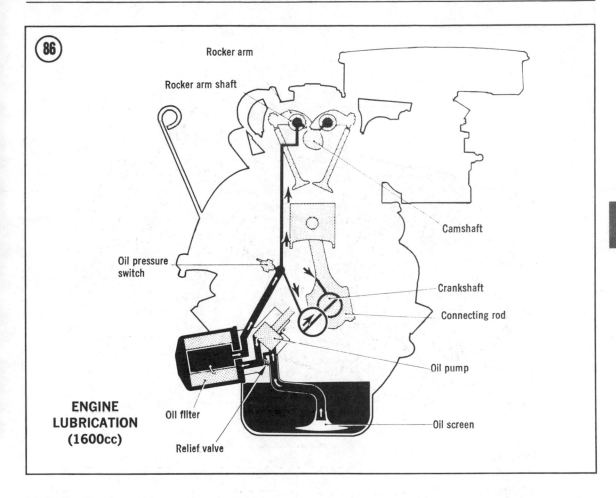

(86)

Rocker arm

Rocker arm shaft

Camshaft

Oil pressure switch

Crankshaft

Connecting rod

Oil pump

ENGINE LUBRICATION (1600cc)

Oil filter

Oil screen

Relief valve

90 ft.-lb. On the 1600cc engine, bolt holes are arranged at an unequal pitch. The flywheel installation can be done by using the standard bolt hole shown in **Figure 85**. Reuse of tongued washers is not recommended.

23. Fix flywheel and tighten crankshaft bolts to 43 to 50 ft.-lb. (1600cc engine) or 80 to 93 ft.-lb. (2000/2600cc engine).

24. Install the engine support bracket. Torque to 29 to 36 ft.-lb.

ENGINE LUBRICATION SYSTEM

Oil Pump

The oil pump differs in location and construction between the 1600cc engine and 2000/2600cc engine. On the 1600cc engine the oil pump is of a trochoid gear type, built inside the bottom of the timing chaincase. Inside the pump is a relief valve which opens at a discharge pressure of 56.9 to 71.1 psi, connecting the incoming and discharge sides in order to prevent oil pressure rise over the prescribed pressure.

The oil screen is installed inside the cylinder block. It traps larger particles of sludge and dirt present in the oil in the oil pan. This filtered oil passes through the oil hole in the chaincase to the oil pump, which sends the oil to the oil filter located on the oil pump cover. **Figure 86** shows the path of the lubricating oil on the 1600cc engine.

On the 2000/2600cc engine the oil pump is located inside the oil pan under the timing chaincase. It is driven by power from the engine through the crankshaft gear and driven gear. Engine oil is drawn into the pump via the oil screen and, after being regulated to 56.9-71.1 psi by the relief valve, is sent on to the oil filter. **Figure 87** shows the path of lubricating oil on the 2000/2600cc engine.

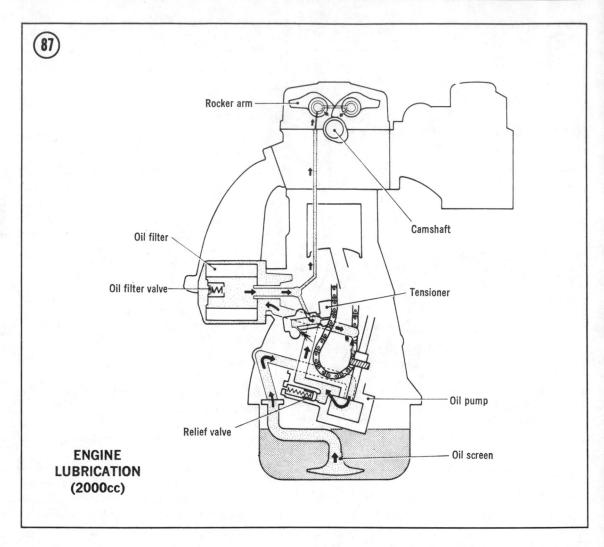

(87)

Rocker arm

Camshaft

Oil filter

Oil filter valve

Tensioner

Oil pump

Relief valve

Oil screen

**ENGINE
LUBRICATION
(2000cc)**

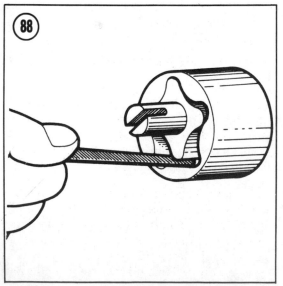

(88)

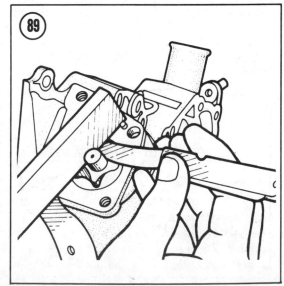

(89)

Oil Pump Removal (1600cc Engine)

1. Remove under cover from body.

2. Remove oil filter.

3. Remove the oil pump cover bolts and rotor assembly, together with cover.

Oil Pump Inspection (1600cc Engine)

1. Check the oil pump shaft claw for excessive wear or damage. Replace if necessary. The chaincase-to-shaft clearance should be 0.0008 to 0.0022 in. The service limit is 0.005 in.

2. Check inner and outer rotors for wear or damage. Check clearance between inner and outer rotor. If clearance exceeds the standard dimension (0.0047 in. or less with a service limit of 0.01 in.) replace the rotor assembly. See **Figure 88**.

3. Check rotor-to-cover end-play. If play exceeds standard dimension (0.0008 to 0.0039 in. with service limit of 0.008 in.) replace rotor assembly or the cover. See **Figure 89**.

> NOTE: *This measurement can be done with gasket attached to the body side. Replace the cover if it has step wear or damage at the rotor section.*

4. Check clearance between outer rotor and chaincase. If clearance exceeds standard dimension (0.0039 to 0.0063 in. with service limit of 0.012 in.) replace rotor assembly. See **Figure 90**.

5. Check oil pump relief plunger movement. Also check the oil passageway and sliding sur-

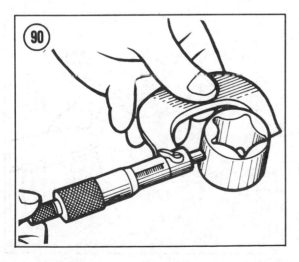

faces for damage. Replace part that is defective. The free length of the relief spring should be 2.352 in. and the tension 17.2 lb. at 1.696 in. length with a service limit of 16.5 lb. at 1.696 in.

Oil Pump Installation (1600cc Engine)

1. Insert rotor assembly into chaincase and install cover. Tighten bolts to 11 to 14 ft.-lb. The oil pump cover gasket is made of special 3-sheet packing material impregnated with liquid packing. Be sure to clean oil and grease from both packing attaching surfaces (chaincase and oil pump cover). Coat cover gasket with sealant but do not apply more than necessary.

2. Install oil filter.

Oil Pump Removal (2000/2600cc Engine)

1. Remove oil pan drain plug. Let engine oil drain thoroughly.

2. Remove oil pan and gasket. Throw gasket away.

3. Remove oil pump assembly by loosening oil pump attaching bolts.

Oil Pump Inspection (2000/2600cc Engine)

1. Remove cover by loosening bolts. Throw away cover gasket.

2. When replacing rotor assembly or gear, remove caulked part of gear fitting pin with a drill, then drive pin off.

> CAUTION
> *Replace outer and inner rotors and shaft as an assembly.*

3. Relief spring and plunger can be removed by removing the plug.

4. See **Figure 91**. Check clearance between inner and outer rotor (**Figure 92**). If clearance exceeds standard dimension (0.0047 in. or less with service limit of 0.010 in.) replace rotor assembly.

5. Check clearance from rotor to cover (**Figure 93**). If clearance exceeds 0.0008 to 0.0079 in. with service limit of 0.008 in., replace rotor assembly or cover. To check clearance attach gasket on the body side. Replace cover if it has groove wear or damage in the rotor sliding part.

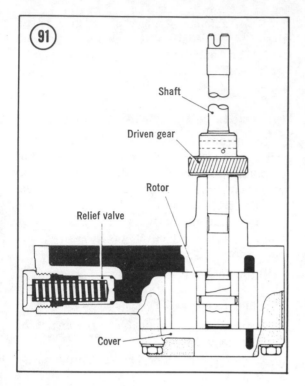

Shaft

Driven gear

Rotor

Relief valve

Cover

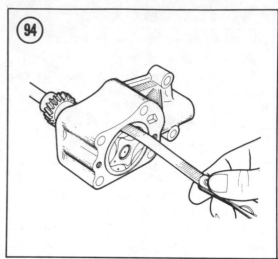

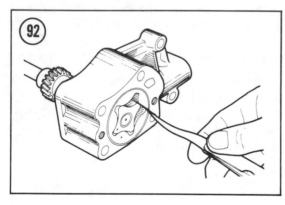

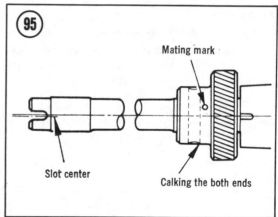

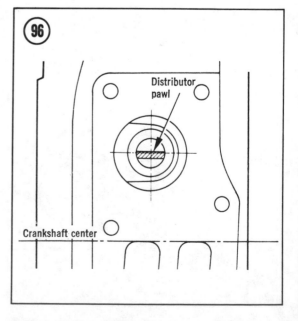

Mating mark

Slot center

Calking the both ends

Distributor pawl

Crankshaft center

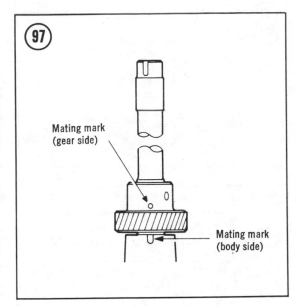

Mating mark (gear side)

Mating mark (body side)

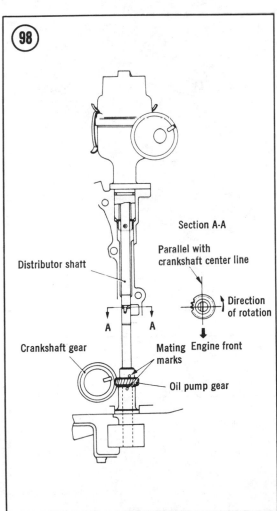

Distributor shaft

Crankshaft gear

Section A-A

Parallel with crankshaft center line

Direction of rotation

A   A

Mating marks

Engine front

Oil pump gear

6. Check clearance from outer rotor to chaincase (**Figure 94**). If clearance exceeds 0.0039 to 0.0063 in. with service limit of 0.012 in., replace rotor assembly.

7. Check relief plunger for sliding motion. Check oil passage and sliding surface for damage. Replace plunger if defective.

8. Check valve spring for breakage or deterioration. The free length of the relief spring should be 2.3516 in., the tension 17.2 lb. @ 1.697 in.

9. Replace cover packing with new part.

10. Caulk both ends of gear lock pin after installing the gear on the shaft, whenever oil pump shaft gear has been removed. See **Figure 95**. When gear is installed, the mating mark on gear should be in relative position of the slot in the forward end of shaft.

Oil Pump Installation (2000/2600cc Engine)

1. Turn crankshaft clockwise to set piston of No. 1 cylinder to TDC on compression stroke.

2. Remove distributor cap. Set rotor to No. 1 position. Be sure distributor shaft pawl is in position shown in **Figure 96**.

3. See **Figure 97**. Align mating mark of oil pump body with that of the gear. Insert oil pump assembly until oil pump shaft gear meshes with crankshaft gear and is engaged with the distributor pawl. When pawl is hard to engage, turn distributor rotor slightly clockwise and counterclockwise. Use a new oil pump gasket. Refer to **Figure 98**.

Oil Filter

The cartridge type oil filter has a built-in valve that opens if the element becomes dirty and clogged and the difference in oil pressure between, before, and after the element becomes 11.4 to 17.0 psi, thus bypassing the filter.

The interior of the filter requires no cleaning but the assembly should be replaced every 8,000 miles or every second oil change.

Oil Filter Removal

1. Place an oil receiving pan beneath the filter.

2. If filter cannot be removed by hand use an oil filter wrench as illustrated in **Figure 99**.

Oil Filter Installation

1. Tighten new filter by hand. Then torque to 8 to 9 ft.-lb. (Vaseline should be applied lightly to the O-ring gasket before installation.) Be sure the O-ring is not twisted during installation.

2. Fill the engine with engine oil after filter replacement.

3. Crank engine over to check filter for oil leaks.

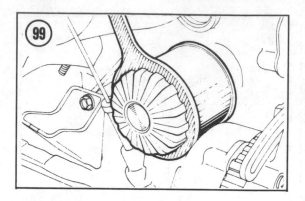

Oil Pressure Switch

The oil pressure switch is mounted at the center of the right-hand side of the engine. If the lubricating system pressure drops below 2.8 to 5.7 psi during normal operation the oil pressure warning lamp lights to give warning to the driver.

Oil Pressure Switch Removal

1. Remove and install the oil pressure switch (1600cc engine, see **Figure 100**) with a one inch, 12-point deep socket.

2. On the 2000/2600cc engine (see **Figure 101**) remove the switch after removing the tag.

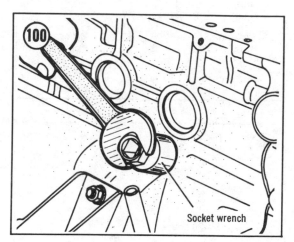

Socket wrench

Oil Pressure Switch Inspection

Check oil pressure switch as illustrated in **Figure 102**. Replace switch if it does not satisfy the standard value of 2.8 to 5.7 psi or less.

Oil Pressure Switch Installation

1. On the 1600cc engine apply sealant to the threaded portion before installing.

2. On the 2000/2600cc engine install the switch, then reinstall the tag (refer to **Figure 101**).

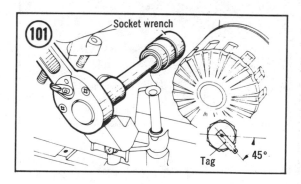

Socket wrench

Tag   45°

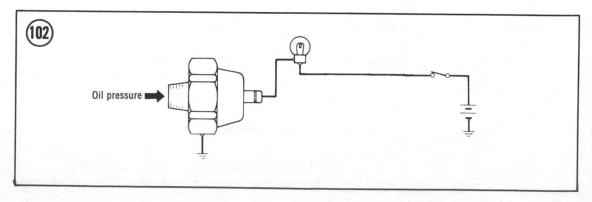

Oil pressure

Table 1   GENERAL ENGINE SPECIFICATIONS

Type	In-line, OHV, OHC
No. of cylinders	4
Bore	
1600cc	3.03 in. (77 mm)
2000cc	3.31 in. (84 mm)
2600cc	3.59 in. (91 mm)
Stroke	
1600cc	3.39 in. (86 mm)
2000cc	3.54 in. (90 mm)
2600cc	3.59 in. (91 mm)
Piston displacement	
1600cc	97.5 cu.-in. (1600cc)
2000cc	121.7 cu.-in. (2000cc)
2600cc	155.9 cu.-in. (2600cc)
Compression ratio	
1600/2000cc	8.5:1
2600cc	8.2:1
Firing order	1-3-4-2
Basic ignition timing	Refer to emission control information label on vehicle
Valve timing	
Intake valve (opens BTDC)	1600cc, 20°; 2000cc, 25°; 2600cc, 25°
Intake valve (closes ABDC)	1600cc, 48°; 2000cc, 59°; 2600cc, 59°
Exhaust valve (opens BBDC)	1600cc, 51°; 2000cc, 70°; 2600cc, 64°
Exhaust valve (closes ATDC)	1600cc, 17°; 2000cc, 14°; 2600cc, 20°
Jet valve (opens BTDC)	1600cc, 20°; 2000cc, 25°; 2600cc, 25°
Jet valve (closes ABDC)	1600cc, 48°; 2000cc, 59°; 2600cc, 59°
Valve overlap	
1600cc	37°
2000cc	39°
2600cc	45°
Intake valve duration	
1600cc	248°
2000/2600cc	264°
Exhaust valve duration	
1600cc	248°
2000/2600cc	264°
Jet valve duration	
1600cc	248°
2000/2600cc	264°

4

Table 2   TIGHTENING TORQUES

Description	1600cc (Ft.-lb.)	2000/2600cc (Ft.-lb.)
Front insulator to crossmember	22-29	22-29
Front insulator to engine bracket	10-14	10-14
Rear insulator to engine support bracket	4-7	10-14
Rear insulator to transmission	14-17	14-17
Engine support bracket to car body	7	7
Cylinder block to engine bracket	43.5-50.5	29-36
Cylinder head bolts (cold engine)	51-54	65-72
Cylinder head bolts (hot engine)	58-61	72-79
Camshaft bearing cap	14-15	13-14
Camshaft sprocket	43.5-57.5	36.5-43
Spark plugs	14.5-21.5	18-21.5
Rocker cover	4-5	4-5
Heater joint	14.5-28.5	14.5-28.5
Main bearing caps	36.5-39.5	54.5-61
Connecting rod caps	23.5-25	33-34.5
Flywheel (manual transmission)	94.5-101	94.5-101
Drive plate (automatic transmission)	83.5-90	83.5-90
Crank pulley	7.5-8.5	80-94
Crankshaft sprocket bolt	43.5-50.5	—
Oil pump sprocket	25-28.5	22-28.5
Timing belt tensioner nut	16-21.5	—
Oil pan	4.5-5.5	4.5-5.5
Oil pan drain plug	43.5-57.5	43.5-57.5
Oil filter	8-9	8-9
Oil pump cover	11-13	—
Oil pump	—	6-7
Intake/exhaust manifold	11-14	11-14
Front exhaust pipe-to-exhaust manifold connecting bolts	11-18	11-18
Counterbalance chamber cover	—	3-4
Counterbalance shaft bolt	—	22-28.5
Oil pressure switch and gauge	11-15.5	11-15.5
Front case	11-13	—
Jet valve	13.5-15.5	13.5-15.5
Oil screen	13.5-18	—

CHAPTER FIVE

FUEL AND EXHAUST SYSTEMS

This chapter provides information on the fuel and exhaust systems. Information on the exhaust emission control system is given in Chapter Seven.

The fuel and exhaust systems consist of the fuel tank, fuel lines, fuel separator, fuel pump, fuel strainer, carburetor, air cleaner, intake and exhaust manifolds, exhaust pipe, muffler, and tailpipe.

FUEL SYSTEM

The fuel system components used on the various Colt models are shown in **Figures 1, 2, 3, and 4**.

FUEL TANK

NOTE
Chrysler Corporation has indicated that the fuel tank retaining straps on some 1977-1978 models may be faulty. Return the car to a dealer for inspection and correction if you have not already done so.

The fuel tank is installed under the luggage compartment floor. The fuel tanks used on 1971-1973 models are shown in **Figure 5**; 1974 models in **Figures 6 and 7**; 1975-1977 models in **Figure 8**; and 1978-1979 models in **Figures 9-11**.

Removal

1. Drain fuel tank by removing the drain plug.

2. Loosen main and return fuel hose clamps (front in the case of sedan, hardtop and coupe, and left in the case of station wagon). Disconnect fuel hoses from fuel tank.

3. Disconnect each vent line tube by loosening clamp at separator tank side.

4. Disconnect filler hose by loosening clamp at tank side.

5. Remove rear floor cover. Remove harness from fuel gauge.

6. Remove fuel tank mounting bolts. Lower the fuel tank slightly. Loosen each vent line tube and remove fuel tank.

Inspection and Maintenance

Check fuel tank and fuel pipes for leaks, rust, corrosion, damage and cracks. Replace the fuel tank if its interior has been seriously corroded or damaged.

WARNING
Exercise extreme caution when servicing the various parts of the fuel system to minimize the danger of fire or explosion. Before servicing the fuel tank or lines, make sure the fuel is completely drained into a suitable sealed container. Residual gases in the fuel tank should be expelled by filling the tank completely with an inert gas or, as a last resort, water. Soldering or welding the tank should be done with it full of inert gas or water. If water is used, be certain to dry the inside of the tank thoroughly before refilling with fuel.

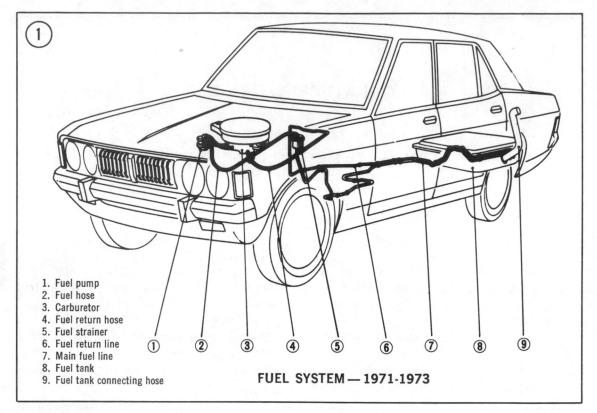

1. Fuel pump
2. Fuel hose
3. Carburetor
4. Fuel return hose
5. Fuel strainer
6. Fuel return line
7. Main fuel line
8. Fuel tank
9. Fuel tank connecting hose

FUEL SYSTEM — 1971-1973

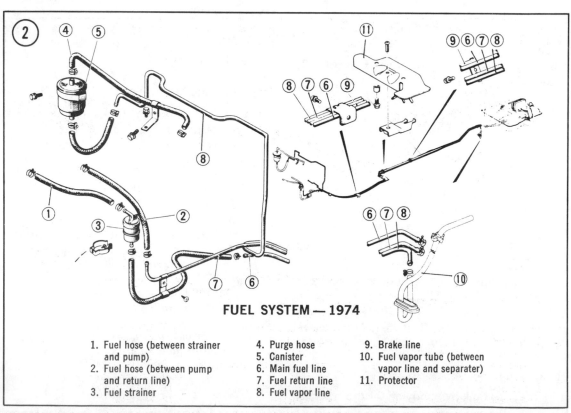

FUEL SYSTEM — 1974

1. Fuel hose (between strainer and pump)
2. Fuel hose (between pump and return line)
3. Fuel strainer
4. Purge hose
5. Canister
6. Main fuel line
7. Fuel return line
8. Fuel vapor line
9. Brake line
10. Fuel vapor tube (between vapor line and separater)
11. Protector

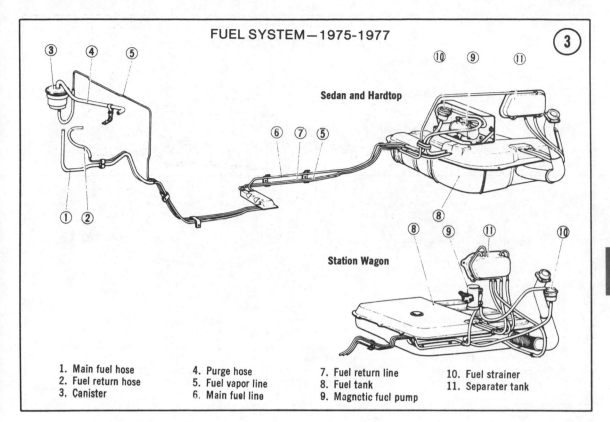

FUEL SYSTEM—1975-1977

③

Sedan and Hardtop

Station Wagon

1. Main fuel hose
2. Fuel return hose
3. Canister
4. Purge hose
5. Fuel vapor line
6. Main fuel line
7. Fuel return line
8. Fuel tank
9. Magnetic fuel pump
10. Fuel strainer
11. Separater tank

5

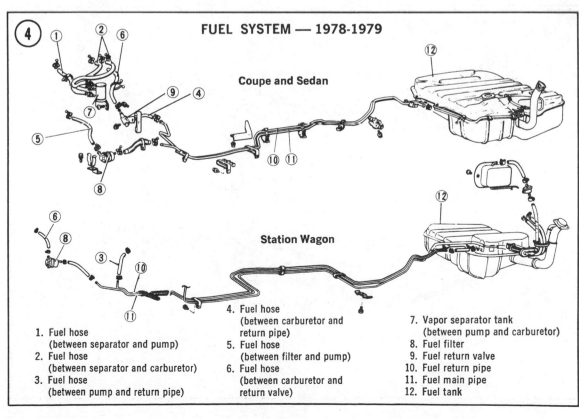

④   **FUEL SYSTEM — 1978-1979**

Coupe and Sedan

Station Wagon

1. Fuel hose
   (between separator and pump)
2. Fuel hose
   (between separator and carburetor)
3. Fuel hose
   (between pump and return pipe)
4. Fuel hose
   (between carburetor and
   return pipe)
5. Fuel hose
   (between filter and pump)
6. Fuel hose
   (between carburetor and
   return valve)
7. Vapor separator tank
   (between pump and carburetor)
8. Fuel filter
9. Fuel return valve
10. Fuel return pipe
11. Fuel main pipe
12. Fuel tank

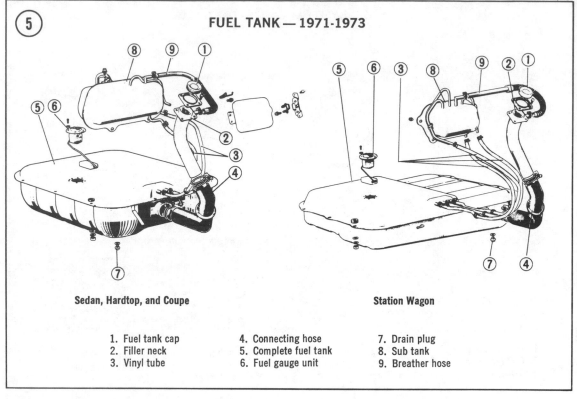

⑤   FUEL TANK — 1971-1973

Sedan, Hardtop, and Coupe   **Station Wagon**

1. Fuel tank cap   4. Connecting hose   7. Drain plug
2. Filler neck   5. Complete fuel tank   8. Sub tank
3. Vinyl tube   6. Fuel gauge unit   9. Breather hose

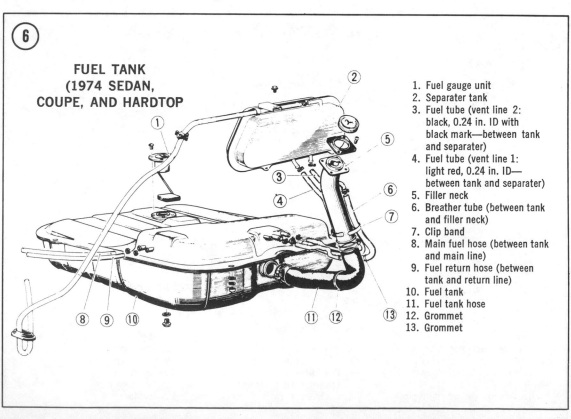

⑥

FUEL TANK
(1974 SEDAN,
COUPE, AND HARDTOP

1. Fuel gauge unit
2. Separater tank
3. Fuel tube (vent line 2: black, 0.24 in. ID with black mark—between tank and separater)
4. Fuel tube (vent line 1: light red, 0.24 in. ID— between tank and separater)
5. Filler neck
6. Breather tube (between tank and filler neck)
7. Clip band
8. Main fuel hose (between tank and main line)
9. Fuel return hose (between tank and return line)
10. Fuel tank
11. Fuel tank hose
12. Grommet
13. Grommet

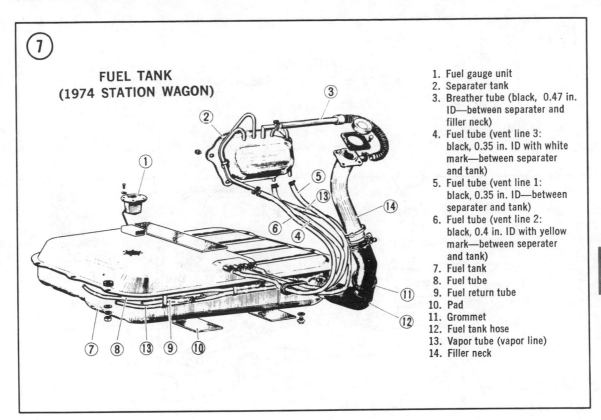

(7)

FUEL TANK
(1974 STATION WAGON)

1. Fuel gauge unit
2. Separater tank
3. Breather tube (black, 0.47 in. ID—between separater and filler neck)
4. Fuel tube (vent line 3: black, 0.35 in. ID with white mark—between separater and tank)
5. Fuel tube (vent line 1: black, 0.35 in. ID—between separater and tank)
6. Fuel tube (vent line 2: black, 0.4 in. ID with yellow mark—between seperater and tank)
7. Fuel tank
8. Fuel tube
9. Fuel return tube
10. Pad
11. Grommet
12. Fuel tank hose
13. Vapor tube (vapor line)
14. Filler neck

5

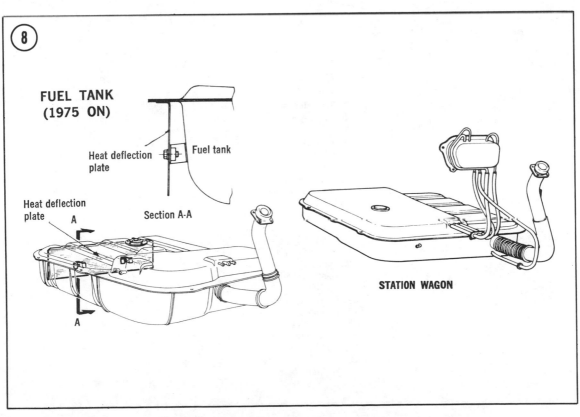

(8)

FUEL TANK
(1975 ON)

Heat deflection plate

Fuel tank

Heat deflection plate

A

Section A-A

A

STATION WAGON

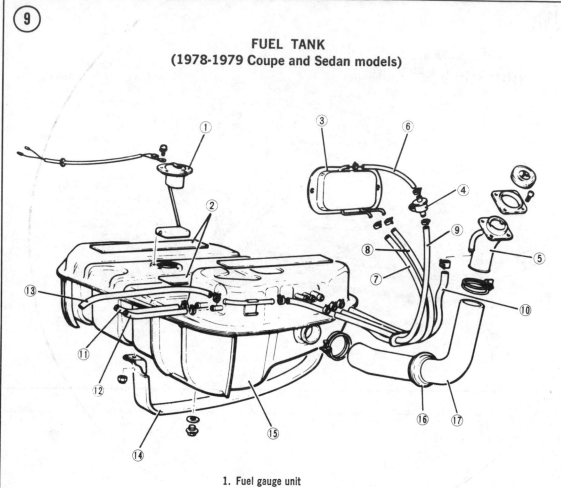

FUEL TANK
(1978-1979 Coupe and Sedan models)

1. Fuel gauge unit
2. Pad
3. Separator tank
4. Two-way valve
5. Filler neck
6. Tube, soft vinyl
   (between separator tank
   and 2-way valve)
7. Tube, soft vinyl
   (between separator tank and
   fuel tank)
8. Tube, soft vinyl
   (between separator tank and
   fuel tank)
9. Tube, soft vinyl
10. Tube, soft vinyl
    (between fuel tank and
    filler neck)
11. Fuel hose, return
12. Fuel hose, main
13. Tube, soft vinyl
14. Tank band
15. Fuel tank
16. Grommet
17. Fuel tank hose

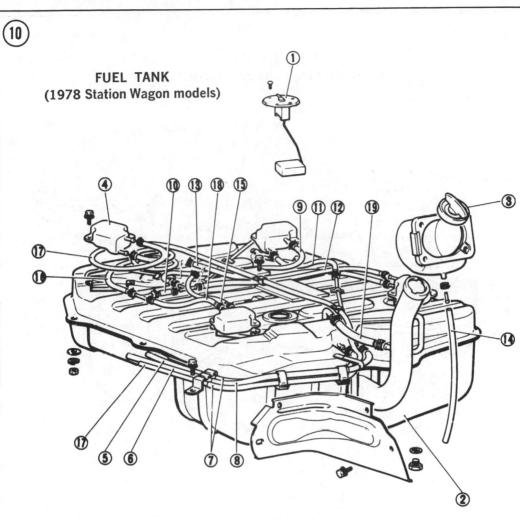

FUEL TANK
(1978 Station Wagon models)

5

1. Fuel gauge unit
2. Fuel tank (4 pieces)
3. Fuel tank cap
4. Separator tank
5. Fuel hose, return
6. Fuel hose, main
7. Tube, soft vinyl
8. Tube, soft vinyl
9. Vapor hose
10. Vapor hose
11. Vapor hose
12. Vapor hose
13. Vapor hose
14. Tube, soft vinyl
15. Vapor hose
16. Vapor hose
17. Fuel hose, vapor
18. Vapor hose
19. Breather hose

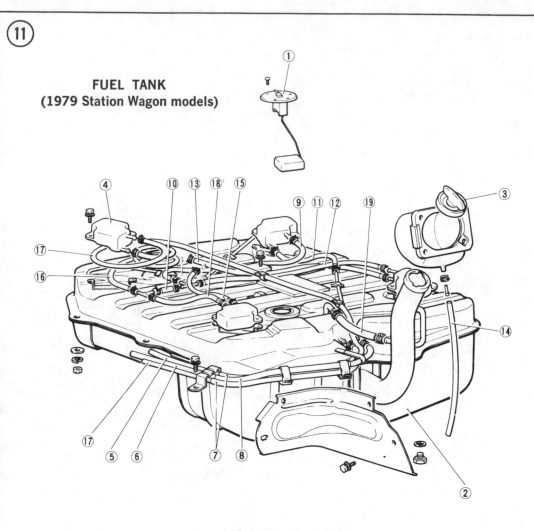

FUEL TANK
(1979 Station Wagon models)

1. Fuel gauge unit
2. Fuel tank
3. Fuel tank cap
4. Separator tank (4 pieces)
5. Fuel hose, return
6. Fuel hose, main
7. Tube, soft vinyl
8. Tube, soft vinyl
9. Vapor hose
10. Vapor hose
11. Vapor hose
12. Vapor hose
13. Vapor hose
14. Tube, soft vinyl
15. Vapor hose
16. Vapor hose
17. Fuel hose, vapor
18. Vapor hose
19. Breather hose

Installation

1. Install and connect the main and return fuel hoses and vent line tubes properly. When laying fuel tubes and pipes, each pipe can be identified by the color paint (or tape) provided at both ends.

2. Apply a sealant to both sides of the gauge unit packing.

3. Apply sealant to grommets for tubes and hoses to be installed in the car body.

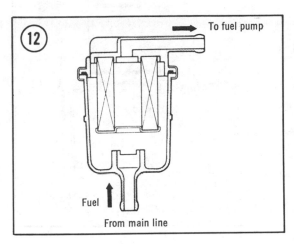

FUEL STRAINER

The cartridge type fuel strainer should be replaced every 12,000 miles or 12 months. The filter can be purged of minor debris by removing the strainer, pointing the outlet downward, and blowing compressed air into the inlet. See **Figure 12**.

VAPOR SEPARATOR

A vapor separator tank is used to lower the fuel temperature and ensure a constant supply of fuel to the engine. **Figure 13** shows the vapor separator used on the 2000cc/2600cc 1974 models. **Figure 14** shows the version used on all 1975-1977 models; **Figure 15**, the 1978-1979 versions.

Removal/Installation

1. Connect fuel hoses by observing the color coding used on the vapor separator nipples (each hose should be connected between nipples

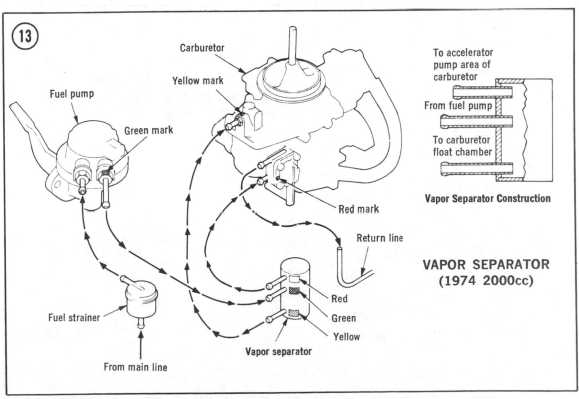

**VAPOR SEPARATOR
(1974 2000cc)**

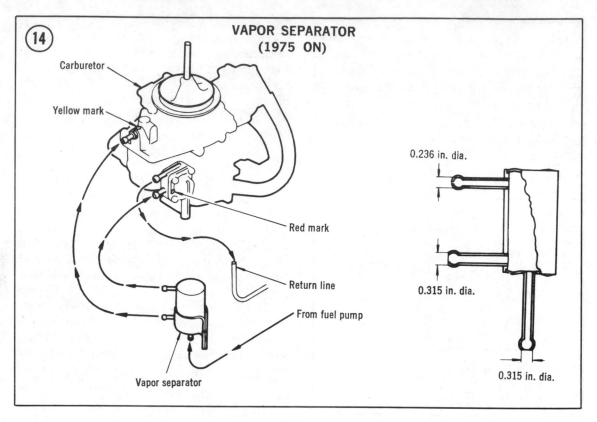

⑭ **VAPOR SEPARATOR**
(1975 ON)

Carburetor

Yellow mark

Red mark

Return line

From fuel pump

Vapor separator

0.236 in. dia.

0.315 in. dia.

0.315 in. dia.

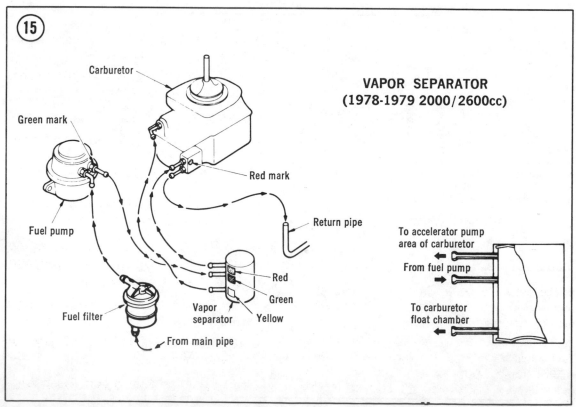

⑮

Carburetor

VAPOR SEPARATOR
(1978-1979 2000/2600cc)

Green mark

Red mark

Return pipe

Fuel pump

To accelerator pump
area of carburetor

From fuel pump

Red

Green

Fuel filter

Vapor
separator

Yellow

To carburetor
float chamber

From main pipe

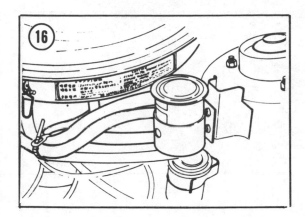

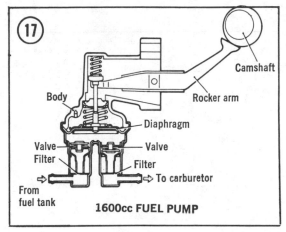

1600cc FUEL PUMP

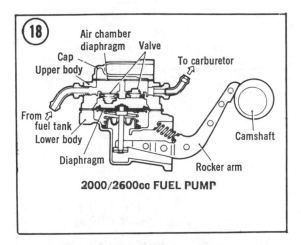

2000/2600cc FUEL PUMP

of the same color). When installing the vapor separator, position the red side upward (**Figure 16**).

2. To eliminate the possibility of connecting fuel hoses improperly, the outer diameter (OD) of the upper nipple differs from that of the lower nipple. Install the vapor separator with the bottom nipple down.

3. Tighten all hose clamps securely after hoses are connected.

MECHANICAL FUEL PUMP

NOTE
Chrysler Corporation has indicated that the fuel pump on some 1978 models may be faulty, allowing fuel leakage into the engine compartment. Return the vehicle to a dealer for inspection and correction if you have not already done so.

The mechanical fuel pump uses a diaphragm which is moved up and down by the rocker arm that is actuated by an eccentric cam on the camshaft, which causes fuel to be sucked into the pump from the fuel tank and discharged from the pump to the carburetor. A fuel return valve which operates when the fuel temperature rises above 122 degrees F , is installed admitting fuel back into the fuel tank after cooling the accelerator pump area of the carburetor. See **Figures 17 and 18**.

Removal

1. Remove fuel pump inlet and outlet return pipes.

2. Loosen body attaching bolts. Remove pump assembly, insulator, and gasket.

Disassembly

1. Remove cap and diaphragm from upper body.

2. Remove upper body from lower body.

> NOTE: *The valve has been caulked to the body and should not be removed.*

3. Pull off rocker arm pin and disassemble pump into the diaphragm assembly, insulator, rocker arm, and diaphragm spring.

4. Do not disassemble return valve installed in upper body.

5. Check the diaphragm for any signs of cracks, deterioration, etc.

6. Check valve for motion and closed condition.

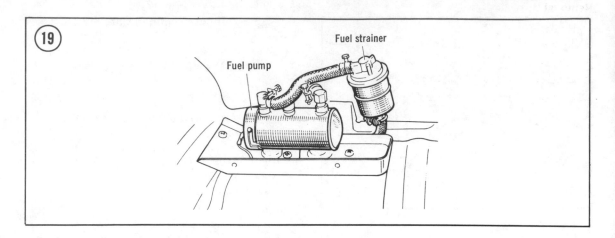

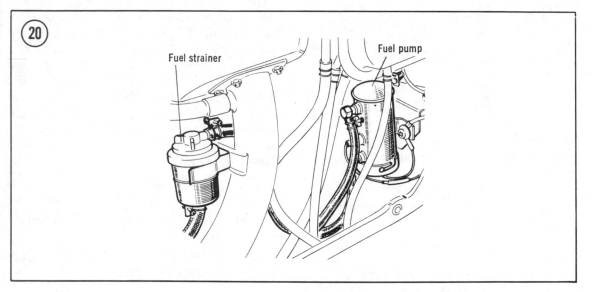

7. Check rocker arm end where camshaft eccentric cam rotates, for wear.

8. Move rocker arm to check spring for deterioration, and the pin section for wear.

9. Check pump body and cover for damage.

Reassembly

To reassemble, reverse the disassembly procedures. In addition, observe the following:

1. Assemble diaphragm assembly with the diaphragm pushed down at the center. No folded or bent diaphragm should be used.

2. After reassembly, check the rocker arm for motion. It should move smoothly without distortion.

Installation

1. Install the pump assembly to cylinder head through the insulator and gasket. Replace 2 gaskets with new ones, coating each side of the gaskets with sealant.

2. Install inlet and outlet return fuel pipes.

ELECTRIC FUEL PUMP

The electric fuel pump is mounted in the trunk in some sedans and hardtops, and in the left rear wheel housing in some station wagons. See **Figures 19 and 20**. The fuel strainer is situated beside the pump. A fuel control relay is installed on the left side of the engine compartment (beside the ignition coil) so that the fuel supply stops if the engine stalls, even though the ignition switch is in the ON position.

Removal/Installation

1. Be careful not to make a wrong connection to the battery when removing and installing the fuel pump.

2. Connect electrical wiring positively.

3. Do not operate fuel pump without fuel.

4. Never apply over-voltage.

Inspection

1. Make sure the fuel pump clicks when the ignition switch is turned to START.

2. If pump fails to click, apply 12 volts directly to the pump (but for no more than one minute). If no click is produced, replace pump.

3. Check fuel strainer for clogging.

CARBURETOR

The carburetor is a 2-barrel downdraft carburetor which supplies the air/fuel mixture at the proper ratio over the entire engine speed range. The carburetor used on models through 1973 is shown in **Figure 21**; the 1974 carburetor in **Figure 22**. Carburetors from 1975 on vary slightly from previous models: The carburetor for automatic transmission cars is provided with an idle adjuster, while the carburetor for manual transmission cars uses a dashpot (as on the 1974 model).

Carburetor Adjustment

Refer to Chapter Three, *Engine Tune-up* section, for procedures.

ACCELERATOR PEDAL

Removal

Refer to **Figures 23 and 24**.

1. Loosen lever (A) locking bolt and pull off lever (A) from accelerator rod.

2. Remove the 2 accelerator arm support locking bolts.

3. Remove accelerator arm split pin. Remove accelerator arm support if necessary.

Installation

1. Before installing pedal support, apply liquid packing (No. 2) to threaded holes for sealing.

2. Tighten throttle rod and lever locking bolts to 7-11 ft.-lb.

3. On 97.5 cid models only, mount the rod with its white-painted side facing lever (A).

Accelerator Rod Adjustment

Refer to **Figures 25 and 26**.

1. With accelerator pedal released (carburetor throttle valve fully closed), insert forward end of lever (A) into the accelerator rod until the prescribed distance shown is obtained between the rear end of the accelerator rod and lever (A).

2. Turn lever (A) until clearance between lever (B) and stopper is the correct distance shown in **Figure 20** (after the engine warm-up operation, and after releasing the automatic choke).

3. Tighten the accelerator rod-to-lever bolt to 7-11 ft.-lb.

> CAUTION
> *Make certain at least 0.4 in. clearance exists between lever (A) and the toe board insulator.*

EXHAUST SYSTEM

The exhaust system should not be removed except when absolutely necessary to replace a damaged muffler, exhaust pipe, or other part of the exhaust system. **Figure 27** shows the exhaust system used on Dodge Colt models through 1973. **Figure 28** shows the 1974 system; **Figure 29** the 1975 on system. The addition of emission control components to the 1975-on system complicates the replacement of exhaust system parts — always one of the more tedious, time-consuming jobs facing the home mechanic.

With the advent of the specialized muffler repair shops, where there is seldom a charge for the actual replacement of the muffler, exhaust pipe, etc., it is recommended that repair or replacement of exhaust system components be left to a shop that specializes in such work.

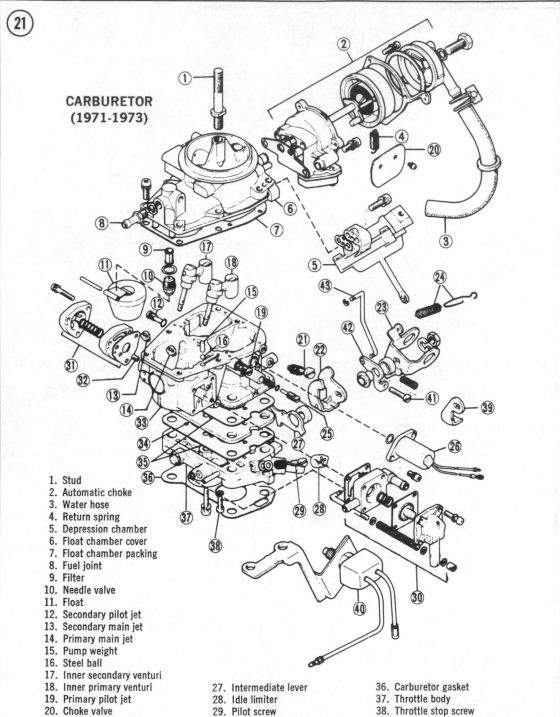

**CARBURETOR
(1971-1973)**

1. Stud
2. Automatic choke
3. Water hose
4. Return spring
5. Depression chamber
6. Float chamber cover
7. Float chamber packing
8. Fuel joint
9. Filter
10. Needle valve
11. Float
12. Secondary pilot jet
13. Secondary main jet
14. Primary main jet
15. Pump weight
16. Steel ball
17. Inner secondary venturi
18. Inner primary venturi
19. Primary pilot jet
20. Choke valve
21. Throttle stop screw
22. Abatement plate
23. Throttle lever
24. Throttle return spring
25. Bypass screw
26. Fuel cut solenoid

27. Intermediate lever
28. Idle limiter
29. Pilot screw
30. Accelerator pump
31. Enrichment body
32. Enrichment jet
33. Main body
34. Insulator
35. Throttle chamber packing

36. Carburetor gasket
37. Throttle body
38. Throttle stop screw
39. Lever (automatic transmission)
40. Kickdown switch
    (automatic transmission)
41. Screw
42. Lever
43. Choke rod

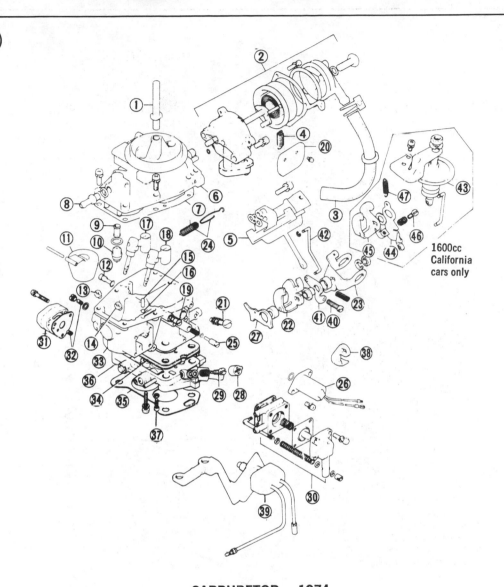

CARBURETOR — 1974

1. Stud
2. Automatic choke
3. Water hose
4. Return spring
5. Depression chamber
6. Float chamber cover
7. Float chamber packing
8. Fuel inlet nipple
9. Filter
10. Needle valve
11. Float
12. Secondary pilot jet
13. Secondary main jet
14. Primary main jet
15. Valve weight
16. Check valve

17. Inner secondary venturi
18. Inner primary venturi
19. Primary pilot jet
20. Choke valve
21. Throttle stop screw
22. Abatement plate
23. Throttle lever
24. Throttle return spring
25. Bypass screw
26. Fuel cut solenoid
27. Intermediate lever
28. Idle limiter
29. Pilot screw
30. Accelerator pump
31. Enrichment body
32. Enrichment jet

33. Main body
34. Insulator
35. Carburetor gasket
36. Throttle body
37. Throttle stop screw
38. Lever (automatic transmission)
39. Kickdown switch
    (automatic transmission)
40. Screw
41. Lever
42. Choke rod
43. Dashpot
44. Lever
45. Abatement plate
46. Adjusting screw
47. Lever spring

5

1600cc
California
cars only

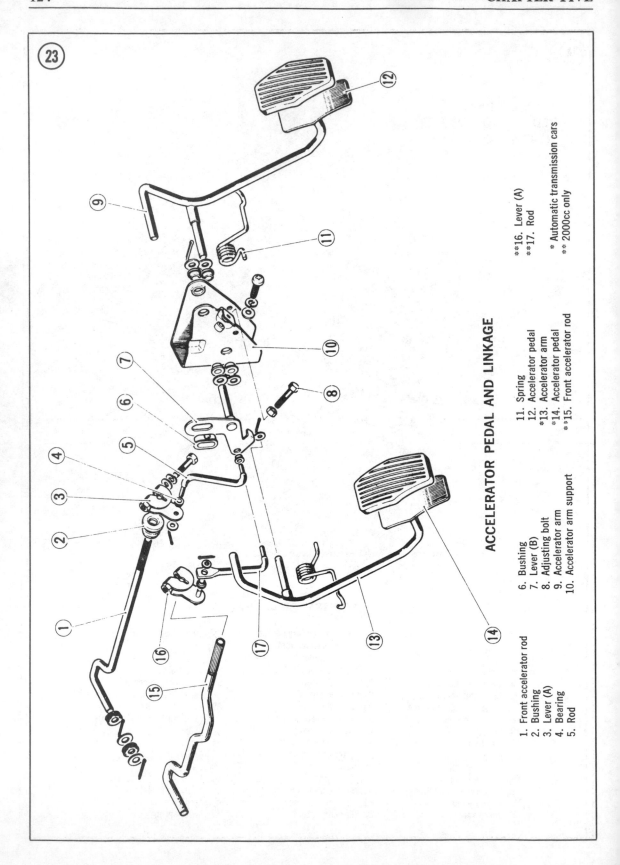

23

ACCELERATOR PEDAL AND LINKAGE

1. Front accelerator rod
2. Bushing
3. Lever (A)
4. Bearing
5. Rod
6. Bushing
7. Lever (B)
8. Adjusting bolt
9. Accelerator arm
10. Accelerator arm support
11. Spring
12. Accelerator pedal
*13. Accelerator arm
*14. Accelerator pedal
**15. Front accelerator rod
**16. Lever (A)
**17. Rod

* Automatic transmission cars
** 2000cc only

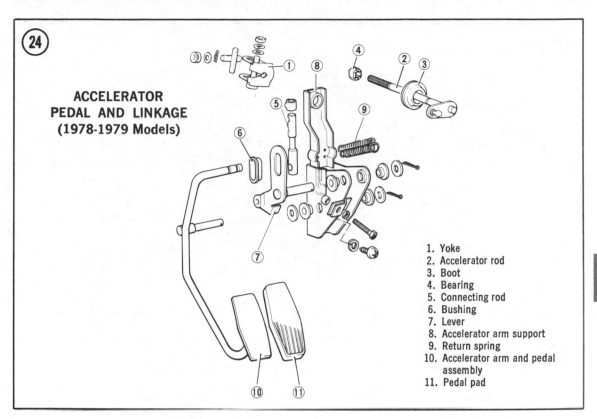

ACCELERATOR PEDAL AND LINKAGE (1978-1979 Models)

1. Yoke
2. Accelerator rod
3. Boot
4. Bearing
5. Connecting rod
6. Bushing
7. Lever
8. Accelerator arm support
9. Return spring
10. Accelerator arm and pedal assembly
11. Pedal pad

5

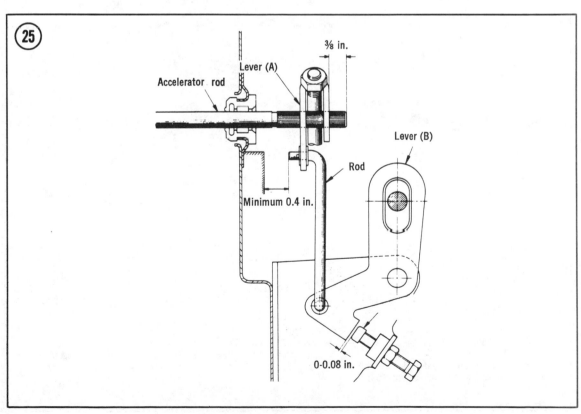

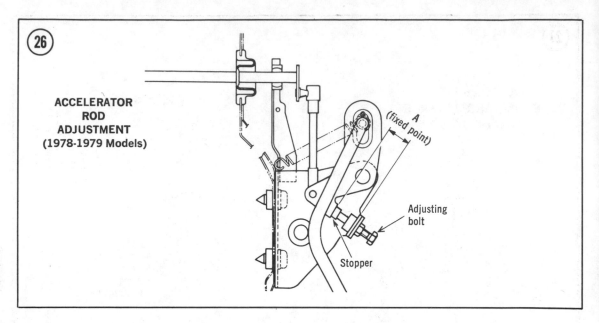

ACCELERATOR
ROD
ADJUSTMENT
(1978-1979 Models)

A
(fixed point)

Adjusting
bolt

Stopper

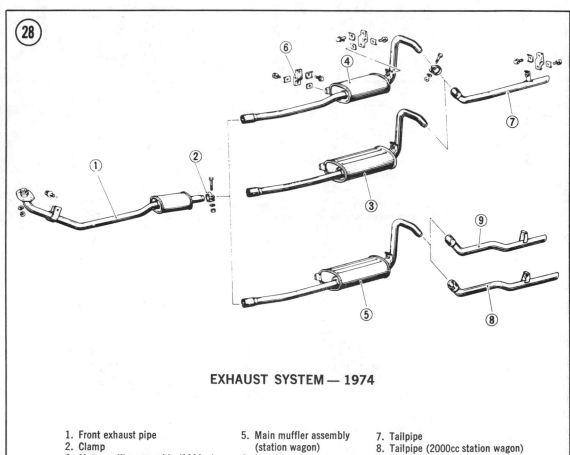

EXHAUST SYSTEM — 1974

1. Front exhaust pipe
2. Clamp
3. Main muffler assembly (1600cc)
4. Main muffler assembly (2000cc)

5. Main muffler assembly
   (station wagon)
6. Hanger

7. Tailpipe
8. Tailpipe (2000cc station wagon)
9. Tailpipe (1600cc station wagon)

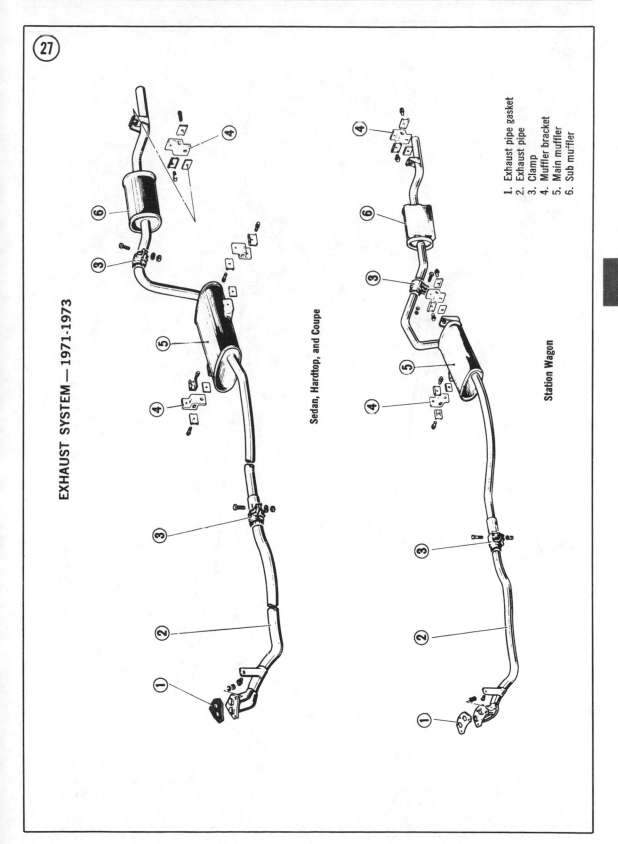

㉗

EXHAUST SYSTEM — 1971-1973

1. Exhaust pipe gasket
2. Exhaust pipe
3. Clamp
4. Muffler bracket
5. Main muffler
6. Sub muffler

Sedan, Hardtop, and Coupe

Station Wagon

5

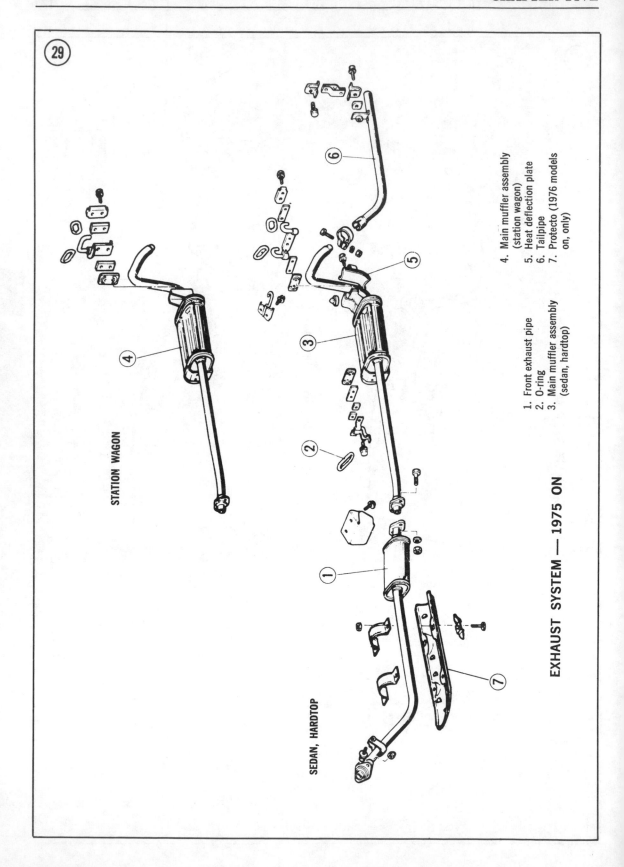

㉙

STATION WAGON

SEDAN, HARDTOP

1. Front exhaust pipe
2. O-ring
3. Main muffler assembly
   (sedan, hardtop)
4. Main muffler assembly
   (station wagon)
5. Heat deflection plate
6. Tailpipe
7. Protecto (1976 models
   on, only)

EXHAUST SYSTEM — 1975 ON

CHAPTER SIX

COOLING AND HEATING SYSTEMS

The cooling system is a water-cooled, pressurized, forced circulation type utilizing a centrifugal impeller type water pump, corrugated fin type radiator, wax type thermostat, and Siamese type cylinder block and head. The radiator has a cap with a pressure reducing button to ensure operational safety. A transmission oil cooler is built into the lower part of the radiator used on automatic transmission equipped cars.

The heater is a hot water type which circulates engine coolant through a small radiator behind the instrument panel. Air is taken in through cowl vents and forced through the radiator to obtain heat.

This chapter includes service procedures for the thermostat, radiator, fan, fan clutch, water pump, and heater. Cooling system flushing, pressure checking, and fan belt tension adjustment procedures are described.

COOLING SYSTEM

Figure 1 shows the cooling system for the 97.5 cid (1600cc) engine; **Figure 2**, the cooling system for the 121.7 cid (2000cc) and 155.9 cid (2600cc) engines. Cooling system specifications are given in **Table 1** at the end of the chapter. **Figure 3** shows the radiator components used

on 1973 and earlier Dodge Colts; **Figure 4** shows 1974 radiator components.

The radiator for the 1975 model on is the same as that for the 1974 model except for the following changes: the lower hose has been modified to provide clearance between the air pump and alternator. The lower hose from the 1974 model will not fit the 1975 on model; the 2000cc (121.7 cid) and 2600cc (155.9 cid) models use a radiator shroud; the 1600cc (97.5 cid), 2000cc (121.7 cid) and 2600cc (155.9), cid engines use Torque-Flite automatic transmissions. Transmission oil is cooled through the bottom tank of the radiator. The radiator hoses and tubes are routed along the left-hand side of the engine. Radiator components are nearly the same for both engines. Differences are shown in **Figure 5**.

Coolant Change

1. The coolant should be changed every 24,000 miles or 2 years. Flush the engine and radiator with radiator cleaning fluid, after draining the coolant completely.

2. Refill the system with a high quality ethylene glycol anti-freeze coolant and water. A convenient ratio for mixing is 50:50 anti-freeze and water.

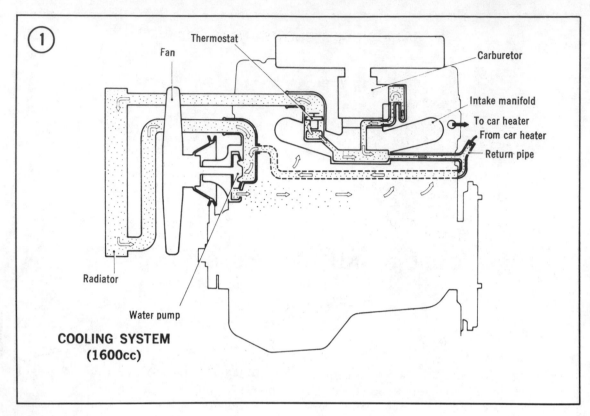

COOLING SYSTEM
(1600cc)

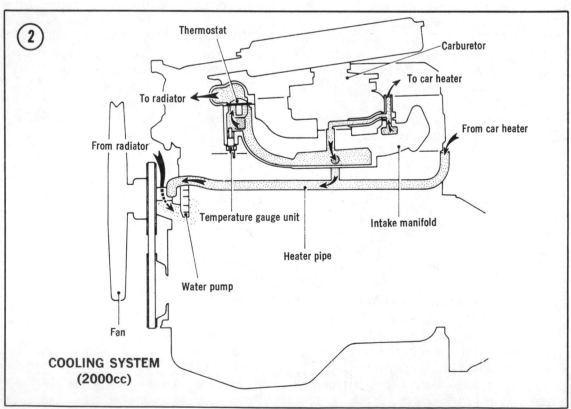

COOLING SYSTEM
(2000cc)

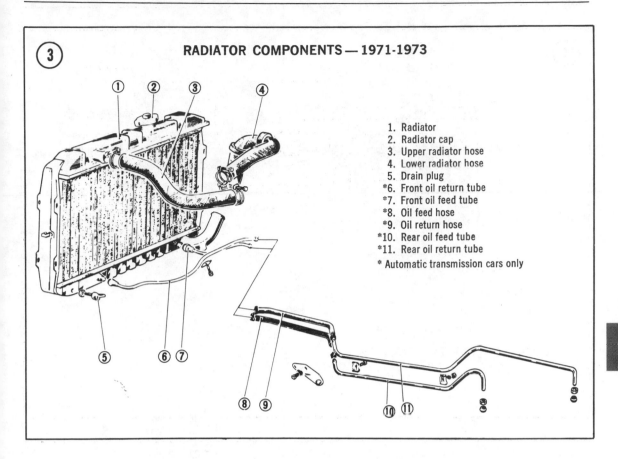

③ **RADIATOR COMPONENTS — 1971-1973**

1. Radiator
2. Radiator cap
3. Upper radiator hose
4. Lower radiator hose
5. Drain plug
*6. Front oil return tube
*7. Front oil feed tube
*8. Oil feed hose
*9. Oil return hose
*10. Rear oil feed tube
*11. Rear oil return tube
* Automatic transmission cars only

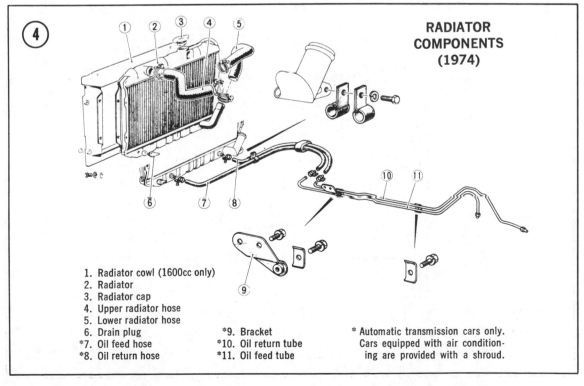

④ **RADIATOR COMPONENTS (1974)**

1. Radiator cowl (1600cc only)
2. Radiator
3. Radiator cap
4. Upper radiator hose
5. Lower radiator hose
6. Drain plug
*7. Oil feed hose
*8. Oil return hose

*9. Bracket
*10. Oil return tube
*11. Oil feed tube

* Automatic transmission cars only.
Cars equipped with air condition-
ing are provided with a shroud.

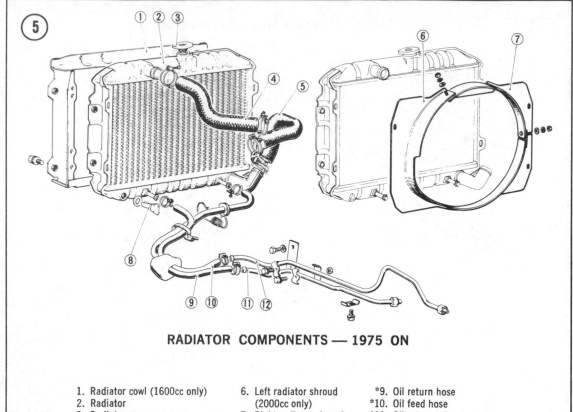

RADIATOR COMPONENTS — 1975 ON

1. Radiator cowl (1600cc only)
2. Radiator
3. Radiator cap
4. Upper radiator hose
5. Lower radiator hose
6. Left radiator shroud (2000cc only)
7. Right radiator shroud (2000cc only)
8. Drain plug
*9. Oil return hose
*10. Oil feed hose
*11. Oil return tube
*12. Oil feed tube
* Automatic transmission cars only.

Table 2   RELATIONSHIP BETWEEN ANTI-FREEZE CONCENTRATION AND SPECIFIC GRAVITY

Concentration of Anti-freeze in Coolant (by Volume)	Specific Gravity and Temperature of Coolant When Specific Gravity is Measured									Freezing Point
	50°F	59°F	68°F	77°F	86°F	95°F	104°F	113°F	122°F	
5%	1.010	1.009	1.007	1.006	1.004	1.003	1.001	1.000	0.998	
10%	1.016	1.015	1.014	1.013	1.011	1.010	1.008	1.006	1.004	
15%	1.025	1.024	1.022	1.020	1.018	1.016	1.014	1.012	1.010	
20%	1.032	1.031	1.029	1.027	1.025	1.023	1.021	1.019	1.016	
25%	1.040	1.038	1.036	1.034	1.032	1.030	1.028	1.025	1.023	
30%	1.047	1.045	1.043	1.041	1.039	1.037	1.034	1.032	1.029	
35%	1.055	1.053	1.051	1.049	1.046	1.043	1.041	1.038	1.035	
40%	1.063	1.060	1.058	1.055	1.053	1.050	1.048	1.045	1.042	
45%	1.070	1.068	1.066	1.063	1.060	1.057	1.054	1.051	1.048	
50%	1.078	1.075	1.072	1.069	1.067	1.064	1.061	1.058	1.055	—34°F
55%	1.083	1.080	1.078	1.075	1.072	1.069	1.066	1.063	1.059	—49°F

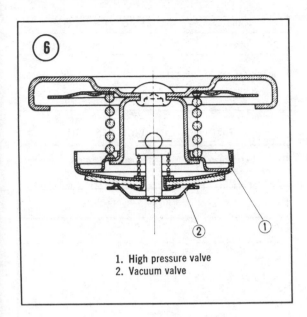

1. High pressure valve
2. Vacuum valve

Table 3   PRESSURE TEST

Model	Standard Value
1971-1973 All models	22.8 psi
1974-1977 All models	22.7 psi
1978-1979 1600cc 2000 and 2600cc	22.7 psi 25.6 psi

Table 4   VALVE OPENING PRESSURE

Description	Standard Value
Radiator cap valve opening pressure	
High pressure side	11.4 to 14.2 psi
Vacuum side	—0.7 to —1.4 psi

3. Run the engine until the water is thoroughly mixed and warmed, then check the water level. Add water until the radiator is filled to the specified level.

Anti-freeze

Using a hydrometer, measure the temperature and specific gravity of the coolant and determine the concentration and safe working temperature with reference to **Table 2**. If the coolant is short of anti-freeze, add anti-freeze up to a concentration of 50%.

RADIATOR

Removal

1. Remove the under-cover and drain the coolant from radiator.

2. Disconnect radiator hose at the engine side.

3. Remove the oil tube (front) on automobiles equipped with automatic transmissions. Place a cover over the tube to prevent foreign matter from entering.

4. On models so equipped, remove the shroud.

Inspection/Maintenance

1. Check radiator hoses for leaks, loose clamps, and deterioration. Replace where necessary.

2. Correct any radiator leaks by soldering or replacement. After repair, perform the pressure proof test (see **Table 3**).

3. Check the radiator for clogging. Flush if necessary.

4. Check the radiator cap valve and spring for deterioration and broken packing. Check valve opening pressure (**Table 4**) and replace radiator cap if necessary. See **Figure 6**.

Installation

1. Insert radiator hoses firmly onto the radiator and engine couplings. Clamp securely so that they will not leak.

CAUTION
When replacing the lower radiator hose in the 1600cc (97.5 cid) model, install the new hose with the white paint mark directed to the engine.

2. In the 1600cc (97.5 cid) model equipped with automatic transmission, install the oil tube, then fit the spring securely between the oil feed tube grommet and radiator cowl front section to obtain proper clearance between the cooling fan and tube.

CAUTION
Maintain a clearance of 0.59 in. or greater between the fan and shroud. In addition, provide more than 0.55 in. clearance between the shroud edge and lower hose. See Figure 7.

6

3. Replenish the transmission oil up to the specified amount on automobiles equipped with automatic transmission. See **Table 5**.

FAN CLUTCH

The fan utilizes a torque type clutch designed to lower the fan speed without regard to atmospheric temperature as the pulley speed increases, thus regulating the volume of cooling air to reduce a loss of output during high-speed travel. See **Figures 8 and 9**.

FAN AND FAN BELT

Removal

1. Loosen the fan bolt and remove the fan.

2. Move the generator or alternator to lessen fan belt tension. Remove fan belt.

Inspection

1. Check fan belt for cracks or stretch. Replace if necessary.

2. Check fan for damage. Replace if necessary.

Installation

To install the fan and fan belt, reverse removal procedure and include the following step.

Move the generator or alternator, when fitting the belt, so that the specified deflection can be obtained when a tensile force of 22 lb. is applied at right angles to the belt at the middle point. See **Table 6**.

WATER PUMP
(1600cc MODELS)

The centrifugal impeller-type water pump is attached to the cylinder block. The pump body is made of aluminum, and uses a double row radial ball bearing, which requires no lubrication. Refer to **Figure 10**.

Removal

1. Drain cooling system (refer to *Cooling System* section, preceding).

2. Disconnect battery ground cable.

Table 5   TRANSMISSION CAPACITY

Description	Standard Quantity
Borg-Warner A/T model	5.8 U.S. qt. (5.5 liters)
Torque-Flite A/T model	6.8 U.S. qt. (6.4 liters)

Table 6   FAN BELT TENSION

Description	Standard Dimension
Deflection of fan belt	0.276 - 0.354 in. (1973 and earlier)
	0.28-0.35 in. (1974 on)

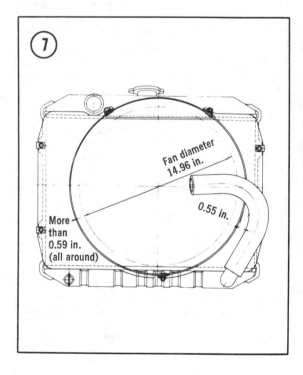

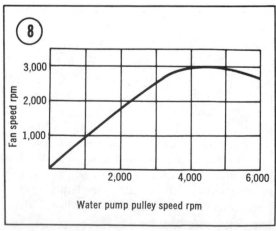

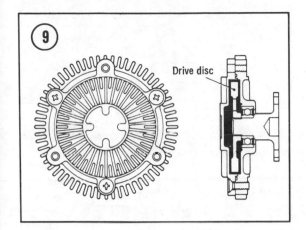

Drive disc

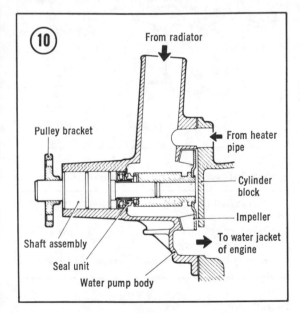

From radiator

Pulley bracket

From heater pipe

Cylinder block

Impeller

To water jacket of engine

Shaft assembly

Seal unit

Water pump body

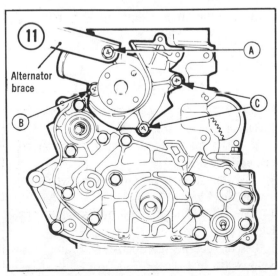

Alternator brace

A

C

B

3. Remove fan shroud (if so equipped), and lower radiator hose.

4. Remove drive belt, cooling fan and pulley (refer to *Fan and Fan Belt* section, later in this chapter).

5. Place piston in No. 1 cylinder at TDC, on the compression stroke.

6. Remove crankshaft pulley, timing belt covers, belt, camshaft sprocket and timing belt tensioner (refer to Chapter Four for procedures).

7. Remove 4 water pump mounting bolts, then remove water pump.

Inspection

1. Check pump for cracks, damage or wear. Replace if necessary.

2. Check bearing for damage, sluggish rotation, noise, etc. Replace if necessary.

3. Check seal for leaks. Replace pump assembly if necessary.

Installation

Install pump by reversing *Removal* procedure, preceding. Install a new water pump gasket. Evenly tighten the 4 bolts illustrated in **Figure 11**, as follows: Bolt A (8x70mm); B (8x55mm); and C (8x28mm).

WATER PUMP
(2000/2600cc Models)

The water pump is a centrifugal impeller type. Its body is attached to the timing chaincase and the water passage portion built integral with the chaincase. The pump body is made of aluminum alloy, which contributes to weight reduction. The pump features a double row of radial ball bearings which require no greasing. The water pump ratio is 1:1. See **Figure 12**.

Removal

1. Drain cooling system (refer to *Coolant Change* section, earlier in this chapter).

2. Disconnect battery ground cable.

3. Remove fan shroud (if so equipped), and lower radiator hose.

6

4. Remove drive belt, cooling fan, fan clutch, and pulley (refer to appropriate sections in this chapter for procedure).

5. Remove water pump assembly.

Inspection

Refer to *Inspection* procedure in *Water Pump (1600cc Models)* section, preceding.

Installation

To install water pump reverse *Removal* procedure, preceding.

> NOTE: *Be sure to install a new water pump gasket. Tighten all mounting bolts evenly to avoid leakage.*

THERMOSTAT

The Dodge Colt cooling system uses a thermostat equipped with a jiggle valve. The design is such that the valve opening temperature cannot be affected by the pressure in the water jacket.

The jiggle valve prevents leakage through the bleed hole and allows the engine to warm up quickly.

Removal

1. Drain the coolant below the level of the thermostat bearing.

2. Remove the water outlet hose from the water outlet fitting.

3. Remove the water outlet fitting. Remove the thermostat.

Inspection

1. Immerse the thermostat in water and raise the temperature by heating it. Measure the valve opening temperature and the valve lift at full opening position. See **Table 7**. If the thermostat does not test satisfactorily, replace it.

2. Replace the thermostat if the valve is open at all at room temperature, or if external damage is found to be excessive. The valve will remain closed if the thermostat sensor is broken.

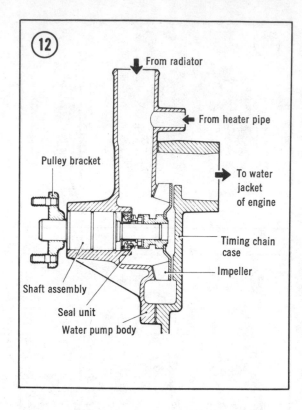

Table 7 THERMOSTAT OPERATING TEMPERATURE

Description	Standard Value
Valve opening temperature	177 to 183°F
Wide-open temperature	203°F
Valve lift at full open position	More than 0.315 in.

Installation

Install the thermostat by reversing the removal steps. Apply sealant to both sides of the gasket.

HEATER ASSEMBLY

Removal

1. Drain the radiator.

2. Remove the glove box, instrument cluster, and console box.

3. Disconnect each heater control wire at the heater. See **Figure 13**.

4. Remove the heater control assembly. See **Figure 14**.

5. Disconnect heater ducts and water hoses. Remove the heater.

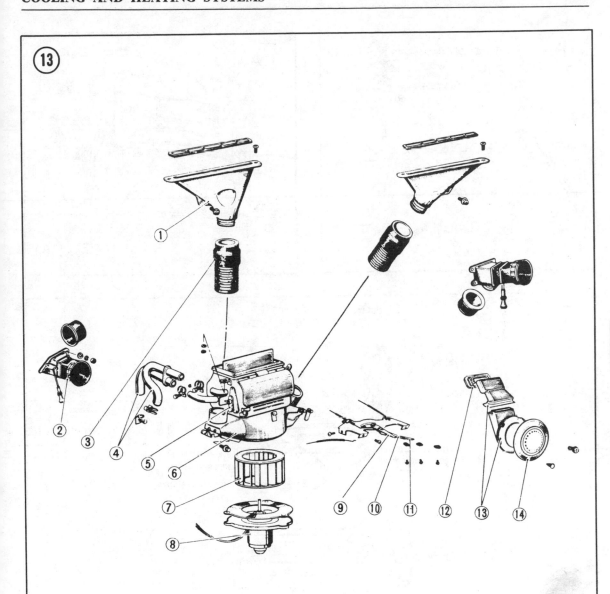

HEATER ASSEMBLY

1. Defroster nozzle
2. Ventilator duct assembly
3. Air duct
4. Water hose
5. Water valve assembly
6. Heater assembly
7. Turbo fan
8. Motor
9. Heater/defroster lever
10. Water valve lever
11. Air control lever
12. Valve (sedan, hardtop, and coupe)
13. Duct assembly (sedan, hardtop, and coupe)
14. Ventilator garnish (sedan, hardtop, and coupe)

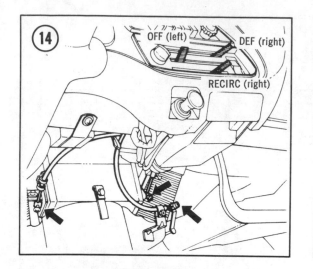

(14)

OFF (left)   DEF (right)

RECIRC (right)

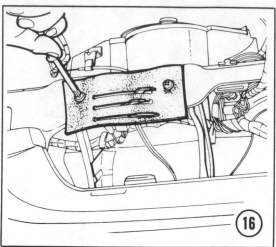

(16)

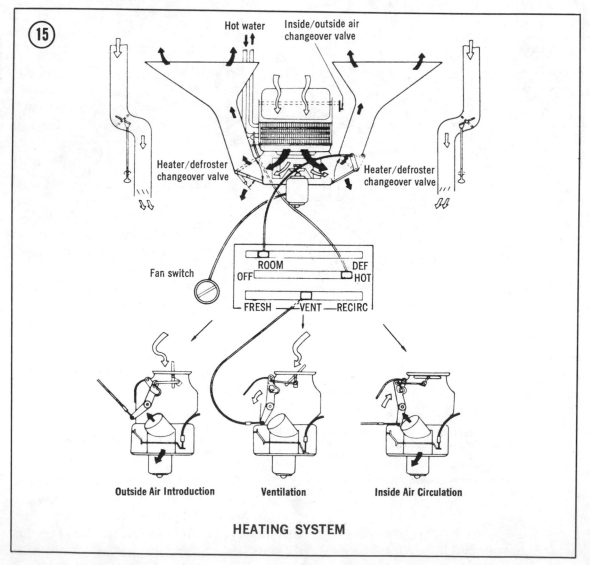

(15)

Hot water   Inside/outside air
changeover valve

Heater/defroster
changeover valve

Heater/defroster
changeover valve

Fan switch

ROOM   DEF
OFF   HOT

FRESH — VENT — RECIRC

Outside Air Introduction   Ventilation   Inside Air Circulation

HEATING SYSTEM

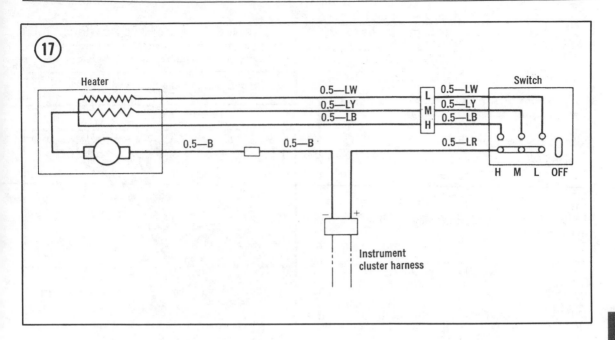

(17)

Heater | 0.5—LW | 0.5—LW | Switch
0.5—LY | 0.5—LY
0.5—LB | 0.5—LB
0.5—B | 0.5—B | 0.5—LR

L M H

H M L OFF

Instrument
cluster harness

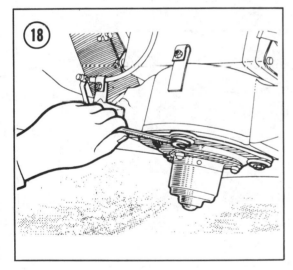

(18)

Installation

1. To install the heater, reverse the removal steps. Be certain to insert the water hose fully into the pipe and securely clamp it so it does not leak.

CAUTION

The water hose in the 2000/2600cc models should be installed with the end having a white paint mark on the engine side.

2. Fill the radiator with water by running water into the radiator until it is full, then with the water valve open, run the engine to circulate the cooling water sufficiently to purge air from inside the heater and engine cooling system. Add water after the engine has stopped.

Adjustment

See **Figure 15**. Adjust the heater control wire as follows:

1. Refer to **Figure 16**. Place the air control lever in RECIRC position (right). Close the heater unit outside air inlet port, and open the air outlet ports. Tighten the wire.

2. With the water valve lever in the OFF position (left), and with the water valve fully closed, tighten the wire. After tightening, run the engine to make sure no hot water leaks.

3. With the heater-defroster lever in the DEF position (right), and with the heater unit butterfly on the DEF side (room side, closed), tighten the wire.

HEATER MOTOR

Removal

1. See **Figure 17**. Disconnect cable between motor and heater unit at the connectors.

2. See **Figure 18**. Remove motor assembly.

3. Remove fan from motor shaft by loosening fan locknut.

4. See **Figure 19**. Pull out armature by loosening attaching screws.

Inspection

See **Table 8**. Inspect brushes and commutator for wear and damage. Replace any part that is defective.

Installation

Install the heater motor by reversing the removal steps. After installing fan on motor shaft, operate the motor to see that the fan turns smoothly.

DEFROSTER NOZZLE

Removal

1. Remove glove box, instrument cluster, and defroster garnish.

2. A special screwdriver is needed to remove the upper attaching screw. See **Figure 20**. This screwdriver is available through your local dealer. After removing the screw, loosen the lower attaching screw and remove the defroster nozzle.

Installation

Install the defroster nozzle by reversing the removal steps. Install an insert (cap) to the screw attaching area to prevent damage to wiring inside the instrument panel.

SIDE VENTILATOR

Removal

1. Remove the glove box to remove the right-hand ventilator. Remove instrument cluster to remove left-hand ventilator.

2. Remove side ventilator knob by turning.

3. Remove ventilator locking bolts. Remove side ventilator. See **Figure 21**.

REAR VENTILATOR
(SEDAN, HARDTOP, AND COUPE)

Removal

1. After removing rear pillar trim, remove the valve by inserting a screwdriver. At the same time, remove the duct. See **Figure 22**.

Table 8	BRUSH	SPECIFICATIONS
Description	Standard Value	Service Limit
Height of brush	0.43 in.	0.28 in.

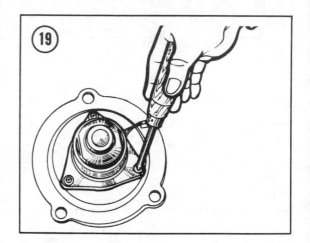

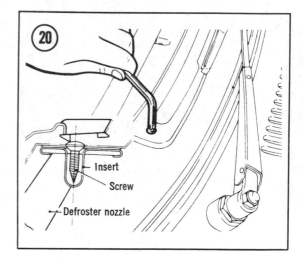

Insert
Screw
Defroster nozzle

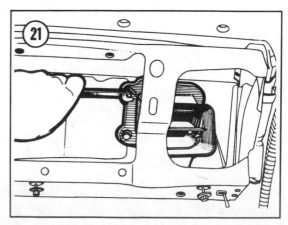

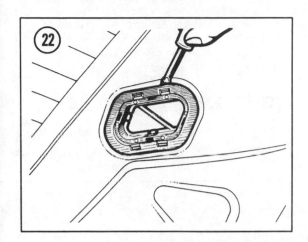

2. Remove ventilator garnish from outside of car. Loosen duct assembly attaching screws, then take off the duct assembly outward.

Inspection

Check valve screen for damage. Replace if necessary.

Installation

When installing rear ventilator, the screws holding the duct should be coated with a sealer to ensure water-tightness. Also apply the sealer between the duct and the outer panel.

6

Table 1   COOLING SYSTEM SPECIFICATIONS

System type	Water cooled, pressurized, forced circulation
Radiator	Pressurized
Water pump	Impeller or centrifugal type
Fan	Seven-blade fan (six-blade fan on cars for Canada)
Fan clutch	Torque type
Thermostat	Wax type
Total quantity of coolant	
1600cc (1973)	7.2 U.S. qt. (6.8 liters)
1600cc (1974-1975)	6.4 U.S. qt. (6.0 liters)
1600cc (1976-1979)	7.7 U.S. qt. (7.3 liters)
2000cc (through 1975)	8.0 U.S. qt. (7.6 liters)
2000cc (1976-on)	9.5 U.S. qt. (9 liters)
2000/2600cc (1978-on)	9.5 U.S. qt. (9 liters)

CHAPTER SEVEN

EMISSION CONTROL SYSTEMS

The Dodge Colt is equipped with the Chrysler Cleaner Air System for controlling crankcase, evaporative, and exhaust emissions. This section explains the function of each component, plus removal, inspection, maintenance, and installation procedures where practical.

EVAPORATION CONTROL SYSTEM

The Evaporation Control System prevents hydrocarbons from escaping into the atmosphere from the fuel tank due to normal vaporization. An activated charcoal canister is installed between the air cleaner and fuel tank. Gasoline vapors are routed to this canister for temporary storage. Outside air is drawn through the canister while the engine is running, purging the vapors from the charcoal. The air/vapor mixture is then routed to the engine combustion chambers through the air cleaner. The carburetor is vented internally or through the charcoal canister, preventing the escape of gasoline vapors into the atmosphere. See **Figure 1**.

SUB TANK

Removal/Installation

See **Figure 2**. The sub tank momentarily reduces the overflow of gasoline in the fuel tank

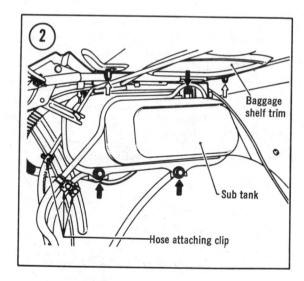

caused by temperature rise, and also prevents gasoline from entering the vapor line in extreme cornering situations.

1. See **Figure 3**. In the station wagon, remove the left rear side trim.

2. Pull hose off the tube after removing the attaching clip.

3. Take off left side trim (toward the car interior) after removing trim retainer on left of package shelf trim (sedan, hardtop, and coupe). See **Figure 4**.

4. Remove attaching bolts. Take out sub tank body.

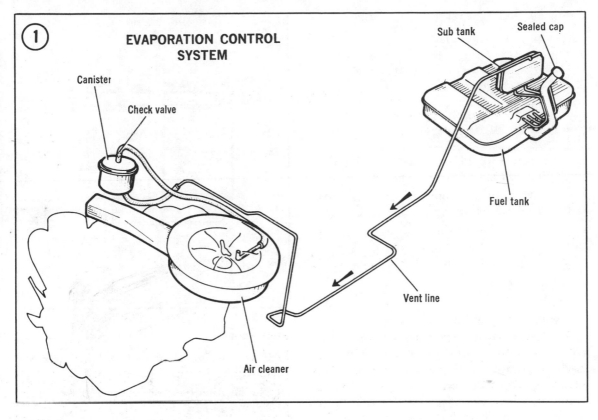

① **EVAPORATION CONTROL SYSTEM**

Canister

Check valve

Sub tank

Sealed cap

Fuel tank

Vent line

Air cleaner

7

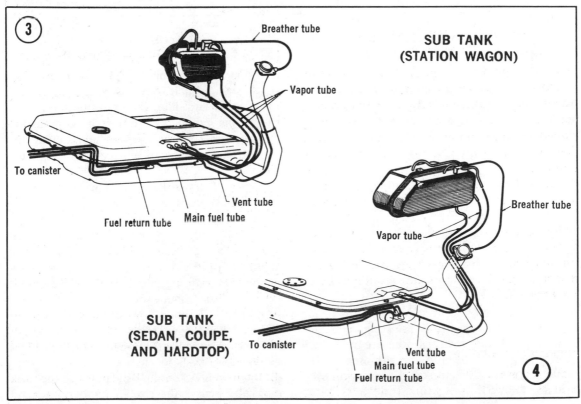

③ Breather tube

SUB TANK (STATION WAGON)

Vapor tube

To canister

Vent tube

Fuel return tube   Main fuel tube

Breather tube

Vapor tube

SUB TANK (SEDAN, COUPE, AND HARDTOP)

To canister

Vent tube

Main fuel tube

Fuel return tube

④

5. Installation is the reverse of these steps.

NOTE: *Do not confuse vapor tubes and pipes when laying them. The vapor pipe can be identified by white paint or tape laid on the ends.*

CANISTER

Removal

See **Figure 5** for 1971-1973 canister, **Figure 6** for 1974, and **Figure 7** for 1975 models on.

1. Remove clamp on canister side of the hose leading to the air cleaner.

2. On canister side of the vapor hose from the sub tank, remove the clamp coupling.

3. Remove canister band tightening bolt.

Installation

1. Replace any hose that shows signs of deterioration or damage. Apply a small amount of grease to the end of the tube and install into the hose.

2. Tighten clamp securely.

Maintenance

1. See **Figure 8**. Every 12,000 miles or 12 months, disconnect both ends of the line and blow air through it.

2. Dust will accumulate around the air suction port to reduce the quantity of purge air and lower the capacity of the canister. Clean it every 12,000 miles or 12 months.

3. Replace interior filter every 24,000 miles or 24 months. At the same time, replace the rubber and vinyl hoses.

4. Inspect check valve (1975 models on) for clogging. If necessary, wash it so that the check ball can move freely.

POSITIVE CRANKCASE VENTILATION SYSTEM (PCV)

Blow-by gas in the crankcase containing carbon monoxide and hydrocarbons are prevented from being released into the atmosphere by means of a positive crankcase ventilation system. See **Figure 9**.

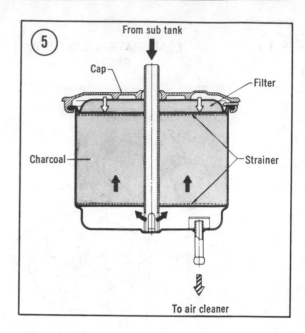

Maintenance

1. Check crankcase ventilation breather hoses for clogging. Replace if necessary.

2. The breather hoses should be replaced every 24,000 miles or 2 years.

EXHAUST GAS RECIRCULATION (EGR)

Dodge Colts from 1974 on incorporate an EGR system, which recirculates part of the exhaust gases and dilutes the air/fuel mixture in the engine cylinders to lower the combustion temperatures for the purpose of reducing the generation of oxides of nitrogen in the exhaust gases.

Figure 10 shows the EGR system in operation. The exhaust gases to be recirculated are fed by the EGR pipe from exhaust ports through the EGR control valve and into the intake manifold. The EGR valve remains inoperative until the engine is thoroughly warmed up. It also remains closed during idling or low speed operation, even after engine warm-up, in order to ensure good drivability and reduce oxides of nitrogen. See **Figures 11 and 12**.

The thermo valve (**Figures 13, 14, and 15**) is designed to react to engine coolant temperature. On the 1974 models, the pellet of the thermo valve senses the rise in temperature and

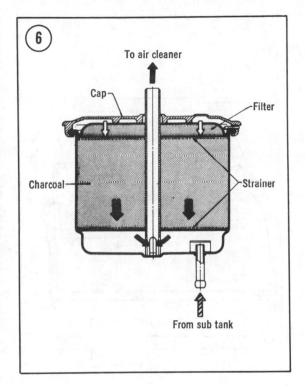

6

To air cleaner

Cap

Filter

Charcoal

Strainer

From sub tank

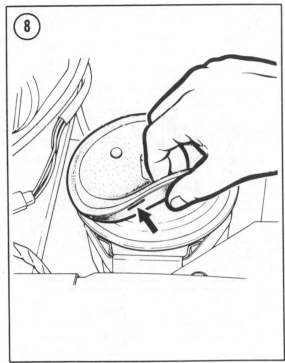

8

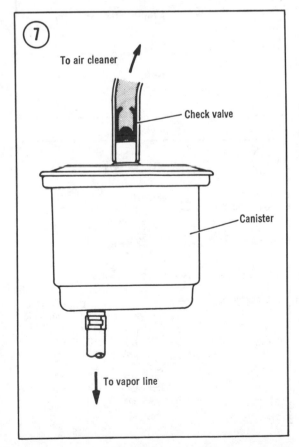

7

To air cleaner

Check valve

Canister

To vapor line

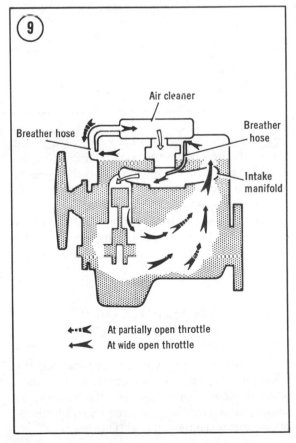

9

Air cleaner

Breather hose

Breather hose

Intake manifold

At partially open throttle
At wide open throttle

7

⑩   **EGR SYSTEM**

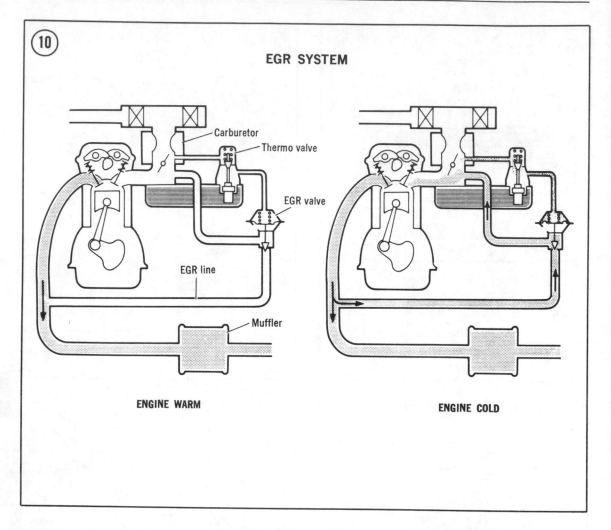

ENGINE WARM   **ENGINE COLD**

pushes up to the valve to open the passage and transmits the carburetor boost to the EGR valve. On 1974 models, the valve controls the vacuum acting on the retard side of the distributor and the vacuum acting on the EGR valve.

The thermal reactor (1975 on California cars only) is used to continue combustion of carbon monoxide and hydrocarbons contained in exhaust gases. See **Figure 16**.

EGR MAINTENANCE WARNING DEVICE

A visual warning device is incorporated in the speedometer assembly, which alerts the driver when it is time for EGR system maintenance by means of a read lamp situated in the speedometer or instrument cluster (**Figure 17**).

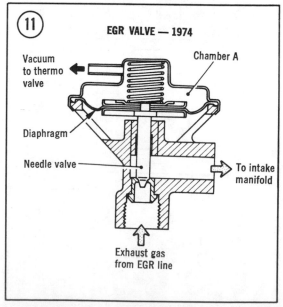

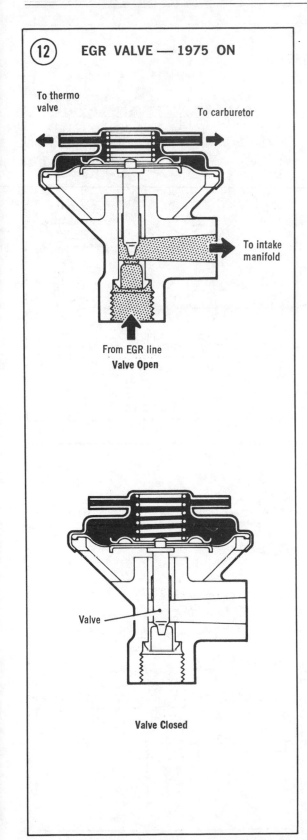

(12) **EGR VALVE — 1975 ON**

To thermo valve

To carburetor

To intake manifold

From EGR line
Valve Open

Valve

Valve Closed

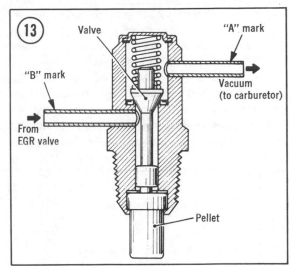

(13) Valve

"A" mark

"B" mark

Vacuum (to carburetor)

From EGR valve

Pellet

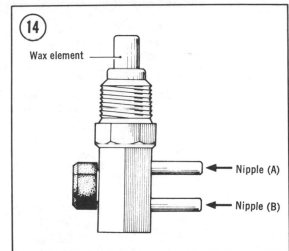

(14) Wax element

Nipple (A)

Nipple (B)

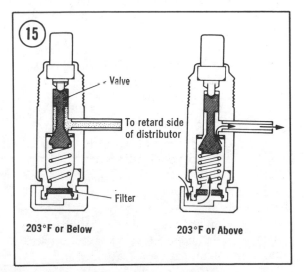

(15) Valve

To retard side of distributor

Filter

203°F or Below   **203°F or Above**

7

The warning device has a mileage sensor, which interlocks with the odometer. The light is turned on at 15,00 miles (24,000 km), and every 15,000 miles (24,000 km) thereafter.

The warning light may be turned off with the reset switch placed under the junction of the speedometer cable, after the EGR maintenance has been completed. This requires the removal of the speedometer, and all adjustment must be carried out by your dealer or garages specified by law.

EGR VALVE

Removal

1. Pull vacuum hose out of EGR valve.
2. Disconnect EGR pipe from EGR valve.
3. Remove EGR valve.

Inspection

1. Check EGR valve diaphragm for damage.
2. Check valve inside EGR valve for sticking.
3. Check EGR valve operation by warming engine to operating temperature and setting

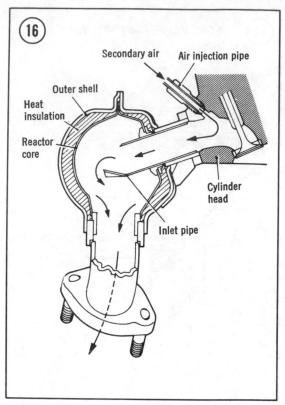

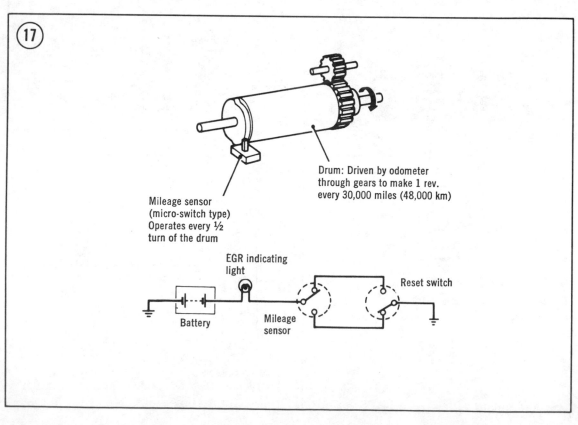

Mileage sensor
(micro-switch type)
Operates every ½
turn of the drum

Drum: Driven by odometer
through gears to make 1 rev.
every 30,000 miles (48,000 km)

EGR indicating
light

Reset switch

Battery

Mileage
sensor

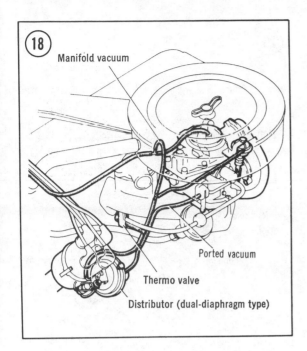

Manifold vacuum

Ported vacuum

Thermo valve

Distributor (dual-diaphragm type)

engine speed to 3,000-3,200 rpm. Connect and disconnect vacuum hose. When hose is disconnected, diaphragm should lower. When hose is connected, diaphragm should rise. If not, EGR valve is unsatisfactory.

4. Check EGR pipe and vacuum pipe for damage, clogging, etc.

Installation

1. To install EGR valve, reverse the removal order. In addition, be sure to install vacuum pipe positively.

2. When connecting EGR pipe to EGR valve, be certain nut is tightened to 22-25 ft.-lb. torque.

THERMO VALVE

Removal

1. Pull vacuum hose off.

2. Remove thermo valve.

Inspection
(1974 Models)

Do not remove valve for this procedure.

1. Increase engine speed from idle to 2,000 to 3,000 rpm.

2. Check to be sure valve is closed while engine is cold (coolant temperature 140°F or lower),

and open to allow EGR flow in warm engine. Refer to **Figure 13**.

Inspection
(1975 on U.S.A. Cars)

1. After removal, allow thermo valve to cool down to room temperature. Install a vinyl tube on each nipple of thermo valve. Refer to **Figure 14**.

2. Blow into each tube. Nipple (A) should allow air to pass without resistance. Nipple (B) should allow no air to pass through.

Inspection
(1975 on Canadian Cars)

1. Remove thermo valve and allow to cool down to room temperature.

2. Refer to **Figure 15**. Blow air into nipple of thermo valve. Valve must remain closed.

Installation

1. Apply a sealer to the threads and securely install the valve.

2. Connect vacuum hoses, using care to see they are installed on the proper nipples.

IGNITION TIMING CONTROL SYSTEM

The ignition timing control system consists of a distributor, thermo valve, and vacuum pipe. See **Figure 18**.

When the engine is operating at low speed, decelerating, under a light load, or idling, the exhaust gas temperature is low. See **Figure 19**. This results in poor combustion of carbon monoxide and hydrocarbons within the thermal reactors. To prevent this, ignition timing is retarded to maintain high exhaust gas temperature, which improves thermal reactor performance. See **Figure 20**.

When the engine is idling, decelerating, under light load, or operating at low speed, the throttle valve is slightly open. In this condition, no vacuum acts on the advance side diaphragm, therefore the diaphragm is depressed left by spring (A). The manifold vacuum is applied to

7

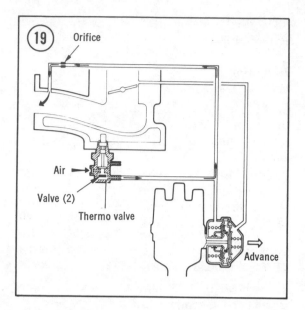

Orifice
Air
Valve (2)
Thermo valve
Advance

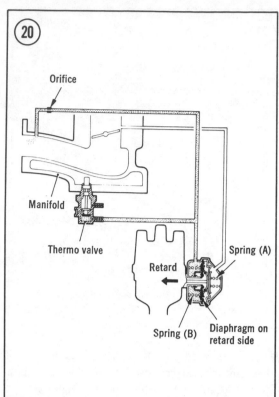

Orifice
Manifold
Thermo valve
Retard
Spring (A)
Spring (B)
Diaphragm on retard side

the diaphragm chamber on the retard side which moves diaphragm toward the left. The ignition control rod moves left relative to the amount of force generated by the manifold vacuum and spring (A), versus the force exerted by spring (B) on the retard side. This movement causes retardation of spark timing.

The manifold vacuum is too low when the engine is being cranked over with the starter to actuate the ignition timing control system, which retards ignition timing. This ensures good engine starting.

A thermo valve is used to protect against engine coolant overheating caused by high ambient temperatures, long periods of operation with the engine idling, or engine overload. The valve is installed in the coolant manifold and connected into the vacuum hose, which runs from the vacuum to the retard diaphragm chamber on the distributor (**Figure 20**). When the coolant temperatures are normal, the valve is closed and vacuum acts on the retard side of the diaphragm chamber. When temperatures exceed 203°F, the valve operates, venting the diaphragm to the atmosphere. This advances ignition timing, which increases engine speed (fan speed), which decreases engine coolant temperature. The valve closes as coolant temperature decreases, which allows vacuum to again act on the retard diaphragm, which retards ignition timing and reduces engine speed.

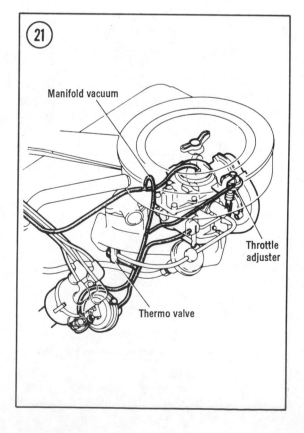

Manifold vacuum
Throttle adjuster
Thermo valve

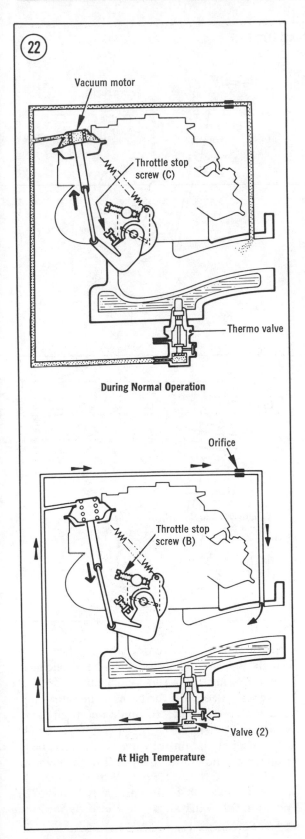

During Normal Operation

At High Temperature

For removal, inspection, and installation of the thermo valve, see procedures described earlier in this chapter under the *Exhaust Gas Recirculation (EGR)* section.

IDLE SPEED CONTROL SYSTEM
(Automatic Transmission Cars Only)

The idle speed control system consists mainly of the thermo valve and carburetor throttle adjuster. See **Figure 21**. If coolant temperature has risen above 203°F, the spark timing is advanced, causing the idle speed to increase. This system prevents the idle speed increase in order to prevent "creep" during idle and hard shifting.

The idle speed control system is designed to operate in conjunction with the dual-diaphragm distributor. When the retard unit remains inoperative, the amount of throttle valve opening at idle is automatically reduced.

During normal idling, the manifold vacuum acts on the vacuum motor and the throttle valve is open the normal amount. See **Figure 22**. When the coolant temperature increases to 203°F, the valve (2) in the thermo valve opens to vent the manifold vacuum to the atmosphere. At this time the retard unit also becomes inoperative and ignition timing is advanced. Consequently, the vacuum which has been acting on the vacuum motor changes to atmospheric pressure and the throttle valve opening is decreased because of spring (B). The opening of the throttle valve is regulated by the throttle stop screw (B) which prevents engine speed from increasing by the advance of ignition timing, and by air (functioning as an idle compensator) flowing into the intake manifold.

Throttle Adjuster

The throttle adjuster consists of a vacuum motor, link, throttle arm, and throttle stop screw. See **Figure 23**. It is located on the carburetor. When manifold vacuum is applied to vacuum motor, throttle arm (B) is pulled up and throttle valve opening is set to the standard idle position by means of the throttle stop screw (C). When manifold vacuum is removed from

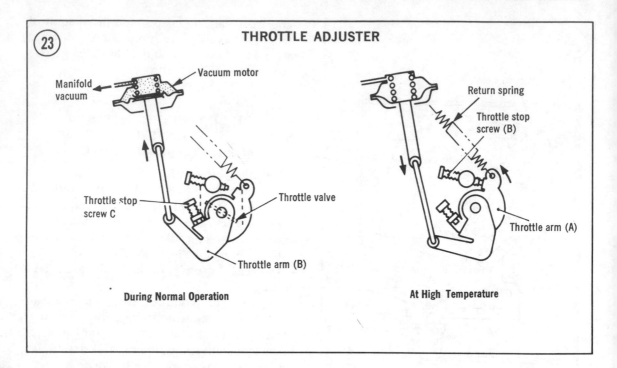

THROTTLE ADJUSTER

Manifold vacuum

Vacuum motor

Throttle stop screw C

Throttle valve

Throttle arm (B)

During Normal Operation

Return spring

Throttle stop screw (B)

Throttle arm (A)

At High Temperature

vacuum motor, throttle arm (A) is moved by the throttle spring and the throttle valve opening is set by the throttle stop screw (B) to a slightly closed position.

System Inspection

1. Check the vacuum motor diaphragm for damage.

2. Check to be sure throttle adjuster linkage operates smoothly. Clean and lubricate hinge points with small amount of engine oil (see **Figure 24**).

3. Remove and install plug on retard side of distributor with engine idling to see if throttle adjuster operates properly. When the plug is removed the vacuum motor rod should lower and the throttle valve close. When the plug is installed the vacuum motor rod should rise and the throttle valve open.

4. After completing inspection, securely insert distributor plug.

HEATED AIR INTAKE SYSTEM

Cold incoming intake air generally results in a too-lean air/fuel mixture, resulting in lowered engine output. To overcome this, the thermal

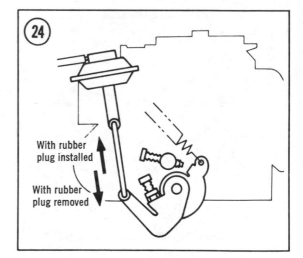

With rubber plug installed

With rubber plug removed

reactor (**Figure 25**) is covered with a heat cowl which preheats the air going to the air cleaner. The air cleaner inlet snorkel has an air control valve which controls the path of the intake air. The valve responds to underhood air temperature. When the air temperature is below 41°F the hot air control valve is in the (A) position which allows heated air to flow through the cowl and into the air cleaner. When the temperature is above 108°F, the valve moves to the (B) position, allowing air to flow directly into the air cleaner.

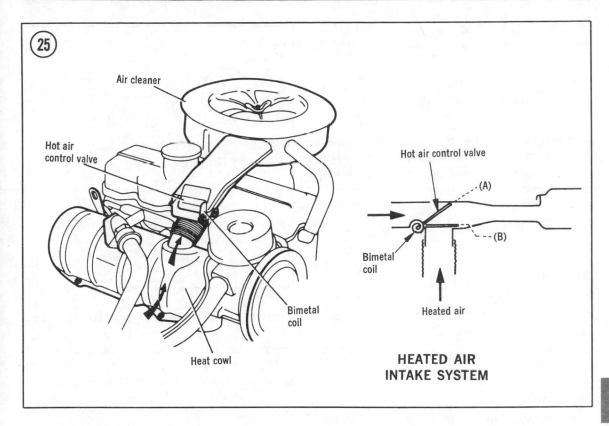

HEATED AIR
INTAKE SYSTEM

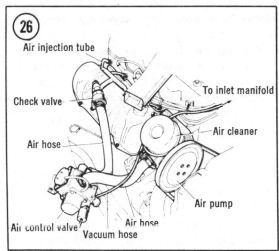

3. Check air cleaner packing and seal washers of the cover and case for damage or air-tightness.

4. Clean or replace air cleaner when necessary (proper cleaning interval is 12,500 miles; proper replacement interval is 25,000 miles).

AIR INJECTION SYSTEM
(1975 and Later U.S.A. Cars Only)

The air injection system supplies secondary air needed for continued combustion of unburned exhaust gases in the thermal reactor. The system consists of an air control valve, check valve, air injection pipe, and an air pump. See **Figure 26**.

AIR PUMP

Inspection

1. Inspect air hoses for deterioration or damage. Be sure hose clamps are tight.

2. Disconnect air hose on discharge side of air pump, with engine idling, to be sure air is being discharged.

Inspection

1. Allow air cleaner to cool down. Crank the engine and see if the hot air control valve operates properly. Also check to see if the heated air intake port is fully closed at an underhood air temperature of 108°F or more.

2. Check air cleaner cover and case for damage or deformation.

3. With air pump running, check for abnormal sounds. Replace the air pump assembly if necessary.

CAUTION
Do not admit engine oil or other foreign substances into air pump.

4. Clean air cleaner every 12,500 miles; replace every 25,000 miles. To clean, tap lightly on wooden block or blow from the inside out with compressed air.

5. Check drive belt for damage.

6. Adjust drive belt tension when necessary (see **Figure 27**).

Removal

1. Disconnect air hose.

2. Remove drive belt after loosening air pump support bolts and brace bolts.

3. Remove support and brace bolts, then take off air pump.

Installation

1. When installing air pump, tighten each bolt as follows: air pump support bolt, 22-30 ft.-lb.; air pump brace bolt, 10-14 ft.-lb.

2. Tighten the air cleaner assembly securely by hand.

3. Install air hoses on nipples. Clamp securely.

4. The belt must deflect 0.3-0.4 in when pulled with a force of 22 lb. as illustrated in **Figure 27**. If belt tension is wrong, loosen pump support and brace bolts and adjust tension by moving the air pump. After adjustment, tighten the bolts as specified under Step 1, above.

AIR CONTROL VALVE

The air control valve consists of a relief valve, air shutoff valve, air shutoff solenoid, and an orifice, which automatically controls the quantity of secondary air fed to the thermal reactor (**Figure 28**).

The relief valve operates when the relief valve spring force is overcome by the manifold vacuum (California model only) and the air pump discharge pressure.

The air shutoff valve functions to divert secondary air to the relief side when a difference in

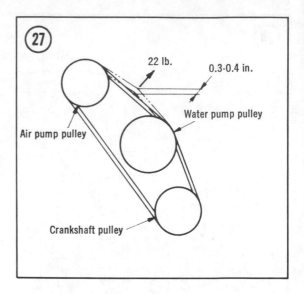

vacuum between vacuum pressure chambers (A) and (B) exists, or when air pump discharge pressure has acted on vacuum chamber (B).

The air shutoff solenoid incorporates a speed sensor (California model only) or a thermo sensor. When the sensor opens the electrical circuit, the air shutoff solenoid plunger moves to the position indicated by the broken line in **Figure 28** to admit pump discharge pressure into vacuum chamber (B).

When manifold vacuum suddenly increases, the orifice controls the vacuum acting on vacuum chamber (B) to decrease it below the manifold vacuum acting on vacuum chamber (A).

Inspection

1. Check air discharge with engine idling. Disconnect air hose from check valve. Valve is in satisfactory condition if air is being discharged. No air should leak on the relief side.

2. Check air shutoff valve to see if air shutoff solenoid is energized when ignition switch is turned on. Remove air hose on discharge side. With engine running at 3,000 rpm, disconnect air shutoff solenoid coupler. See **Figure 29**. If air is being discharged only on relief side, the air shutoff valve is operating properly.

3. Check the relief valve operation (**Figure 30**) by increasing engine idle speed gradually from idle to 3,500 rpm. If air is discharged from relief port at this time, relief valve is operating normally.

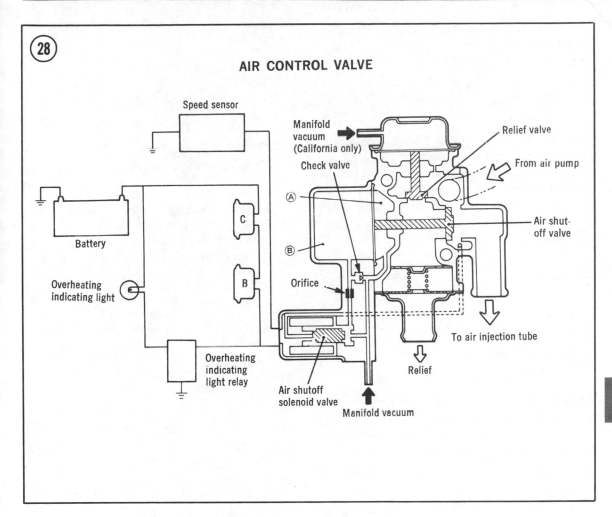

(28)

AIR CONTROL VALVE

Speed sensor

Manifold vacuum (California only)

Check valve

Relief valve

From air pump

Air shut-off valve

Battery

(A)

(B)

Overheating indicating light

C

B

Orifice

To air injection tube

Overheating indicating light relay

Air shutoff solenoid valve

Relief

Manifold vacuum

7

(29)

Air shutoff solenoid coupler

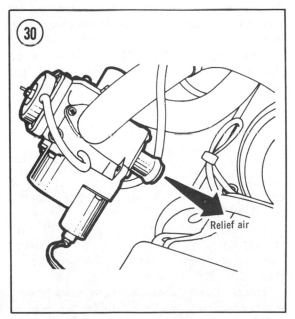

(30)

Relief air

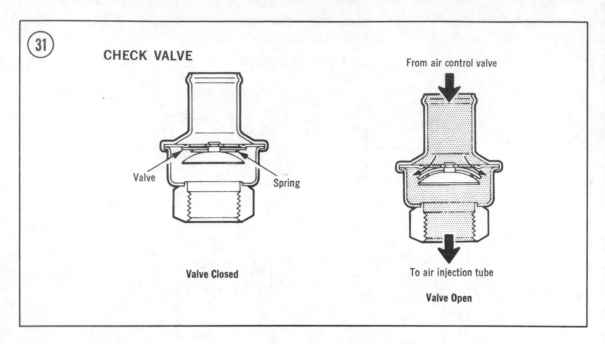

Removal/Installation

1. Remove air shutoff solenoid coupler.

2. Disconnect vacuum hose and air hose from air control valve.

3. Remove air control valve.

4. Installation is the reverse of these steps.

CHECK VALVE

The check valve prevents exhaust gases from flowing back to the air control valve and air pump. See **Figure 31**. When air pressure is applied from air pump side, the check valve opens to allow the flow of air. If pressure is applied from the thermal reactor or exhaust manifold side, the valve seats, thus closing the passageway.

Inspection

1. Check air hose and air control valve for damage or defect.

2. Remove air hose from check valve and race engine to check for exhaust gas blow-by. If no blow-by takes place, the check valve is in satisfactory condition.

Removal/Installation

1. Unclamp air hose from check valve and remove valve.

2. Installation is the reverse of removal. Tighten check valve to 25-28 ft.-lb. and make sure clamp is tight.

JET AIR SYSTEM

On all models from 1978 on (except Canada models), a jet valve has been designed into the hemispherical combustion chamber which draws a super lean fuel mixture (or air) into the combustion chamber. This mixes with the conventional incoming fuel/air mixture in a swirling pattern (**Figures 32 and 33**) to provide more efficient combustion.

Jet Valve Removal/Installation

1. Remove breather hoses and purge hose from air cleaner.

2. Remove air cleaner; rocker cover; camshaft bearing cap retaining bolts; rocker arms, rocker shafts and bearing caps (as an assembly); and the jet valve assembly (use Dodge special tool MD998310 or equivalent, as shown in **Figure 34**).

CAUTION
Be sure that the wrench is not tilted with respect to the center of the jet valve, or the valve stem might be bent by the force exerted on the valve spring retainer.

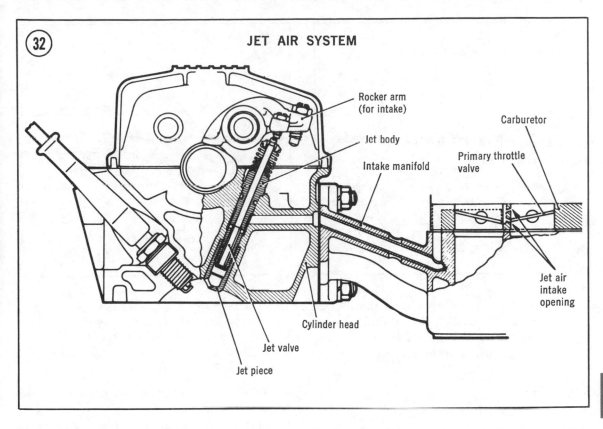

JET AIR SYSTEM

Rocker arm (for intake)

Jet body

Intake manifold

Carburetor

Primary throttle valve

Jet air intake opening

Cylinder head

Jet valve

Jet piece

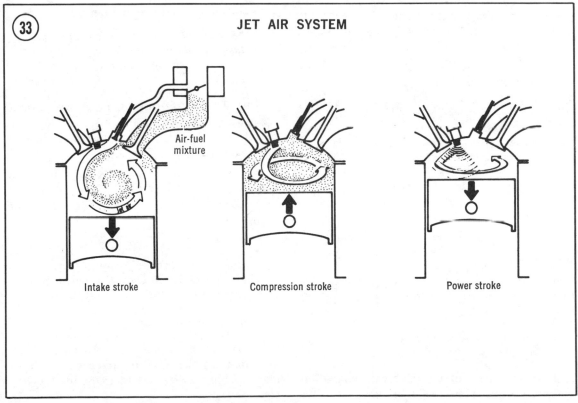

JET AIR SYSTEM

Air-fuel mixture

Intake stroke

Compression stroke

Power stroke

Jet valve socket wrench

Jet valve

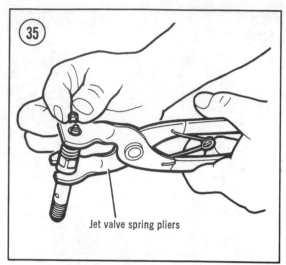

Jet valve spring pliers

3. Remove the jet valve spring retainer lock with Dodge special tool MD998309 (or equivalent), as shown in **Figure 35**. Remove the valve spring retainer and valve spring.

Inspection

1. Check to be sure that the jet valve is inserted in the jet body so that it slides smoothly, with no play. Do not disturb the jet valve/jet body combination. Replace jet valve and jet body as an assembly.

2. Check jet valve face and jet body seat for damage. Replace if defective.

3. Check jet valve spring for weakness, damage, etc. Replace if defective.

> NOTE: *The standard dimension of the jet valve stem (O.D.) is 0.1693 in. (4.3 mm); the valve face angle is 45°; the free length of the jet valve spring is 1.1654 in. (29.6 mm); and the jet valve spring load is 5.5 lb. @ 0.846 in. (3.5 kg @ 21.5 mm).*

Installation

1. Install jet valve stem seal with Dodge tool MD998308 (or equivalent), as shown in **Figure 36**.

> CAUTION
> *Do not reuse old jet valve stem seal.*

2. Lubricate stem of jet valve with engine oil before inserting it into the jet body.

> NOTE: *When valve is inserted, use special care to prevent damage to the new valve stem seal lips. Check to be sure that the valve slides smoothly, after insertion.*

3. Install jet valve spring and jet valve spring retainer. Install retainer lock while compressing the spring with Dodge special tool MD998309 (or equivalent), as shown in **Figure 35**.

> NOTE: *When spring is compressed, take special care to avoid damaging the valve stem with the bottom of the spring retainer.*

4. Install a new O-ring in the groove around the jet body. Lubricate the O-ring with engine oil, then apply engine oil to the threaded area and seat surface of the jet body.

5. Screw the jet valve assembly into the cylinder head, finger-tight. Then tighten to 13.5-15.5 ft.-lb. (18-21.5 N•m), as shown in **Figure 37**.

> CAUTION
> *Hold socket wrench firmly to be sure that it does not tilt in relationship to the center of the jet valve, or the valve stem might be bent by the force exerted on the valve spring retainer.*

6. Install rocker arms, rocker shafts and bearing cap assemblies, and tighten camshaft bearing cap bolts evenly to 14-15 ft.-lb. (19-20.5 N•m).

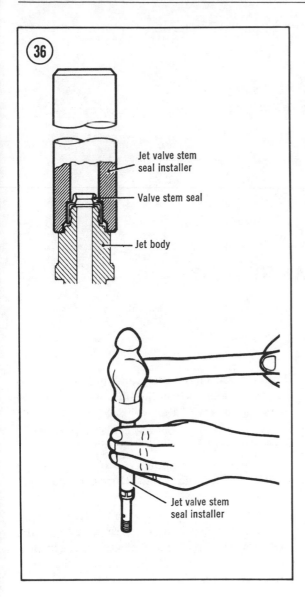

Jet valve stem
seal installer

Valve stem seal

Jet body

Jet valve stem
seal installer

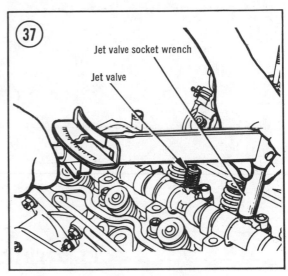

Jet valve socket wrench

Jet valve

7. Temporarily set valve clearance to the following dimensions (cold engine): Jet valve, 0.003 in. (0.07 mm); intake valve, 0.003 in. (0.07 mm); and exhaust valve, 0.007 in. (0.17 mm).

8. Install rocker cover, air cleaner, breather hoses, and purge hose to air cleaner.

9. Start engine and let it idle for 5 minutes. When it reaches normal operating temperature, adjust valve clearance, as follows: Jet valve, 0.006 in. (0.15 mm); intake valve, 0.006 in. (0.15 mm); and exhaust valve, 0.010 in. (0.25 mm).

Jet Valve Adjustment

Refer to Chapter Three, *Engine Tune-Up* section, *Jet Valve Adjustment* procedure.

CHAPTER EIGHT

ELECTRICAL SYSTEM

All models have a 12-volt negative ground electrical system. Fuses provide overload protection. A fusible link melts in the event that an excessive current flows to the electrical system without passing through the fuses. Cars manufactured through 1973 were equipped with a generator (direct current). 1974 and later models use an alternator (alternating current). Details on both types are given in this chapter.

Several electrical testing devices are required for complete diagnosis and adjustment of the charging and starting circuits. However, preliminary diagnosis of these circuits, and most work on the rest of the electrical system, can be done with a voltmeter, ohmmeter, and 12-volt test lamp. Electrical parts can be removed and taken to an automotive electrical shop for testing, adjusting, and repair. This is especially true of the generator or alternator, regulator, and starter motor. Unless you are experienced and have proper equipment for testing, adjustment, and overhaul, refer necessary service to your Colt dealer or automotive electrical shop.

BATTERY

Inspection

1. Inspect the battery frequently for signs of corrosion on top of the battery and on the case. Use a solution of water and baking soda to neutralize any corrosion. Rinse with water and wipe the battery clean.

2. After cleaning, coat battery terminals lightly with Vaseline.

3. Inspect battery connections and battery cables for tightness and corrosion damage. Replace if defective.

4. Check battery condition with a hydrometer, as discussed in Chapter Three. If any of the cells are weak, recharge the battery. If recharging does not return the battery to satisfactory condition, replace it before trouble starts.

Safety Precautions

When batteries are being charged, highly explosive hydrogen gas forms in each cell. Some of this gas escapes through the filler openings and may form an explosive atmosphere around the battery. This explosive atmosphere may exist for several hours. Sparks, open flame, or a lighted cigarette can ignite this gas, causing an internal explosion and possible serious personal injury. The following precautions should be taken to prevent an explosion:

1. Do not smoke or permit any open flame near any battery being charged or which has been recently charged.

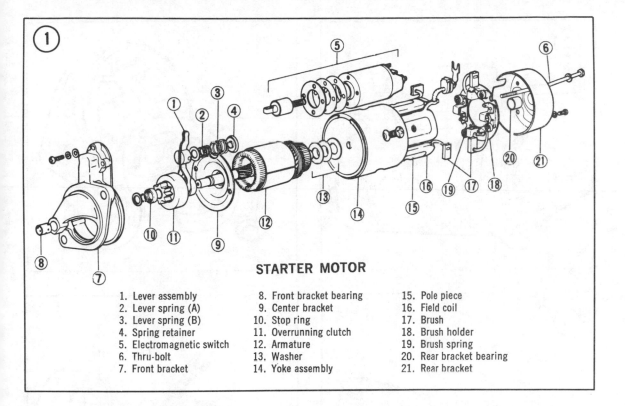

STARTER MOTOR

1. Lever assembly	8. Front bracket bearing	15. Pole piece
2. Lever spring (A)	9. Center bracket	16. Field coil
3. Lever spring (B)	10. Stop ring	17. Brush
4. Spring retainer	11. Overrunning clutch	18. Brush holder
5. Electromagnetic switch	12. Armature	19. Brush spring
6. Thru-bolt	13. Washer	20. Rear bracket bearing
7. Front bracket	14. Yoke assembly	21. Rear bracket

2. Do not disconnect live circuits at battery terminals because a spark usually occurs where a live circuit is broken. Care must always be taken when connecting or disconnecting any battery charger; be sure its power switch is off before making or breaking connections. Poor connections are a common cause of electrical arcs which cause explosions.

Replacement

1. Disconnect battery cables from battery terminals by loosening the nuts and spreading the connectors.

CAUTION
Always remove the negative cable first to prevent possible shorts. Do not twist the cable around the battery poles as damage to the poles or insulation may occur.

2. Remove nuts and battery hold-down bracket.

3. Remove battery from battery holder. Make certain to note which cable connects to the positive terminal and which connects to the negative terminal.

4. Install new battery, battery holder, and cables. Tighten all connections securely. Make certain the battery is full of electrolyte.

5. Coat battery terminals and cable connections with Vaseline.

IGNITION/STARTER SWITCH

Maintenance of the ignition/starter switch is not required. A defective switch must be replaced.

STARTER MOTOR

Removal

1. Disconnect battery terminals.

2. Disconnect starter motor wiring.

3. Loosen the 2 starter motor mounting bolts. Remove starter motor.

Disassembly

See **Figure 1** for this procedure.

1. Remove terminal (M) and then remove the 3 electromagnetic switch mounting screws. Remove the electromagnetic switch. See **Figure 2**.

8

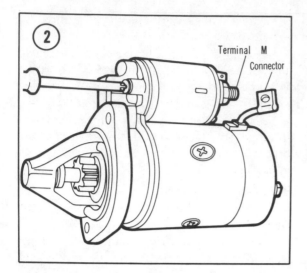

②

Terminal M

Connector

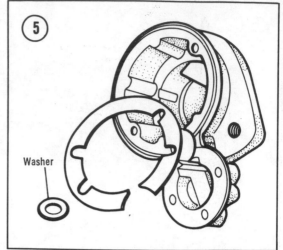

⑤

Washer

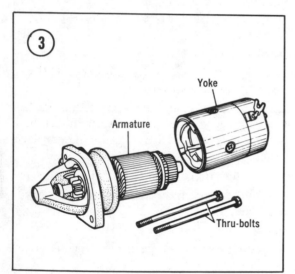

③

Yoke

Armature

Thru-bolts

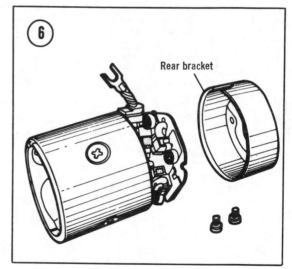

⑥

Rear bracket

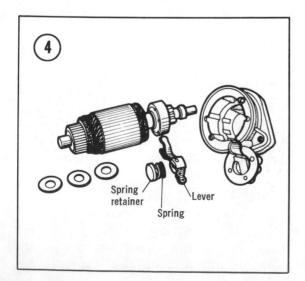

④

Spring
retainer

Lever

Spring

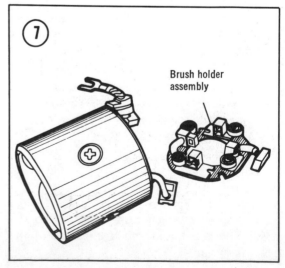

⑦

Brush holder
assembly

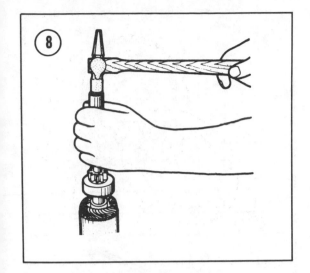

8

2. Remove the 2 thru-bolts (see **Figure 3**). Separate the armature and yoke.

3. See **Figure 4**. Carefully take out the armature and lever from the front bracket. Keep in mind the direction of the lever and the order in which the spring and spring holder are inserted.

4. See **Figure 5**. Remove the small washer from armature shaft end. Do not lose it (it is often left behind inside the front bracket).

5. See **Figure 6**. Remove the rear bracket after loosening the 2 screws.

6. Remove the brush holder assembly (see **Figure 7**).

7. Remove the overrunning clutch by striking the stop ring toward the clutch side until it gets out of position. See **Figure 8**.

8. Remove clutch together with the stop ring.

Brush Replacement

1. Check the brush for wear (**Figure 9**). If excessive, replace with a new one.

2. With a VOM meter, check for continuity between the (+) side of the brush holder and brush holder base. If there is continuity, replace the holder assembly (**Figure 10**).

Assembly

Reverse the disassembly procedure. In addition, perform the following steps:

1. See **Figure 11**. Assemble the armature, yoke, and brush holder.

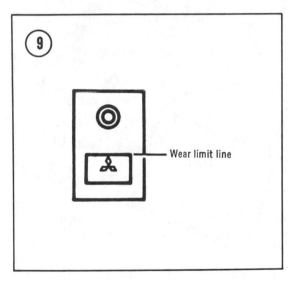

Wear limit line

8

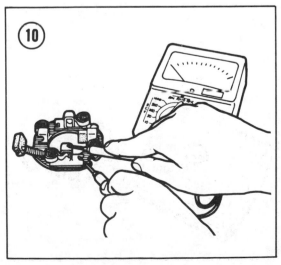

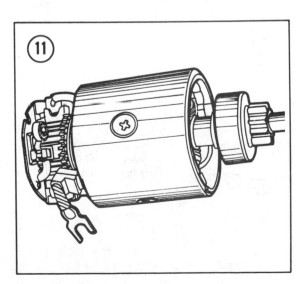

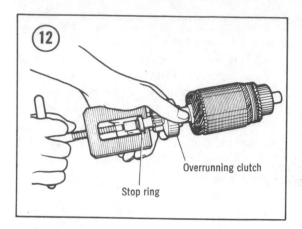

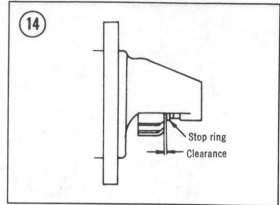

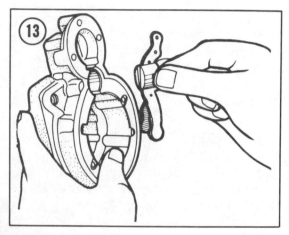

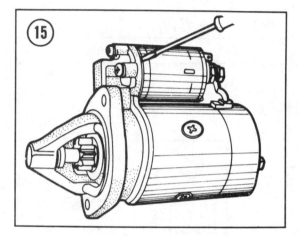

2. Mount the overrunning clutch by allowing the snap ring to hold the shaft firmly, then fitting the stop ring. See **Figure 12**.

3. See **Figure 13**. Pay attention to the direction of the lever when mounting.

4. Check the position where the piston springs out after reassembly (see **Figure 14**). With the pinion in its outermost position, measure the clearance between the end surface of the pinion and stop ring. If the clearance exceeds 0.020 to 0.079 in. (0.5-2.0 mm), adjust it by changing the position of the electromagnetic switch and increasing or decreasing the number of packings. See **Figure 15.** If clearance is too wide, increase the number of packings; if too narrow, decrease the number.

Installation

Reverse the removal procedure. Tighten the mounting bolts so that the starter motor will be parallel with the central axis of the engine in all directions. The starter motor attaching bolts should be torqued to 14-21 ft.-lb.

ALTERNATOR/GENERATOR (MODELS THROUGH 1978)

Removal

1. Disconnect the battery terminals and alternator or generator wires.

2. Remove brace bolts.

3. Remove mounting bolts and alternator or generator.

Disassembly/Assembly

1. See **Figures 16 and 17.** Remove the 3 thrubolts. Insert a screwdriver between the rear bracket and stator core.

CAUTION
Do not insert the screwdriver too deep as it could cause damage to stator coil.

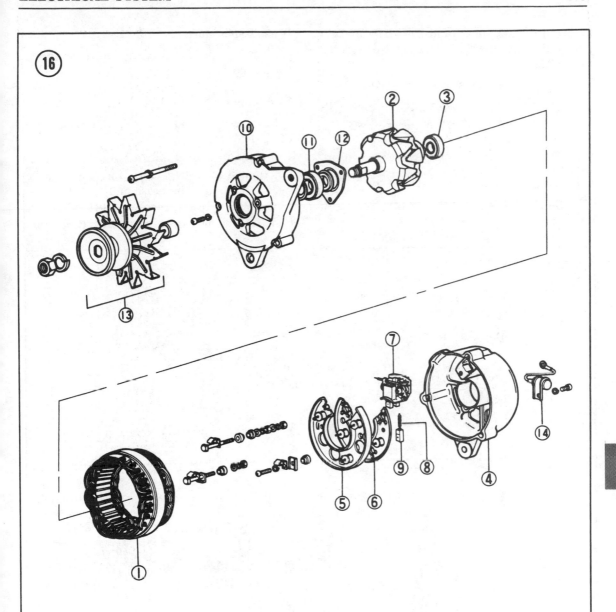

ALTERNATOR—1971-1978

1. Stator
2. Rotor
3. Ball bearing
4. Rear bracket
5. Complete heat sink (+)
6. Complete heat sink (−)
7. Brush holder assembly
8. Brush spring
9. Brush
10. Front bracket
11. Ball bearing
12. Bearing retainer
13. Pulley
14. Condenser

8

2. Separate the stator and rotor by carefully prying the two apart with the screwdriver. See **Figure 18**.

3. Assembly is the reverse of these steps.

> NOTE: *When inserting the rotor into the rear bracket, keep the brushes lifted with a piece of wire as shown in Figure 19.*

Brush Replacement

If the brush is excessively worn, replace it with a new one. See **Figure 20**.

Brush Replacement

If the brush is excessively worn, replace it with a new one. See **Figure 20**.

Installation

Reverse the removal steps. In addition, observe the following.

1. Position the alterantor or generator but do not tighten mounting bolts. Insert a shim between the timing chaincase and each front leg of the alternator or generator bracket to determine the thickness of shims needed. (Each shim

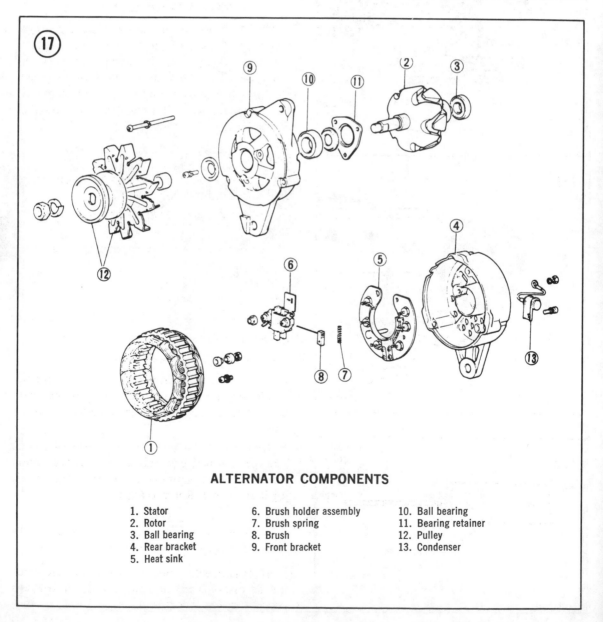

ALTERNATOR COMPONENTS

1. Stator	6. Brush holder assembly	10. Ball bearing
2. Rotor	7. Brush spring	11. Bearing retainer
3. Ball bearing	8. Brush	12. Pulley
4. Rear bracket	9. Front bracket	13. Condenser
5. Heat sink		

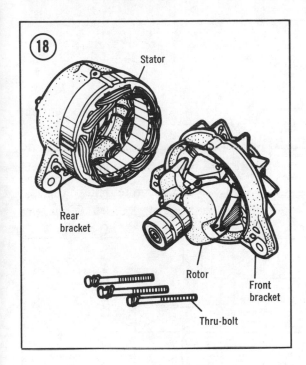

⑱

Stator

Rear
bracket

Rotor

Front
bracket

Thru-bolt

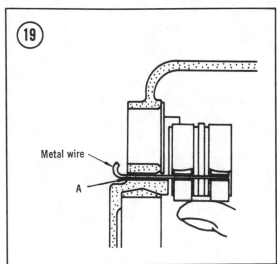

⑲

Metal wire

A

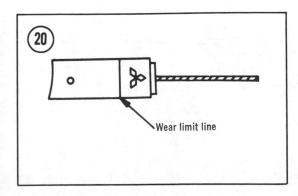

⑳

Wear limit line

must not fall when released.) Insert shims as required and install bolts and nuts. Torque the mounting bolts to 18-21 ft.-lb. The required shim is 0.0078 in. (0.198 mm).

2. After installation is complete, adjust the cooling fan belt tension (see Chapter Six, *Fan Belt Installation*).

3. Be careful to ground the regulator securely and connect the generator or alternator and battery correctly.

ALTERNATOR
(1979 MODELS ON)

All 1979 models use an electronic voltage regulator in place of the conventional contact point type used previously. Due to the use of integrated circuits, the compact electronic voltage regulator is either built into the rear bracket of the alternator, or mounted externally on the rear bracket (refer to **Figure 21**).

Removal

1. Turn ignition switch to OFF position, then disconnect battery ground cable.

2. Disconnect cable from B terminal of alternator.

3. Remove alternator brace bolt and support bolt nut.

4. Remove support bolt, then remove alternator.

Disassembly/Assembly

Refer to **Figures 22 and 23**.

1. On models with externally mounted regulators, remove regulator cover from rear bracket, then remove electronic voltage regulator.

2. Remove 3 through bolts, then insert a screwdriver between the front bracket and stator. Remove front bracket and stator by prying it gently off. Refer to **Figure 18**.

CAUTION
Do not insert screwdriver too deep, or stator coil might be damaged.

3. If brush replacement is necessary, perform the necessary steps as listed in the following procedure, *Brush Replacement*.

8

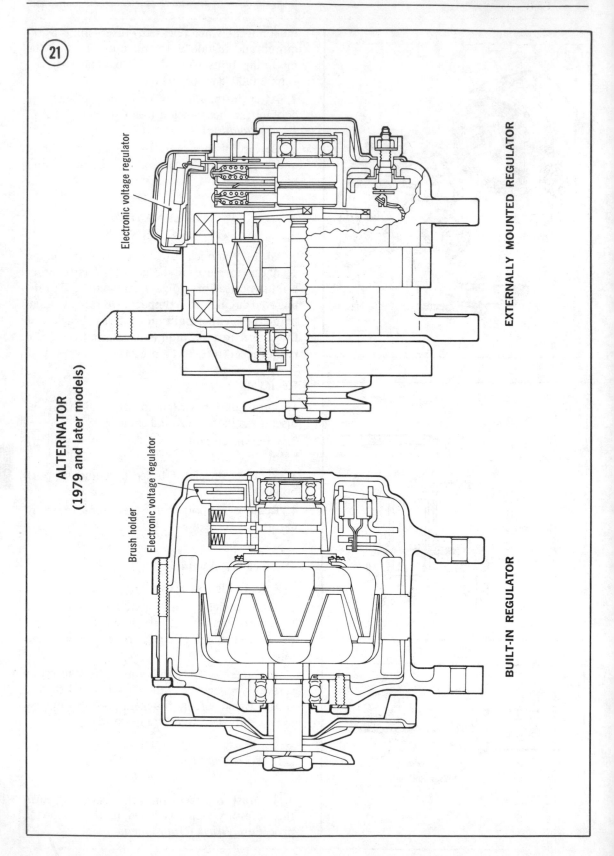

(21)

ALTERNATOR
(1979 and later models)

Electronic voltage regulator

EXTERNALLY MOUNTED REGULATOR

Brush holder

Electronic voltage regulator

BUILT-IN REGULATOR

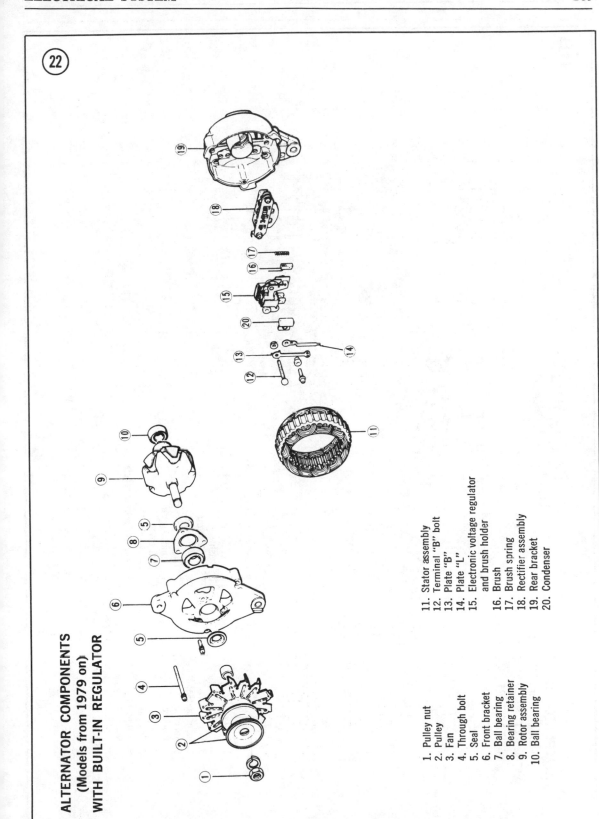

ALTERNATOR COMPONENTS
(Models from 1979 on)
WITH BUILT-IN REGULATOR

1. Pulley nut
2. Pulley
3. Fan
4. Through bolt
5. Seal
6. Front bracket
7. Ball bearing
8. Bearing retainer
9. Rotor assembly
10. Ball bearing

11. Stator assembly
12. Terminal "B" bolt
13. Plate "B"
14. Plate "L"
15. Electronic voltage regulator
    and brush holder
16. Brush
17. Brush spring
18. Rectifier assembly
19. Rear bracket
20. Condenser

8

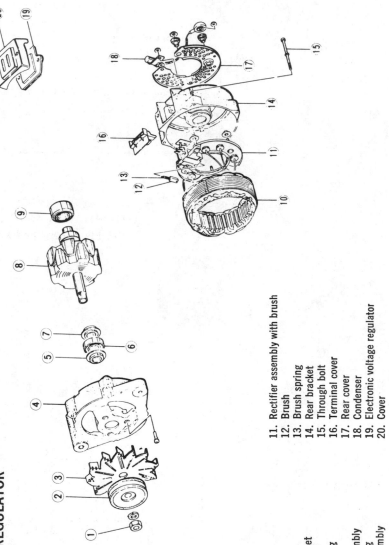

ALTERNATOR COMPONENTS
(Models from 1979 on)
WITH EXTERNALLY-MOUNTED
VOLTAGE REGULATOR

1. Pulley nut
2. Pulley
3. Fan
4. Front bracket
5. Spacer
6. Ball bearing
7. Spacer
8. Rotor assembly
9. Ball bearing
10. Stator assembly

11. Rectifier assembly with brush
12. Brush
13. Brush spring
14. Rear bracket
15. Through bolt
16. Terminal cover
17. Rear cover
18. Condenser
19. Electronic voltage regulator
20. Cover

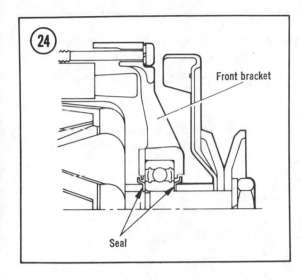

Front bracket

Seal

4. To assemble the alternator, perform the following steps:

    a. Install seals in front of and behind the front bearing (**Figure 24**).

    b. Push the brushes into the brush holder, then insert a wire to hold them in raised position (**Figures 25 and 26**). Install the rotor, then remove the wire.

Installation

1. Align holes in the alternator leg and the front case (on 1600cc engines) or timing chain case (2000 and 2600cc engines), then insert alternator support bolt from the front bracket side.

8

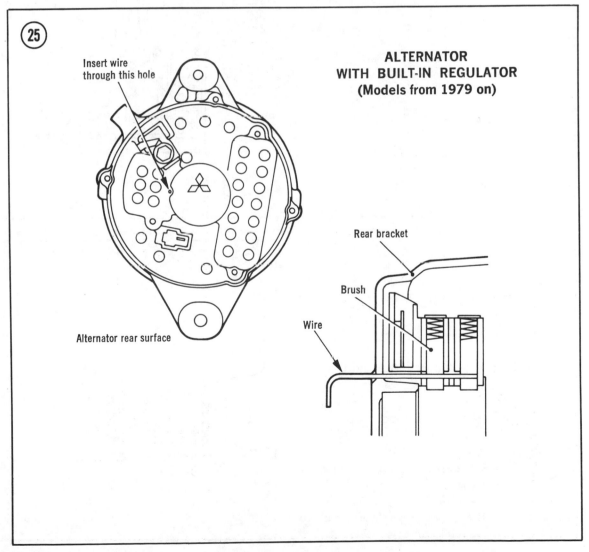

Insert wire through this hole

ALTERNATOR WITH BUILT-IN REGULATOR (Models from 1979 on)

Rear bracket

Brush

Wire

Alternator rear surface

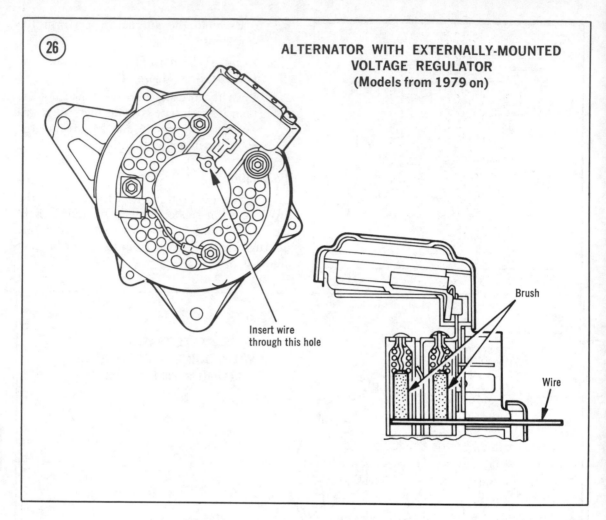

ALTERNATOR WITH EXTERNALLY-MOUNTED
VOLTAGE REGULATOR
(Models from 1979 on)

Insert wire
through this hole

Brush

Wire

2. Install brace bolt.

3. Install belt.

4. Push alternator toward the front of the engine. Refer to **Figure 27** and perform the following steps:

    a. Check clearance (A) between alternator leg and front case or timing chain case. If more than 0.008 in. (0.2 mm), insert spacers 0.0078 in. (0.198 mm), as required.

    b. Remove alternator support bolt, then insert spacers selected in Step 4a, preceding. Reinsert bolt, then tighten nut.

    c. Adjust belt tension (refer to Chapter Three, *Gas Stop Checks* section, *Drive Belts* procedure).

    d. Tighten alternator support bolt nut to 15-18 ft.-lb. and brace bolt to 9-10 ft.-lb.

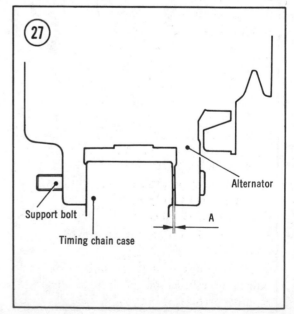

Alternator

Support bolt

Timing chain case

A

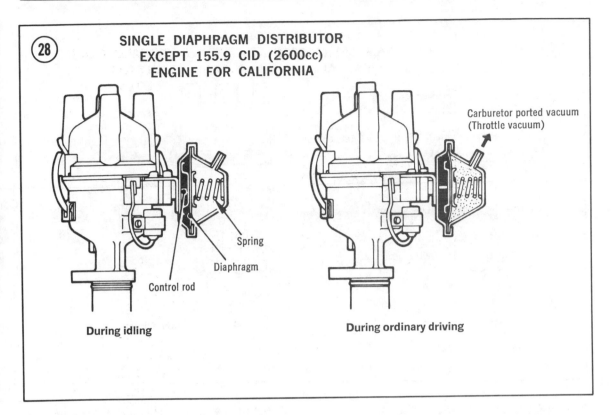

(28)
SINGLE DIAPHRAGM DISTRIBUTOR
EXCEPT 155.9 CID (2600cc)
ENGINE FOR CALIFORNIA

Carburetor ported vacuum
(Throttle vacuum)

Spring

Diaphragm

Control rod

During idling

During ordinary driving

Handling Precautions

1. When making battery connections, observe correct polarity.

2. A high voltage tester is not recommended because of danger of damage to diodes.

3. Disconnect the battery terminals prior to quick-charging the battery.

4. During high-speed operation do not disconnect battery terminals.

5. Battery voltage is always present at the BAT terminal of the generator or alternator. Disconnect one of the battery terminals before making electrical system checks.

6. When using a steam cleaner (or simply having your car washed), be careful not to get water in the generator or alternator.

7. Oil or dust on the slip ring will result in no continuity between the brush and slip ring. Keep slip ring clean always.

8. Replace the brush if worn down to the wear limit line.

9. All bearings are sealed ball bearing type requiring no lubrication. If signs of oil shortage, replace bearings.

VOLTAGE REGULATOR

Due to critical adjustment procedures and tolerances necessary in repairing the regulator, procedures are not given here. If trouble is suspected in the regulator, refer service to your dealer or automotive electrical shop or replace with a new one.

CONVENTIONAL IGNITION SYSTEM

The distributor is the heart of the ignition system, which consists of the distributor, contact breaker points, condenser, coil, and high and low tension circuit parts. The low tension (primary) circuit consists of the power source (battery), contact breaker points, condenser, and ignition coil primary winding. The high tension (secondary) circuit consists of ignition coil secondary winding, rotor arm, distributor cap electrical contacts, high tension cables, and spark plugs.

There are 2 types of distributors in use, a single diaphragm type and a dual diaphragm type. The single diaphragm type is shown in **Figure 28**, and is used nationwide except in

8

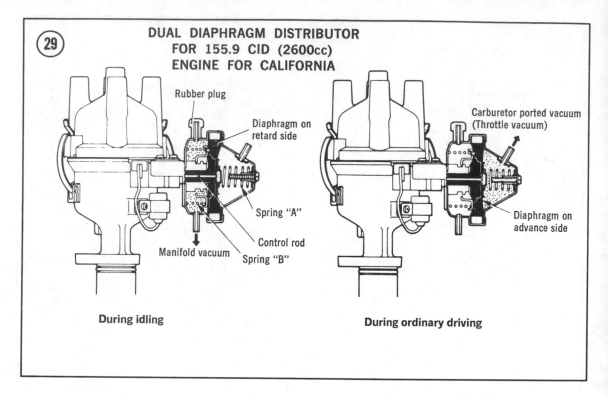

(29) DUAL DIAPHRAGM DISTRIBUTOR
FOR 155.9 CID (2600cc)
ENGINE FOR CALIFORNIA

Rubber plug

Diaphragm on
retard side

Carburetor ported vacuum
(Throttle vacuum)

Spring "A"

Control rod

Manifold vacuum   Spring "B"

Diaphragm on
advance side

During idling   During ordinary driving

2600cc California vehicles, which use the dual diaphragm type shown in **Figure 29**.

The distributor is mounted on the right front of the cylinder head, and is driven by a drive gear mounted to the front end of the camshaft.

Distributor Removal (All Models)

1. Disconnect the high tension wire and spark plug cables.

2. Disconnect primary wire.

3. Disconnect the vacuum hose(s) if so equipped.

4. Remove mounting bolts. Remove distributor from timing chaincase.

Distributor Installation
1600cc (97.5 cid) Models Through 1974

1. Adjust the distributor contact gap to the specified gap before installation (see *Contact Point Adjustment*, this section).

2. Adjust the alignment mark on the timing adjuster to the center position.

3. Rotate the crankshaft until the crank pulley notch is in alignment with the "T" timing mark

of the timing indicator. Check the compression TDC of the No. 1 cylinder. See **Figure 30**.

4. Adjust the oil pump shaft so that shaft groove is at right angles to the center line of the crankshaft. See **Figure 31**.

NOTE: *The oil pump shaft can be rotated easily with a screwdriver.*

5. Adjust the notch position of the crankshaft according to the ignition timing (**Figure 32**).

6. Insert the distributor rotor and main body into the timing chain cover with the center position of the rotor approximately 15 degrees before the No. 1 position. If the distributor shaft and oil pump shaft do not fit each other, rotate the crankshaft slightly until they do.

7. Turn the distributor until the contacts begin to open at the proper engine ignition timing positions. After the adjustments, tighten the bolts holding the distributor in place.

8. Mount the distributor cap and insert the spark plug and coil wires in their proper holes in the distributor cap.

9. Connect primary wire.

10. Set the timing (see Chapter Three, *Engine Tune-up* section).

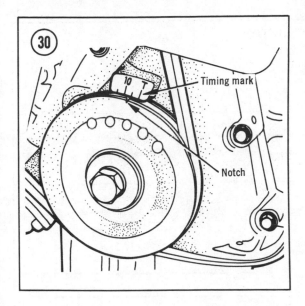

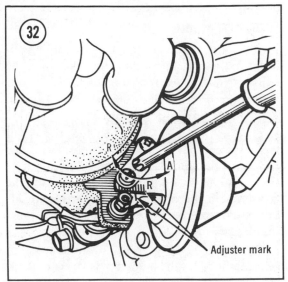

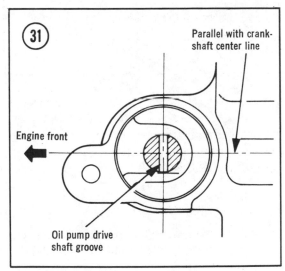

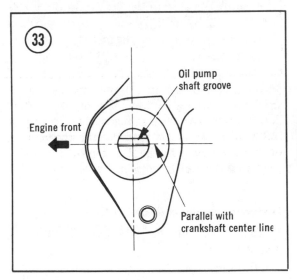

Distributor Installation
2000cc (121.7 cid) Models Through 1974

1. Adjust the distributor contact gap to the specified gap before installation (see *Contact Point Adjustment*, this section).

2. Adjust the alignment mark of the timing adjuster to the center position.

3. Set the piston of the No. 1 cylinder to TDC. Look through the distributor mounting hole to be sure that the groove in the end of the oil pump shaft is in position shown in **Figure 33**. If the oil pump is improperly installed, the distributor cannot be installed correctly.

4. Insert the distributor into the timing chain-case until it engages with the groove of the oil pump shaft. Lock the distributor in position with the locknut.

5. Set notch of crankshaft pulley to ignition timing of enging (3 degrees BTDC/850 rpm).

6. Loosen the distributor locknut and turn the distributor body until the point just begins to open. In this position, tighten the locknut.

7. Install the distributor cap. Install spark plug and coil wires in their proper holes in the distributor cap. Connect primary wire.

8. Set timing (see *Ignition Timing*, this section).

Distributor Installation
(1975-1977 Models)

1. Place the alignment mark of the timing adjuster to the center position. One division of the adjuster equals 4 degrees of crank angle.

2. Rotate the crankshaft until the No. 1 piston is at TDC on the compression stroke.

3. On the 1600cc (97.5 cid) engine, the lug at the lower end of the distributor shaft fits in the groove in the upper end of the oil pump drive shaft. Rotate the oil pump drive shaft until the groove is in the position shown in **Figure 31**. The shaft can be easily turned with a long-shank screwdriver.

4. On the 2000/2600cc engine, the crankshaft gear meshes with the oil pump drive gear. Turning the crankshaft will also turn the oil pump drive shaft. Be certain the groove in the upper end of the oil pump drive shaft is in the position shown in **Figure 33** when the piston in the No. 1 cylinder is at TDC. If it is not, the oil pump has been incorrectly installed.

5. Install the distributor so that the distributor shaft lug fits snugly in the oil pump drive shaft groove. Adjust the distributor position so that the stud will be at the center of the oblong hole in the distributor flange. See **Figure 34**. Install and firmly tighten a nut and washer.

> NOTE: *On the 1600cc (97.5 cid) engine, hold the rotor in the position shown in* **Figure 35** *and insert the distributor into the timing chaincase.*

6. Install the distributor cap, coil wire, and spark plug wires. Connect primary wire.

7. Install the vacuum advance hoses to the nipples: the vacuum hose from the carburetor to the nipple on the advance side and the vacuum hose from the intake manifold to the nipple on the retard side. Set the timing (see Chapter Three, *Engine Tune-up* section, for procedure).

Distributor Installation
(1978 Models)

1. Turn crankshaft until piston is in No. 1 cylinder at TDC on compression stroke.

2. Align mating marks on the distributor housing and the distributor driven gear (**Figure 36**).

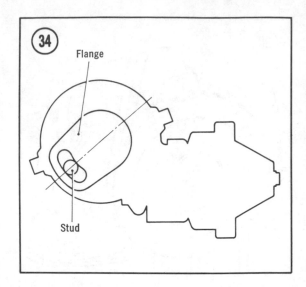

(34) Flange
Stud

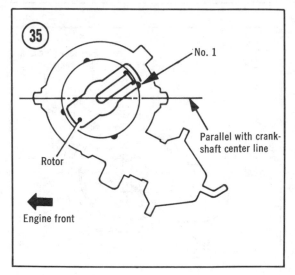

(35) No. 1
Parallel with crankshaft center line
Rotor
Engine front

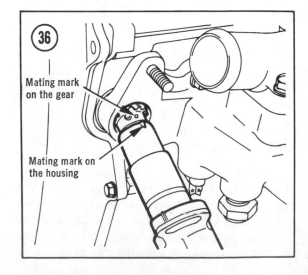

(36) Mating mark on the gear
Mating mark on the housing

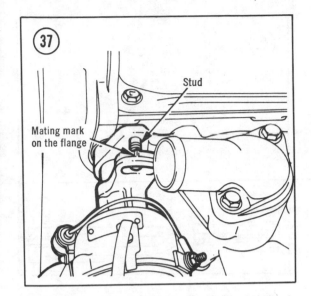

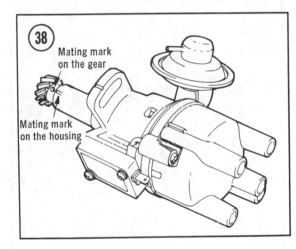

NOTE: *Be sure that the vacuum hoses fit the nipple of the vacuum control unit securely.*

7. Adjust the ignition timing. Refer to Chapter Three, *Engine Tune-up* section, for procedure.

Ignition Timing

Refer to Chapter Three, *Engine Tune-up* section, for ignition timing procedures for this type distributor.

ELECTRONIC IGNITION SYSTEM (EIS) (2000/2600cc ENGINES FROM 1979 ON)

The electronic ignition system, used on the 2000 and 2600cc engines beginning with the 1979 models, consists of a battery, ignition switch, breakerless electronic ignition control unit, ignition coil, spark plugs, and wiring. The electronic ignition control unit switches the primary current in response to timing signals produced by a distributor magnetic pickup.

The distributor is equipped with both vacuum and centrifugal advance mechanisms.

Distributor Removal/Installation

1. Disconnect battery ground cable.

2. Disconnect wiring harness from distributor control unit, and high tension cables from distributor cap. Remove the high tension cables (pull on the cable caps).

3. Disconnect vacuum hose from vacuum control unit.

4. Remove distributor mounting nut and lift distributor off the engine.

5. To install, refer to **Figure 38**. Turn engine crankshaft until the position of the piston in the No. 1 cylinder is at TDC on the compression stroke.

6. Align the mating line on the distributor housing with the mating punch mark on the distributor driven gear.

7. Refer to **Figure 39**. Install the distributor on the cylinder head.

NOTE: *Align the mating mark on the distributor attaching flange with the center of the distributor installation stud. Tighten the nuts evenly.*

3. Install distributor in the cylinder head while keeping mating marks on the distributor attaching flange and the center of the distributor installing stud aligned. Tighten the nuts (**Figure 37**).

NOTE: *The 2000/2600cc engines have no mating mark on the distributor attaching flange. Therefore, insert the distributor in the cylinder head while aligning the mating marks as described in Step 3, preceding.*

4. Adjust breaker point gap. Refer to Chapter Three, *Engine Tune-up* section, for procedure.

5. Install distributor cap, then connect high tension cable and spark plug cables.

6. Connect vacuum hoses.

8

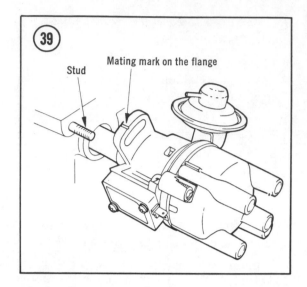

(39)

Stud

Mating mark on the flange

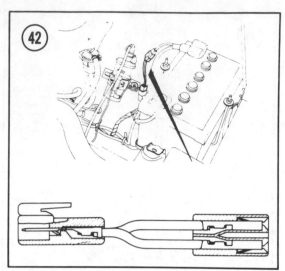

(42)

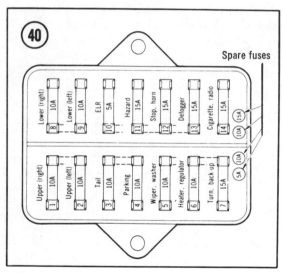

(40)

Spare fuses

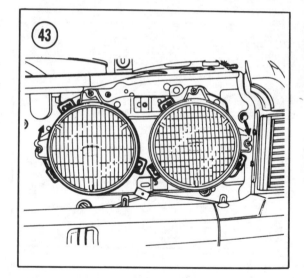

(43)

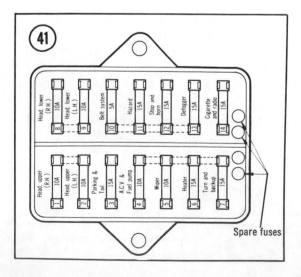

(41)

Spare fuses

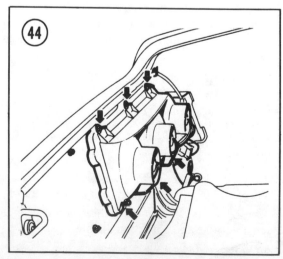

(44)

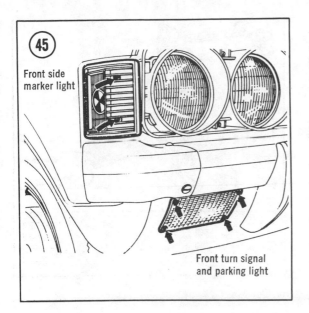

(45)

Front side
marker light

Front turn signal
and parking light

Ignition Timing

Refer to Chapter Three, *Engine Tune-up* section, for ignition timing procedure for this type distributor.

FUSES

Fuses are installed in a multi-pole fuse block fixed to the cowl trim to the left of the driver's seat. **Figure 40** shows the fuse block used on 1974 and earlier Colts; **Figure 41** shows the 1975 models on.

1. Locate cause when a fuse has been burned out and eliminate the defect before replacing the fuse.

2. Always use fuses of the correct amperage. It is dangerous to use larger capacity fuses. When additional electrical equipment is connected to the power source add a larger fuse.

3. A fuse holder that becomes loose is heated to such a point that the fuse may be burned out. Check the fuse holders for contact. When a fire holder is found defective, replace it or the entire fuse block assembly.

FUSIBLE LINK

A fusible link protects the electrical system from excessive current flowing through the cir-

cuits without passing through the fuses. See **Figure 42**.

A current as high as 100-150 amperes will burn out the fusible link within 15 seconds after power is applied. Do not use any fusible link with a capacity larger than the original. A melted fusible link can be detected by a swelling or discoloring of the harness covering.

CAUTION
Do not cover a fusible link with vinyl tape.

LIGHTING SYSTEM

Headlight Replacement

1. Remove front grille.

2. Remove connector on rear side of headlight unit. See **Figure 43**.

3. Loosen the retaining ring clamp screw, turn clockwise, and pull out retaining ring and headlight unit. Replace with a fresh sealed beam unit (do not disturb headlight adjusting screw).

Taillight Replacement

1. Remove fasteners and take off taillight assembly. See **Figure 44**.

2. Turn the socket on the rear side of taillight body when replacing bulb and turn it counterclockwise. Turn it counterclockwise while pushing in the bulb to free it. Remove bulb.

3. On the station wagon, remove screws from behind taillight body when exchanging lens.

Front Turn Signal, Side Marker Light, and Parking Light Replacement

1. Remove attaching screws and lens. See **Figure 45**.

2. Push in bulb while turning it counterclockwise when replacing bulb, and pull it out.

3. The front side marker light assembly can be removed by loosening attaching bolts after front grille is removed.

8

Rear Side Marker Light Replacement

1. Turn socket counterclockwise when replacing bulb and pull it out from behind lens. Pull bulb out by pushing it in and turning it counterclockwise.

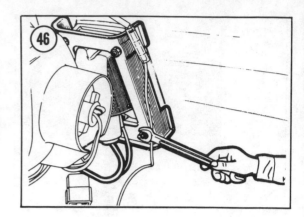

2. Remove rear side marker lights by removing the attaching nuts in the luggage compartment (**Figure 46**).

3. Loosen screws on rear side of light body. Take out lens.

CHAPTER NINE

CLUTCH , TRANSMISSION AND DRIVE SHAFT

This chapter covers the clutch assembly, manual transmission, and drive shaft. Checks and adjustments for the automatic transmission are given as appropriate for the average home mechanic. Overhaul or major service to automatic transmission should be referred to your dealer or transmission specialist.

Special tools are needed in many cases to work on the manual transmission. While a well-equipped mechanic may be able to substitute or fabricate equivalent tools as required, we recommend major overhaul be left to a transmission specialist after removal of the defective unit from the car.

CLUTCH ASSEMBLY

The clutch is a single dry disc type with a diaphragm spring. See **Figure 1**. The pedal force transfers to the control lever, shift arm, and release bearing through the cable to actuate the clutch.

See **Figure 2**. The clutch disc contains 4 torsion springs, cushion rubbers, and cushioning plate located between 2 facings. The facing is made of woven material.

The pressure plate is fastened together with rivets and cannot be disassembled. No adjustment is required within the normal service life of the facing.

See **Tables 1 and 2** for clutch specifications.

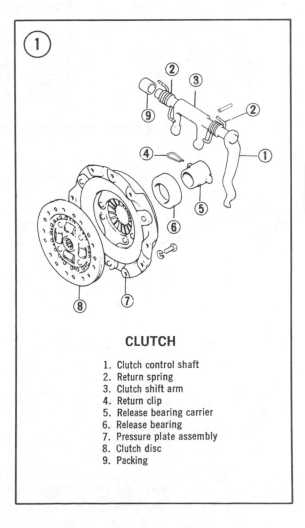

CLUTCH

1. Clutch control shaft
2. Return spring
3. Clutch shift arm
4. Return clip
5. Release bearing carrier
6. Release bearing
7. Pressure plate assembly
8. Clutch disc
9. Packing

9

Table 1   CLUTCH SPECIFICATIONS (THROUGH 1974 MODELS)

Clutch control method	Cable type
Clutch disc	
Facing (outer diameter x inner diameter x thickness)	7.874 in. x 5.512 in. x 0.138 in.
Facing surface area	51.2 sq. in.
Facing material	Special woven
Pressure plate assembly	
Type	Diaphragm spring strap drive type
Setting load	794 lb. (through 1973); 800 lb. (1974)

Table 2   CLUTCH SPECIFICATIONS — 1975 AND LATER MODELS

Description	1600cc (97.5 cid) Engine	2000cc (121.7 cid) Engine
Clutch control method	Cable type	Cable type
Clutch disc		
Facing (outer diameter x inner diameter x thickness)	7.874 x 5.512 x 0.138 in.	8.465 x 5.906 x 0.138 in.
Facing material	Special woven	Special woven
Pressure plate assembly		
Type	Diaphragm spring strap drive type	Diaphragm spring strap drive drive type
Setting load	800 lb.	882 lb.

Clutch Removal

1. Remove the transmission (see *Transmission Removal* under *Manual Transmission* in this chapter).

2. Insert the clutch center guide (Colt Part No. MD998017) into the center hole to prevent dropping the clutch disc. Loosen 6 bolts, one by one, holding the pressure plate assembly diagonally. Remove the pressure plate assembly. See **Figure 3**.

3. Remove the clutch disc.

4. Remove the release bearing carrier and bearing after removing the return clip on the transmission side.

5. Remove the shift arm spring pin and control lever assembly using a $\frac{3}{16}$ in. punch. Remove the shift arm and return spring (2 each).

Clutch Inspection

1. Do not use cleaning solution to clean the release bearing (it is permanently lubricated and sealed). Blow it clean with air. Replace the release bearing if it shows evidence of damage, noise, sluggish rotation, burn, or abnormal wear of meshing face against the diaphragm spring claw.

2. If the contact face against the shift arm of the bearing carrier is worn abnormally, replace it.

3. Check the bearing carrier clip for deformation, deterioration, or damage. Replace if necessary.

4. Check the contact face against the bearing carrier of the shift arm for unusual wear. Replace if necessary.

5. Replace the shaft if bend exceeds 0.0016 in., and bearing if clearance between shaft and bushing exceeds 0.006 in.

6. Clean and check the clutch disc for damage or wear. Replace if necessary.

7. Check the clutch disc for flatness by placing a dial gauge in contact with the facing surface 0.197 in. inside from the outside periphery of

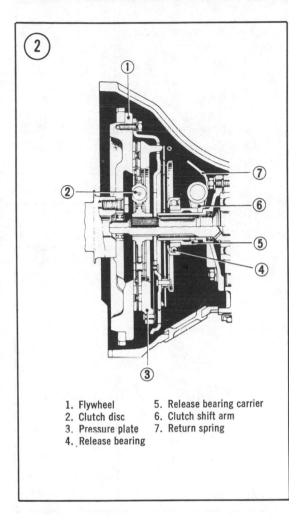

1. Flywheel
2. Clutch disc
3. Pressure plate
4. Release bearing
5. Release bearing carrier
6. Clutch shift arm
7. Return spring

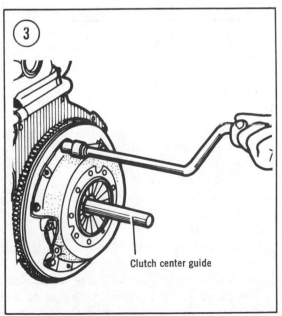

Clutch center guide

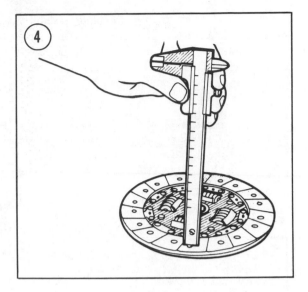

the disc. Read the flatness or runout indicated on the gauge while you slowly rotate the clutch disc. See **Figure 4**. Replace the disc if the flatness exceeds 0.028 in.

8. Check the play of the spline coupled with the main drive gear in the direction of rotation. Replace the main drive gear, clutch disc, or both, if the play is abnormal.

9. Check the facing for loose rivets, uneven facing contact (roughness must be less than 0.016 in.), facing burn, or facing stained with grease or oil.

> NOTE: *Stained facings must be replaced. Occasionally it is possible to remove a slight stain with a cloth moistened in gasoline.*

10. Check the torsion spring, friction washer, and cushion rubbers for deterioration, damage, or play. Replace if necessary.

11. Replace badly worn facing. Measure the wear from the surface of the facing to the rivet head. Standard dimension is 0.055-0.067 in.; service limit is 0.012 in.

12. Inspect the pressure plate assembly carefully. Replace diaphragm if claw plate is less than 0.067 in. thick.

13. Replace the assembly if it has a worn pivot ring (if it makes a noise when it is shaken, the pivot ring is worn).

14. Check the diaphragm spring tension. Replace it if less than 720 lb. During the tension

9

check, apply load to pressure plate assembly, press down until the pressure plate face sinks approximately 0.335 in. below clutch cover face, return pressure plate and read load when pressure plate face reaches 0.311 in.

Clutch Installation

1. Insert control lever into transmission. Install return springs (2 each), felt packing, and shift arm. Lock shift arm to the shaft with the spring pin.

> NOTE: *Fill the oil seal of the shaft with grease. Fit the spring pin so that the mating ends are lined up in the axial direction. The felt packing should be installed after impregnating it with oil.*

2. Install release bearing carrier and bearing. Install return clip.

3. Coat the clutch disc spline with grease. Install disc and pressure plate assembly on flywheel with the aid of Colt clutch center guide tool MD 998107. Tighten attaching bolt 11-15 ft.-lb.

> NOTE: *Install disc with longer boss facing the transmission. The pressure plate can be installed by mating the flywheel notch, for it is perfectly balanced.*

4. Install transmission (see *Transmission Installation*, this chapter). Adjust clutch after installing (see *Clutch Adjustment*, this chapter).

CLUTCH CONTROL

Clutch Cable Removal

Refer to **Figure 5** for the following procedure.

1. Loosen the cable adjusting wheel inside engine compartment.

2. Loosen clutch pedal adjusting bolt locknut. Back out the adjusting bolt.

3. Disconnect cable from pedal lever.

4. Disconnect cable from clutch shift lever. If broken or damaged, replace.

Clutch Pedal Removal

1. Loosen cable adjusting wheel inside engine compartment.

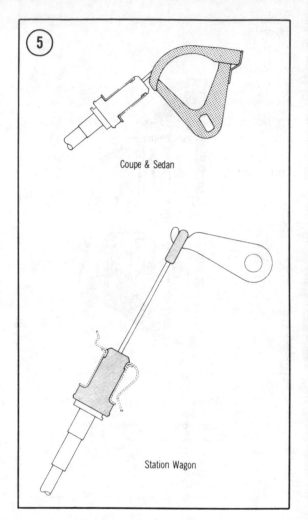

(5)

Coupe & Sedan

Station Wagon

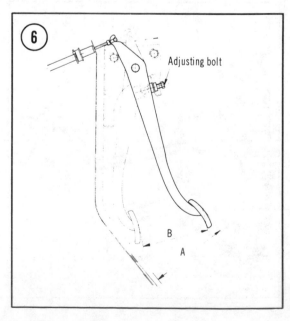

(6)

Adjusting bolt

B

A

2. Loosen clutch pedal adjusting bolt locknut. Back out the adjusting bolt.

3. Remove clutch cable from pedal lever.

4. Remove cable from clutch shift lever.

5. Remove clevis pin connecting the pushrod of the brake master cylinder and the pedal.

6. Remove brake and clutch pedal attaching bracket. Remove pedal assembly.

7. Remove the nut or snap ring on the pedal shaft and disconnect lever from the pedal shaft. Move pedal shaft to the left. Remove the brake pedal and clutch pedal simultaneously.

8. Check pedal shaft bushing. Replace if worn.

Clutch Pedal Installation

1. Reverse the removal steps. Apply grease to the pedal shaft, spacer, bushing, and cable fitting area of the clutch pedal.

2. Apply as much engine oil to the cable as necessary when installing cable.

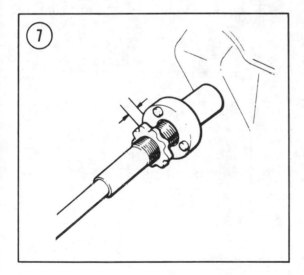

3. After installing cable, install pads at the battery cable area of the starter and at rear of engine front support insulator.

> CAUTION
> *Lubricate cable every 8,000 miles.*

Clutch Pedal Adjustment

1. Adjust the distance from the toe board to the top face of the pedal, and the difference in height between the clutch and brake pedals (refer to **Table 3**) by means of the adjusting bolt (**Figure 6**).

> CAUTION
> *Insufficient pedal stroke results in insufficient clutch release.*

2. Slightly pull the outer cable from the cable holder of the toe board. Make adjustment by means of the adjusting nut. See **Figure 7**. Check to see that the pedal has the correct free stroke and specified distance from the floor to the clutch pedal in the released position (**Table 3**).

> CAUTION
> *Check the clutch free stroke after the first 600 miles and every 4,000 miles.*

TRANSMISSION

All Dodge Colts are equipped with a 4-speed synchronized manual transmission as standard equipment. An optional 5-speed has been added for 1975 models on. **Figure 8** shows a cutaway view of the 4-speed manual transmission, **Figures 9 and 10**, the 5-speed.

Multipurpose Gear Oil, SAE 80 as defined by API GL-5 (MIL-L-2105B) should be used in all manual transmissions.

Table 3   CLUTCH ADJUSTMENT SPECIFICATIONS

Description	Standard Value	Remarks
Distance A	6.8 in. (175 mm)	1600cc and 2000cc engines
Distance A	7.2 in. (185 mm)	2600cc engines
Distance B	5.5 in. (140 mm)	1600cc and 2000cc engines
Distance B	5.9 in. (150 mm)	2600cc engines
Adjusting nut-to-insulator free play	0.12-0.16 in. (3-4 mm)	All models

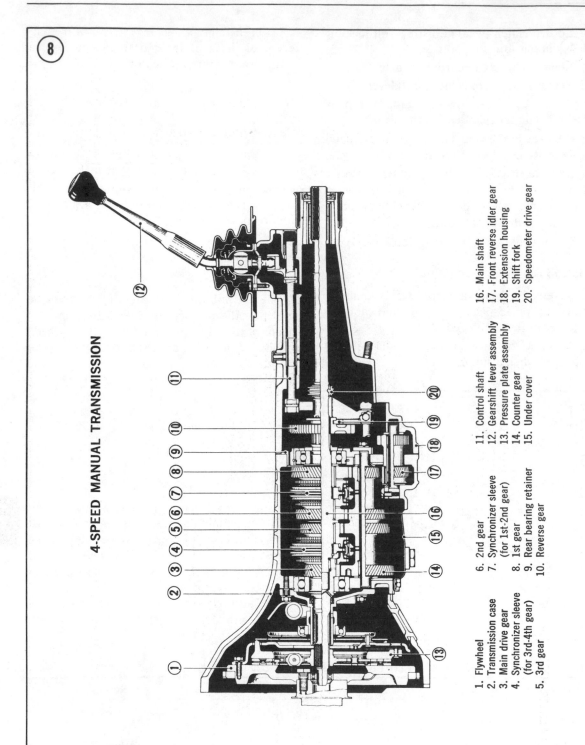

4-SPEED MANUAL TRANSMISSION

⑧

1. Flywheel
2. Transmission case
3. Main drive gear
4. Synchronizer sleeve
   (for 3rd-4th gear)
5. 3rd gear
6. 2nd gear
7. Synchronizer sleeve
   (for 1st-2nd gear)
8. 1st gear
9. Rear bearing retainer
10. Reverse gear
11. Control shaft
12. Gearshift lever assembly
13. Pressure plate assembly
14. Counter gear
15. Under cover
16. Main shaft
17. Front reverse idler gear
18. Extension housing
19. Shift fork
20. Speedometer drive gear

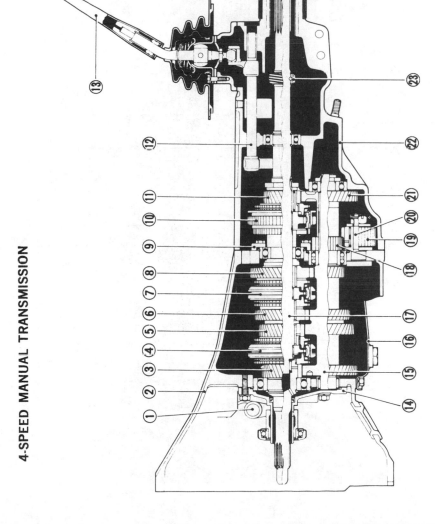

4-SPEED MANUAL TRANSMISSION

1. Clutch control shaft
2. Transmission case
3. Main drive gear
4. Synchronizer
5. 3rd speed gear
6. 2nd speed gear
7. Synchronizer
8. 1st speed gear
9. Rear bearing retainer
10. Synchronizer
11. Overdrive gear
12. Control shaft
13. Control lever
14. Front bearing retainer
15. Countershaft gear
16. Under cover
17. Main shaft
18. Counter reverse gear
19. Reverse idler gear
20. Reverse idler gear shaft
21. Counter overdrive gear
22. Extension housing
23. Speedometer drive gear

9

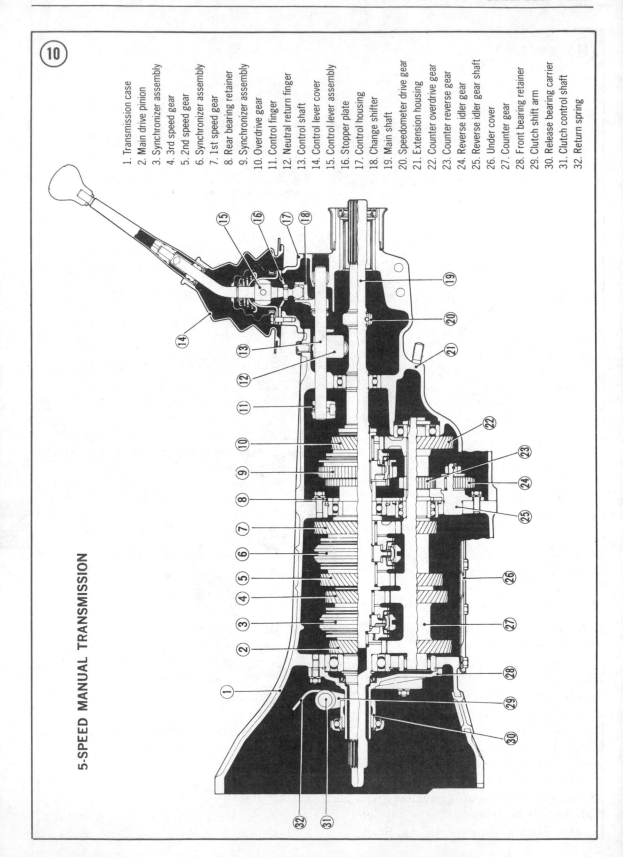

5-SPEED MANUAL TRANSMISSION

1. Transmission case
2. Main drive pinion
3. Synchronizer assembly
4. 3rd speed gear
5. 2nd speed gear
6. Synchronizer assembly
7. 1st speed gear
8. Rear bearing retainer
9. Synchronizer assembly
10. Overdrive gear
11. Control finger
12. Neutral return finger
13. Control shaft
14. Control lever cover
15. Control lever assembly
16. Stopper plate
17. Control housing
18. Change shifter
19. Main shaft
20. Speedometer drive gear
21. Extension housing
22. Counter overdrive gear
23. Counter reverse gear
24. Reverse idler gear
25. Reverse idler gear shaft
26. Under cover
27. Counter gear
28. Front bearing retainer
29. Clutch shift arm
30. Release bearing carrier
31. Clutch control shaft
32. Return spring

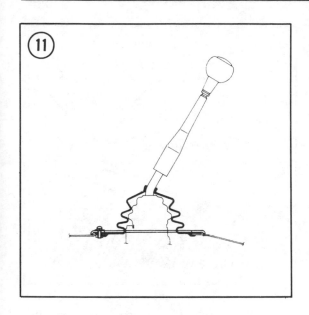

Manual Transmission Removal

1. Remove the air cleaner.

2. Disconnect the battery cables from the starter motor. Unclip them at the transmission and move them away to give access to transmission.

3. Remove the starter motor.

CAUTION
Battery terminals should be disconnected prior to removal of the starter motor.

4. Remove 2 bolts from the top of transmission.

5. Lift the console box upward after removing lock screws. (In a car without the console box, pull the carpet upward.)

6. Remove the dust cover retaining plate upward by removing lock screws.

7. Lift up the dust cover. Remove 4 attaching bolts at the lower part of the extension housing. Remove the gearshift lever assembly.

8. Jack the car up and support it with jackstands. Drain the transmission oil.

9. Remove the speedometer cable and transmission switch and back-up light switch wiring from the transmission.

10. Remove bolts from the rear of the drive shaft. Pull the shaft out of the transmission.

11. Disconnect muffler pipe from its bracket.

12. Disconnect clutch cables.

13. Support the transmission on a jack. Remove the insulators from members by removing the attaching bolts.

CAUTION
The jack should be placed under the under cover. The under cover supporting area must be as wide as possible.

14. Disconnect each member from the frame. Pull it off toward the side.

15. Remove bell housing cover.

16. Remove remaining locking bolts from the transmission. Pull the transmission rearward from the engine.

CAUTION
Be careful you do not bend the front end of the main drive shaft while pulling the transmission rearward.

Manual Transmission Installation

1. To install the transmission, reverse the removal steps. Tighten mounting bolts to 22-30 ft.-lb.

2. When installing the control lever assembly, place the change shifter so that the nylon bushing hole is vertical.

CAUTION
During this operation use care so that no dirt enters the transmission at the control housing mounting section.

3. Be sure the bell housing cover is not bent (a bent cover will not mate correctly with the cylinder block and transmission, resulting in entry of mud into the transmission).

4. Install the gearshift lever dust cover securely into the back bone hole. Attach the retaining plate with screws (**Figure 11**).

5. Adjust the clutch (see *Clutch Adjustment*, this chapter).

6. Place 1.8 U.S. qt. (1.5 Imp. qt.) of transmission fluid into the transmission case.

Disassembly
(4-Speed Transmission)

1. Remove clutch control lever shaft and arm (refer to *Clutch* section, preceding).

9

2. Drain transmission fluid, then remove speedometer locking plate and driven gear assembly.

3. Remove backup light switch and transmission switch. Remove ball with care.

4. Remove extension housing and undercover.

5. Remove speedometer drive gear snap ring, then remove drive gear.

6. Remove main drive gear bearing retainer.

7. Remove countershaft stopper.

8. Withdraw countershaft toward rear of case. Remove counter gear, 40 needle rollers (front and rear), spacer, and 2 thrust washers (front and rear).

9. Remove rear thrust washer, reverse idler gear, needle bearing, spacer, and front thrust washer from reverse idler gear shaft.

10. Remove reverse idler gear shaft locking bolt. Pull shaft backward and out of case.

11. Remove 3 plugs on right-hand side of case. Remove poppet springs and balls.

12. Remove reverse gear, and reverse shift rail and fork.

13. Drive shift rail and fork spring pins off with a $\frac{3}{16}$ in. punch (**Figure 12**).

14. Pull each shift rail (with selector) rearward, out of the case. Remove shift fork. (The shift rail and selector should not be disassembled, but should be kept together as an assembly.)

> NOTE: *The interlock plungers (2 pieces) might drop out of the transmission case when the shift rail is withdrawn. Do not lose them.*

15. Pull main shaft assembly rearward, along with the rear bearing retainer. Remove this assembly, along with the main drive gear synchronizer ring and pilot needle bearing.

16. Disassemble main shaft assembly (refer to **Figure 13**), as follows:

   a. Expand snap ring with a pair of pliers, then pull rear bearing retainer off of the bearing (**Figure 14**).

   b. Remove locking nut.

   c. Hold main shaft assembly with front end pointing downward, and strike it gently against a hard surface, to cause the bearing to slip off.

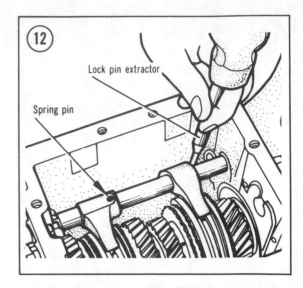

Lock pin extractor

Spring pin

d. Remove spacer, first gear, needle bearing, spacer bushing, synchronizer ring, first/second gear synchronizer assembly, synchronizer ring, second gear, and needle bearing (**Figure 15**).

e. Remove snap ring from front of main shaft, then remove 3rd/top speed synchronizer assembly, synchronizer ring, 3rd gear, and needle bearing.

f. Disassemble each synchronizer assembly into 4 parts: synchronizer sleeve, synchronizer hub, springs, and synchronizer pieces.

CAUTION
All parts (except the synchronizer hub) are identical. Be sure to put them in the exact order of removal, so as not to mix them up during reassembly.

17. Pull main drive gear assembly out, toward front of case.

18. Remove each snap ring. Pull bearing off with Colt tool No. MD998056 (bearing puller), or equivalent (**Figure 16**).

19. Disassemble extension housing, as follows:

   a. Remove change shifter and control shaft lock pin with a $\frac{3}{16}$ in. punch (**Figure 17**).

   b. Remove return spring, then pull off control shaft. Remove change shifter.

   c. Disassemble control lever assembly into 3 parts: control housing, stopper plate, and lever assembly.

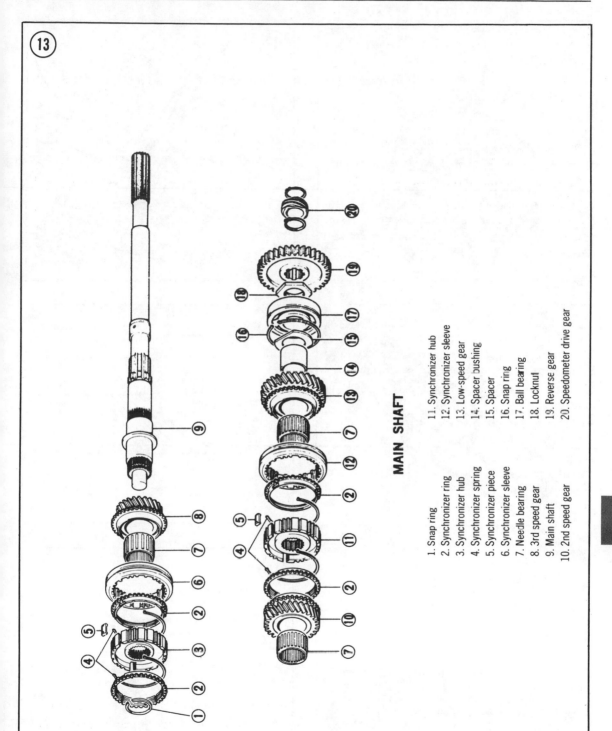

⑬

MAIN SHAFT

1. Snap ring
2. Synchronizer ring
3. Synchronizer hub
4. Synchronizer spring
5. Synchronizer piece
6. Synchronizer sleeve
7. Needle bearing
8. 3rd speed gear
9. Main shaft
10. 2nd speed gear

11. Synchronizer hub
12. Synchronizer sleeve
13. Low-speed gear
14. Spacer bushing
15. Spacer
16. Snap ring
17. Ball bearing
18. Locknut
19. Reverse gear
20. Speedometer drive gear

9

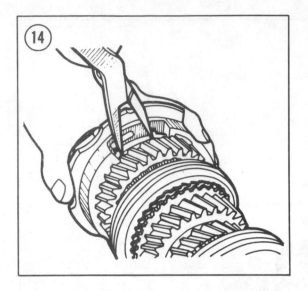

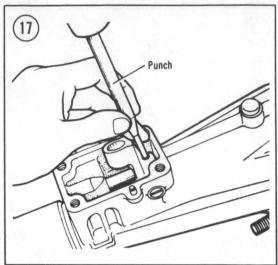

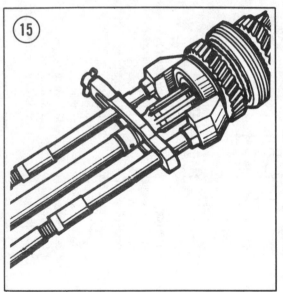

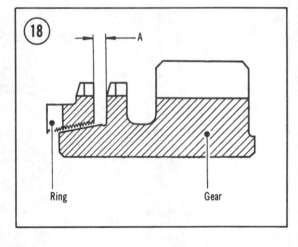

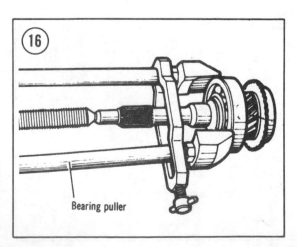

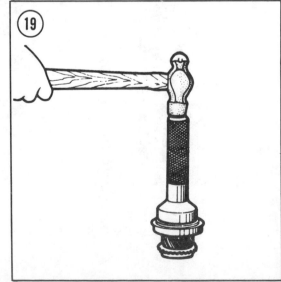

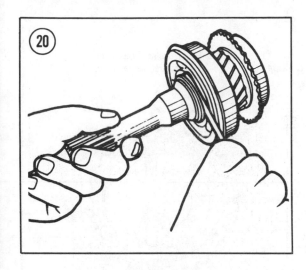

Table 4   SNAP RINGS
(4-SPEED TRANSMISSION)

Thickness	Color
0.098 in. (2.5 mm)	Yellow
0.096 in. (2.45 mm)	Blue
0.094 in. (2.4 mm)	Red
0.093 in. (2.35 mm)	None
0.091 in. (2.3 mm)	White

Inspection

Check transmission case and extension housing for cracks and damage. In addition, perform the following checks:

1. Check main shaft, main drive gear, and all other gears for excessive wear or damage.

2. Check clutch gear teeth for wear and damage.

3. Check synchronizer ring for wear or damaged internal threads. With synchronizer assembled to the cone of each gear, check dimension A, **Figure 18**. If less than 0.032 in. (0.8 mm), replace synchronizer ring.

4. Check shift fork groove in sleeve for wear or damage.

5. Check clearance between the shift fork and fork groove of the synchronizer sleeve and reverse gear. The standard clearance is 0.004-0.012 in. (0.1-0.3 mm).

6. Check the clearance between the selector and change lever. It should be 0.004-0.012 in. (0.1-0.3 mm).

7. Replace any bearing that makes noise when turned, or does not rotate smoothly. Replace any bearing that shows signs of external damage.

8. Check springs for breakage or deterioration. The standard lengths for the various springs are as follows:

   a. Poppet spring (for reverse): free length, 1.236 in. (31.4 mm); load, 8.8 lb. @ 1.091 in. (4kg @ 27.7 mm).

   b. Poppet spring: free length, 0.744 in. (18.9 mm); load, 8.8 lb. @ 0.598 in. (4kg @ 15.2 mm).

   c. Return spring: free length 2.876 in. (73 mm); load, 2.5 lb. @ 3.071 in. (1.1kg @ 78 mm).

Reassembly
(4-Speed Transmission)

When reassembling the transmission, be sure to use new gaskets, oil seals, lock pins, and spring pins. Be sure all components are clean. Apply oil to sliding and rotating parts of bearings and gears. Fill oil seal lips with fresh grease. Use sealant on gaskets where indicated in the procedural steps.

1. To assemble the main drive gear assembly, proceed as follows:

   a. Press bearing in place with a hammer or press and Colt tool No. MD998029 (Bearing Installer), as shown in **Figure 19**. Install a select fit snap ring (**Table 4**) so that bearing end play is 0-0.002 in. (0-0.06 mm). See **Figure 20**.

   b. Install the bearing and secure it with the snap ring which you just selected from **Table 4**.

2. To assemble the main shaft assembly, proceed as follows:

   a. Assemble the synchronizer hub and sleeve in position (**Figure 21**). Be sure that the front and rear synchronizer springs have their stepped portions installed on the different synchronizer pieces.

   NOTE: *The 1st/2nd speed synchronizer sleeve is identical to that for the 3rd/4th speeds. When the synchronizer is reassembled, be sure that they go back in the*

9

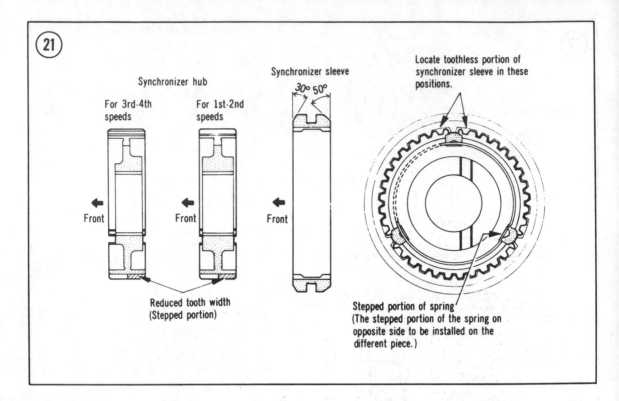

Synchronizer hub

For 3rd-4th speeds

For 1st-2nd speeds

Synchronizer sleeve

30° 50°

Front

Front

Front

Reduced tooth width
(Stepped portion)

Locate toothless portion of
synchronizer sleeve in these
positions.

Stepped portion of spring
(The stepped portion of the spring on
opposite side to be installed on the
different piece.)

*exact reverse order in which they were
removed. Also, the synchronizer sleeve
has an internal tooth missing at 6 places.
Install the sleeve with the toothless portions positioned as shown in* **Figure 21.**

b. After the needle bearing and 3rd speed
gear has been installed on the main shaft
(from its front end), install the synchronizer ring (all rings are identical in
shape) and the top/3rd speed synchronizer assembly.

NOTE: *The direction of installation of
the 1st/2nd speed synchronizer hub is
not specified; accordingly, it must be
reassembled in exactly the reverse order
of disassembly (Figure 22).*

c. Install a snap ring from **Table 5** so that
the synchronizer assembly end play is as
follows: 3rd speed gear end play,
0.001-0.008 in. (0.04-0.20 mm); 3rd/top
speed synchronizer hub end play, 0-0.003
in. (0-0.08 mm). Refer to **Figure 23.**

d. After installing the needle bearing and
2nd speed gear on the main shaft (from
rear end), install synchronizer ring and

Table 5   SNAP RINGS
(4-SPEED TRANSMISSION)

Thickness	Color
0.085 in. (2.15 mm)	None
0.087 in. (2.22 mm)	Yellow
0.090 in. (2.29 mm)	Green
0.093 in. (2.36 mm)	Blue

the 1st/2nd speed synchronizer assembly
on the main shaft.

CAUTION
*Be sure that you assemble the syn-
chronizer on the main shaft in exactly
the same manner as it was removed.*

e. Force the synchronizer assembly forward,
then check the 2nd speed gear end play
(**Figure 24**). It should be 0.001-0.008 in.
(0.04-0.20 mm).

f. Install 1st speed gear spacer ring, needle
bearing, synchronizer ring, 1st speed gear
and spacer. Force these parts forward,
then check 1st speed gear end play (**Figure 25**). It should be 0.001-0.008 in.
(0.04-0.20 mm).

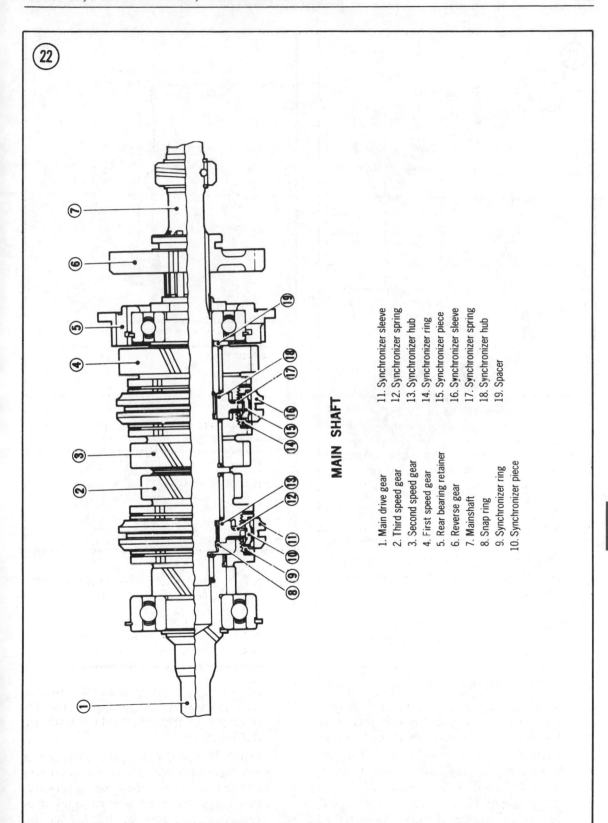

MAIN SHAFT

1. Main drive gear
2. Third speed gear
3. Second speed gear
4. First speed gear
5. Rear bearing retainer
6. Reverse gear
7. Mainshaft
8. Snap ring
9. Synchronizer ring
10. Synchronizer piece
11. Synchronizer sleeve
12. Synchronizer spring
13. Synchronizer hub
14. Synchronizer ring
15. Synchronizer piece
16. Synchronizer sleeve
17. Synchronizer spring
18. Synchronizer hub
19. Spacer

9

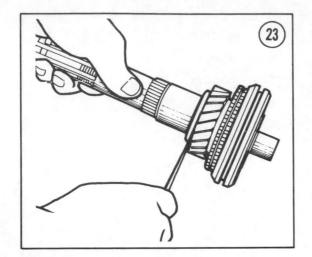

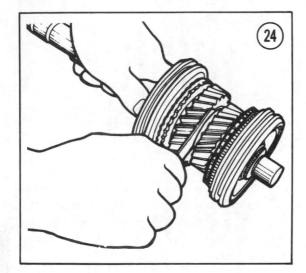

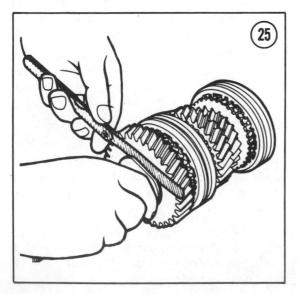

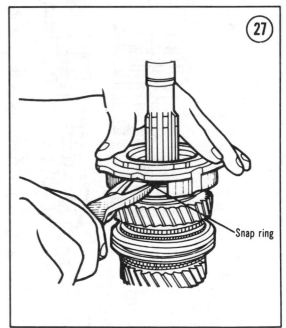

Table 6   SNAP RINGS
(4-SPEED TRANSMISSION)

Thickness	Color
0.057 in. (1.44 mm)	None
0.060 in. (1.53 mm)	Red
0.064 in. (1.62 mm)	White
0.067 in. (1.71 mm)	Yellow
0.071 in. (1.80 mm)	Blue

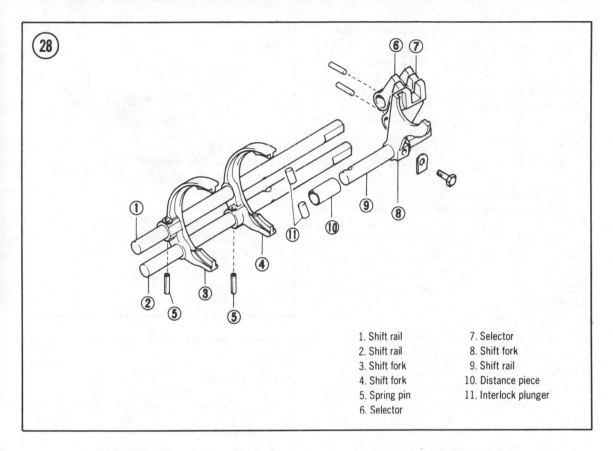

1. Shift rail	7. Selector
2. Shift rail	8. Shift fork
3. Shift fork	9. Shift rail
4. Shift fork	10. Distance piece
5. Spring pin	11. Interlock plunger
6. Selector	

g. Use Colt tool MD998030 (bearing installer) and install main shaft bearing with a hammer or press (**Figure 26**). Tighten locknut to 36-72 ft.-lb. (49.0-98.0 N•m), then lock with a key inserted in the keyway of the main shaft against rotation. Attach nut to main shaft spline with a blunt drift.

h. Install snap ring on rear bearing retainer (**Figure 27**). Expand the snap ring and install the retainer on the bearing. The snap ring should be selected and installed so that the bearing end play (snap ring to bearing retainer play) is 0-0.006 in. (0-0.15 mm). Refer to **Table 6**.

NOTE: *Where it is difficult to check the end play, select a snap ring of the proper thickness by first selecting the thickest ring which fits in the groove with no end play. Then select the next thinner ring (Figure 27).*

3. Place transmission case upside down with under cover facing up. Install main drive gear assembly into the case. (If gear assembly is difficult to install, tap lightly with a soft hammer.)

4. Insert needle bearing into front end of main drive gear and apply grease to it. Install synchronizer ring.

5. Insert main shaft assembly into case (through the rear bore), and install it so that it is in mesh with the main drive gear.

6. Install the main shaft assembly (be sure that the synchronizer ring meshes correctly with the top/3rd speed synchronizer assembly). If rear bearing retainer is difficult to install in the case, tap lightly with a soft hammer.

7. Insert each shift fork into shift fork groove in synchronizer sleeve. Hold the forks by hand inside the case, then insert the top/3rd speed shift rail assembly into the case (through the rear bore), and insert into each fork.

8. Insert interlock plunger into case (through rear bore). Push the plunger into the hole with a screwdriver (through the top opening in the case). See **Figure 28**.

9. Insert the 1st/2nd speed shift rail assembly into the case through the rear bore (central opening). Insert it into each fork, then place in proper position relative to the case. Set the shift forks (with their pin holes aligned with those of the shift rail) in place.

10. Install the shift forks on the shift rail with the spring pins and Colt tool MD998245 (lock pin installer).

> NOTE: *Each spring pin must be driven completely into the hole with its slit placed on the center line of the shift rail.*

11. Insert the remaining interlock plunger from the rear opening of the case.

12. Insert reverse shift fork ends in the groove of the reverse gear. Install the distance piece on the shift rail, then insert the assembled reverse shift rail assembly into the case.

13. Install poppet balls and springs. Install and tighten plugs (apply sealant to the threads first). See **Figure 29**.

14. Install poppet springs with the tapered ends facing the balls.

> NOTE: *The poppet springs differ in overall length: reverse shift fork poppet spring, 1.236 in. (31.4 mm); all others, 0.744 in. (18.9 mm).*

15. Tighten the plugs until their tops are flush with the case surface.

16. Install reverse idler gear shaft, then tighten the lock bolt and bend the tongued washer to lock it in place.

17. Install the thrust washer front, needle bearing, distance piece, and needle bearing on the reverse idler gear shaft.

18. Insert reverse idler gear.

19. Install a select thrust washer from **Table 7**, of the proper thickness (refer to **Figure 30**), as follows:

  a. Measure from rear of case to rear of reverse idler gear shaft hole.

  b. Determine thrust washer thickness by using the following calculation: B + 0.004 in. (0.10 mm), which is the thickness of extension housing gasket, -A-0.002 to 0.012 in. (0.05 to 0.30 mm) equals thrust washer thickness.

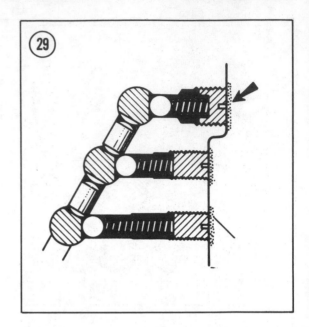

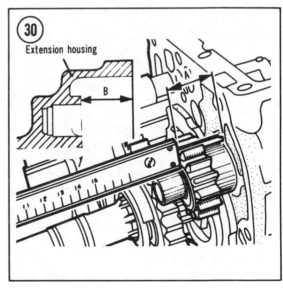
Extension housing

Table 7　REAR THRUST WASHERS
(4-SPEED TRANSMISSION)

Thickness	Identification Mark
0.070 in. (1.79 mm)	None
0.078 in. (1.98 mm)	A
0.082 in. (2.075 mm)	E
0.085 in. (2.17 mm)	B
0.089 in. (2.265 mm)	E
0.093 in. (2.36 mm)	C
0.100 in. (2.55 mm)	D

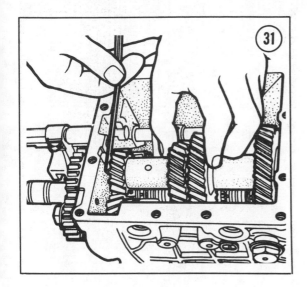

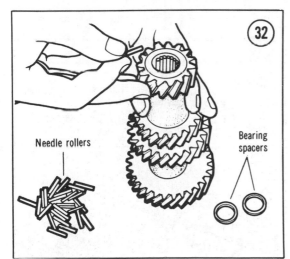

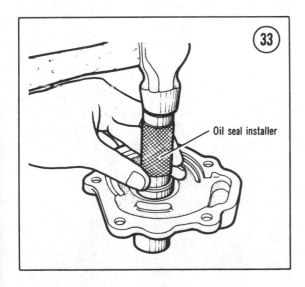

Oil seal installer

20. Install counter gear, as follows:

a. Temporarily install counter gear, front and rear thrust washers and shaft, then measure the end play of the counter gear (**Figure 31**). If end play does not agree with the standard measure of 0.002-0.007 in. (0.05-0.18 mm), correct it by selecting a proper rear thrust washer from **Table 8**. Be sure that the thrust washer tongue fits properly into the slot in the case.

b. Install the needle rollers and bearing spacers in the front and rear bores of the counter gear (**Figure 32**). Apply grease to them, so that they will not drop out. (The number of needle rollers is 42 — 21 for the front and 21 for the rear.) Be sure to install the spacers on the outside of the needle rollers.

c. Attach the front thrust washer and rear thrust washer selected from **Table 8**, to the counter gear with grease. Install counter gear in case, then insert counter gear shaft from the rear of the case. Be sure that the thrust washer tongue fits properly into the slot in the case.

d. Fasten the rear end of the countershaft by tightening the stopper plate.

21. To install the front bearing retainer, proceed as follows:

a. Fill out seal lip with grease, then apply sealant to the gasket. Install the new oil seal with Colt tool MD998031 (oil seal installer). See **Figure 33**.

b. Refer to **Figure 34**. Measure sizes A and B before installing the front bearing re-

9

Table 8   THRUST WASHERS (4-SPEED TRANSMISSION)

Thickness	Identification Mark
0.080 in. (2.04 mm)	A
0.083 in. (2.11 mm)	B
0.084 in. (2.145 mm)	F
0.086 in. (2.18 mm)	C
0.087 in. (2.215 mm)	G
0.089 in. (2.25 mm)	D
0.092 in. (2.33 mm)	E

tainer. Adjust the retainer-to-bearing clearance to 0-0.004 in. (0.01 mm) with a shim selected from **Table 9**. Select the spacer by using the following formula: Spacer thickness + 0-0.004 in. (0-0.1 mm) = B + 0.012 in. (0.3 mm) - A. Be sure to use sealant prior to installing the gasket.

22. Install speedometer driven gear on main shaft.

23. Install extension housing to transmission case (use sealant on gasket and bolts).

> NOTE: *The extension housing is socket-jointed with the rear bearing retainer. The bolt washer must be installed with the convex side facing the bolt head.*

24. Tighten the backup light switch and transmission switch cord clip together.

25. Insert a ball into the backup light switch hole, then install the backup light switch. Install the transmission switch in the same manner.

> NOTE: *Prior to installing either switch, apply sealer to threads.*

26. Attach the backup light switch and transmission switch cords to the clip.

27. Install speedometer driven gear and lock with the locking plate (which must be fully inserted toward the sleeve and secured with a bolt).

28. Install the under cover to the transmission case. Tighten the under cover bolts in a crisscross fashion to 6-7 ft.-lb. (7.8-9.8 N•m).

29. Install the control lever assembly on the transmission case. Before doing this, however, place the gearshift lever in the second speed position, and the nylon bushing in the vertical position. Complete the installation of the control lever from inside the passenger compartment.

> NOTE: *Use sealant on the gaskets. Also, be sure that you use sufficient grease in the change shifter bushing.*

30. Fill the transmission with fluid.

31. Install the clutch and related parts (refer to *Clutch* section, earlier in this chapter).

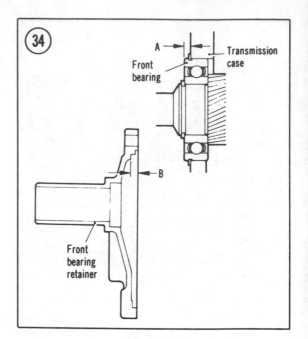

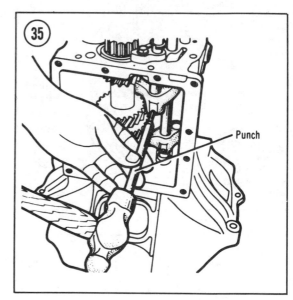

Table 9   SPACERS (4-SPEED TRANSMISSION)

Thickness	Color Code
0.033 in. (0.84 mm)	Black
0.037 in. (0.93 mm)	None
0.040 in. (1.02 mm)	Red
0.044 in. (1.11 mm)	White
0.047 in. (1.20 mm)	Yellow
0.051 in. (1.29 mm)	Blue
0.054 in. (1.38 mm)	Green

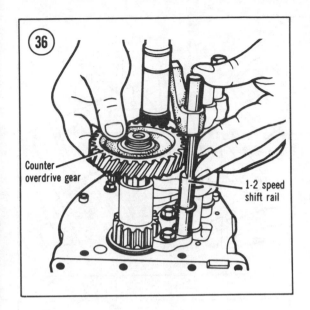

Counter overdrive gear

1-2 speed shift rail

Disassembly
(5-Speed Transmission, KM119)

1. Remove clutch and related parts (refer to *Clutch* section earlier in this chapter).

2. Drain transmission oil and remove inspection cover.

3. Remove backup light switch, then remove steel ball from extension housing.

4. Remove extension housing assembly as follows:

    a. Loosen mounting bolts.

    b. Loosen neutral return plunger B plug, then place gearshift lever in reverse and pull extension housing out rearward.

5. Remove snap ring, speedometer drive gear, and steel ball. Also, remove gear front snap ring.

6. Remove snap ring, main shaft rear bearing, and bearing front snap ring.

7. Remove reverse idler gear and related parts. Pull off split pin, loosen the nut, remove thrust washer, needle bearing, gear, and spacer bushing. Pull reverse idler shaft out of case.

8. Loosen the main shaft intermediate locknut. Loosen and remove countershaft gear rear end locknut.

NOTE: *The main shaft intermediate locknut cannot be removed. Therefore, loosen it only by straightening the lockwasher and loosening the nut. (It*

can be loosened easily by double-engaging the reverse and 2nd gears.)

9. Remove split pin which retains the 1-2 and 3-4 speed shift forks to the respective split rail, with a $\frac{3}{16}$ in. punch (**Figure 35**).

10. Pull 1-2 speed shift rail toward rear of case. Remove counter overdrive gear and ball bearing simultaneously with the rail (**Figure 36**).

11. Pull the 3-4 speed shift rail out toward rear of case, then remove the main shaft nut.

12. Remove overdrive/reverse synchronizer assembly, the overdrive gear, and the overdrive reverse shift rail and shift fork at the same time. Also, remove the spacer.

13. Remove 2 interlock plungers, spacer and counter reverse gear, rear retainer, and front bearing retainer (remove the spacer).

14. Insert Colt special tool MD998244 (Rear Stop Plate) between clutch gear and synchronizer ring of 3rd speed gear, and Colt tool MD998243 (Front Stop Plate) between clutch gear and synchronizer gear of main drive gear.

CAUTION
*The front and rear stop plates mentioned in Step 14 are special tools used to prevent the 3-4 speed synchronizer from damage by the main drive gear bushing and the main shaft gear bushing when these bearings are removed or installed. These tools must be inserted into their respective positions as shown in **Figure 37**. The front stop plate is identified by an "F" mark; the rear stop with an "R" mark.*

15. Remove the main shaft bearing snap ring. Then remove the ball bearing (**Figure 38**). Slide special Colt tool MD998241 (Main shaft Support) in place of the bearing over the main shaft, to support the main shaft (**Figure 39**).

16. Remove the main drive gear bearing snap rings (big and small). Pull off bearing with Colt tool MD998056 (Bearing Puller). See **Figure 40**.

17. Remove special tools front and rear stop plates. Then remove countershaft gear front bearing snap ring and pull off countershaft gear front bearing with Colt tool MD998246 (Countershaft Gear Bearing), as shown in **Figure 41**.

9

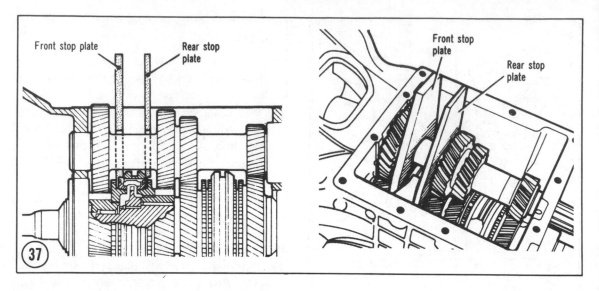

Front stop plate

Rear stop plate

Front stop plate

Rear stop plate

(37)

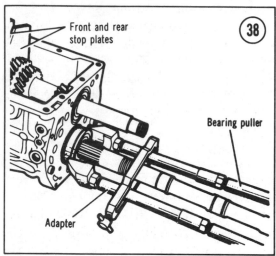

Front and rear stop plates

Bearing puller

Adapter

(38)

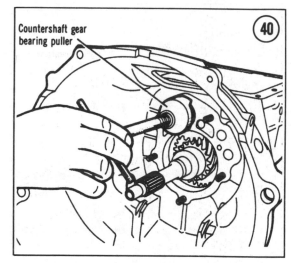

Countershaft gear bearing puller

(40)

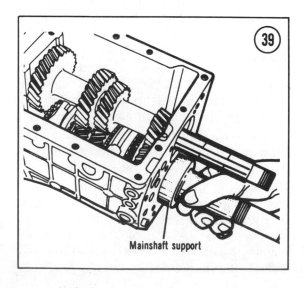

Mainshaft support

(39)

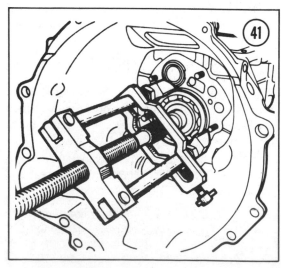

(41)

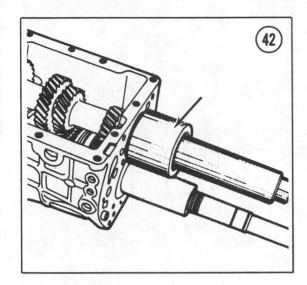

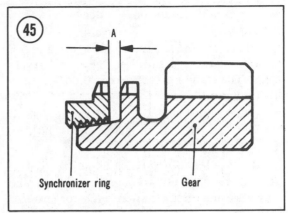

Synchronizer ring   Gear

18. Remove countershaft gear rear bearing snap ring, then remove countershaft gear rear bearing (**Figure 42**) with special Colt tool MD998192 (Countershaft Gear Bearing Puller).

19. Pull off special tool mainshaft adapter, then lower main shaft assembly and take 1st speed gear rear bearing spacer out of the case.

20. Shift 3-4 speed synchronizer sleeve to 3rd speed side to permit easy removal of countershaft gear without interference with the sleeve (**Figure 43**).

21. Remove countershaft gear and washer; snap ring from countershaft gear; sub gear and spring; and 1-2 and 3-4 speed shift forks.

22. Remove main drive gear.

23. Remove main shaft assembly (**Figure 44**). Disassemble main shaft related parts. Be sure to lay out the parts in the exact order in which you disassemble them (the synchronizer hub; sleeve; piece and spring; and bearings for 3-4 speed) to prevent confusion with the 1-2 speed parts.

Inspection

Check transmission case and extension housing for cracks and damage. In addition, perform the following checks:

1. Check main shaft, main drive gear, and all other gears for excessive gear or damage.

2. Check clutch gear teeth for wear and damage.

3. Check synchronizer ring for wear or damaged internal threads. With synchronizer assembled to the cone of each gear, check dimension A, **Figure 45**. If less than 0.032 in. (0.8 mm), replace synchronizer ring.

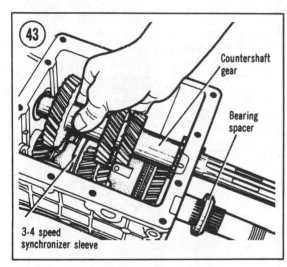

Countershaft gear

Bearing spacer

3-4 speed synchronizer sleeve

9

4. Check shift fork groove in sleeve for wear or damage.

5. Check clearance between shift fork and fork groove of the synchronizer sleeve and reverse gear. The standard clearance is 0.004-0.012 in. (0.1-0.3 mm).

6. Check the clearance between the selector and change lever. It should be 0.004-0.012 in. (0.1-0.3 mm).

7. Replace any bearing that makes noise when turned, or does not rotate smoothly. Replace any bearing that shows signs of external damage.

8. Check springs for breakage or deterioration. The standard lengths for the various springs are as follows:

   a. Poppet spring (for 3-4 speed and R-OT): free length, 0.744 in. (18.9 mm); load, 8.8 lb. @ 0.598 in. (4kg @ 15.2 mm).

   b. Poppet spring (for 1-2 speed): free length, 1.236 in. (31.4 mm); load, 8.8 lb. @ 1.091 in. (4 kg @ 27.7 mm).

   c. Neutral return spring: free length, 1.638 in. (41.6 mm); load, 8.8 lb. @ 1.244 in. (4 kg @ 31.6 mm).

   d. Resistance spring: free length, 1.091 in. (27.7 mm); load, 13.9 lb. @ 0.886 in. (6.3 kg @ 22.5 mm).

Reassembly
(5-Speed Transmission, KM119)

When reassembling the transmission, be sure to use new gaskets, oil seals, lock pins, and spring pins. Be sure all components are clean. Apply oil to sliding and rotating parts of bearings and gears. Fill oil seal lips with fresh grease. Use sealant on gaskets where indicated in the procedural steps.

1. Assemble main shaft assembly as follows:

   a. Slide 3rd speed gear and needle bearing over main shaft (from the front).

   b. Install synchronizer ring, then assemble 3-4 speed synchronizer hub and sleeve. Insert synchronizer pieces, then install springs as shown in **Figure 46**.

   c. Install assembled 3-4 speed synchronizer assembly on main shaft, with synchronizer piece fitted into the ring groove in

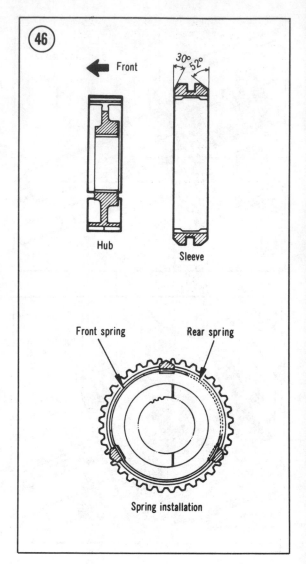

Hub

Sleeve

Front

Front spring　　　　Rear spring

Spring installation

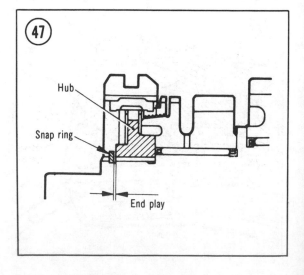

Hub

Snap ring

End play

Table 10   SNAP RINGS (5-SPEED KM119 TRANSMISSION)

Thickness	Identification Color
0.085 in. (2.15 mm)	Blue
0.087 in. (2.22 mm)	None
0.090 in. (2.29 mm)	Brown
0.093 in. (2.36 mm)	White

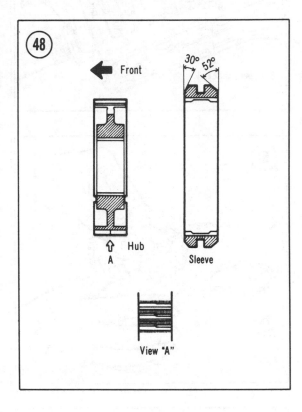

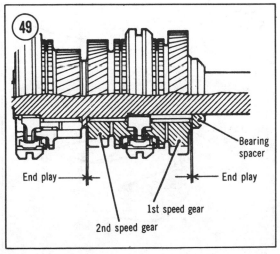

the synchronizer. Install a selected snap ring (from **Table 10**) so that synchronizer hub will have an end play of 0-0.003 in. (0-0.08 mm), and 3rd speed gear will have an end play of 0.001-0.007 in. (0.03-0.019 mm). See **Figure 47**. Check to be sure that 3rd gear rotates smoothly.

d. Slide 2nd speed gear and needle bearing over main shaft from rear end.

e. Install synchronizer ring.

f. Assemble 1-2 speed synchronizer hub and sleeve in direction shown in **Figure 48**. Insert synchronizer piece and install spring. The hub and sleeve should be assembled as shown in **Figure 48**. The spring should be installed in the same manner as the 3-4 speed synchronizer spring.

g. Install assembled 1-2 speed synchronizer assembly on main shaft (be sure that the synchronizer piece fits into the groove in the synchronizer).

h. Install the synchronizer ring on the synchronizer piece. Install 1st speed gear, needle bearing, and sleeve.

i. Install bearing spacer. Check to be sure that the bearing spacer is pressed firmly forward, then turn 1st and 2nd speed gears to see if they rotate smoothly. If these 2 gears have end play in excess of 0.001-0.007 in. (0.03-0.019 mm), check gear and hub ends for wear and replace if necessary (**Figure 49**).

j. Insert the assembled main shaft into transmission case.

k. Install synchronizer ring and needle bearing to main drive gear, then insert main drive gear into transmission case from the front.

l. Slide 2nd speed gear and needle bearing over main shaft (from the rear end). Then install synchronizer ring.

m. Assemble 1-2 speed synchronizer hub and sleeve in direction shown in **Figure 48**. Insert synchronizer piece and install the synchronizer spring. The hub and sleeve should be assembled as shown in **Figure 48**. The spring should be installed in the same manner as the 3-4 speed synchronizer spring.

n. Install assembled 1-2 speed synchronizer assembly on the main shaft, fitting the synchronizer piece into the groove in the synchronizer.

o. Install the synchronizer ring on the synchronizer piece. Install 1st speed gear, needle bearing and sleeve.

p. Install bearing spacer. When bearing spacer is pressed forward, 1st and 2nd speed gears should rotate smoothly. If end play is beyond 0.001-0.007 in. (0.03-0.19 mm), check gear and hub ends for wear, and replace if necessary (**Figure 49**).

2. Insert assembled main shaft into transmission case.

3. Install synchronizer ring and needle bearing to main drive gear, then insert the main drive gear into transmission case from the front.

4. Install 1-2 speed and 3-4 speed shift forks. Then shift the 3-4 speed synchronizer sleeve to 3rd speed side until 1st speed gear rear bearing spacer is out of case (**Figure 50**). After this operation, it is easy to insert the countershaft gear into the case.

5. Install sub gear spring on countershaft gear (**Figure 51**).

> NOTE: *Insert the longer leg of the spring into the countershaft gear (Figure 51).*

6. Install the sub gear and fit the shorter leg of the spring into it (**Figure 52**).

7. Insert a rod 0.315 in. (8 mm) in diameter x 1.4 in. (35 mm) in length into the 0.315 in. (8 mm) diameter hole in the countershaft gear, from the rear. Turn the sub gear in direction of arrow (**Figure 53**) until the 0.315 in. (8 mm) diameter hole is aligned with the rod. Insert the rod.

CAUTION
Do not force the gear tooth to turn the sub gear. Turn it with a rod inserted into one of its 4 holes, 0.236 in. (6 mm) in diameter, as shown in Figure 53.

8. Install a washer in front of the snap ring which is fitted on the countershaft gear forward

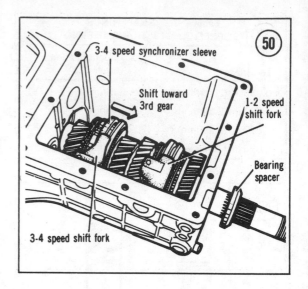
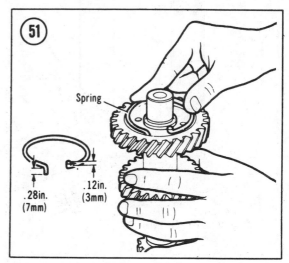
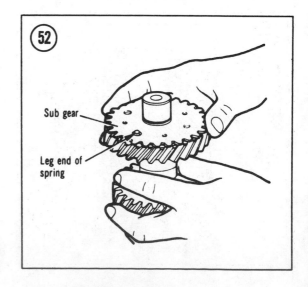

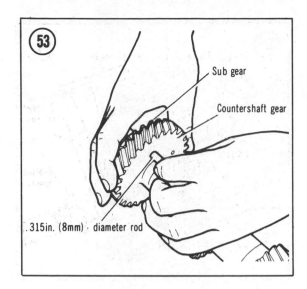

Sub gear

Countershaft gear

.315 in. (8mm) diameter rod

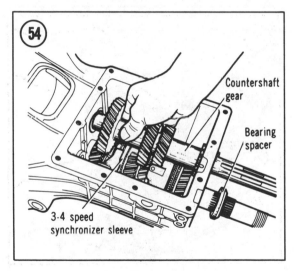

Countershaft gear

Bearing spacer

3-4 speed synchronizer sleeve

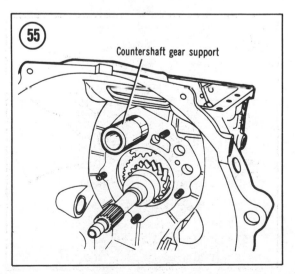

Countershaft gear support

end. Then install the countershaft gear assembly into the transmission case. See **Figure 54**.

> CAUTION
> *Be sure that a washer is installed in front of the countershaft gear. Place a dowel pin under the countershaft gear, to temporarily locate the sub gear (the pin, positioned above or beside the countershaft, will interfere with insertion of a special tool, stopper plate).*

9. Insert Colt tool MD998242 (Countershaft Gear Support) into case to support the counter gear (**Figure 55**).

10. Install the snap ring, then install countershaft gear bearing, using Colt tool MD998199 (Bearing Installer), as shown in **Figure 56**.

11. To install countershaft gear front bearing, install outer race only into the transmission case, then install the needle bearing.

> CAUTION
> *If the outer race and needle bearing is assembled prior to installation, it will damage the countershaft at the time of installation.*

12. To install the countershaft gear bearing, attach snap ring to outer race and drive bearing into place with an aluminum rod, tapping the circumference of the outer race evenly and lightly (**Figure 57**).

> CAUTION
> *Do not force the outer race into position.*

9

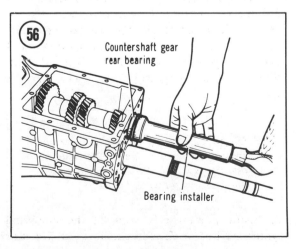

Countershaft gear rear bearing

Bearing installer

13. Install Colt tool MD998241 (Main Shaft Support) on main shaft rear end to support the main shaft (**Figure 58**).

14. Insert Colt tool MD998243 (Front Stop Plate) between main drive gear and synchronizer ring. Then insert Colt tool MD998244 (Rear Stop Plate) between 3rd speed gear and synchronizer ring, with stamped tool number on the tools facing the front of the transmission (**Figure 59**).

15. To Install main drive gear bearing, install snap ring on bearing, then drive bearing into position with Colt tool MD998029 (Bearing Installer), as shown in **Figure 60**. Install small snap ring on main drive gear. This snap ring must be selected and installed to obtain a clearance of 0-0.002 in. (0-0.06 mm) between the bearing inner face and the snap ring (**Figure 61**). Select the snap ring from **Table 11**.

16. Remove Colt Main Shaft Support tool. Then install snap ring on main shaft bearing. With Colt tool MD998067 (Bearing Installer), drive bearing into position (**Figure 62**). Then remove all special tools.

17. Remove dowel pin.

18. Install oil seal in front bearing retainer. Apply grease to oil seal lip and drive in oil seal with Colt tool MD998031 (Oil Seal Installer), as shown in **Figure 63**.

19. Prior to installing front bearing retainer, check clearance between front bearing retainer and main drive gear. Select and install a spacer from **Table 12** which will give a bearing-to-retainer clearance of 0-0.004 in. (0-0.1 mm), as shown in **Figure 64**. To measure this clearance, check amount that the bearing protrudes (A, **Figure 64**) from front end of case, and the depth (B, **Figure 64**) of the retainer. The

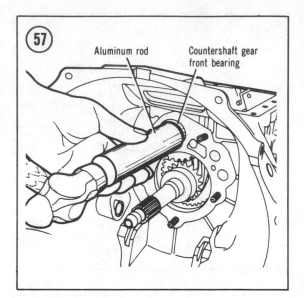

Aluminum rod   Countershaft gear front bearing

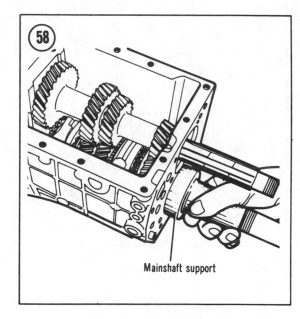

Mainshaft support

Table 11   SNAP RINGS
(5-SPEED KM119 TRANSMISSION)

Thickness	Identification Color
0.087 in. (2.21 mm)	Dark blue
0.089 in. (2.25 mm)	Brown
0.090 in. (2.29 mm)	Orange
0.092 in. (2.33 mm)	Blue
0.093 in. (2.36 mm)	Green

Table 12   SPACERS
(5-SPEED KM119 TRANSMISSION)

Thickness	Identification Color
0.033 in. (0.84 mm)	Black
0.037 in. (0.93 mm)	None
0.040 in. (1.02 mm)	Red
0.044 in. (1.11 mm)	White
0.047 in. (1.20 mm)	Yellow
0.051 in. (1.29 mm)	Blue
0.054 in. (1.38 mm)	Green

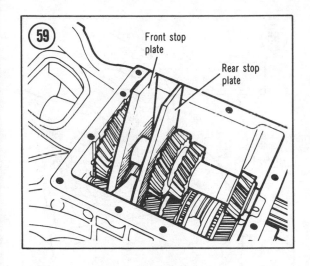

Front stop plate

Rear stop plate

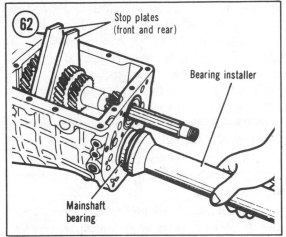

Stop plates (front and rear)

Bearing installer

Mainshaft bearing

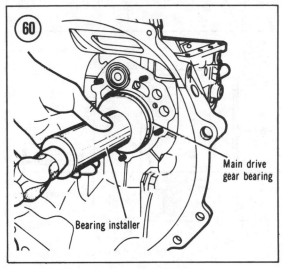

Main drive gear bearing

Bearing installer

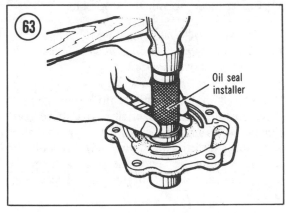

Oil seal installer

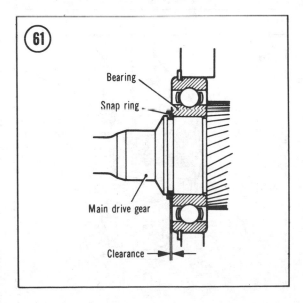

Bearing

Snap ring

Main drive gear

Clearance

9

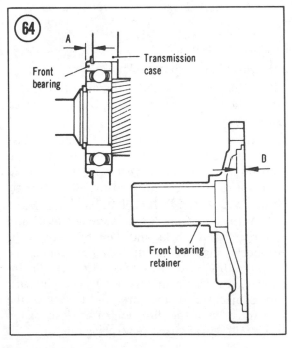

A

Transmission case

Front bearing

D

Front bearing retainer

thickness of the spacer is decided by the following formula: B + 0.3 in. (7.6 mm), which is the thickness of the gasket, − A + clearance.

20. Install front bearing retainer to transmission case. When installing retainer, apply sealant to retainer, then attach the gasket. Apply sealant to the case side of the gasket, then attach the retainer.

21. Install rear retainer.

22. Install counter reverse gear and spacer. Install gear with the relieved side facing the bearing (**Figure 65**).

23. Install 2 interlock plungers. Then assemble the overdrive-reverse synchronizer (**Figure 66**). Install synchronizer hub and sleeve. Install synchronizer piece, spring and stop plate.

> NOTE: *The synchronizer spring should be installed in the same manner as the 3-4 speed synchronizer.*

24. Install spacer on main shaft from the rear. Then install synchronizer ring, overdrive gear, needle bearing and sleeve to the synchronizer assembly (refer to **Figure 66**). Install the assembly, together with the overdrive-reverse shift fork and rod, on the main shaft (**Figure 67**).

> NOTE: *Assemble the shift fork and bar as outlined in Step 28, following. Always use a new spring pin.*

25. Install main shaft locknut.

26. Insert the 3-4 speed shift rail into the case from the rear, then into the 1-2 and 3-4 speed shift forks.

27. Insert the 1-2 speed shift rail into the case from the rear, then into the shift forks. Align the counter overdrive gear with the relieved portion of the shift rail and install both parts together (**Figure 68**). Install the ball bearing.

28. With spring pin holes of the 1-2 speed and 3-4 speed shift forks and their respective rails properly aligned, install spring pins into the holes with Colt tool MD998245 (Lock Pin Installer), as shown in **Figure 69**. The pin must not project out of the fork, and the slit of the pin must be in the direction of the axis of the shift rail. Always use a new spring pin.

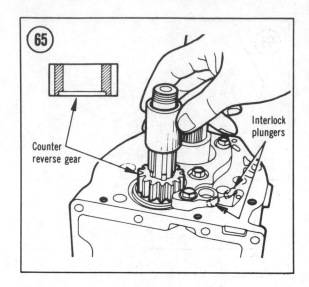

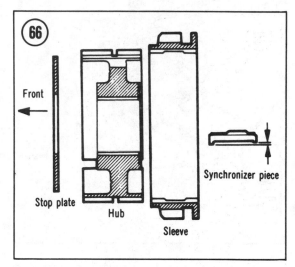

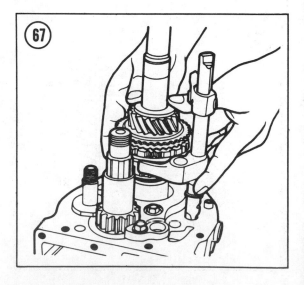

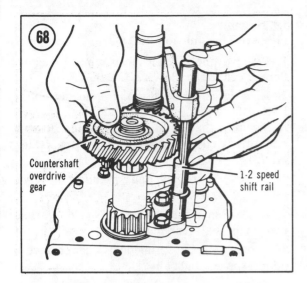

Countershaft overdrive gear

1-2 speed shift rail

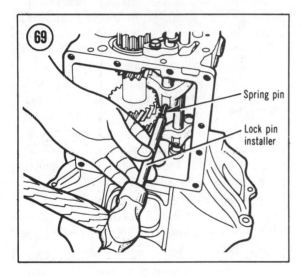

Spring pin

Lock pin installer

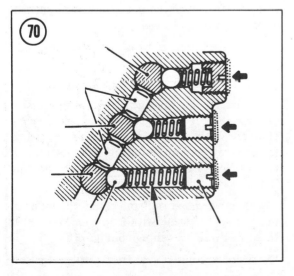

29. Install poppet balls and spring (**Figure 70**), then install plugs until they are flush with case surface. Apply sealant to secure them.

> NOTE: *The springs must be installed with their tapered ends facing inside (on the ball side). The free length of the 1-2 speed poppet spring is approximately 1.236 in. (31.4 mm), while the other springs are 0.744 in. (18.9 mm).*

30. Tighten main shaft locknut to 72-94 ft.-lb. (98.0-127.4 N•m); the countershaft gear locknut to 50-72 ft.-lb. (68.6-98.0 N•m). It is easy to perform these tightening procedures if you double-engage the 2nd speed and reverse gears. Stake the nuts after tightening them.

31. Insert reverse idler shaft into case. Install spacer bushing, gear, needle bearing and thrust washer. Tighten nut to 15-43 ft.-lb. (19.6-58.8 N•m), then align the slit in the nut with the split pin hole of the shaft and insert a split pin to lock the nut in position.

> NOTE: *The thrust washer must be installed with the ground side on the gear side.*

32. Install rear ball bearing on main shaft. Install snap ring, either a red one, 0.0591 in. (1.5 mm), or a white one, 0.0630 in. (1.6 mm), to obtain a clearance of 0-0.007 in. (0-0.17 mm) between bearing inner race and snap ring.

33. Install speedometer drive gear and snap ring.

34. Install extension housing parts as follows:

   a. Insert the control shaft into the extension housing from the front of the housing. Install the neutral return finger and change shifter. Apply grease to the surface of the rear portion of the shaft, then align lock pin holes in control shaft with those in the neutral return finger, and change shifter and insert lock pins into their respective holes (**Figure 71**).

   b. Drive the lock pin into the neutral return finger, through the sealing plug hole in the top of the housing. Insert the sealing plug into the hole and apply sealant.

   c. Insert speedometer driven gear into sleeve and drive spring pin into pin hole with the

9

slit positioned on the opposite side of the driven gear shaft. Replace O-ring with a new one (apply gear oil to the shaft prior to installing the O-ring). See **Figure 72**.

d. Insert speedometer driven gear and sleeve into extension housing. Then install locking plate. Apply sealant to external surface of sleeve.

e. Drive oil seal into rear of extension housing. Tap oil seal evenly around circumference to avoid deforming it. Apply gear oil to oil seal lip.

35. Install extension housing assembly on case. Apply sealant to extension housing side of gasket, and sealant to the other side. Also apply sealant to threads of the 2 lower attaching bolts.

> NOTE: *When installing extension housing, tilt change shifter fully down and to the left (Figure 73) and fit change lever into the groove in the selector. If speedometer drive gear interferes with the speedometer driven gear during installation of extension housing, do not force the housing into position. Instead, rotate speedometer driven gear shaft slightly until the mating is easily completed. Install backup light switch cord fastener at this time.*

36. Install neutral return plungers A and B, springs and steel ball, and resistance spring. Screw in the plugs until their heads are flush with the boss surfaces. Seal plug heads with sealant (**Figure 74**).

> NOTE: *The free length of the resistance spring is approximately 1.10 in. (28 mm), the remaining 2 springs, 1.65 in. (42 mm).*

37. Apply sealant to backup light switch threads prior to installation.

> NOTE: *Be sure to insert the steel ball.*

38. Install under cover and gasket. Tighten bolts to 6-7 ft.-lb. (7.8-9.8 N•m).

39. Install transmission control lever assembly after applying grease to plastic bushing at lower end of control lever and change shifter.

40. Install clutch and related parts (refer to *Clutch* section earlier in this chapter).

Disassembly
(5-Speed Transmission, KM132)

1. Remove under cover, then remove backup light switch (do not lose steel ball).

2. Remove extension housing attaching bolts. Back off the plug of the neutral return plunger B, then turn change shifter down to the left and pull off extension housing to the rear (**Figure 75**).

3. Remove snap ring and speedometer drive gear.

4. Remove snap ring, then remove ball bearing from main shaft rear end.

5. Loosen 3 poppet spring plugs, then remove 3 poppet springs and balls.

6. Pull off 3-4 and 1-2 speed shift fork spring pins (drive out with a $3/16$ in. punch as shown in **Figure 76**). Pull each shift rail off toward rear of transmission case, then remove shift fork. Take out interlock plunger.

7. Pull off overdrive and reverse shift forks spring pins by driving out with a $3/16$ in. punch (**Figure 77**). Then remove shift rails and forks.

8. Bend lockwasher back and loosen locknuts (main shaft and countershaft rear ends). The nuts can be easily loosened by double-engaging the reverse and 2nd gears (**Figure 78**).

9. Pull off counter overdrive gear and ball bearing together, with a commercial puller. Then remove spacer and counter reverse gear (**Figure 79**).

10. Remove overdrive gear and sleeve from main shaft. Then remove overdrive synchronizer assembly and spacer.

11. Remove split pin, loosen the nut, and remove reverse idler gear.

12. Remove rear bearing retainer (**Figure 80**).

13. Drive reverse idler gear shaft from outside the case (**Figure 81**). Remove the front bearing retainer. With counter gear pressed rearward, remove rear bearing snap ring. Then, with Colt tool MD998192, remove counter rear bearing (**Figure 82**).

14. Remove snap ring from counter front bearing. Pull off bearing with Colt tool MD998192 (Bearing Puller), as shown in **Figure 83**.

15. Remove counter gear from inside the case.

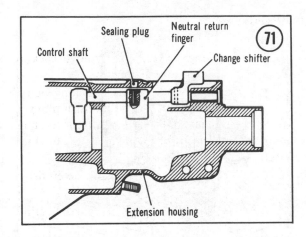

71

Control shaft
Sealing plug
Neutral return finger
Change shifter
Extension housing

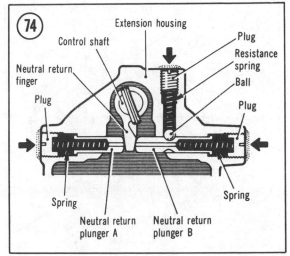

74

Extension housing
Control shaft
Neutral return finger
Plug
Resistance spring
Ball
Plug
Plug
Spring
Spring
Neutral return plunger A
Neutral return plunger B

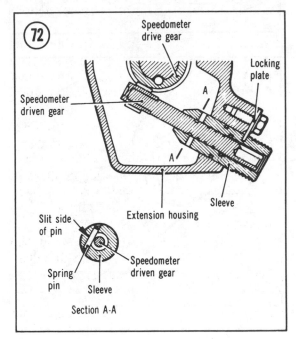

72

Speedometer drive gear
Speedometer driven gear
Locking plate
A
A
Sleeve
Extension housing
Slit side of pin
Spring pin
Sleeve
Speedometer driven gear
Section A-A

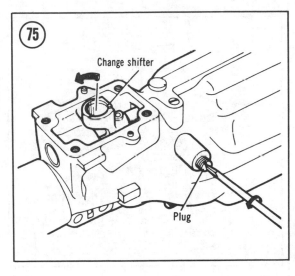

75

Change shifter
Plug

9

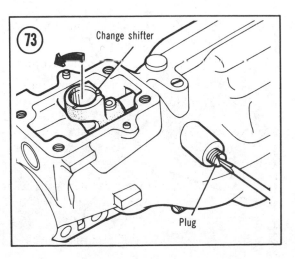

73

Change shifter
Plug

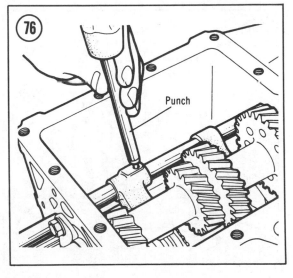

76

Punch

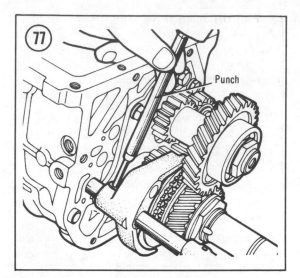

Punch

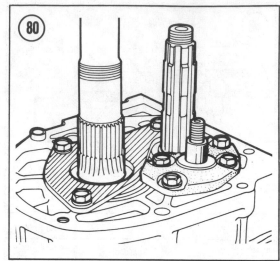

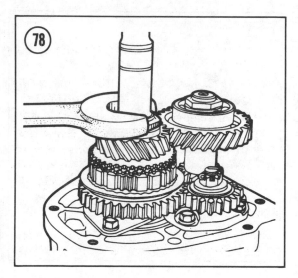

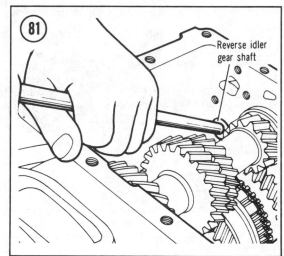

Reverse idler
gear shaft

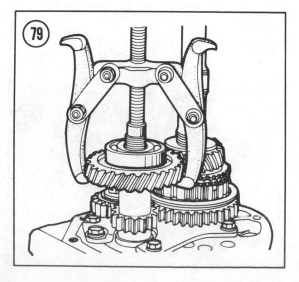

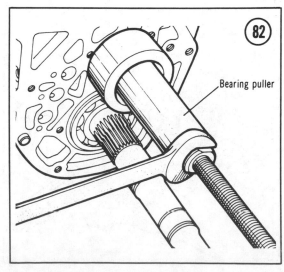

Bearing puller

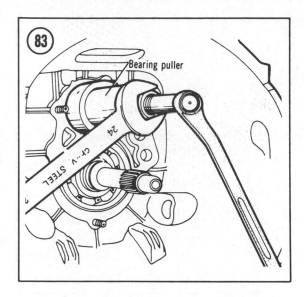

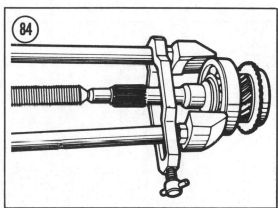

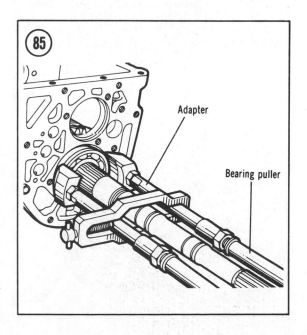

16. Pull off main drive pinion from front of case. To remove bearing from main drive pinion, remove 2 snap rings, then remove bearing with Colt tool MD998056 (Bearing Puller), as shown in **Figure 84**.

17. Remove main shaft bearing snap ring, then remove ball bearing (**Figure 85**).

18. Pull main shaft assembly out of case (**Figure 86**). Disassemble the main shaft in the following order:

   a. Pull off 1st speed gear; 1-2 speed synchronizer; and 2nd speed gear toward rear of main shaft.

   b. Remove snap ring from forward end of main shaft, then remove 3-4 speed synchronizer and 3rd speed gear.

19. To disassemble the extension housing, proceed as follows:

   a. Remove locking plate, then the speedometer drive gear.

   b. Remove plug, then the resistance spring and neutral return plunger (**Figure 87**).

   c. When removing control shaft assembly, pull off lock pin holding the gear shifter in place, with a $\frac{3}{16}$ in. punch. Press the gear shifter forward and pull lock pin off. Do not bend control shaft (**Figure 88**).

Inspection

Refer to *Inspection* section for *5-Speed Transmission (KM119)*, earlier in this chapter. Procedures are identical.

9

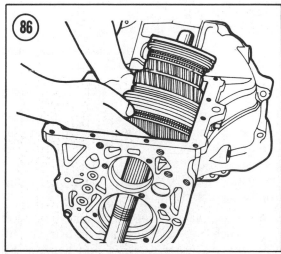

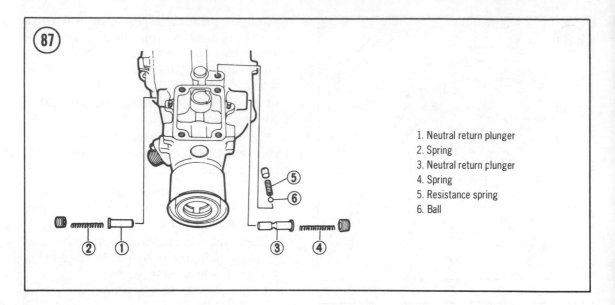

87

1. Neutral return plunger
2. Spring
3. Neutral return plunger
4. Spring
5. Resistance spring
6. Ball

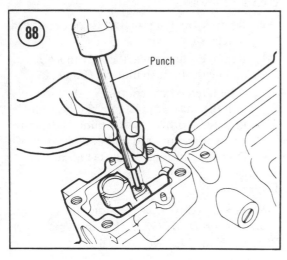

88

Punch

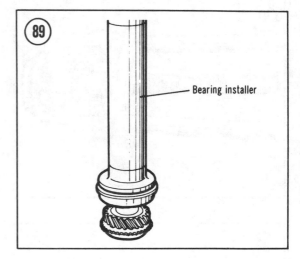

89

Bearing installer

Reassembly
(5-Speed Transmission, KM132)

1. Install ball bearing on main drive pinion with Colt tool MD998029 (Bearing Installer), as shown in **Figure 89**.

2. Install the bearing, then install the snap ring on the drive pinion (**Figure 90**). Install a selective snap ring from **Table 13**, so that the clearance between the snap ring and bearing is 0-0.002 in. (0-0.06 mm).

3. Install the main shaft assembly in the following order (refer to **Figure 91**):

   a. Assemble the 3-4 speed and 1-2 speed synchronizers. The front and rear ends of the synchronizer sleeve and hub can be

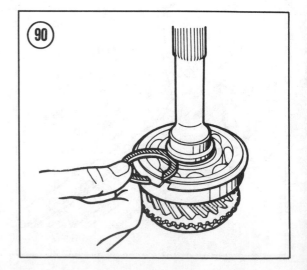

90

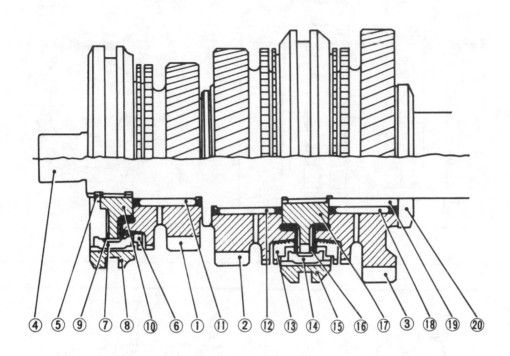

MAIN SHAFT

1. 3rd speed gear
2. 2nd speed gear
3. 1st speed gear
4. Mainshaft
5. Snap ring
6. Synchronizer ring
7. Synchronizer piece
8. Synchronizer sleeve
9. Synchronizer spring
10. Synchronizer hub

11. Needle bearing
12. Needle bearing
13. Synchronizer ring
14. Synchronizer piece
15. Synchronizer sleeve
16. Synchronizer spring
17. Synchronizer hub
18. Needle bearing
19. 1st gear bearing sleeve
20. Bearing spacer

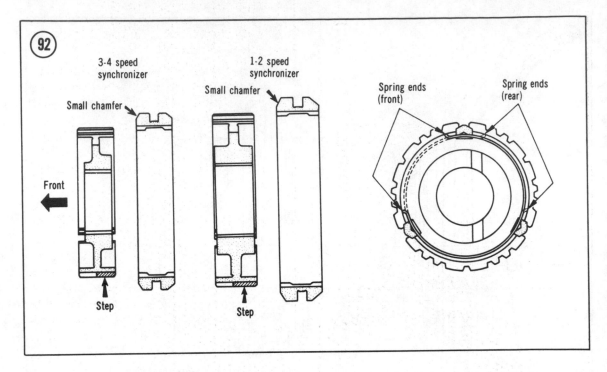

3-4 speed synchronizer

1-2 speed synchronizer

Small chamfer

Small chamfer

Spring ends (front)

Spring ends (rear)

Front

Step

Step

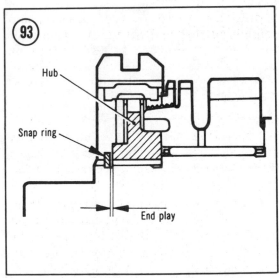

Hub

Snap ring

End play

Table 13   SNAP RINGS
(5-SPEED KM132 TRANSMISSION)

Thickness	Identification Color
0.091 in. (2.30 mm)	White
0.092 in. (2.35 mm)	None
0.094 in. (2.40 mm)	Red
0.096 in. (2.45 mm)	Blue
0.098 in. (2.50 mm)	Yellow

Table 14   SNAP RINGS
(5-SPEED KM132 TRANSMISSION)

Thickness	Identification Color
0.085 in. (2.15 mm)	None
0.087 in. (2.22 mm)	Yellow
0.090 in. (2.29 mm)	Green
0.093 in. (2.36 mm)	White

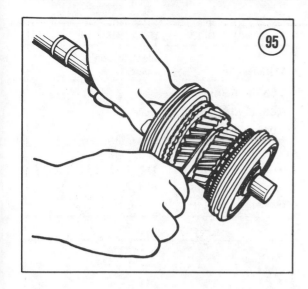

identified by referring to **Figure 92**. The synchronizer spring can be installed as shown in **Figure 92**.

b. Install the needle bearing, 3rd speed gear, synchronizer ring, and the 3-4 speed synchronizer assembly on the main shaft (from the front end).

c. Select a snap ring from **Table 14**, so that the 3-4 speed synchronizer hub end play will be 0-0.003 in. (0-0.08 mm). See **Figure 93**.

d. Check 3rd speed gear end play (**Figure 94**). It should be 0.002-0.008 in. (0.04-0.20 mm).

e. Install needle bearing, 2nd speed gear, synchronizer assembly, bearing sleeve, needle bearing, 1st speed gear, and bearing spacer on main shaft (from rear end). Press bearing spacer forward and check 2nd and 1st speed gear end play (**Figure 95**). It should be 0.002-0.008 in. (0.04-0.20 mm).

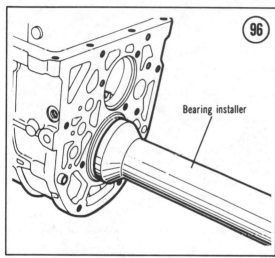

Bearing installer

4. Insert assembled main shaft assembly into transmission case and drive in the main shaft center bearing with Colt MD998067 (Bearing Installer). When installing, hold forward end of main shaft by hand at the front of the case (**Figure 96**).

5. Install needle bearing and synchronizer ring, then insert main drive pinion assembly into case (from the front). With a brush, rub clutch grease onto the splines on which the clutch disc will be installed.

6. Insert countershaft gear into the case. Then, with snap ring fitted to the countershaft front needle bearing, drive bearing into the case by hammering the outer race with a plastic hammer (**Figure 97**).

7. Install snap ring on countershaft rear ball bearing, then install it in place with Colt tool MD998199 (Bearing Installer), as shown in **Figure 98**.

8. Install front bearing retainer. Select and install a spacer from **Table 15**, so that clearance **C, Figure 99,** will be 0-0.004 in. (0-0.10 mm).

Apply sealant to both sides of front bearing retainer gaskets, and gear oil to the oil seal lip. Then install gasket and oil seal.

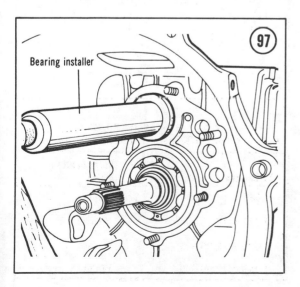

Bearing installer

9

9. Replace front bearing retainer oil seal with Colt tool MD998200 (Oil Seal Installer), **Figure 100**.

10. Install rear bearing retainer.

11. Install reverse idler gear shaft. When installing shaft, install bolts by using a guide as shown in **Figure 101**.

12. Install needle bearing, reverse idler gear, and thrust washer. Lock with a nut and split pin. Check reverse idler gear end play (**Figure 102**). It should be 0.005-0.011 in. (0.12-0.28 mm).

13. Install thrust washer with ground side facing gear side.

14. Assemble overdrive synchronizer, and install spring in same manner as on the 3-4 and 1-2 speed synchronizer springs (**Figure 103**).

15. Install spacer, stop plate, overdrive synchronizer assembly, overdrive gear bearing sleeve, needle bearing, synchronizer ring, and overdrive gear in the order removed (working from the rear end). Tighten locknut, then lock it at the notch of the main shaft. Be sure that overdrive gear end play is 0.004-0.010 in. (0.1-0.25 mm), as shown in **Figure 104**.

16. Install spacer, counter reverse gear, spacer, counter overdrive gear, and ball bearing on the countershaft gear (from the rear). After tightening the nut, lock the nut at the notch at the rear end of the counter shaft gear.

17. Insert 3-4 and 1-2 speed shift forks into respective synchronizer sleeves. Insert each shift rail from rear of case. Lock shift forks and rails with spring pins. Install an interlock plunger between shifter rails.

> NOTE: *The spring pin should be installed with the slit in the axial direction of the shift rail.*

18. Insert ball and poppet spring into each shift rail. Tighten plug to position shown in **Figure 105**. Install poppet spring with small end on ball side. Then seal plug head with sealant.

19. Install ball bearing on rear end of main shaft, then install speedometer drive gear.

20. Apply sealant to both sides of extension housing gasket. Then install gasket on housing, and install extension housing on transmission case.

Table 15	SPACERS (5-SPEED KM132 TRANSMISSION)
Thickness	**Identification Color**
0.033 in. (0.84 mm)	Black
0.037 in. (0.93 mm)	None
0.040 in. (1.02 mm)	Red
0.044 in. (1.11 mm)	White
0.047 in. (1.20 mm)	Yellow
0.051 in. (1.29 mm)	Blue
0.054 in. (1.38 mm)	Green

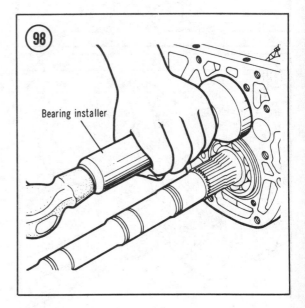

Bearing installer

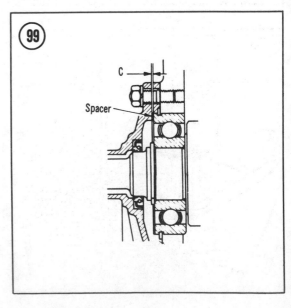

C

Spacer

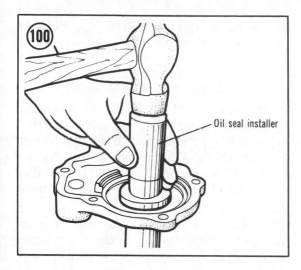

(100)

Oil seal installer

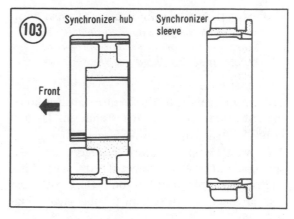

(103) Synchronizer hub   Synchronizer sleeve

Front

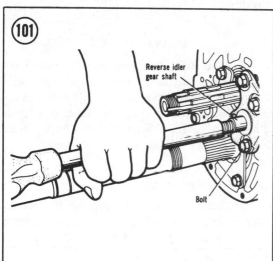

(101)

Reverse idler gear shaft

Bolt

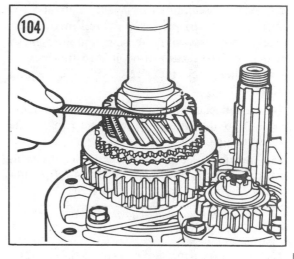

(104)

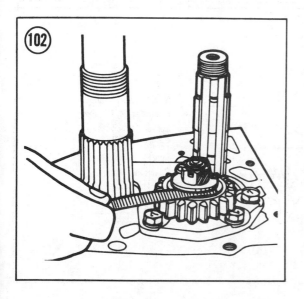

(102)

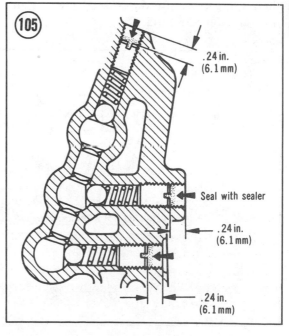

(105)

.24 in. (6.1 mm)

Seal with sealer

.24 in. (6.1 mm)

.24 in. (6.1 mm)

9

NOTE: *When installing housing, turn change shifter fully down to the left. Be sure that the forward end of the control finger is snugly fitted into the shift lug slot.*

21. Apply sealant to threds of extension housing attaching bolts prior to installation. Tighten bolts evenly.

22. Install neutral return plungers and the spring, and the resistance spring and ball. Tighten each plug until its top is flush with boss top surface. Apply sealant to plug head (**Figure 106**).

23. Apply sealant to outside surface of speedometer driven gear sleeve, then insert sleeve into extension housing and into mesh with the drive gear. Insert it into the locking plate, then lock the sleeve with the locking plate.

24. Install back up light switch after applying sealant to the threads. (Be sure to insert the steel ball prior to installation.)

25. Install under cover, then tighten bolts to 6-7 ft.-lb. (7.8-9.8 N•m).

CAUTION
Do not overtighten bolts, or oil leakage will result.

26. Install transmission control lever assembly, then fill gear shifter area with grease, and transmission with fluid.

27. Install clutch and related parts. Refer to *Clutch* section earlier in this chapter.

AUTOMATIC TRANSMISSION

Maintenance and repair of the automatic transmission is complex and should be referred to your dealer or transmission specialist.

Figure 107 is a cutaway of the Borg-Warner automatic transmission used in 1973 and earlier Colts; **Figure 108** is the Torque-Flite automatic used in 1974 and later models.

See Chapter Three, *Lubrication, Maintenance, and Tune-up,* for checks and maintenance instructions which will save costly repairs if followed faithfully.

DRIVE SHAFT

The drive shafts for manual and automatic transmissions differ in length and have different sleeve yokes. Needle bearings are maintenance-free, sealed-for-life units that require no lubrication except when they have been disassembled. See **Figure 109**.

Drive Shaft Removal

1. Withdraw the bolts connecting the flange yoke to the differential pinion flange. Remove the drive shaft by pulling it out at its sleeve yoke end.

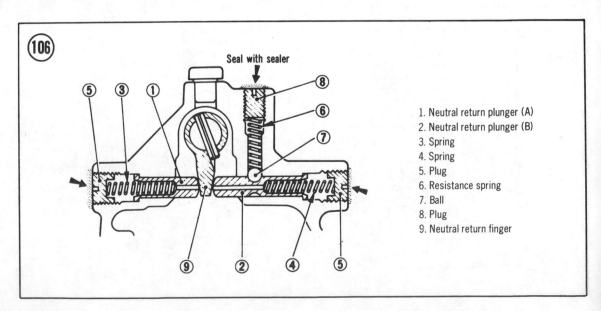

(106)

Seal with sealer

1. Neutral return plunger (A)
2. Neutral return plunger (B)
3. Spring
4. Spring
5. Plug
6. Resistance spring
7. Ball
8. Plug
9. Neutral return finger

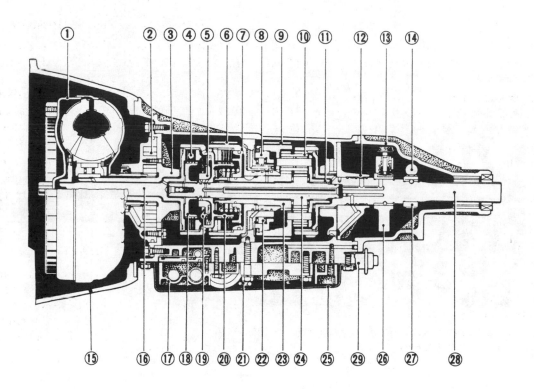

BORG-WARNER AUTOMATIC TRANSMISSION — 1971-1973

1. Torque converter
2. Oil pump gear
3. Pump adapter and converter support
4. Front clutch plate
5. Front clutch piston
6. Front brake band
7. Front drum
8. One-way clutch outer race
9. Rear brake band
10. Long pinion
11. Planet cover
12. Rear adapter
13. Extension housing
14. Speedometer driven gear

15. Conveter housing
16. Input shaft
17. Valve body assembly
18. Front clutch hub
19. Front clutch spring
20. Front clutch cylinder
21. Oil tube
22. One way clutch assembly
23. Reverse sun gear
24. Forward sun gear
25. Oil pan
26. Governor assembly
27. Speedometer drive gear
28. Output gear
29. Vacuum diaphragm

9

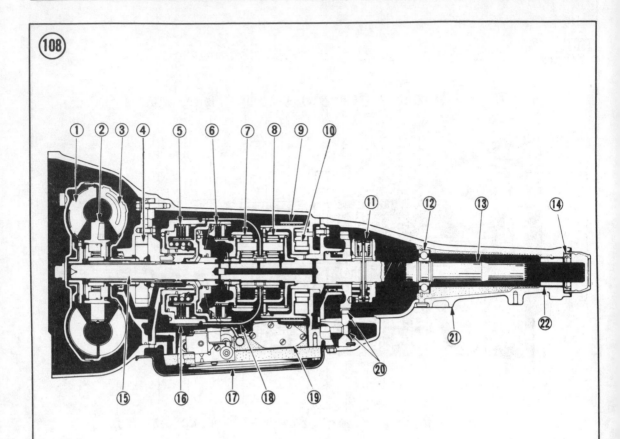

TORQUE-FLITE AUTOMATIC TRANSMISSION — 1974 ON

1. Turbine	12. Bearing
2. Stator	13. Output shaft
3. Impeller	14. Seal
4. Oil pump	15. Input shaft
5. Front clutch	16. Kickdown band
6. Rear clutch	17. Oil filter
7. Front planetary gear set	18. Sun gear driving shell
8. Rear planetary gear set	19. Valve body
9. Low and reverse band	20. Parking lock assembly
10. Overrunning clutch	21. Extension housing
11. Governor	22. Bushing

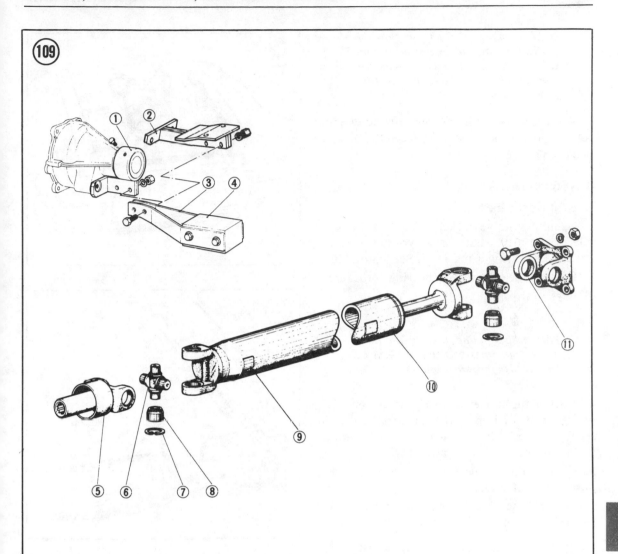

9

DRIVE SHAFT

1. Damper bracket
   (Borg-Warner type)
2. Damper bracket
   (Torque-Flite type)
3. Damper arm
4. Damper weight
5. Sleeve yoke
6. Universal joint journal
7. Snap ring
8. Needle roller bearing
9. Balance weight
10. Drive shaft
11. Flange yoke

NOTE: *Transmission oil will flow out of the transmission extension housing when the drive shaft has been removed, if the front end of the car is raised too high.*

2. When removing the drive shaft, be careful not to damage the oil seal lip. Keep the oil seal clean.

Drive Shaft Disassembly

1. Remove the snap ring.

2. Using a suitable socket applied to the outside of the drive shaft flange yoke, force out one needle bearing using a vise. See **Figure 110**.

3. Remove the other needle bearing in the same manner.

> CAUTION
> *When disassembling, note the positions of the snap rings so that they may be reinstalled in the same position.*

4. Inspect the universal joints. If evidence of pitting, rust, or impressions of needle roller is seen, replace both the universal joint journals and needle bearings as an assembly.

5. Replace the needle bearing assembly if the dust seal is defective.

6. Replace the sleeve yoke and transmission main shaft splines if worn or damaged.

Drive Shaft Assembly

1. Pack grease into each grease pit of the universal joint journals. Apply a thin coat of grease evenly to the needle bearings and journals.

> CAUTION
> *The bearing cap (outer race) will not fit in position properly if too much grease is placed in the grease pit.*

2. Apply a thin even coat of grease to the dust seal lips before assembly.

3. Install the needle bearings on the universal joint journals in the similar manner as provided for the removal of the needle bearings, using suitable sockets and a vise to reassemble each universal joint.

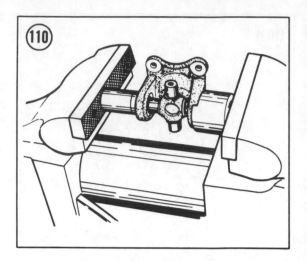

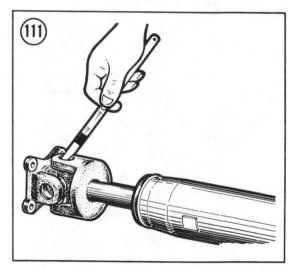

Table 16   SNAP RING SIZES

Part No.	Thickness	Color code
MA180905	0.0504 ± 0.0006 in.	
MA180906	0.0516 ± 0.0006 in.	Yellow
MA180907	0.0528 ± 0.0006 in.	Blue
MA180908	0.0539 ± 0.0006 in.	Purple

4. After the installation of the needle bearings, select 4 kinds of snap rings to adjust the snap ring-to-bearing end clearance to the standard value (**Table 16**).

> CAUTION
> *If possible, select snap rings of the same thickness on each pair of yokes in order to provide adequate balance to the drive shaft. See Figure 111.*

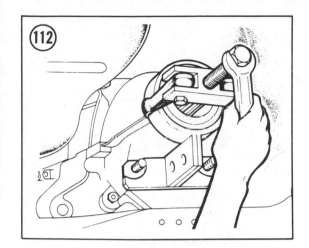

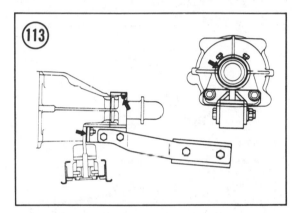

Drive Shaft Installation

1. Reverse the *Drive Shaft Removal* steps to install the drive shaft. Clean the outside surface of the sleeve yoke very carefully, apply gear oil, then install.

2. Tighten the flange yoke bolts to 18-21 ft.-lb. (1600cc and 2000cc engines) or 22-26 ft.-lb. (2600cc engines).

DYNAMIC DAMPER
(BORG-WARNER
AUTOMATIC TRANSMISSION)

Dynamic Damper Removal

1. Remove drive shaft.

2. Loosen damper arm connections. Remove damper.

3. Remove the damper bracket with a puller after loosening the bolt nuts connecting the damper bracket to the extension housing. See **Figure 112**.

CAUTION
DO NOT use a hammer to remove the damper bracket. The extension housing could be cracked or damaged. Use only a puller.

4. Check the damper bracket and arm for damage. Replace defective parts. Check each bolt nut for looseness. Tighten the loose nut to the standard torque value (**Table 17**).

Dynamic Damper Installation

1. Clean the faces of the extension housing and damper bracket (**Figure 113**). Remove all grease and oil. Apply a sufficient amount of adhesive to the faces, then insert the bracket. Clean and apply adhesive at the damper bracket and extension housing, the damper bracket and rear insulator bracket, and the threads of the damper bracket mounting bolts. Three-Bond 105Q or 103KG (Thread Lock Cement Super) adhesive is recommended.

NOTE: *Do not use gasoline or trichloroethylene to remove oil and grease from the joint faces.*

2. Tighten each mounting bolt to the standard torque value as found in **Table 5** within 15 minutes after applying the adhesive.

CAUTION
Avoid running the engine at high speeds (over 3,000 rpm) until the adhesive is fully set (about 3 hours).

DYNAMIC DAMPER
(TORQUE-FLITE
AUTOMATIC TRANSMISSION)

Dynamic Damper Removal

1. Remove drive shaft.

2. Remove damper by loosening the damper arm joint.

3. Remove damper bracket.

4. Check dynamic damper bracket and arm for damage or wear. Replace any defective part. Check each part for looseness.

Dynamic Damper Installation

Tighten the dynamic damper-to-extension housing locking bolts to 25-33 ft.-lb.

9

CHAPTER TEN

FRONT SUSPENSION AND STEERING

The Dodge Colt uses the strut-type front suspension which has a shock absorber made integral with a knuckle spindle and mounted with a coil spring. It is fixed to the wheelhouse at its upper end, and to the steering knuckle arm (wheel spindle) at its lower end. An oilless ball bearing is provided at the upper end of the strut assembly, and an oilless ball-joint at its lower end to allow smooth swing of the steering knuckle.

The front caster angles and wheel camber are fixed and require no alignment.

Road irregularities are absorbed by the coil spring installed on the respective shock absorbers and rebound of the coil springs is absorbed by the shock absorbers. A stabilizer bar is provided with the front suspension system to minimize body roll. Highly rigid shaped steel lower arms protect the front suspension from shocks applied to them along the car's longitudinal axis. See **Figure 1**.

The steering system uses a recirculating-ball steering gear of variable ratio, a height-adjustable tilting steering wheel, and a collapsible steering tube for safety in the event of an accident.

Ball-joints in the steering linkage utilize resin bearings which require no lubrication. See **Figure 2**.

FRONT AXLE HUB

Removal

Refer to **Figure 3** when performing the following procedure.

1. Set the parking brake and block rear wheels. Jack up front of car and support with jackstands.

2. Remove front wheel(s).

3. Examine **Figure 3** to familiarize yourself with the construction of the front axle hub assembly.

4. Remove hub cap, split pin and cap (locknut), and caliper assembly **(Figure 4)**.

5. Pull out brake disc and wheel hub, being careful not to drop outer wheel bearing cone.

6. Remove dust cover and disc brake adapter.

7. Service wheel bearings as described in *Wheel Bearing* section, this chapter.

Installation

1. Insert inner bearing into hub. Press in an oil seal as deep as the end of the hub with the lip directed inward.

2. Install wheel hub assembly on wheel spindle. Do not damage oil seal. Install outer bearing, plain washer, and the nut.

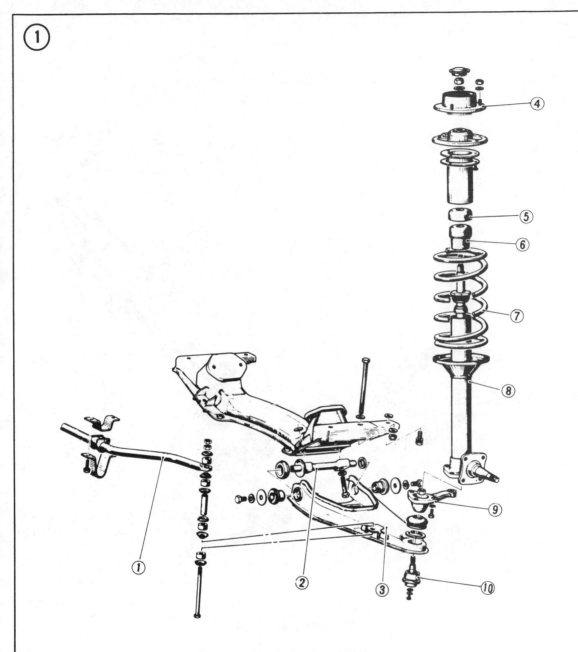

FRONT SUSPENSION

1. Stabilizer	6. Bumper rubber
2. Lower arm shaft	7. Front spring
3. Lower arm	8. Strut assembly
4. Strut insulator	9. Knuckle arm
5. Spacer	10. Lower ball-joint

10

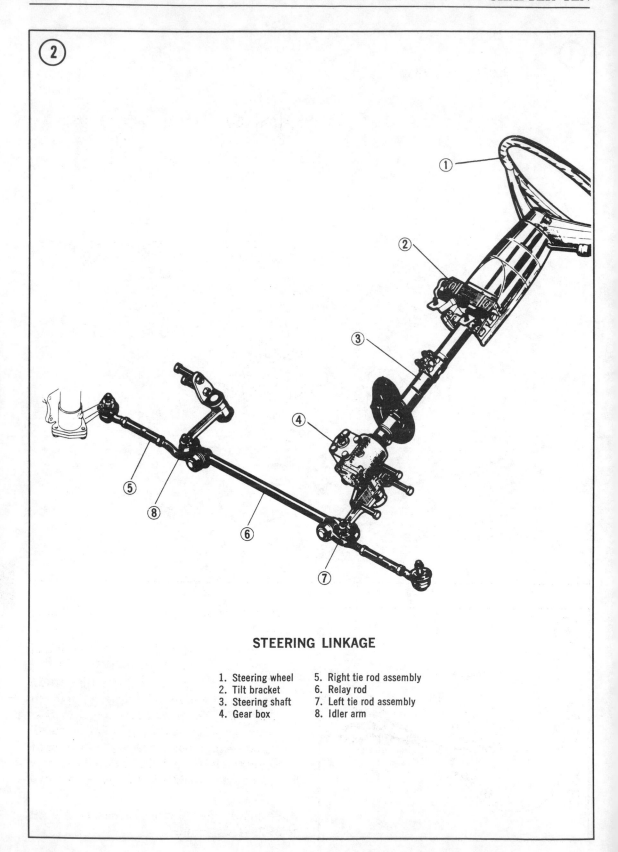

STEERING LINKAGE

1. Steering wheel
2. Tilt bracket
3. Steering shaft
4. Gear box

5. Right tie rod assembly
6. Relay rod
7. Left tie rod assembly
8. Idler arm

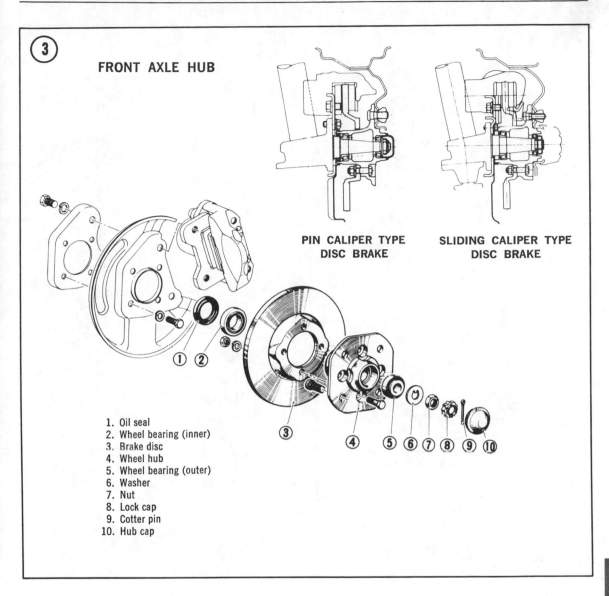

③

FRONT AXLE HUB

PIN CALIPER TYPE
DISC BRAKE

SLIDING CALIPER TYPE
DISC BRAKE

① ②

③

④ ⑤ ⑥ ⑦ ⑧ ⑨ ⑩

1. Oil seal
2. Wheel bearing (inner)
3. Brake disc
4. Wheel hub
5. Wheel bearing (outer)
6. Washer
7. Nut
8. Lock cap
9. Cotter pin
10. Hub cap

10

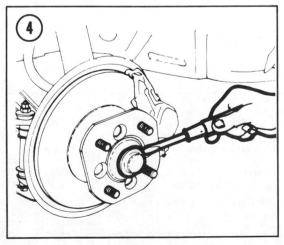

④

3. Adjust the bearing preload in the following manner:

   a. Tighten nut to 14.5 ft.-lb. to "settle" all assembled parts. Loosen to 0.0 ft.-lb.

   b. Tighten the nut again, this time to 3.6 ft.-lb. torque. Install the cap and split pin. Split the pin. However, if holes cannot be aligned after shifting position of the installed cap, loosen nut until a flute on the nut meets the split pin hole on the spindle. The nut should not be backed off over 15°.

4. Install disc brake caliper assembly. Tighten to 25-29 ft.-lb. torque.

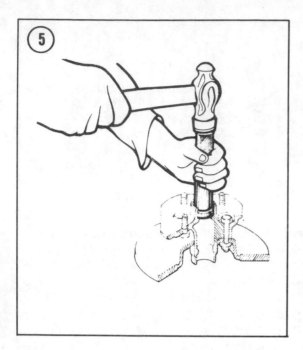

⑤

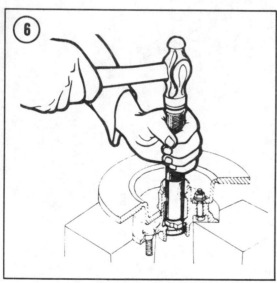

⑥

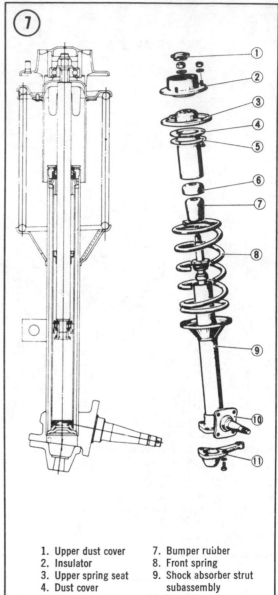

⑦

1. Upper dust cover
2. Insulator
3. Upper spring seat
4. Dust cover
5. Dust cover plate
6. Spacer
7. Bumper rubber
8. Front spring
9. Shock absorber strut subassembly
10. Knuckle
11. Knuckle arm

Table 1   WHEEL HUB AND BEARING GREASING

Description	Application
Bearing	Spread grease over and into rollers, using your fingers.
Oil seal	Apply just enough grease to provide proper lubrication without overflowing grease lip and dust lip.
Wheel hub	Coat evenly over inner wall.
Wheel hub cap	Fill cap completely.

Table 2   STRUT ASSEMBLY TORQUES

Description	Torque
Bolts retaining strut assembly to wheelhouse	7 - 10 ft.-lb.
Bolts retaining strut assembly to knuckle arm	29 - 36 ft.-lb.

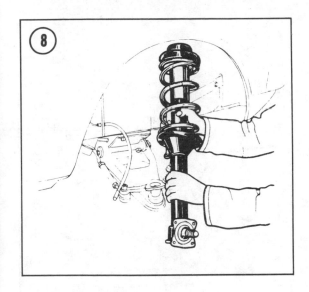

WHEEL BEARING

Removal

1. In order to work on the wheel bearing, perform Steps 1 through 6 in the *Front Axle Hub* section, preceding.

2. Remove grease inside wheel hub. Drive out bearing outer race (outer bearing), using a suitable drift pin as shown in **Figure 5**. The inner bearing outer race should be removed together with the oil seal.

Inspection

Inspect bearing for looseness, rough rotation, and damage of rollers and race curvature. Replace if necessary.

1. Coat grease evenly over outer surface of the bearing race.

2. Using a suitable drift pin, drive in the bearing outer race (**Figure 6**).

3. Pack grease in the bearing and wheel hub as specified in **Table 1**.

STRUT ASSEMBLY

Removal

1. Remove front wheel, caliper assembly, front hub with disc wheel, and dust cover (Steps 1 through 6, *Front Axle Hub* section, this chapter). See **Figure 7**.

2. Disconnect stabilizer link (see *Stabilizer*, this chapter). Remove strut assembly, knuckle arm,

and strut insulator retaining bolts. Remove strut assembly from wheelhouse (**Figure 8**).

> NOTE: *Special tools are required for disassembly of the strut. It is recommended that the strut assembly be taken to your dealer for servicing of the strut (coil spring/shock absorber) assembly.*

Installation

1. Fasten top of strut assembly to mounting bracket on wheelhouse. Apply a sealer (Three-Bond No. 4 or equivalent) to lower end of assembly. Connect it with bolts to the knuckle arm, with the dowel pins in their proper holes in the arm's flange surface. See **Table 2** for proper torque values.

2. Pack upper strut bearing with SAE J310a Multipurpose Lubricant (or equivalent). Install the dust cap.

3. Install stabilizer, hub assembly, and wheel.

STABILIZER

Removal

1. Set parking brake and block rear wheels. Jack up front of car and support with jackstands.

2. Remove front wheel(s). Slightly jack up lower part of lower arm and disconnect stabilizer link from lower arm.

3. Loosen stabilizer fixture locking bolts. Remove stabilizer.

Inspection

1. Check the stabilizer for cracks. Replace if defective.

2. Check stabilizer bushings and cushion rubber for cracks or deterioration. Replace any defective part.

Installation

1. Tighten stabilizer fixture to 7-10 ft.-lb. See **Figure 9**.

2. See **Figure 9**. When connecting both ends of the stabilizer, set the gap between the nut (A) and the top end of the bolt to 0.16-0.28 in. Hold the nut (A) with a wrench and securely tighten the nut (B).

10

LOWER ARM

Special tools are required to disassemble the lower arm assembly. However, since only a tie rod end puller (Special Tool CT-1116) is required to remove the lower arm, the following removal and installation steps are given. Actual disassembly of the lower arm assembly is best left to your dealer. See **Figure 10**.

Removal

1. Disconnect the stabilizer from the lower arm (see *Stabilizer* section, this chapter). Remove the strut assembly.

2. Using the tie rod end puller (Special Tool CT-1116, available from your Colt dealer), disconnect the steering knuckle arm and tie rod ball-joint (**Figure 11**).

3. Remove bolts holding lower arm to the sub-frame. Remove lower arm assembly.

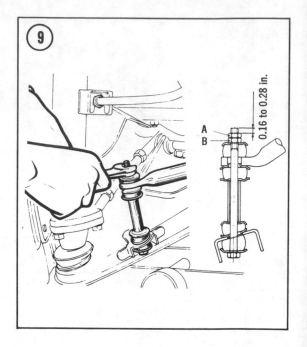

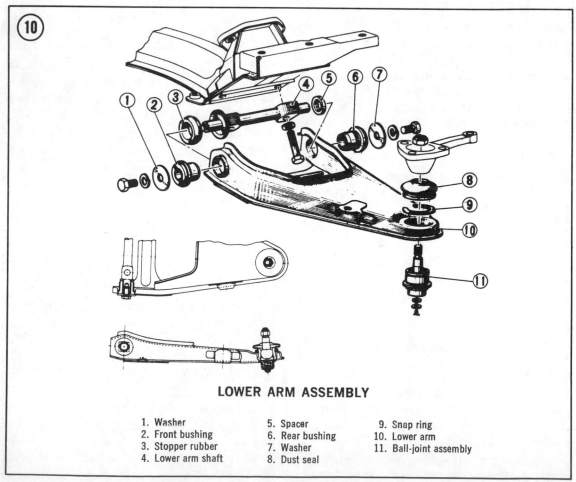

LOWER ARM ASSEMBLY

1. Washer	5. Spacer	9. Snap ring
2. Front bushing	6. Rear bushing	10. Lower arm
3. Stopper rubber	7. Washer	11. Ball-joint assembly
4. Lower arm shaft	8. Dust seal	

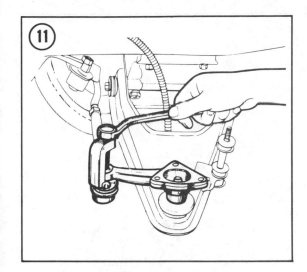

Installation

1. Install lower arm assembly to the crossmember by tightening the mounting bolts 58-65 ft.-lb. Make certain that the special nut is installed with the chamfered end toward the rounded surface of the bracket, and not riding over the rounded part of the crossmember. See **Figure 12**.

2. Install the knuckle arm to the tie rod end. Tighten the locknut to 29-36 ft.-lb. Install a split pin, then open the cotter pin as shown in **Figure 13**.

3. Attach stabilizer fixture to the stabilizer through a bushing, then to the frame, tightening to 7-10 ft.-lb. Subsequently install to lower arm through the link.

STEERING ADJUSTMENT

1. Check the steering wheel play with the front wheels jacked up and the steering wheel in the straight ahead position. The recommended play is one inch; it should not exceed 2 inches. See **Figure 14**.

2. If the steering needs adjusting, do so by means of the steering gear housing adjusting bolt (**Figure 15**). Do not tighten the bolt too much or more steering effort will be necessary than normal.

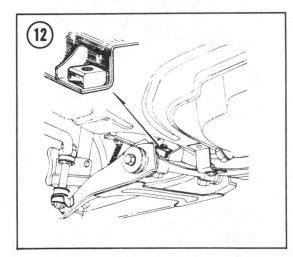

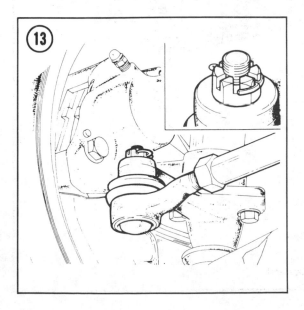

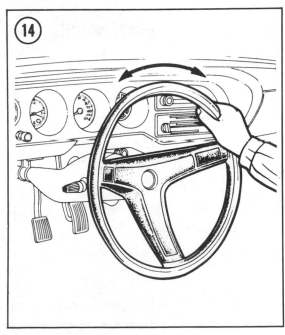

10

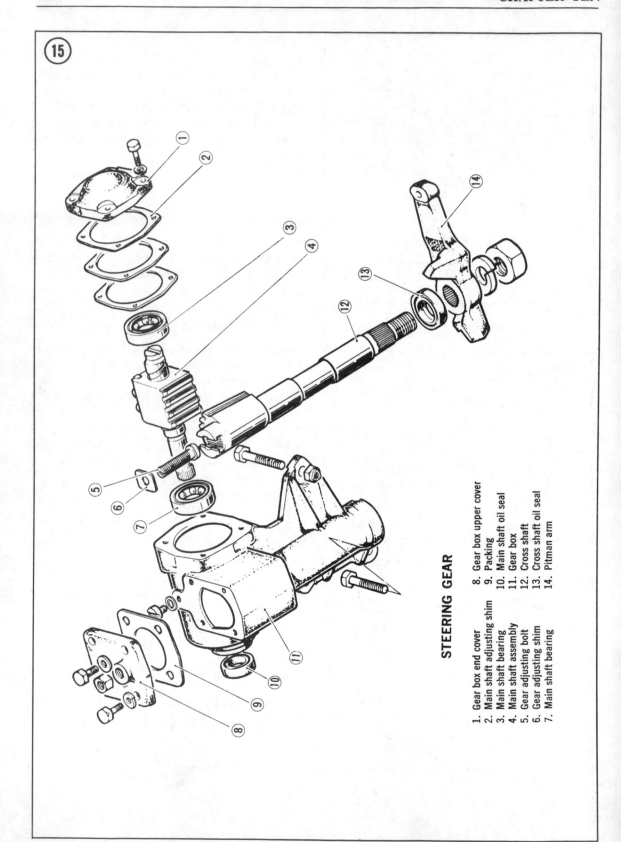

STEERING GEAR

1. Gear box end cover
2. Main shaft adjusting shim
3. Main shaft bearing
4. Main shaft assembly
5. Gear adjusting bolt
6. Gear adjusting shim
7. Main shaft bearing
8. Gear box upper cover
9. Packing
10. Main shaft oil seal
11. Gear box
12. Cross shaft
13. Cross shaft oil seal
14. Pitman arm

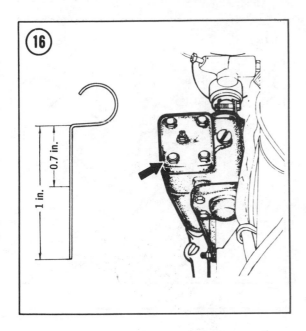

3. Remove the bolt at the right lower corner of the upper cover and check the oil level. The oil should be kept to about 0.7 in. from the bolt hole. Use the special gauge or a screwdriver in absence of the level gauge. See **Figure 16**.

STEERING LINKAGE

Special tools are needed to remove the tie rods, relay rod, idler arm, and pitman arm. Generally speaking, the tie rod ends wear faster than the other steering linkage parts and are fairly easy to replace for the average home mechanic. Therefore, only the removal and installation procedures for the tie rod assembly are given in this chapter. Other work on steering linkage is best left to your dealer or a qualified front-end alignment shop. See **Figure 17**.

10

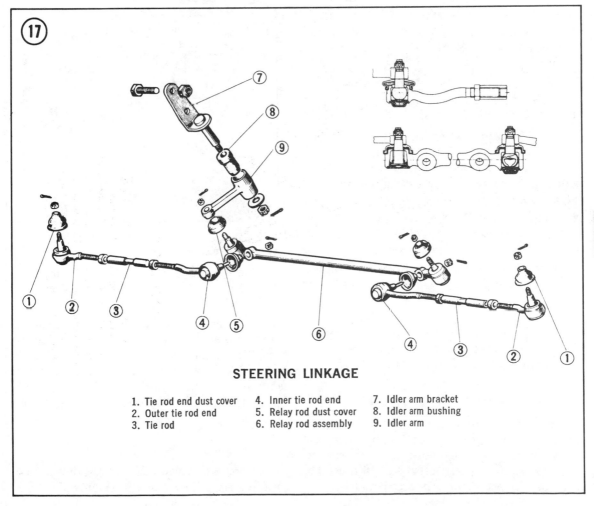

STEERING LINKAGE

1. Tie rod end dust cover
2. Outer tie rod end
3. Tie rod
4. Inner tie rod end
5. Relay rod dust cover
6. Relay rod assembly
7. Idler arm bracket
8. Idler arm bushing
9. Idler arm

Tie Rod Removal

1. Disconnect the tie rod ends with Special Tool CT-1116. See **Figure 18**.

> NOTE: *If the disc brake pad is badly worn, the caliper will interfere with the special tool. Remove the worn pad and move the caliper outward.*

2. Remove the tie rod ends from the tie rods.

> NOTE: *The tie rod end (outer) is provided with the left-hand screw thread; the tie rod end (inner), the right-hand screw thread. The tie rod end socket is calked with the plug and can't be disassembled.*

Tie Rod Inspection

1. Check tie rod ends for cracks and other damage. Replace if necessary.
2. Check the axial free-play of the tie rod end socket and stud. Replace if free-play is excessive.
3. Check dust covers for damage or wear.

Tie Rod Installation

1. Coat cover lip with grease. Fill inside of dust cover with grease before installing a new dust cover. Apply a sealer (Three-Bond No. 4 or equivalent) to tie rod mounting surface. See **Figure 19**.
2. Temporarily tighten so the distance between the stud bolts at both ends of the tie rod ends is 12.250 ± 0.008 in. See **Figure 20**. Apply a small amount of Multipurpose Lubricant to the tie rod threaded ends.
3. When connecting tie rod assembly to knuckle arm, tighten to 29-36 ft.-lb. Install a split pin, then open the split pin as shown in **Figure 21**. Make the toe-in adjustment and tighten the locknut to 36-40 ft.-lb.

WHEELS AND TIRES

Since tire air pressure has a direct bearing on handling, riding comfort, tire life, braking, fuel consumption, and road noise, it is necessary to keep the tires properly inflated at all times (24 psi front, 30 psi rear; all years and models).

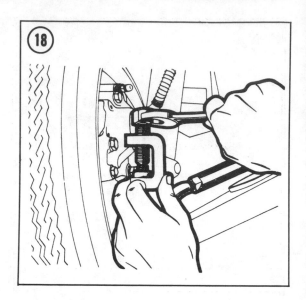

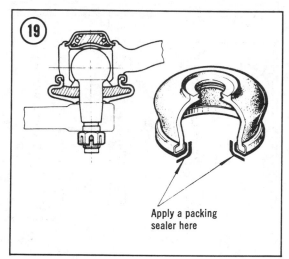

Apply a packing sealer here

Wheel/Tire Inspection

1. Check the tightness of the wheel lug nuts. Torque to 51-58 ft.-lb., tightening in a diagonal sequence.
2. Jack the car up so that wheels clear the floor. Rotate each wheel by hand. If excessive wobble is apparent to the eye, replace the wheel. A wheel should not deflect more than 0.06 in. Tire deflection should not exceed 0.12 in., and the wheel should have a flatness within 0.01 in.

Tire Rotation

To prevent uneven wear of tires, they must be rotated every 8,000 miles. See **Figure 22**.

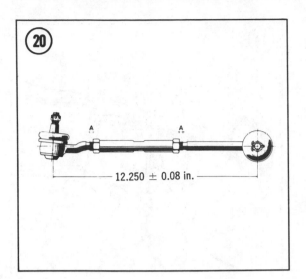

12.250 ± 0.08 in.

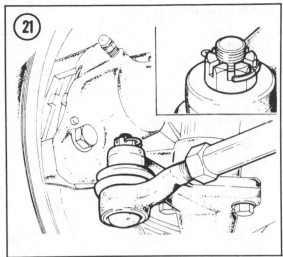

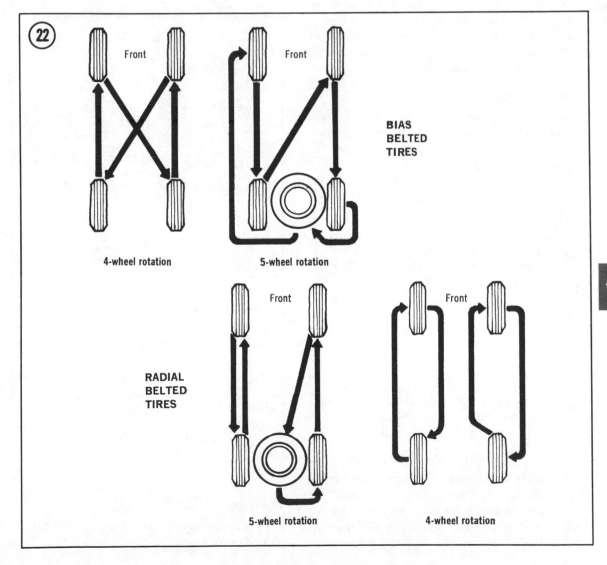

Front

Front

BIAS
BELTED
TIRES

4-wheel rotation

5-wheel rotation

RADIAL
BELTED
TIRES

Front

Front

5-wheel rotation

4-wheel rotation

10

Wheel Balancing

Whenever a tire has been repaired or rotated, have it balanced. Before doing so, read the section on wheel balancing in Chapter Three.

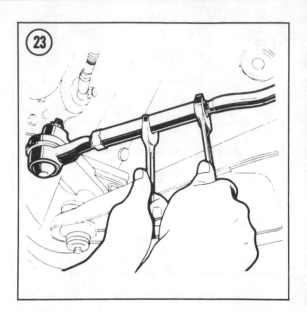

WHEEL ALIGNMENT

Toe-in Adjustment

Toe-in can be adjusted by screwing the turn buckle of the tie rod in or out. The amount of toe-in on the left side front wheel can be reduced by turning the tie rod turn buckle toward the front of the car, and the toe-in on the right side front wheel by turning it toward the rear of the car. See **Figure 23**. The turn buckles should always be tightened or loosened the same amount between the two. The difference of tie rod length should not exceed 0.2 in. (5 mm), when adjusted. Standard toe-in is 0.08-0.24 in. (2.0-6.0 mm). The tie rod turn buckle locking nut should be torqued to 36-40 ft.-lb.

Camber Adjustment

The steering knuckle (part of the strut assembly) is set to a specified camber at the factory and requires no adjustment. See **Figure 24**. Camber should be $1° \pm \frac{1}{2}°$ (coupe and sedan); $1°28' \pm \frac{1}{2}°$ (station wagon). Difference between both wheels: within $\frac{1}{2}°$.

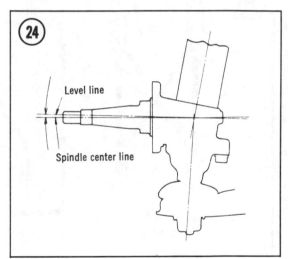

Caster Adjustment

The caster needs no adjustment. However, fine adjustment may be made to eliminate sideways free-play of the bolt retaining the lower arm to the crossmember. See **Figure 25**. Caster should be $2°05' \pm \frac{1}{2}°$ for coupe and sedan models; $2°38' \pm \frac{1}{2}°$ for station wagon models.

Steering Angle Adjustment

The steering angle is fixed by the stoppers provided for the pitman arm (which are fixed at designed positions). No adjustment is necessary.

The standard value for the inner wheel on sedan and coupe models is $35° \pm 1°$; the outer wheel, $30° \pm 1°$. The standard value for the inner wheel on station wagon models is $39° \pm +0°$, $-3°$; the outer wheel, $30° 30'$, $+1°$, $-2°$.

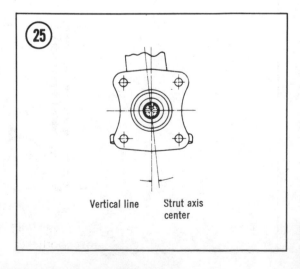

CHAPTER ELEVEN

REAR AXLE, DIFFERENTIAL,
AND REAR SUSPENSION

This chapter deals with the rear axle, differential, and rear suspension. Complete removal, disassembly, inspection, repair, reassembly, and installation procedures are given where practical.

The rear axle housing is of the banjo type, featuring light weight construction, joining "Y" split tubular housing with center covers welded to the axle housing, and hypoid drive gear. See **Figure 1**.

Axle shafts are semifloating, supported with grease-packed bearings at each end of the axle shafts. The oil seals are installed on the bearing retainers to prevent overflow of the differential gear oil to the bearing side. See **Figure 2**.

All 1600cc models use the same rear axle. All 2000/2600cc rear axles are basically the same except for the axle ratio in the 1975 and later models with 5-speed transmission. The rear axle for the 1600cc engine is not interchangeable with the rear axle for the 2000/2600cc engine.

The rear suspension is shown in **Figures 3-5**.

REAR AXLE ASSEMBLY

Removal

1. Loosen lug nuts on both rear wheels. Jack up the differential case. Remove both rear wheels. Support the car on jackstands positioned in front of the rear spring front bracket. The jack should be left holding the rear axle assembly slightly up.

2. Loosen the drive shaft. See Chapter Nine for procedure.

3. Disconnect the brake hose and brake line. Pull out the stops to disconnect the brake hose. See **Figure 6**.

4. Disconnect both ends of the parking brake cable from the wheel brakes. Remove the parking brake cable lever assembly from the rear axle housing.

5. Remove the shock absorbers and spring seats after removing U-bolts. See *Rear Suspension Removal*, this chapter.

6. Remove the spring shackle pin nuts, then the shackle plate (**Figure 7**). Be careful that the axle housing is not moved as it could drop off the jack since the rear springs are removed while the housing is resting on the jack alone.

7. Lower the jack with the axle housing resting on the jack saddle and supported by a helper.

Installation

To install the rear axle assembly, reverse the removal steps. In addition, bleed the brake

11

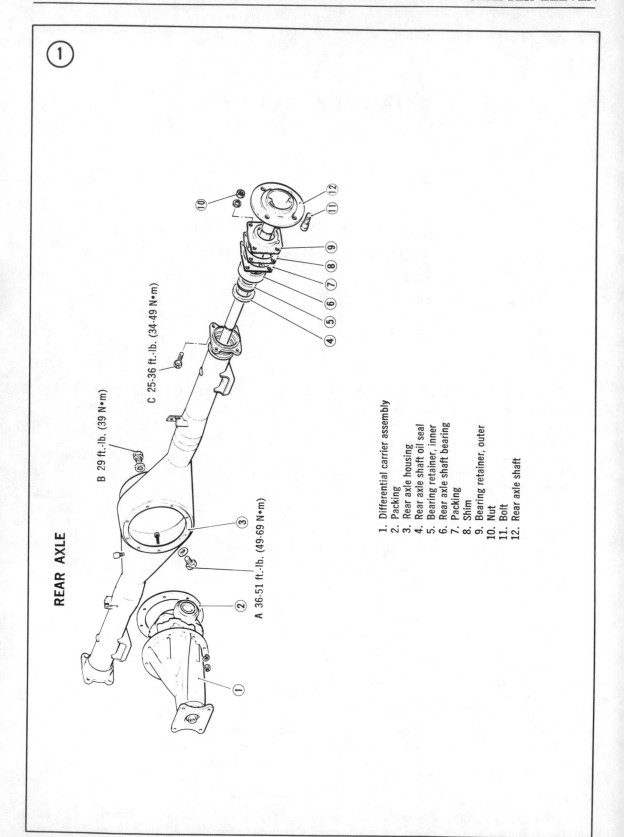

REAR AXLE

A 36-51 ft.-lb. (49-69 N•m)

B 29 ft.-lb. (39 N•m)

C 25-36 ft.-lb. (34-49 N•m)

1. Differential carrier assembly
2. Packing
3. Rear axle housing
4. Rear axle shaft oil seal
5. Bearing retainer, inner
6. Rear axle shaft bearing
7. Packing
8. Shim
9. Bearing retainer, outer
10. Nut
11. Bolt
12. Rear axle shaft

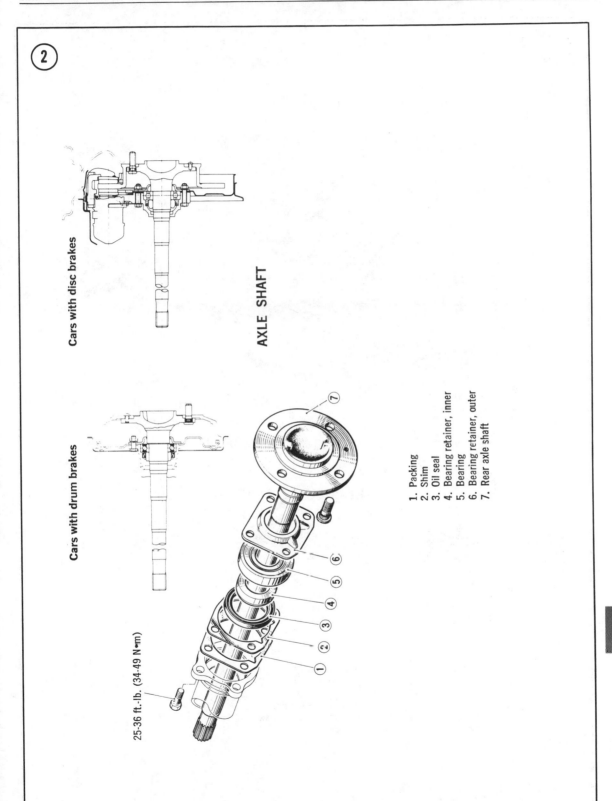

Cars with disc brakes

Cars with drum brakes

AXLE SHAFT

25-36 ft.-lb. (34-49 N•m)

1. Packing
2. Shim
3. Oil seal
4. Bearing retainer, inner
5. Bearing
6. Bearing retainer, outer
7. Rear axle shaft

11

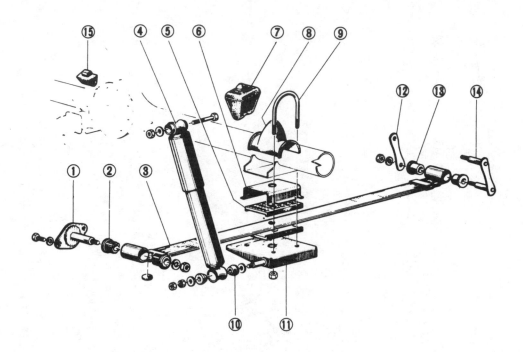

REAR SUSPENSION

1. Spring pin assembly
2. Eye bushing
3. Leaf spring assembly
4. Shock absorber
5. Spring pad
6. Bracket
7. Axle bumper (for sedan, hardtop, and coupe)
8. Stopper rubber (for station wagon)
9. U-bolt
10. Bushing rubber
11. U-bolt seat
12. Shackle plate
13. Shackle bushing
14. Rear spring shackle
15. Carrier bumper

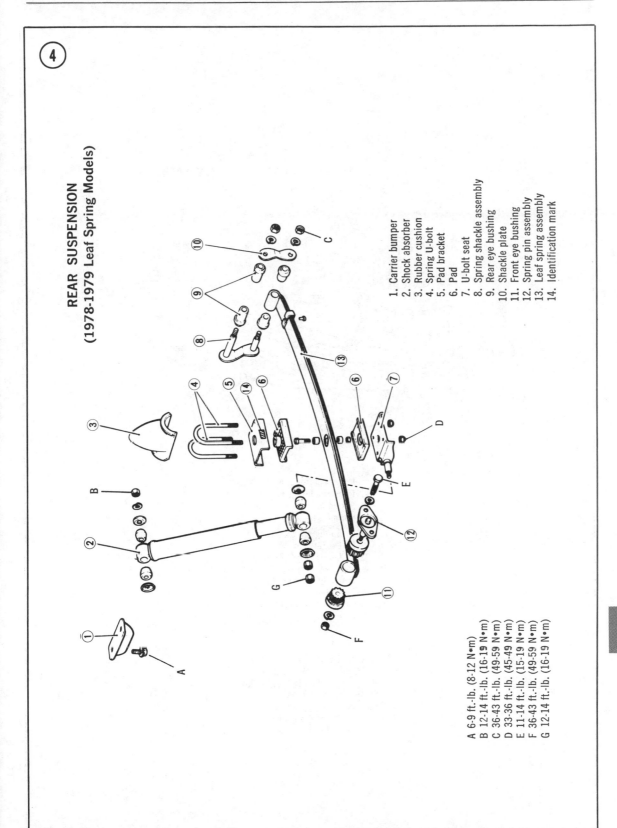

REAR SUSPENSION
(1978-1979 Leaf Spring Models)

1. Carrier bumper
2. Shock absorber
3. Rubber cushion
4. Spring U-bolt
5. Pad bracket
6. Pad
7. U-bolt seat
8. Spring shackle assembly
9. Rear eye bushing
10. Shackle plate
11. Front eye bushing
12. Spring pin assembly
13. Leaf spring assembly
14. Identification mark

A 6-9 ft.-lb. (8-12 N•m)
B 12-14 ft.-lb. (16-19 N•m)
C 36-43 ft.-lb. (49-59 N•m)
D 33-36 ft.-lb. (45-49 N•m)
E 11-14 ft.-lb. (15-19 N•m)
F 36-43 ft.-lb. (49-59 N•m)
G 12-14 ft.-lb. (16-19 N•m)

11

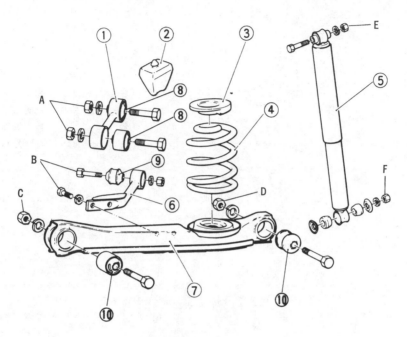

1. Upper control arm
2. Rear axle bumper
3. Spring pad
4. Spring
5. Shock absorber
6. Assist link
7. Lower control arm
8. Upper control arm bushing
   (with embossed ring)
9. Assist link bushing
   (with embossed ring)
10. Lower control arm bushing

A 94-123 ft.-lb. (128-167 N•m)
B 36-43 ft.-lb. (49-59 N•m)
C 94-123 ft.-lb. (128-168 N•m)
D 94-123 ft.-lb. (128-168 N•m)
E 47-58 ft.-lb. (64-78 N•m)
F 12-14 ft.-lb. (16-19 N•m)

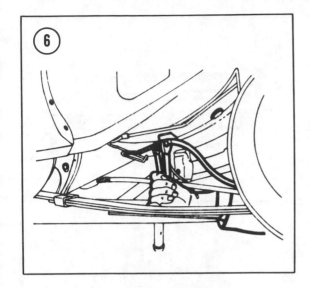

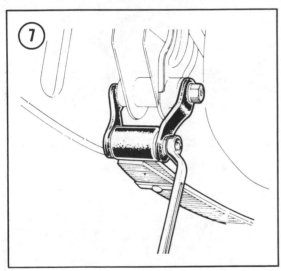

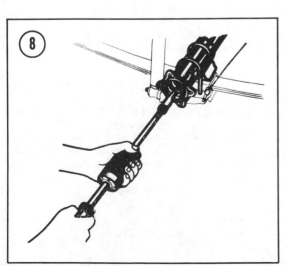

pipeline thoroughly (see Chapter Twelve). Also refer to *Rear Suspension, Installation,* this chapter.

REAR AXLE SHAFT

Removal

1. Loosen lug nuts on both rear wheels. Jack up the differential case. Support the car on jackstands positioned in front of the rear spring front bracket. The jack should be left holding the rear axle assembly slightly up. Remove both rear wheels.

2. Remove the brake backing plate retaining nuts and disconnect the brake line from the wheel cylinder.

3. Remove the rear axle shaft assembly by pulling on the shaft.

4. Leave the parking brake cable connected with the brake backing plate. Set the backing plate out of the way.

5. Remove axle shaft oil seal. See **Figure 8**.

> NOTE: *The average home mechanic may not have the proper tool for the axle shaft oil seal removal step. Dodge Colt dealers use special tool Sliding Hammer C-637. If the oil seal can be reused, do not damage it during its removal.*

6. Remove the axle shaft bearing inner retainer by thinning down a point on the retainer to a thickness of 0.04-0.06 in. (1.0-1.5 mm) with a grinder. See **Figure 9**.

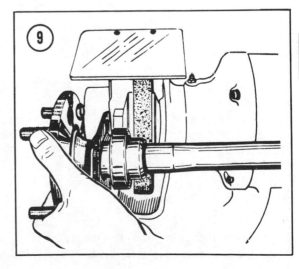

7. Crack the ground portion of the bearing retainer with a chisel. Be certain the retainer is held in position parallel with the working block to avoid bending the axle shaft. Remove the bearing retainer.

8. Remove the bearing with a bearing puller. This portion of the job may have to be performed by your Colt dealer with special tool Bearing Puller CT-1120 (**Figure 10**).

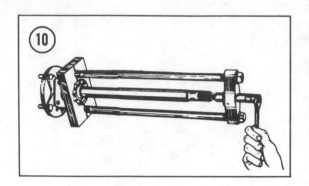

Inspection

1. Check the axle shaft for bend, the splined shaft and seal lip sliding area for wear and cracks.

2. Check the rear axle shaft bearing for noise, excessive play in axial or radial direction, and general condition. Replace if in doubt as to the axle shaft or bearing condition.

3. Check wheel hub bolts for tightness, the bearing retainer (outer) for deformation, and packings and oil seal for damage.

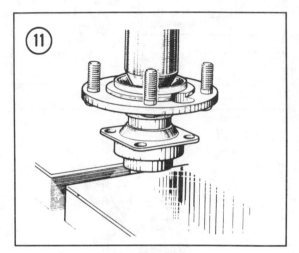

Installation

1. Install the outer retainer with its flat side toward the splined end of the shaft. Install bearing and retainer (inner) on the shaft.

2. Press the bearing retainer in with the smaller chamfered side toward the bearing side. See **Figure 11**. Begin the pressing operation with an initial pressure of 6,600 lb. or more and a final pressure of 13,000 lb. or more. Be sure the bearing retainer edge completely touches the bearing.

3. Apply a thin coat of chassis grease to the rear axle housing where the oil seal seats. Using the Dodge Colt special tool Oil Seal Installer (DT-1007B or equivalent) and special tool Bar (CT-1008 or equivalent), force the axle shaft oil seal into the rear axle housing (see **Figure 12**). Apply a thin coat of bearing grease (containing 50% or more molybdenum disulfide) over the oil seal lip. Apply grease to the surface which the oil seal lip contacts when the axle shaft is installed.

4. When tightening the rear axle shaft bearing (outer) to the axle housing flange, refer to **Table 1** to obtain a 0-0.01 in. (0-0.3 mm)

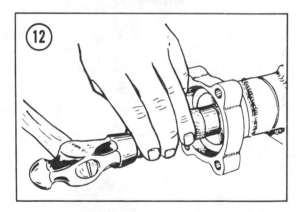

Table 1   BEARING RETAINER TO BEARING CLEARANCE

Formula	Clearance	Number of Packings	Number of Shims
C—(A+B) =	Less than 0.0098 in.	0	0
	0.0098 - 0.0197 in.	1	0
	0.0197 - 0.0295 in.	2	0
	0.0295 - 0.0394 in.	2	1
	0.0394 - 0.0492 in.	2	2

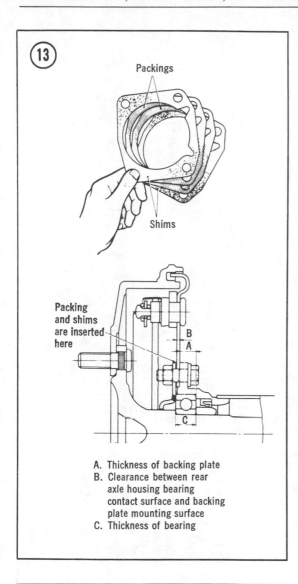

A. Thickness of backing plate
B. Clearance between rear
   axle housing bearing
   contact surface and backing
   plate mounting surface
C. Thickness of bearing

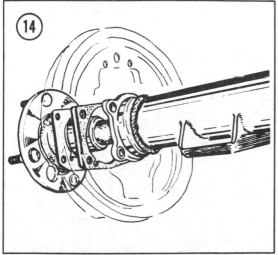

clearance between the bearing retainer and the bearing by installing packing(s) and shim(s). See **Figure 13**.

5. After installing packing(s) and shim(s) and the brake backing plate on rear axle shaft assembly, insert axle shaft assembly into axle housing, using care not to damage oil seal. See **Figure 14**. Fit splined end of axle shaft into differential side pinion. Align oil escape holes of the packing and the outer bearing retainer. Temporarily tighten bearing retainer to axle housing flange using the bolts with spring washers.

6. Tighten nuts for bearing retainer (outer) bolts to 25-29 ft.-lb. in diagonal sequence. Connect brake tube to wheel cylinder and bleed air from the brake.

7. Fill gear housing with Multipurpose gear oil conforming to API GL-5 (MIL-L-2105B). Fill with SAE 90 if temperature above − 10°F; SAE 80 if as low as − 30°F; or SAE 75 if below − 30°F. Tighten the drain plug to 51 ft.-lb., and the level plug to 29 ft.-lb.

DIFFERENTIAL

NOTE: *Disassembly and overhaul of the differential is complex and should be referred to your dealer.*

Removal

1. See **Figure 15**. Drain oil from differential gear housing. Disconnect drive shaft (see Chapter Nine for procedure).

2. Pull out right and left rear axle shafts by over 2 in. (refer to *Rear Axle Assembly, Removal*, this chapter).

3. Remove differential gear housing retaining nuts. Demount gear carrier (**Figure 16**). The gear carrier is fixed to the gear housing with sealing compound. Lightly tap gear carrier with a mallet while pulling on it.

Installation

1. Apply a sealer to the gear carrier/gear housing mating surfaces after cleaning the surfaces thoroughly. Install the differential assembly with bolts to the rear axle housing.

11

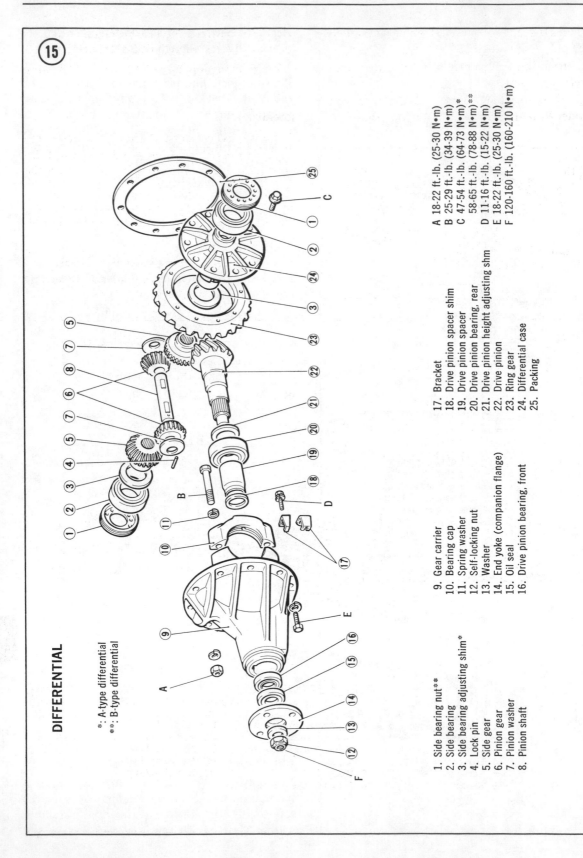

DIFFERENTIAL

*: A-type differential
**: B-type differential

1. Side bearing nut**
2. Side bearing
3. Side bearing adjusting shim*
4. Lock pin
5. Side gear
6. Pinion gear
7. Pinion washer
8. Pinion shaft

9. Gear carrier
10. Bearing cap
11. Spring washer
12. Self-locking nut
13. Washer
14. End yoke (companion flange)
15. Oil seal
16. Drive pinion bearing, front

17. Bracket
18. Drive pinion spacer shim
19. Drive pinion spacer
20. Drive pinion bearing, rear
21. Drive pinion bearing height adjusting shm
22. Drive pinion
23. Ring gear
24. Differential case
25. Packing

A 18-22 ft.-lb. (25-30 N•m)
B 25-29 ft.-lb. (34-39 N•m)
C 47-54 ft.-lb. (64-73 N•m)*
   58-65 ft.-lb. (78-88 N•m)**
D 11-16 ft.-lb. (15-22 N•m)
E 18-22 ft.-lb. (25-30 N•m)
F 120-160 ft.-lb. (160-210 N•m)

2. Insert rear axle shafts. Tighten brake backing plate locknuts to 25-29 ft.-lb.

3. Bleed brake hydraulic system thoroughly (refer to Chapter Twelve).

4. Fill axle housing with gear oil (refer to Step 7 under *Rear Axle Shaft, Installation,* above).

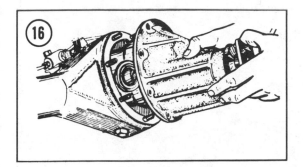

REAR SUSPENSION (LEAF SPRING MODELS)

Refer to **Figures 17 and 18** for the following procedures.

Removal

1. Loosen wheel nuts. Place a jack under the center of the rear axle and jack up the car. Support body side frame on jackstands. Lower the jack slowly. See **Figure 19**.

2. Disconnect upper end of shock absorbers, then lower end installed to the spring U-bolt seat.

> NOTE: *If it is not necessary to remove shock absorbers, leave lower end connected to the spring U-bolt seat.*

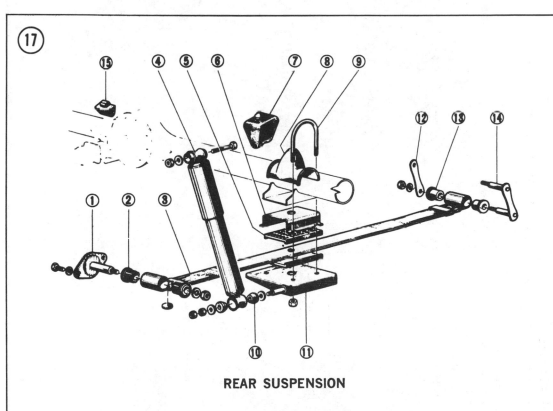

REAR SUSPENSION

1. Spring pin assembly
2. Eye bushing
3. Leaf spring assembly
4. Shock absorber
5. Spring pad
6. Bracket
7. Axle bumper (for sedan, hardtop, and coupe)
8. Stopper rubber (for station wagon)
9. U-bolt
10. Bushing rubber
11. U-bolt seat
12. Shackle plate
13. Shackle bushing
14. Rear spring shackle
15. Carrier bumper

11

REAR SUSPENSION
(1978-1979 Leaf Spring Models)

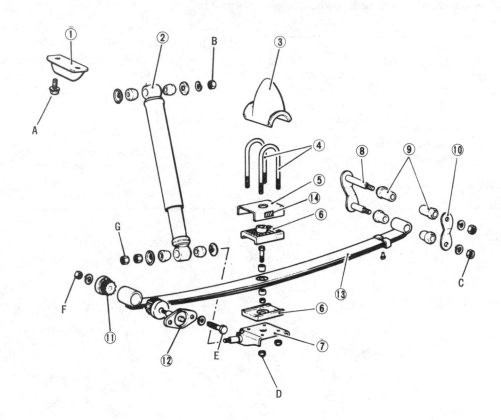

1. Carrier bumper
2. Shock absorber
3. Rubber cushion
4. Spring U-bolt
5. Pad bracket
6. Pad
7. U-bolt seat
8. Spring shackle assembly
9. Rear eye bushing
10. Shackle plate
11. Front eye bushing
12. Spring pin assembly
13. Leaf spring assembly
14. Identification mark

A 6-9 ft.-lb. (8-12 N•m)
B 12-14 ft.-lb. (16-19 N•m)
C 36-43 ft.-lb. (49-59 N•m)
D 33-36 ft.-lb. (45-49 N•m)
E 11-14 ft.-lb. (15-19 N•m)
F 36-43 ft.-lb. (49-59 N•m)
G 12-14 ft.-lb. (16-19 N•m)

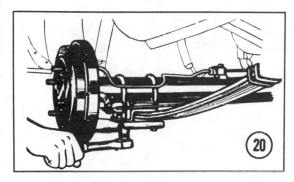

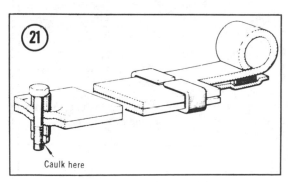

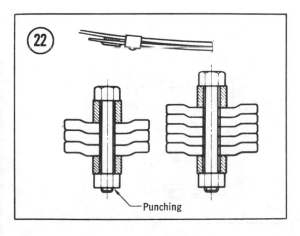

3. See **Figure 20**. Loosen U-bolt nut. Jack up rear axle housing until axle housing clears the spring seat. Remove the spring pad and the spring seat.

4. Demount spring assembly after removing spring pin at front end, and spring shackle pin at rear end.

Disassembly

Open the spring leaf clamp bands and remove center bolts. Separate spring leaves.

Inspection

1. Check each spring leaf, clamp, rubber bushing, and silencer rubber for wear or damage. Replace if necessary.

2. Check shock absorbers for leaks caused by damaged packing and seal. Inspect rod for bend.

3. Remove rust from spring leaves, using a wire brush. Apply "chassis black" to each leaf.

Assembly

1. Replace silencers with new ones. Assemble spring leaves and with center bolt collars installed at both ends of the bolts, securely tighten the nuts. See **Figure 21**.

2. Punch the center bolt threads to lock the nut against rotation (**Figure 22**).

3. Install leaf clips and securely bend them.

4. Check axle bumpers (sedan, hardtop, and coupe), stopper bumper (station wagon), and carrier bumper for cracks and loss of expansion force.

Installation

1. The No. 1 leaf spring has a camber identification mark (+, 0, −). Be certain the leaves carrying the same mark are installed on both sides of the car. See **Table 2**.

NOTE: *Leaf spring camber for the 1975 sedan and hardtop series has been changed. The station wagon series remains unchanged.*

CAUTION
If the car tilts over 0.6 in. to the right or left (measure the height of the lamp),

11

select and install springs, considering the rear spring camber.

2. Install spring front eye bushings from both sides of the eye with bushing flanges facing out. Insert spring pin assembly from body side. Secure to the hanger bracket with the bolt. Temporarily tighten spring pin nut. See **Figure 23**.

3. Install rear eye bushing to the spring and spring bracket the same as the spring front eye bushings. Press shackle assembly in from outside the car body. Temporarily install nuts through shackle plate from inside. Refer to **Figure 23**.

4. Install upper spring pad and pad bracket with center holes aligned with spring center bolt. Attach assembled spring and spring seat on the axle housing. Install lower spring pad and U-bolt seat in a similar manner. Insert U-bolt from above the axle housing into the U-bolt seat. See **Figure 24**. Tighten spring U-bolt nuts to 33-36 ft.-lb. (45-49 N•m). After tightening the nuts, make certain the pad bracket and U-bolt seat are in firm contact with each other.

5. Tighten the upper shock absorber mounting nuts to 12-14 ft.-lb. for coupe and sedan models; 47-58 ft.-lb. for station wagon model. Tighten the lower mounting nut.

6. Lower car to the floor. Tighten the spring pins and shackle pins.

7. New carrier bumpers should be torqued to 6-9 ft.-lb.

REAR SUSPENSION (1978-1979 4-LINK TYPE)

The suspension shown in **Figure 25** is used on Colt station wagons. Refer to that when performing the following procedures.

Removal

1. Support car body with jackstands, then raise rear axle slightly with a jack (**Figure 26**). Remove wheels.

2. Disconnect parking brake cable from extension lever.

3. Remove shock absorbers, then lower jack and remove both coil springs (**Figure 27**).

4. Jack the axle up slightly, then remove lower control arm, assist link, and upper arm.

Table 4   LEAF SPRING COMBINATIONS

Sedan, Hardtop, and Coupe		Station Wagon	
Left	Right	Left	Right
(+)	(+)	(+)	(+)
(0)	(0)	(0)	(0)
(—)	(—)	(—)	(—)

Note: Solid line = Desirable combination.
Dotted line = Undesirable but unavoidable combination.

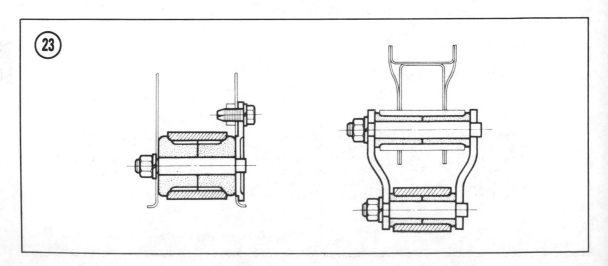

(23)

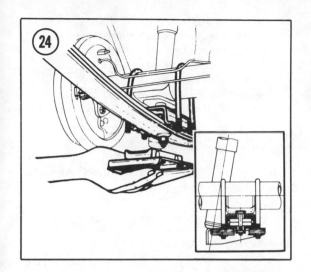

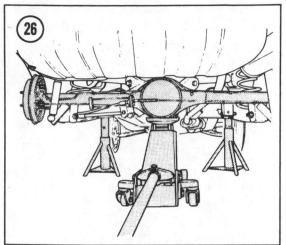

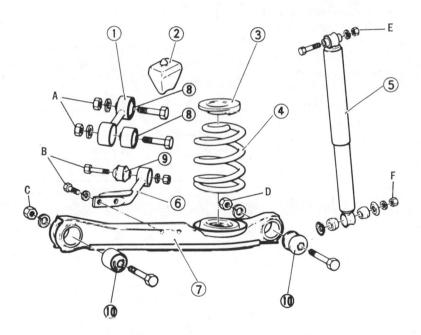

1. Upper control arm
2. Rear axle bumper
3. Spring pad
4. Spring
5. Shock absorber
6. Assist link

7. Lower control arm
8. Upper control arm bushing
   (with embossed ring)
9. Assist link bushing
   (with embossed ring)
10. Lower control arm bushing

A 94-123 ft.-lb. (128-167 N•m)
B 36-43 ft.-lb. (49-59 N•m)
C 94-123 ft.-lb. (128-168 N•m)
D 94-123 ft.-lb. (128-168 N•m)
E 47-58 ft.-lb. (64-78 N•m)
F 12-14 ft.-lb. (16-19 N•m)

11

Inspection

Check springs and shock absorbers for signs of wear, fluid leakage, bends, damage, etc.

LOWER CONTROL ARM

Disassembly/Assembly

1. Remove front bushings with Dodge special tool MB990641 (or equivalent), as shown in **Figure 28**; remove rear bushings with Dodge special tool MB990649 (or equivalent), as shown in **Figure 29**.

2. To install the bushings, use the same special tools required for Step 1, preceding, and observe the following note:

> NOTE: *When installing the front bushing, press it into the bushing hole in the control arm with the chamfered end of the bushing hole facing up, and the bushing hole positioned as shown in Figure 30.*
>
> *When installing the rear bushing, apply neutral detergent solution sufficiently to the bushing and bushing hole. When the bushing is installed, be sure that the right and left bushings project out from the arm as follows: front bushing, 0.06 in. (1.5 mm) or less; rear bushing, 0.08 in. (2.0 mm) or less.*

UPPER CONTROL ARM

Disassembly/Assembly

Remove the bushing with Dodge special tool MB990645 (or equivalent) and a press, as shown in **Figure 31**. Use the same tool to install the new bushing.

> NOTE: *After installation, be sure that the right and left bushing ends do not project more than 0.04 in. (1.0 mm) from the upper control arm.*

ASSIST LINK

Disasembly/Assembly

Remove the bushing with Dodge special tool MB990653 and a press (**Figure 32**). Install the new bushing with the same tool.

> NOTE: *When installing the bushing, be sure to apply a neutral detergent solution to the bushing and bushing hole in the arm. When the bushing is installed, be sure that the right and left bushings project out from the arm no more than 0.08 in. (2.0 mm).*

Rear Suspension Installation

1. Jack the rear axle up and support it. Temporarily install the upper and lower control arms and assist link.

> NOTE: *Each coil spring is color coded. Be sure that you install coil springs coded with 2 yellow marks (station wagon springs). See Figure 33.*

2. Lower rear axle, then install spring pad to the upper end of the spring. Insert lower end of spring into spring groove in the spring seat of the lower control arm.

3. Install shock absorbers.

4. Install parking brake cable, and adjust its stroke. Refer to Chapter Twelve, *Parking Brakes* section.

5. Keep car in unladened condition, then tighten all nuts and bolts of upper and lower control arms, and the assist link.

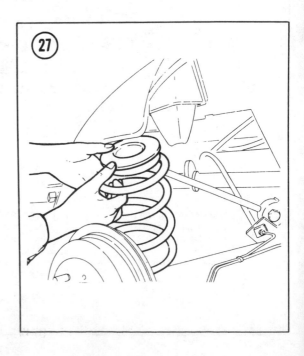

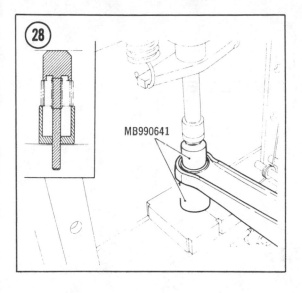

28

MB990641

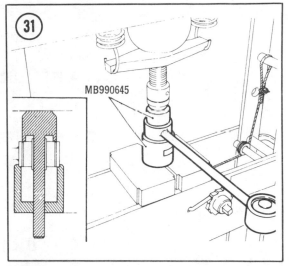

31

MB990645

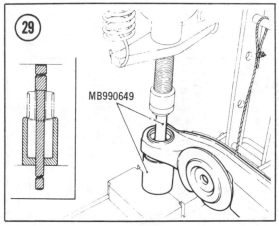

29

MB990649

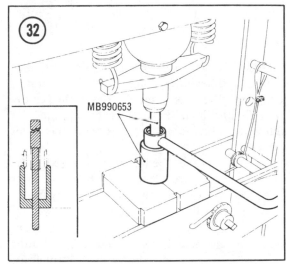

32

MB990653

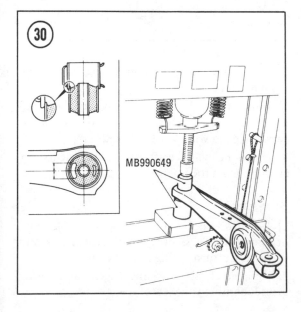

30

MB990649

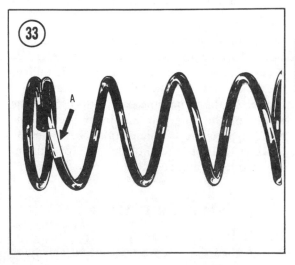

33

A

11

CHAPTER TWELVE

BRAKES

Dodge Colts are fitted with front disc brakes and leading-trailing rear shoe brakes. The front disc brake calipers are attached to the knuckle and hold the wheel cylinders on both sides. The brake disc rotates with the front wheel.

As the brake pedal is depressed, the hydraulic pressure generated in the master cylinder is exerted on the wheel cylinders through brake lines. See **Figure 1**.

The master cylinder is a tandem unit consisting of independent front and rear hydraulic systems — even if one hydraulic system fails, the remaining one will bring the car safely to a stop.

The parking brakes are mechanical expansion types acting on the 2 rear wheels. See **Figure 2**. When parking brake lever is pulled, the inner cable is pulled to lock the right-hand brake. At the same time, a lever located at the center of the rear axle housing moves to the right, locking the left-hand brake. See **Figure 3**.

Refer to **Table 1** (end of chapter) for tightening torque recommendations.

MASTER CYLINDER

Removal

1. See **Figure 4**. Depress the pedal slowly to

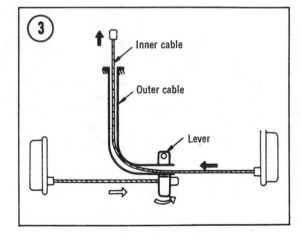

drain the fluid, after disconnecting brake tube from master cylinder.

2. Pull off the clevis pin connecting the pedal with the master cylinder pushrod (except on cars equipped with Master-Vac).

3. Clean the cylinder after removing the master cylinder from toe board.

Disassembly

1. Remove boots and stopper rings, and primary piston assembly, secondary piston, and secondary return spring in that order.

2. Remove check valve and check valve spring after loosening valve case.

① BRAKE SYSTEM

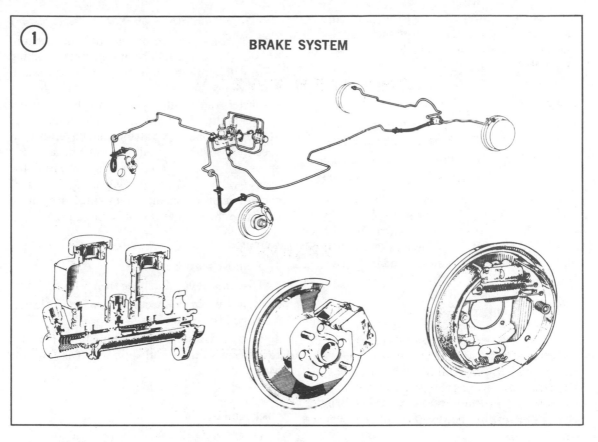

②

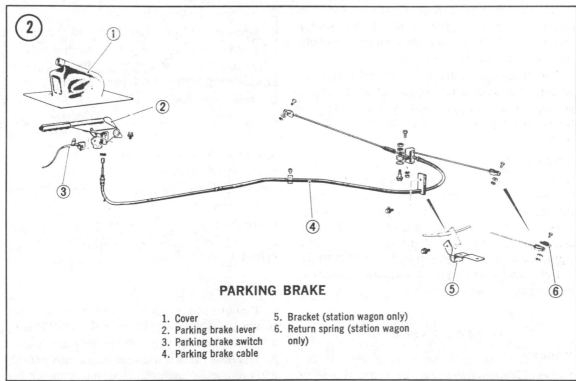

PARKING BRAKE

1. Cover
2. Parking brake lever
3. Parking brake switch
4. Parking brake cable

5. Bracket (station wagon only)
6. Return spring (station wagon only)

12

3. Wash master cylinder, piston, and cups in clean brake fluid. Do not damage parts in handling. Do not disassemble primary piston assembly.

Inspection

1. Check outer surface of piston and inner surface of master cylinder for damage or wear.

2. Check master cylinder-to-piston clearance (see **Table 2**). Replace defective part(s) if necessary.

3. Check piston cup for wear or damage.

4. Check free length of each master cylinder spring. Replace if free length is less than 1.55 in. (the standard dimension is an ideal 1.68 in.).

CAUTION
When any part such as the return spring, piston cup, and piston requires replacement, replace piston assembly.

Assembly

1. Apply brake fluid to bore of master cylinder and piston cup before assembling master cylinder.

2. Tighten the check valve cap to 17-25 ft.-lb., the check valve case to 29-36 ft.-lb., piston stopper to 1.1-2.2 ft.-lb., and the fluid reservoir band to 1.7-2.9 ft.-lb.

3. After master cylinder is assembled, check to be sure that return port is not blocked by the piston cup, when piston is in returned position.

Installation

1. Tighten master cylinder to 6-9 ft.-lb., brake tube flare nuts to 9-12 ft.-lb., and master cylinder connector bolts to 14-18 ft.-lb. (18-25 ft.-lb. on 1975 and later models).

2. On cars equipped with Master-Vac, the master cylinder should be installed after being certain there is 0-0.03 in. clearance between back of master cylinder piston and Master-Vac pushrod.

3. After master cylinder is installed, adjust brake pedal (see *Brake Pedal, Adjustment*, this chapter) and bleed hydraulic system (see *Brake Bleeding*, this chapter).

MASTER-VAC

Some cars are equipped with a vacuum booster (Master-Vac) to obtain greater braking force with a minimum of brake pedal pressure. See **Figure 5**.

Master-Vac trouble can easily be confused with a faulty check valve. To determine if the Master-Vac or check valve is defective, disconnect the Master-Vac side vacuum hose at the check valve and crank the engine. Hold the check valve with your fingers and feel if vacuum is produced and maintained. Replace a defective check valve if that is the cause.

Removal

1. Remove master cylinder.

2. Disconnect vacuum hose from Master-Vac.

3. Remove pin connecting pedal and Master-Vac operating rod.

4. Loosen Master-Vac attaching nuts (fastened together with the pedal support). Take out the Master-Vac.

Disassembly

1. Hold front shell flange in a vise.

2. Remove clevis and locknut.

3. Draw mating marks on front and rear shells.

4. Hold neck of rear shell from both sides with pipes and remove rear shell by turning counterclockwise. See **Figure 6**. Diaphragm spring can be removed at same time.

5. Remove diaphragm plate from rear shell. The plate is made of plastic; handle carefully to avoid damage.

6. Disassemble Master-Vac into rear shell and seal assembly, diaphragm plate assembly, and front shell assembly, as follows:

  a. To disassemble rear shell and seal assembly, see **Figure 7**. Pull off retainer with a driver. Remove bearing and valve body seal.

  b. To disassemble the diaphragm plate assembly, remove the silencer retainer from diaphragm plate with a screwdriver. Then remove silencer filter and silencer. Remove valve plunger stop key. Slowly pull off valve rod and plunger assembly

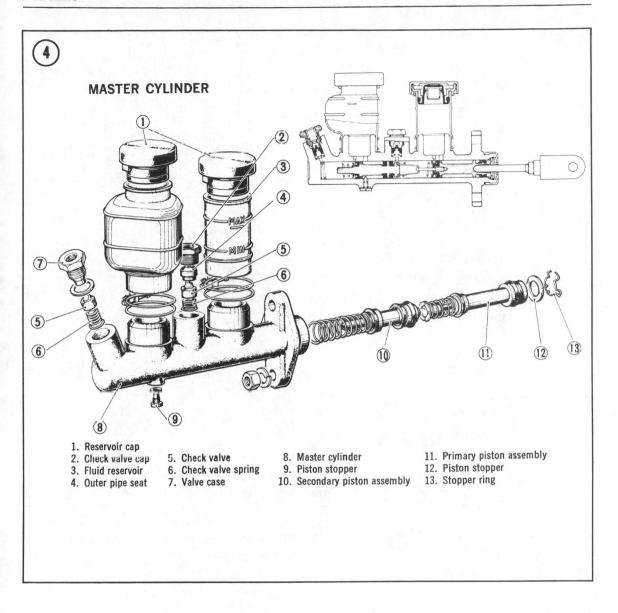

④

MASTER CYLINDER

1. Reservoir cap
2. Check valve cap
3. Fluid reservoir
4. Outer pipe seat
5. Check valve
6. Check valve spring
7. Valve case
8. Master cylinder
9. Piston stopper
10. Secondary piston assembly
11. Primary piston assembly
12. Piston stopper
13. Stopper ring

Table 2   MASTER CYLINDER TO PISTON CLEARANCE

Description	Standard Value	Service Limit	Remarks
Master cylinder inner diameter	11/16 - 0.6891 in. (17.46 - 17.503mm)		
	13/16 - 0.8146 in. (20.64 - 20.692mm)		Fitted with Master-Vac
Piston outer diameter	0.6851 - 0.6861 in. (17.401 - 17.428mm)		
	0.8097 - 0.8110 in. (20.567 - 20.60mm)		Fitted with Master-Vac
Cylinder-to-piston clearance	0.0014 - 0.0040 in.	0.0059 in.	
	0.0016 - 0.0049 in.	0.0059 in.	Fitted with Master-Vac

12

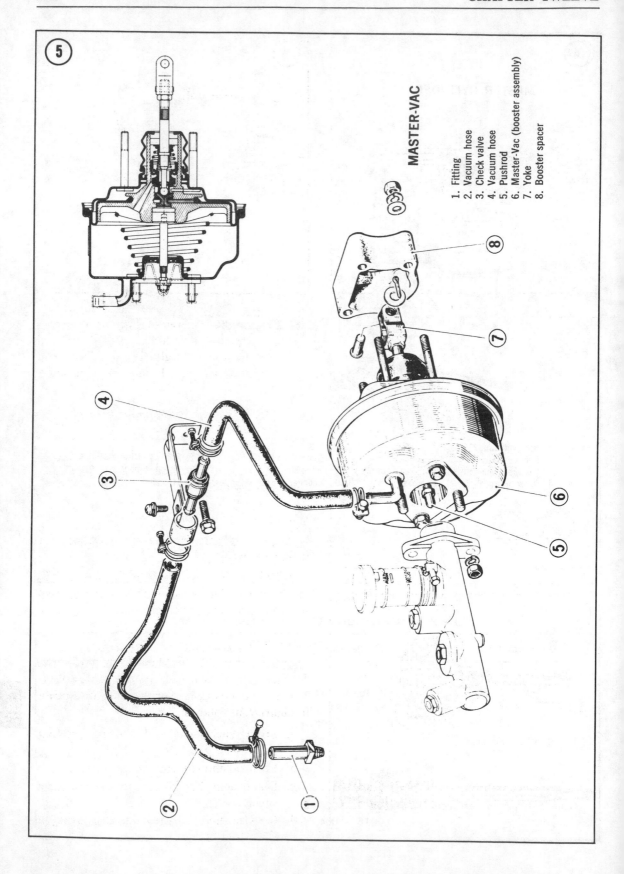

MASTER-VAC

1. Fitting
2. Vacuum hose
3. Check valve
4. Vacuum hose
5. Pushrod
6. Master-Vac (booster assembly)
7. Yoke
8. Booster spacer

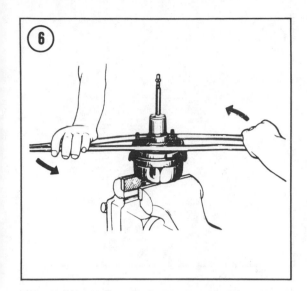

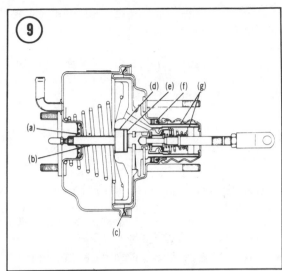

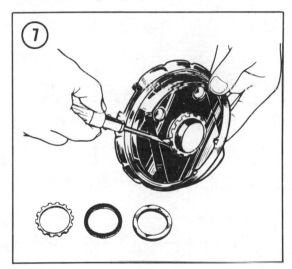

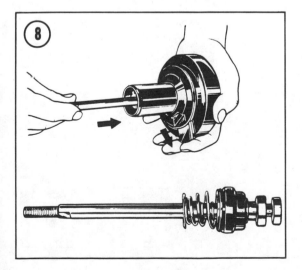

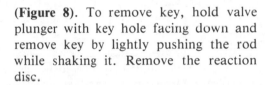

(**Figure 8**). To remove key, hold valve plunger with key hole facing down and remove key by lightly pushing the rod while shaking it. Remove the reaction disc.

NOTE: *The valve rod plunger assembly cannot be disassembled.*

c. To disassemble front shell, remove flange from front shell, then pull off plate and seal assembly.

Inspection

1. Wipe each part clean and dry and check for damage or wear.

2. Check pushrod for bend and damage.

3. Check part into which stud bolts are pressed for cracks, damage, and deformation.

Assembly

1. When assembling Master-Vac, use the silicone grease furnished in the Dodge Colt Master-Vac repair kit to grease the parts shown in **Figure 9**, as follows:

    a. Front shell seal and pushrod sliding surfaces.

    b. Pushrod and seal contact surfaces.

    c. Diaphragm lug-to-rear shell contacting surface.

    d. Outside surface of reaction disc (apply a thin coat of grease).

12

3. Gently install valve rod and plunger assembly to diaphragm plate.

4. Insert chamfered end of valve plunger stop key toward piston side. Pull plunger assembly to be sure valve plunger is securely locked by the key. See **Figure 10**.

> CAUTION
> *If the stop key is installed wrong, it will be hard to remove during the next disassembly.*

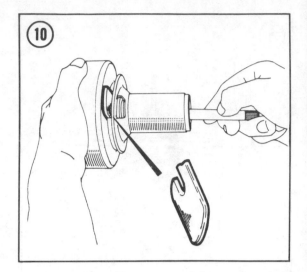

5. Install reaction disc and diaphragm to diaphragm plate. Be sure diaphragm is securely inserted in the groove in plate. Be careful not to stain diaphragm with oil.

6. Insert silencer filter and silencer into rear of diaphragm plate. Press in the retainer. See **Figure 11**. The diaphragm will not function correctly if filter and silencer are installed incorrectly.

7. Install diaphragm plate into rear shell. Install valve body guard to rear shell, inserting rear of guard into the end of the retainer.

8. Insert plate and seal assembly into front shell. Install pushrod and install flange to front shell. The flange can be pressed in identical to front shell seal.

9. Hold rear shell with its mating mark aligned with mating mark on front shell. Turn rear shell until its notch touches the stopper.

10. Check clearance from Master-Vac pushrod to back of master cylinder piston. If standard clearance cannot be obtained, adjust the length of the pushrod (see **Table 3** and **Figure 12**).

11. Install yoke onto threaded end of operating rod (**Figure 13**). Yoke to operating rod clearance should be 0.51 in. (+0.08 −0.016 in.).

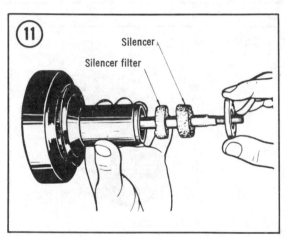

Silencer

Silencer filter

    e. Reaction disc inserting part of diaphragm plate.

    f. Rear shell seal and diaphragm plate sliding surfaces.

    g. Interior of piston plate into which plunger assembly is inserted, and seal sliding surfaces.

2. Press in retainer after inserting seal, bearing, and retainer into rear shell. Do not apply too much pressure to retainer.

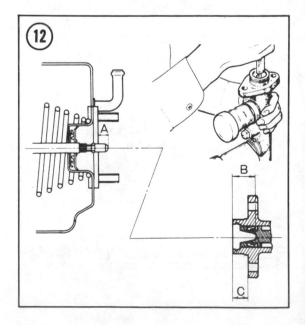

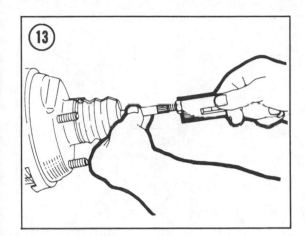

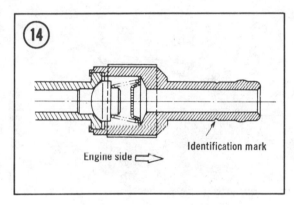

Identification mark

Engine side ⟹

Table 3   **PUSHROD TO MASTER CYLINDER CLEARANCE**

Description	Standard Value
Pushrod length A	0.315 —0.010 in.
Master cylinder piston end gap B-C	0.315 +0.020 in.
Pushrod-to-master cylinder piston end clearance (B-C)-A	0 - 0.3 in.

Installation

1. Apply a sealer (Cemedine 366E or equivalent) to the Master-Vac mounting surfaces (toe board and Master-Vac surfaces). Tighten Master-Vac to 6-9 ft.-lb., master cylinder to 6-9 ft.-lb., and the brake tube flare nut to 9-12 ft.-lb.

2. Follow instructions on the label affixed to the top of the check valve when installing check valve. See **Figure 14**.

3. Apply a sealer (Three-Bond No. 4 or equivalent) to the fitting so no air will leak. Install fitting and tighten to 11-13 ft.-lb.

4. Install vacuum hoses securely.

5. Connect Master-Vac operating rod to brake pedal. Adjust brake pedal (see *Brake Pedal, Adjustment,* this chapter).

6. Bleed hydraulic brake system (see *Brake Bleeding*, this chapter).

BRAKE PEDAL

Removal

1. Pull off clevis pin connecting pushrod with the pedal. Remove master cylinder. In car with Master-Vac, remove Master-Vac unit.

2. Disconnect pedal support. Remove clutch pedal shaft attaching snap ring and disconnect clutch pedal from pedal support. See **Figure 15**.

3. Remove the pedal support, then remove the brake pedal.

Inspection

1. Check pedal shaft, bushing, and rod for wear or damage.

2. Check pedals for bend, cracks, and other damage.

Installation

1. Apply chassis grease to pedal shaft (**Figures 16 and 17**). Apply grease to clutch cable fitting area at forward end of clutch pedal arm.

2. Tighten pedal support to support member to 10-13 ft.-lb., and the pedal support to Master-Vac (toe board) to 6-9 ft.-lb.

3. Install master cylinder. Bleed hydraulic system (see *Brake Bleeding*, in following section).

Adjustment (Cars Without Master-Vac)

1. Adjust distance from pedal top to toe board to 6.9-7.1 in. by means of the pedal stopper (which also serves as stoplight switch). See **Figure 18**.

2. Adjust master cylinder piston-to-pushrod end clearance to 0.004-0.020 in. by adjusting the turnbuckle.

3. Check pedal free-play (**Figure 18**).

12

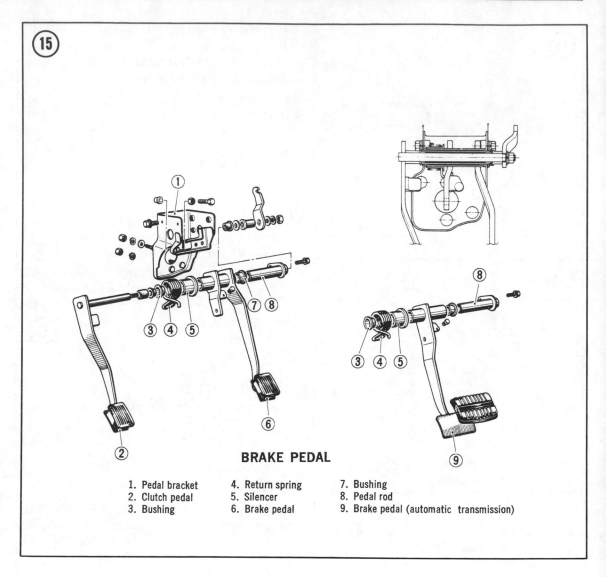

BRAKE PEDAL

1. Pedal bracket
2. Clutch pedal
3. Bushing
4. Return spring
5. Silencer
6. Brake pedal
7. Bushing
8. Pedal rod
9. Brake pedal (automatic transmission)

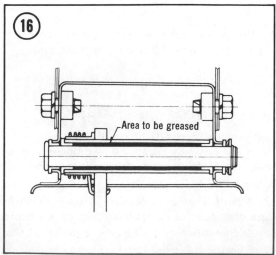

Area to be greased

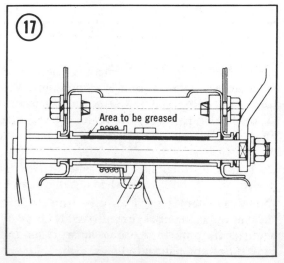

Area to be greased

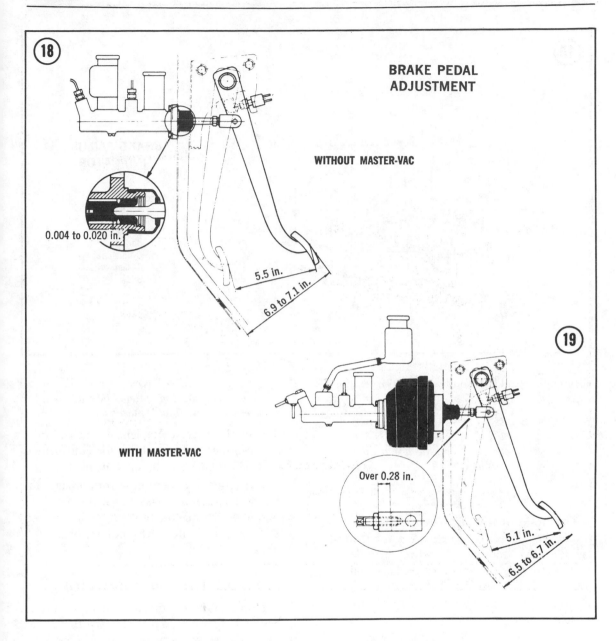

**BRAKE PEDAL
ADJUSTMENT**

WITHOUT MASTER-VAC

0.004 to 0.020 in.

5.5 in.

6.9 to 7.1 in.

WITH MASTER-VAC

Over 0.28 in.

5.1 in.

6.5 to 6.7 in.

Adjustment (Cars With Master-Vac)

1. Remove pin connecting Master-Vac operating rod to pedal. Adjust pedal height to 6.5-6.7 in. (**Figure 19**) by means of the pedal stopper.

> NOTE: *It is advisable to back out the pedal stopper a little.*

2. Install operating rod to pedal with the hole of the operating rod yoke aligned with pedal hole (in the position in which the operating rod is in the returned position).

CAUTION
If operating rod is set to the pedal in the pushed position, the vacuum valve is closed to operate Master-Vac, causing brakes to drag. Use care when connecting rod to pedal. Adjust pedal height to the recommended distance, otherwise insufficient entrance length of the operating rod end in the yoke will result.

3. Perform adjustment by turning in pedal stopper until it touches the pedal. The stopper should be adjusted to the degree that the brake pedal is not pushed inward.

12

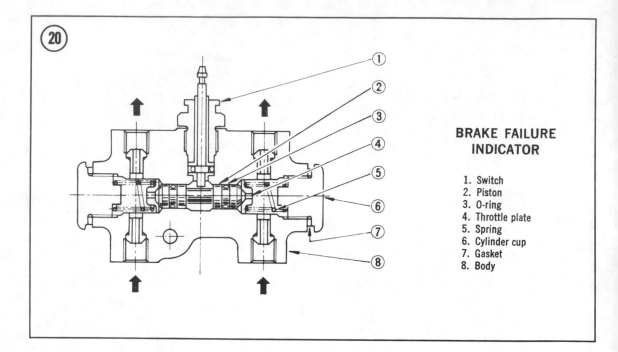

⑳

**BRAKE FAILURE
INDICATOR**

1. Switch
2. Piston
3. O-ring
4. Throttle plate
5. Spring
6. Cylinder cup
7. Gasket
8. Body

4. Check pedal free-play (**Figure 19**).

> *CAUTION*
> *If pedal has an excessively long stroke, check master cylinder-to-Master-Vac pushrod clearance and the brake shoe-to-drum clearance.*

BRAKE BLEEDING

The brake hydraulic system should be bled whenever the brake hose, brake tube, master cylinder, Master-Vac, or wheel cylinder has been removed, or whenever brake pedal feels spongy when depressed. The bleeding sequence should be: left rear wheel, right rear wheel, left front wheel, right front wheel.

1. Fill master cylinder fluid reservoir with brake fluid, if low.

2. Remove bleed screw cap of wheel cylinder. Connect one end of a vinyl pipe to the bleed screw and place the other end into a glass container of approximately 30 cu. in. capacity, half full of brake fluid.

3. Slowly depress brake pedal several times. Turn bleed screw back a little with pedal in the depressed position. Tighten bleed screw while fluid is flowing in the vinyl pipe. Keep repeating until no air bubbles can be seen in the brake fluid coming out of the vinyl pipe.

> *CAUTION*
> *While bleeding the system, be sure to keep sufficient fluid in master cylinder.*

4. Install bleed screw. Replenish fluid in brake master cylinder reservoir. Use fluid conforming to SAE J1703 (70R3 Type) or equivalent.

5. Check brake tube and hose for damage, interference, rust, and leaks. Tighten the bleed screws to 4-7 ft.-lb., the brake tube flare nut to 9-12 ft.-lb., and the 3-way connector to 6-9 ft.-lb.

BRAKE FAILURE INDICATOR

The brake failure indicator operates a brake indicator light which lights to warn the driver when a failure has occurred somewhere in the brake system. The indicator is located between the master cylinder and wheel cylinders. See **Figure 20**.

FRONT DISC BRAKES

Brake Pad Removal
(1971-1973 Models)

1. Remove the wheel.

2. Disconnect brake pipe from brake hose. Remove connector bolt for the flexible hose connected to the caliper.

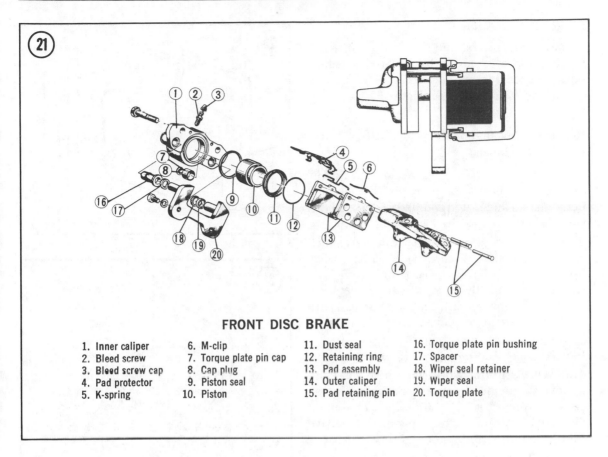

FRONT DISC BRAKE

1. Inner caliper
2. Bleed screw
3. Bleed screw cap
4. Pad protector
5. K-spring
6. M-clip
7. Torque plate pin cap
8. Cap plug
9. Piston seal
10. Piston
11. Dust seal
12. Retaining ring
13. Pad assembly
14. Outer caliper
15. Pad retaining pin
16. Torque plate pin bushing
17. Spacer
18. Wiper seal retainer
19. Wiper seal
20. Torque plate

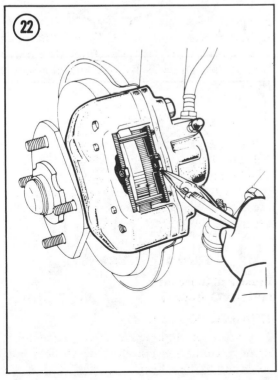

3. Pull out the clip and remove retaining pin and cross spring.

4. Hold the backing plate of the pad with pliers. Remove pad assembly and shim.

**Brake Pad Removal
(1974 and Later Models)**

1. Remove the wheel.

2. Remove the protector (see **Figure 21**) by prying up edge of clip at center of pad protector with a screwdriver.

3. Detach the M-clip from pad and its ends from the retaining pins while holding the center of the M-clip. Take off the M-clip.

4. Pull off retaining pins from caliper assembly. Remove K-spring.

5. Take out pad assembly by grasping back plate area of the pad with pliers. See **Figure 22**.

CAUTION
The caliper is of a floating type; therefore the torque plate shaft should be kept clean.

12

Brake Pad Inspection

Check pad for oil and wear. If worn, pads for both wheels should be replaced at same time. The ideal lining thickness is 0.38 in., and the service limit 0.08 in. See **Figure 23**.

Brake Pad Installation
(1971-1973 Models)

1. Spread piston with Colt special tool Piston Spreader (C-3992). Insert pad with the shim between pad and piston with arrow mark on the shim facing forward. See **Figure 24**.

2. To install cross spring, insert pin into caliper with the (A) part (**Figure 25**) of cross spring hooked on retaining pin and fasten it in position with a clip. Be sure pad shim is between cross spring flanges (B). Firmly press (C) part of spring onto the retaining pin with the hand.

3. Tighten connector bolt to 14.5-18 ft.-lb. Bleed brakes (see *Brake Bleeding*, this chapter).

4. To check for brake dragging, drive the car at a slow speed and apply the parking brakes. Check brakes for excessive drag. If found, disassemble piston and check piston sliding part for dirt and rust, and piston seal for elasticity.

Brake Pad Installation
(1974 and Later Models)

1. Spread the piston with Colt special tool Piston Spreader (C-3992). Insert pad through the shim. See **Figure 24**.

2. Install K-spring and M-clip as shown in **Figure 26**. Use care not to confuse their positions.

3. Install pad protector in proper direction as illustrated in **Figure 27**.

4. To check for brake dragging, drive the car at a slow speed and apply the parking brakes. Check the brakes for excessive drag. If found, disassemble piston and check the piston sliding part for dirt and rust, and the piston seal for elasticity.

Brake Caliper Removal

1. Remove disc brake pad (see Steps 1-5 under *Brake Pad Removal*, preceding).

2. Pull off brake hose clip from strut area. Disconnect brake hose from caliper.

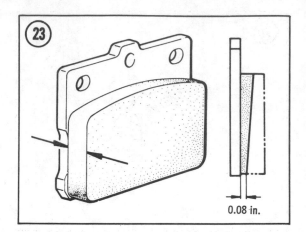

(23)

0.08 in.

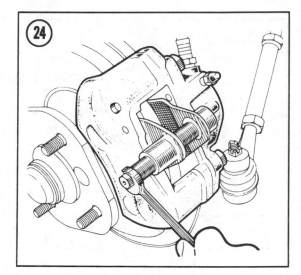

(24)

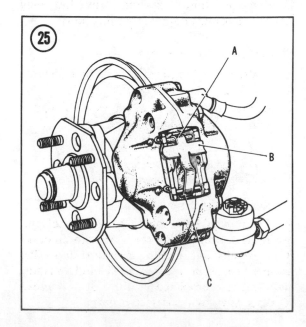

(25)

A

B

C

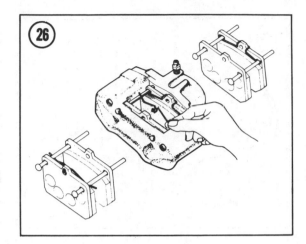

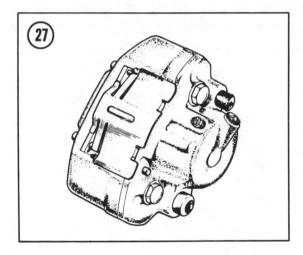

3. Remove caliper assembly by loosening torque plate and adapter mounting bolts.

Brake Caliper Disassembly

1. Loosen attaching bridge bolts and separate outer caliper from inner caliper.

2. Remove dust seal. Remove piston by applying compressed air at brake hose fitting.

CAUTION
Do not apply high pressure suddenly. The piston could fly out, causing injury.

3. Remove piston seal carefully.

4. Clean metal parts in non-petroleum solvent, alcohol, or brake fluid; the piston seal in brake fluid or alcohol; and the dust seal and other rubber parts in alcohol. (Alcohol washing should be completed within 30 seconds.) Replace any worn or defective parts.

Brake Caliper Assembly

1. Whenever the caliper assembly has been disassembled, reassemble using a new piston seal and dust seal. When replacing inner parts, use special Colt kit parts which are available for this purpose. The kits include rubber grease (red) and special grease (yellow) which are ideal for disassembly and servicing.

2. Apply rubber grease (red) to the piston seal brake fluid to the piston cylinder inner diameter (ID). Insert piston seal into piston. Be careful not to twist the seal during installation.

3. Clean torque plate shaft and caliper shaft bore whenever torque plate has been removed from inner caliper. Apply special grease (yellow) to the rubber bushing, wiper seal inner surface, and torque plate shaft before assembly. Apply grease to the threaded portion of the torque plate shaft. Use care to apply the rubber grease (red) and special grease (yellow) to proper parts. Do not confuse them.

4. Tighten inner and outer caliper bridge bolts to 58-69 ft.-lb.

Brake Caliper Installation

1. Tighten caliper assembly (torque plate) to the adapter (29-36 ft.-lb. for 1971-1973 models; 51-65 ft.-lb. for 1974 models; 58-72 ft.-lb. on 1975 and later models).

2. Tighten the brake hose to 9-12 ft.-lb. Bleed the brake hydraulic system (see *Brake Bleeding*, this chapter).

CAUTION
The wheel cylinder uses a large piston. The smallest amount of air will affect the brake pedal stroke. The bleeding operation is critical and should be performed with precision. Tighten the bleed screw to 4-7 ft.-lb. after bleeding is completed.

Disc Removal

1. Remove the wheel and brake caliper.

2. Remove hub assembly from the knuckle. Disconnect hub from disc by capturing disc in a vise. Avoid holding the disc in direct contact with the jaws of the vise (use soft copper or aluminum plates between them).

12

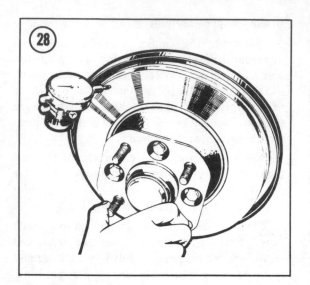

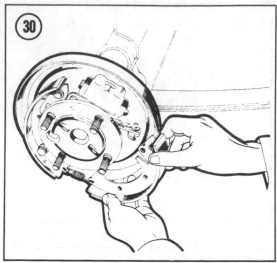

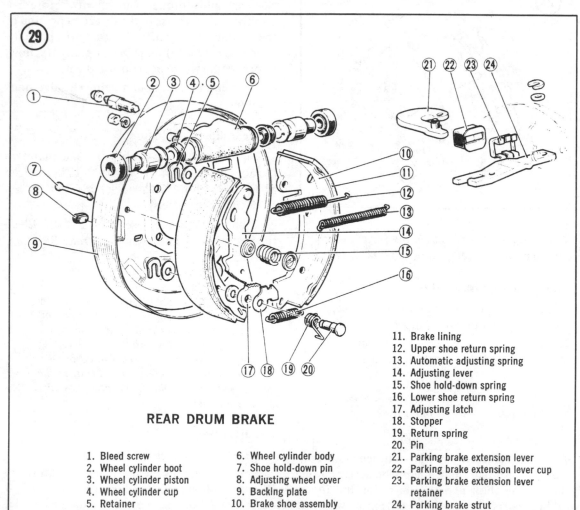

REAR DRUM BRAKE

1. Bleed screw
2. Wheel cylinder boot
3. Wheel cylinder piston
4. Wheel cylinder cup
5. Retainer
6. Wheel cylinder body
7. Shoe hold-down pin
8. Adjusting wheel cover
9. Backing plate
10. Brake shoe assembly
11. Brake lining
12. Upper shoe return spring
13. Automatic adjusting spring
14. Adjusting lever
15. Shoe hold-down spring
16. Lower shoe return spring
17. Adjusting latch
18. Stopper
19. Return spring
20. Pin
21. Parking brake extension lever
22. Parking brake extension lever cup
23. Parking brake extension lever retainer
24. Parking brake strut

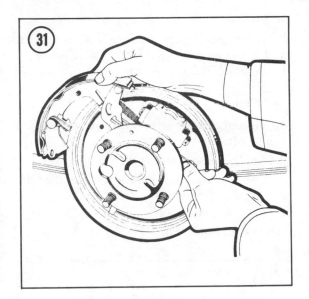

Disc Inspection

Check disc for wear and damage. The standard thickness of 1974 and later discs is 0.51 in., the service limit is 0.45 in.; 1971-1973 discs are 0.39 in. thick with a service limit of 0.33 in.

Disc Installation

1. Tighten caliper adapter and dust cover to the knuckle (29-36 ft.-lb. torque).

2. Tighten disc to hub (25-29 ft.-lb. torque).

3. Install front hub assembly (see Chapter Ten).

4. The disc deflection should be less than 0.006 in. If beyond, change its location on the hub and check again. If deflection cannot be corrected, replace the disc. See **Figure 28**.

5. Install caliper assembly to adapter by tightening to 51-65 ft.-lb. torque.

REAR DRUM BRAKES

Removal

1. After removing wheel, remove brake drum.

2. Remove shoe hold-down spring (**Figure 29**).

3. Detach shoe return spring (upper) end hook and strut-to-shoe spring from trailing shoe. Remove brake shoe assembly together with lower shoe return spring. See **Figure 30**.

4. Hold the adjusting latch down. Pull adjusting lever toward center of brake and remove leading shoe assembly. See **Figure 31**.

5. Remove shoe return spring (upper) and strut-to-shoe spring.

6. Remove wheel cylinder from backing plate after disconnecting brake line from the wheel cylinder.

7. Disconnect parking brake cable from extension lever by pulling the clevis pin off.

8. Pull parking brake extension lever and parking brake strut from the backing plate.

9. Pull the axle shaft and remove backing plate (see Chapter Eleven).

Inspection

1. Inspect linings for excessive wear.

2. Inspect wheel cylinders for leaks.

3. Check adjusting lever and latch for damage and wear.

4. Check brake drum for cracks or grooves. The standrd dimension for the brake drum ID is 9.0 in. The repair limit is 9.079 in.

Installation

1. Install wheel cylinder to backing plate. Tighten to 4-7 ft.-lb. torque.

2. Apply brake grease (Plastilube No. 2 or equivalent) to the backing plate ledge surface, wheel cylinder, and anchor plate shoe contact surfaces, and parking strut joints and contact surfaces.

3. Pull adjusting lever fully toward center of brake. Adjust amount of engagement of the lever with the strut. Note that the adjusting lever and latch spring differ between left and right: left lever is white; right is yellow; the left latch spring is black; the right is light blue.

4. Install one end of the strut-to-shoe spring to the strut and the other end to the shoe. The left spring is white; the right a different color. See **Figure 32**.

5. Return the adjusting lever until it touches the shoe rim.

6. Tighten the brake tube to 9-12 ft.-lb. torque. Bleed the hydraulic system (see *Brake Bleeding*, this chapter). Tighten bleed screw to 4-7 ft.-lb.

7. Depress the brake pedal several times. This will automatically adjust the brake shoe lining-to-drum clearance. The adjuster is designed to

12

operate approximately every 0.003 in. of lining wear. The normal brake shoe lining-to-drum clearance is 0.018-0.027 in.

PARKING BRAKES

Removal

1. Disconnect cable from extension lever after pulling off clevis pins from both sides of the rear brake. Disconnect cable by loosening nut at center of axle housing. See **Figure 33**.

2. Loosen parking brake mounting bolts and take parking brake out by lifting upward. See **Figure 34**. Remove snap ring from front end of outer cable. Disconnect cable from parking brake lever.

Inspection

Inspect parking brake lever for latch wear and cable damage. Replace any defective or borderline parts.

Installation

1. Tighten cable lever to center of axle housing to 11-14 ft.-lb.

2. Apply chassis grease to each sliding part.

3. Install each cable clip (be sure the clip doesn't interfere with a rotating part).

4. Tighten attaching nut of cable lever shaft at center of axle housing to 11-14.5 ft.-lb.

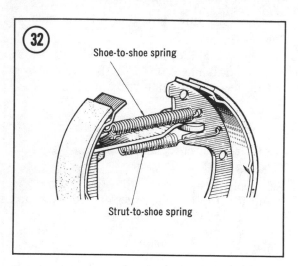

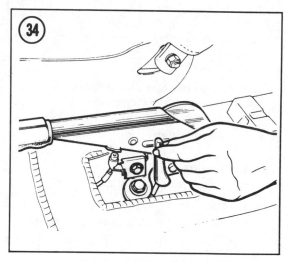

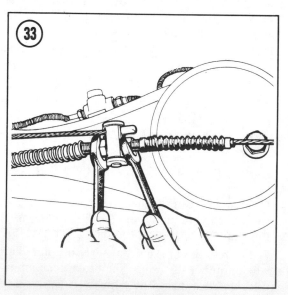

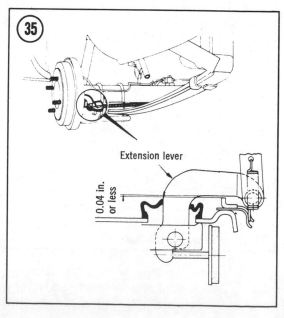

Adjustment

1. Release parking brakes.

2. Adjust extension lever-to-stopper clearance to 0-0.04 in. with the cable adjusting nut. See **Figure 35**. Loosen both the cable lever attaching bolt and the adjusting nut and move cable lever to the right. Set the left cable and tighten cable lever to 11-14 ft.-lb. torque. Tighten adjusting nut and set the right cable.

3. Check parking brake lever free stroke and brake drag (8-12 notches, and brakes must be applied fully when lever is pulled with 66 lb. force).

CAUTION
If, after above adjustment, the parking brake lever free stroke is more than 8-12 notches, rear brake automatic adjusters are malfunctioning. Disassemble and check brakes.

NOTE: *The parking lever switch requires no adjustment.*

Table 1   TIGHTENING TORQUES

Part	Ft.-lb.	N•m
Service brakes		
Pedal support to support member	6-9	8-12
Pedal support to power brake (toe board)	6-9	8-12
Master cylinder		
Check valve cap	17-25	23-34
Check valve case	29-36	39-49
Piston stopper	1.1-2.2	1.5-3.0
Reservoir tank band	1.7-2.9	2.3-3.9
Master cylinder connector bolts (1971-1974)	14-18	19-25
Master cylinder connector bolts (1975-on)	18-25	25-34
Power brake hose fitting	11-13	15-18
Power brake installation bolts	6-9	8-12
Bleeder screw	4-7	6-9
Brake hose	9-12	12-16
Combination valve	6-9	8-12
Brake tube flare nut	9-12	12-16
Disc brake		
Caliper inner and outer bridge bolt	58-69	79-93
Caliper assembly (torque plate) installation bolts	51-65	69-88
Caliper adapter installation bolts	29-36	40-49
Disc rotor to hub connection	25-29	34-39
Leading/trailing brake		
Wheel cylinder installation bolts	4-7	6-9
Parking brakes		
Cable lever installation	11-14	15-19

12

CHAPTER THIRTEEN

BODY

This chapter covers basic removal and installation procedures for the more commonly damaged body parts: hood, trunk lid, doors, etc.

HOOD

Removal/Installation

Refer to **Figures 1 and 2** for the following procedure.

1. Disconnect washer tube, remove hook, and remove hinge attaching bolts.

2. Remove hood from body (**Figure 3**), then remove hood lock and disconnect release cable (**Figure 4**).

3. Pull off release cable by disconnecting it from bracket. Remove stand from bracket.

4. To install, insert release cable through the hole in the light support. Then clip cable to body at 5 points (**Figure 5**, all except station wagon).

5. Install release cable through spring house and tighten release cable and bracket (Colt Station Wagon only). See **Figure 6**.

6. Install release cable in grommet. Apply sealer in space between grommet and cable.

Adjustment

1. Adjust hood position by loosening attaching

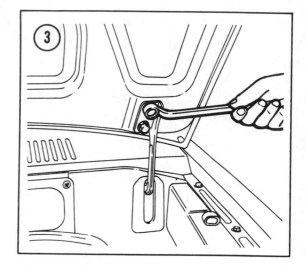

nuts and sliding hood front or rear, or side to side in the oblong holes in the hinges.

2. Adjust vertical position of hood with bumper screws (**Figure 7**).

3. Adjust hood lock-to-hook alignment by loosening mounting screws and sliding in direction required, as shown in **Figure 8**. Tighten screws after adjustment.

> NOTE: *The hook engagement is affected by the length of the lock bolt. The standard is 2.2 in. (56 mm) for the coupe and sedan, and 2.1 in. (53 mm) for the station wagon* (**Figure 9**).

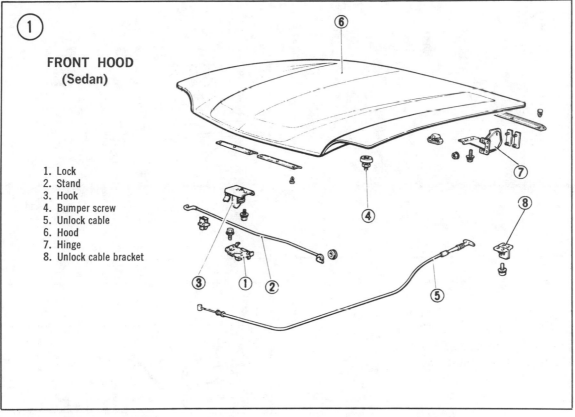

① FRONT HOOD (Sedan)

1. Lock
2. Stand
3. Hook
4. Bumper screw
5. Unlock cable
6. Hood
7. Hinge
8. Unlock cable bracket

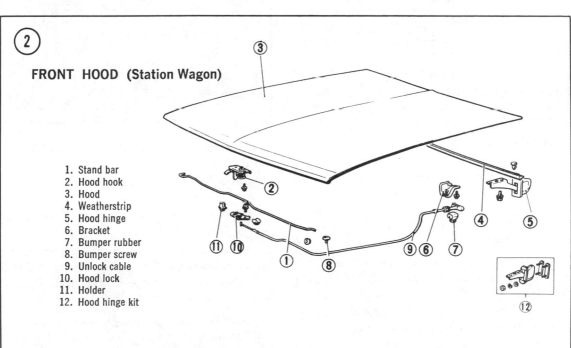

② FRONT HOOD (Station Wagon)

1. Stand bar
2. Hood hook
3. Hood
4. Weatherstrip
5. Hood hinge
6. Bracket
7. Bumper rubber
8. Bumper screw
9. Unlock cable
10. Hood lock
11. Holder
12. Hood hinge kit

13

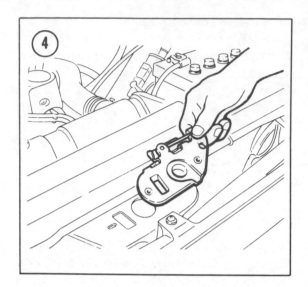

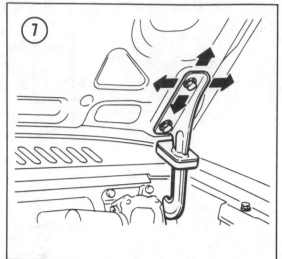

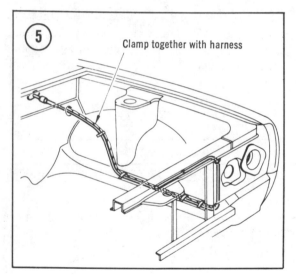

Clamp together with harness

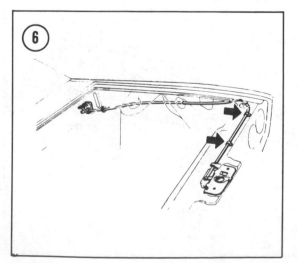

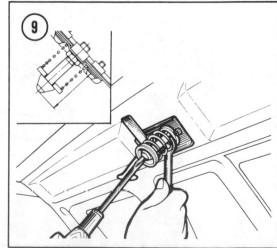

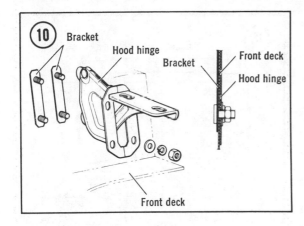

⑩ Bracket

Hood hinge

Bracket

Front deck

Hood hinge

Front deck

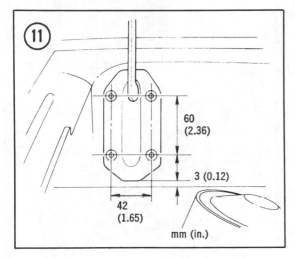

⑪

60
(2.36)

3 (0.12)

42
(1.65)

mm (in.)

Hinge Replacement
(Station Wagon)

The hood hinge is welded to the front deck. To replace it, proceed as follows, referring to **Figure 10**:

1. Cut away the spot weld at the junction of the hinge and front deck with a drill bit 0.31 in. (8 mm) in diameter, and remove the hood hinge.

2. Mark centers of the hinge attaching positions on the front deck, as shown in **Figure 11**. Drill 4 hinge mounting holes with a 0.31 in. (8 mm) drill bit.

3. Remove access hole cover or wiper motor, then insert bracket from inside the front deck and loosely tighten the hood hinge.

4. Apply adhesive to contacting surfaces of front deck and bracket (be sure that the area is smooth) before mounting the bracket. Mount the hinge.

DECK LID

Removal
(Coupe and Sedan)

Refer to **Figure 12** for the following procedure:

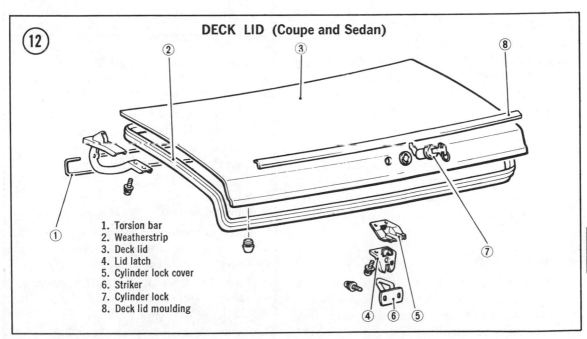

⑫ **DECK LID (Coupe and Sedan)**

1. Torsion bar
2. Weatherstrip
3. Deck lid
4. Lid latch
5. Cylinder lock cover
6. Striker
7. Cylinder lock
8. Deck lid moulding

13

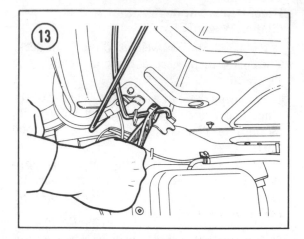

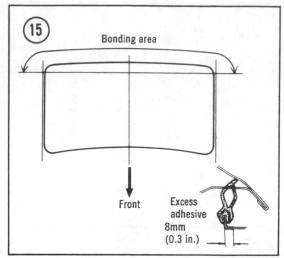

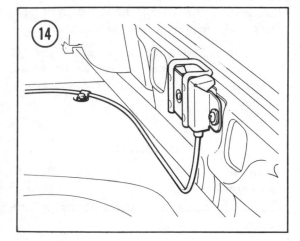

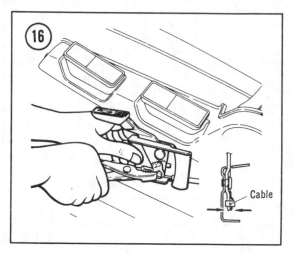

1. Remove lid latch, cylinder lock, and lid moulding.

2. Remove lid hinge attaching bolts, then remove lid from body.

3. Remove torsion bar by removing it from the bar supporting area of central bracket, and prying bar off of the bar fitting area at the side (**Figure 13**).

4. Remove striker from rear panel, then remove weatherstripping.

5. Remove all traces of adhesive at the body flange.

Removal
(Station Wagon)

1. Remove lid latch, cylinder lock, and antenna lead-in terminal and striker.

2. Remove lid hinge attaching bolts, then remove lid from body.

3. Remove torsion bar from lid hinge side, then withdraw cable locking snap ring and disconnect cable from latch.

4. Remove release handle from cable and withdraw cable (**Figure 14**).

5. Remove weatherstripping from body, and all traces of adhesive at body flange.

Installation
(Coupe and Sedan)

1. Apply adhesive to bonding area to attach the weatherstripping. Where necessary, attach weatherstrip in the flanging (**Figure 15**).

2. To install lid moulding, place adhesive in moulding attachment area, then attach moulding.

3. Install damper with water drain hole at rear.

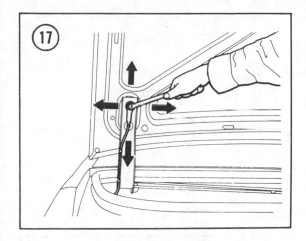

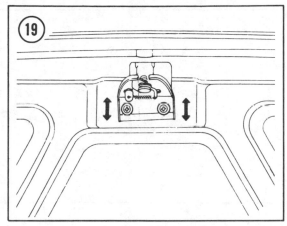

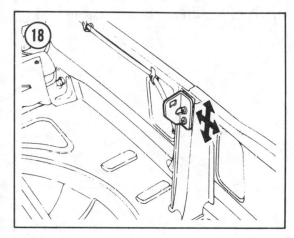

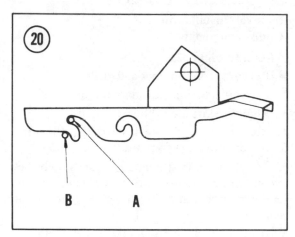

B   A

Installation
(Station Wagon)

1. Use special care to insulate the lid from the body, as it also serves as the antenna. Install the torsion bar collar at the center of the upper torsion bar, then apply grease to the turning and sliding latch surfaces.

2. Tighten the release handle and cable connection in directions of arrows (**Figure 16**). Use pliers to be sure that cable does not come off.

3. Apply adhesive to bonding part of weatherstripping, then fit it snugly into the flange (refer to **Figure 15**).

Lid Adjustment

1. Adjust the lid position by loosening mounting bolts and sliding hood in the oblong holes at the lid fitting area (**Figure 17**). Tighten bolts when through.

2. Adjust vertical position of lid by inserting a washer in the hinge fitting area on the body side.

Latch and Striker Adjustment
(Coupe and Sedan)

1. Adjust lateral and vertical positions of striker by loosening attaching screws (**Figure 18**). Tighten after adjustment.

2. Adjust longitudinal position of latch by loosening latch attaching screws (**Figure 19**). Tighten after adjustment.

Torsion Bar Adjustment

To increase or decrease the effort required to open and close the trunk lid, change the position of the bars on the torsion bar support bracket (**Figure 20**). Place the right and left torsion bars in the A area, then move one of the bars to the B area if the bar holding pressure is less than desired.

13

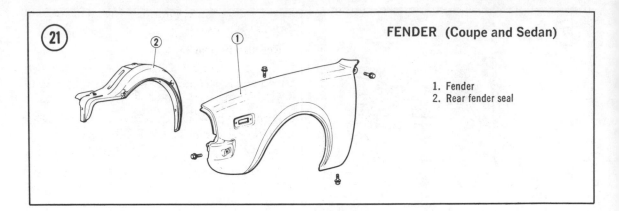

FENDER (Coupe and Sedan)

1. Fender
2. Rear fender seal

FENDERS

**Removal/Installation
(Coupe and Sedan)**

Refer to **Figure 21**.

1. Remove front bumper and grille.

2. Disconnect front side marker light wiring.

3. Remove skirt moulding front clips.

4. Remove fender attaching bolts, then the fender by moving it forward.

5. To install, insert fender gasket snugly between fender and body, then apply adhesive to fender rear seal and attach seal to rear end of fender.

6. Install front seal and upper seal with clips to the body.

**Removal/Installation
(Station Wagon)**

Refer to **Figure 22**.

1. Disconnect wiring at the front combination light, then remove front bumper.

2. Remove radiator grille, lower grille, and front turn signal light.

3. Remove front step panel.

4. Remove fender and fender shield plate.

5. Remove fender attaching bolts, then the fender assembly by moving it forward.

6. To install, touch up fender inner surface if the coating is damaged.

7. Improper sealing of wheel cut portion will cause corrosion, so be sure to install fender shield plate and rubber. See **Figure 23**.

8. Reverse preceding steps to complete installation procedure.

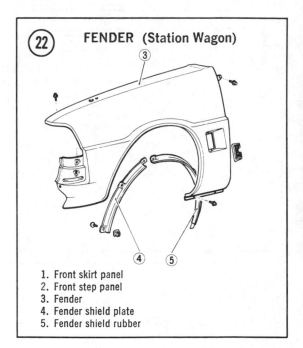

FENDER (Station Wagon)

1. Front skirt panel
2. Front step panel
3. Fender
4. Fender shield plate
5. Fender shield rubber

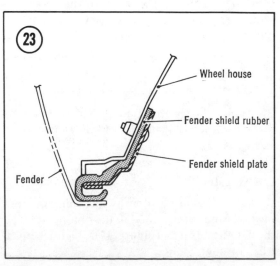

Wheel house

Fender shield rubber

Fender shield plate

Fender

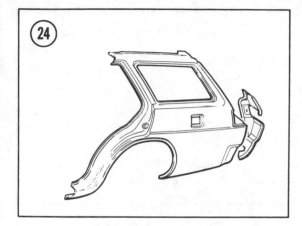

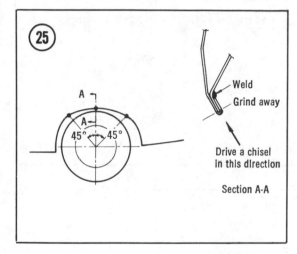

Weld
Grind away

Drive a chisel
in this direction

Section A-A

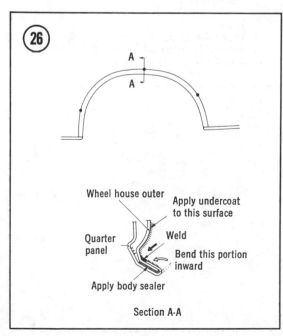

Wheel house outer
Apply undercoat
to this surface

Quarter
panel
Weld

Bend this portion
inward

Apply body sealer

Section A-A

Rear Quarter Panel Removal/Installation (Station Wagon)

Refer to **Figure 24**.

1. Grind away all 3 welded points and hatched portion (all around) with a portable hand grinder.

2. Drive a chisel in direction of arrow (**Figure 25**), then remove adhesive all around.

3. To install, be sure that spot welding is done properly, because if wheel cut portion is weak, strain will certainly develop in the outer panel. After the welding is done, be sure that the quarter panel and 3 wheel house inner panels are welded.

4. An improperly sealed wheel cut portion can cause corrosion, so be sure to apply undercoating and body sealer (**Figure 26**). Be sure to clean and degrease the surfaces to be undercoated or sealed, prior to application of the undercoating and body sealer.

5. If coated film on inside surface of quarter panel has been damaged, be sure to apply paint to prevent rust formation.

DOORS

Refer to **Figures 27 through 32** when performing the following procedures.

Door Assembly and Door Hinges Removal/Installation

1. Remove door-to-hinge attaching bolts, then remove door assembly.

2. Remove hinge-to-pillar attaching bolts.

3. Remove hinge assemblies. See **Figure 33**.

4. To install, temporarily attach the upper and/or lower hinges to the pillars.

5. Install the door on the hinges.

6. Adjust position of door at hinge-to-body attaching bolts to provide a uniform clearance between door and body.

7. Adjust lateral position of body by installing shims between hinges and body.

8. Be sure to tighten all bolts after adjustment.

13

Door Adjustment

Use Colt tool CT-1127 (Door Adjusting Wrench) if available, to adjust the door.

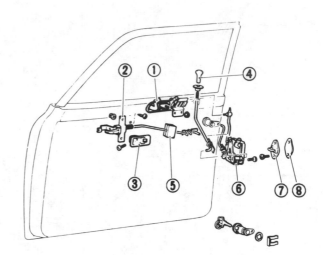

1. Door outer handle
2. Door inner handle
   and lock assembly
3. Cover
4. Lock knob
5. Inside rod cushion
6. Door latch
7. Door striker
8. Shim

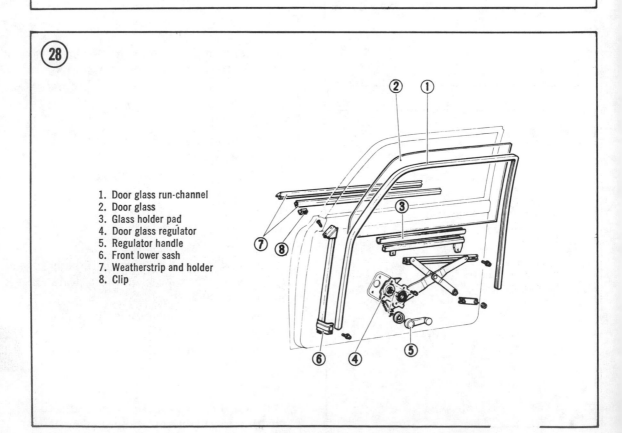

1. Door glass run-channel
2. Door glass
3. Glass holder pad
4. Door glass regulator
5. Regulator handle
6. Front lower sash
7. Weatherstrip and holder
8. Clip

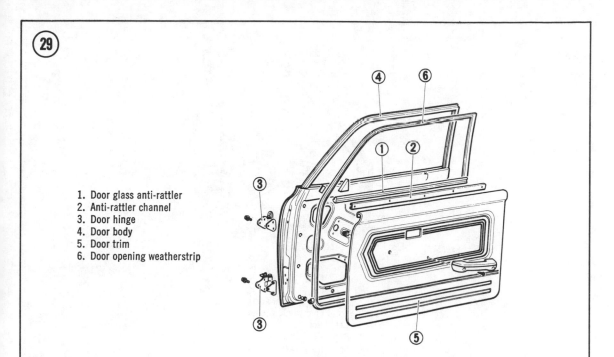

1. Door glass anti-rattler
2. Anti-rattler channel
3. Door hinge
4. Door body
5. Door trim
6. Door opening weatherstrip

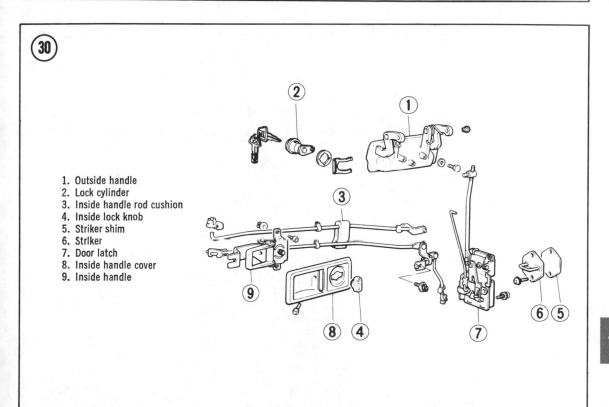

1. Outside handle
2. Lock cylinder
3. Inside handle rod cushion
4. Inside lock knob
5. Striker shim
6. Strlker
7. Door latch
8. Inside handle cover
9. Inside handle

13

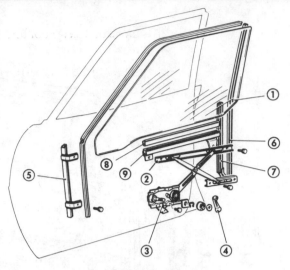

1. Front door window glass
2. Front door window roller
3. Regulator
4. Regulator handle
5. Front lower sash
6. Run channel
7. Rear lower sash
8. Door glass pad
9. Window glass holder

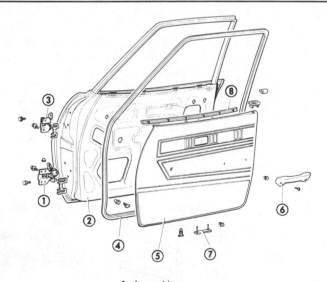

1. Lower hinge
2. Door body
3. Upper hinge
4. Weatherstrip
5. Door trim
6. Arm rest
7. Drain hole seal
8. Anti-rattler

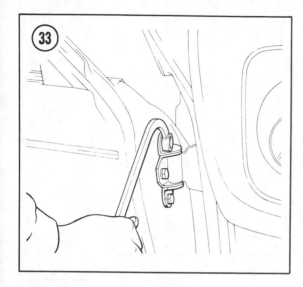

Loosen hinge attaching bolts on body side and adjust door position to provide a uniform clearance between door and body (**Figure 34**).

Door Striker Adjustment

1. Adjust position of striker by loosening its attaching screws.

2. Adjust longitudinal position of door striker by inserting a shim, Colt part number MB019009, for station wagon, which gives 0.02-0.04 in. (0.5-1.0 mm); or Colt MB037131, for coupe and sedan, which gives 0.031 in. (0.8 mm) in the striker attaching section (**Figure 35**).

Door Glass and Winding Mechanism (Removal/Installation, Coupe and Sedan)

1. Remove arm rest, then pull off inside lock knob and remove inside handle cover.

2. Insert a screwdriver between door trim and the escutcheon, and open up clearance between these parts. Pull clip off, then remove handle.

3. Remove door trim and waterproof film.

4. With door glass fully lowered, remove weatherstripping and holder, along with the clip (hold the clip up from the inside with a screwdriver, as shown in **Figure 36**).

5. Remove screws holding glass holder to the arm.

6. Remove door glass upward (**Figure 37**).

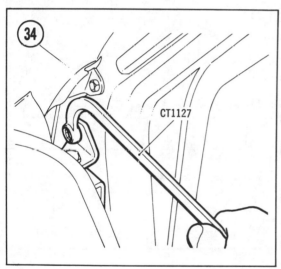

CT1127

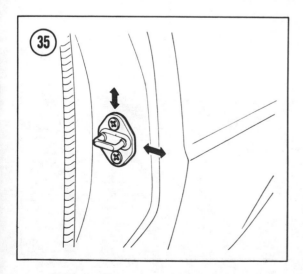

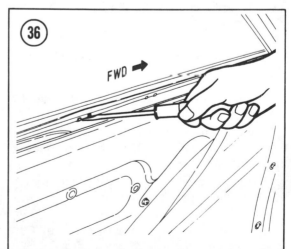

FWD

13

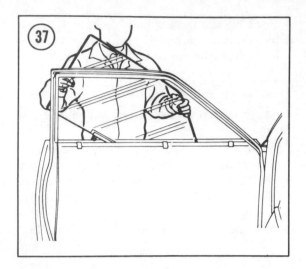

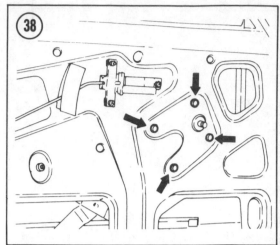

7. Remove winder sub-roller guide and the winder body attaching screws, then remove the winder. See **Figure 38**.

8. Remove front lower sash.

9. Check winder pinion and driven gear for wear and damage.

10. To install, apply grease to all revolving and sliding parts such as the driven gear rollers and winder pinion.

11. Attach waterproof film with butyl tape.

12. Install the glass assembly on the winder mechanism, and raise glass as high as it will go to see if it slides smoothly in the channels. If glass is loose in the longitudinal direction, adjust by shifting winding guide up or down (**Figure 39**).

13. With glass in fully closed position, install handle so that knob is 30° above the level position, facing forward.

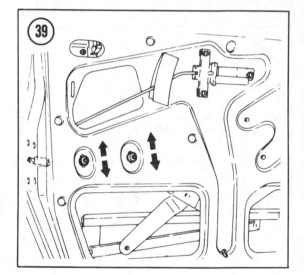

Door Glass and Winding Mechanism (Removal/Installation, Station Wagon)

1. Remove arm rest and inside door handle cover.

2. Open door trim and escutcheon with a screwdriver, then pull off clip and remove winder handle.

3. Turn to remove door inside lock knob, then remove trim retainer and trim with a screwdriver.

4. Remove door inside panel waterproof film from door body.

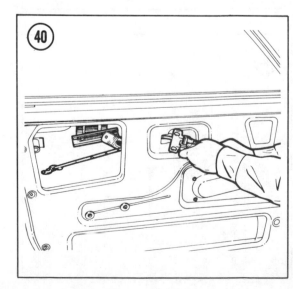

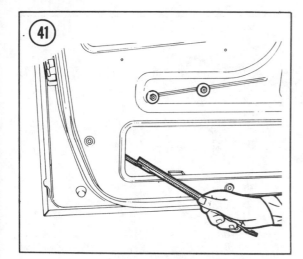

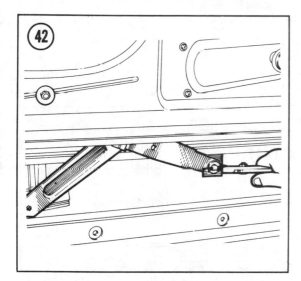

5. Remove inside handle rod on door lock side, then remove inside handle (**Figure 40**).

6. Remove door sash (rear) lower screws, then pull sash downward and off (**Figure 41**).

7. Lower door glass as low as possible, then remove glass holder pin from winder arm (**Figure 42**).

8. Hold the glass and pull off the winder arm roller from the glass roller guide. Remove glass by lifting upward and outward, slowly, with the rear end up (**Figure 43**).

9. Remove the winder sub-roller guide, then remove the winder (**Figure 44**).

10. Check winder pinion and driven gear for wear and damage.

11. To install, apply grease to all sliding and rotating parts such as the winder driven gear and pinion, glass holder pin and rollers.

12. Use adhesive for bonding areas such as weatherstripping (A, **Figure 45**), door inside panel waterproof film (B, **Figure 45**), and bumper (C, **Figure 45**).

13. Insert each clip exactly in the clip hole when installing the weatherstripping. Place the top of the weatherstripping along the sash.

14. Install the winder handle so that the knob is in the fully closed position, with the handle 30° up over the horizontal and forward.

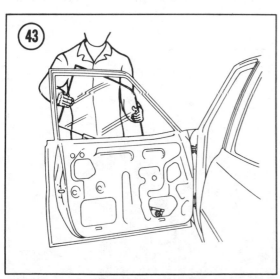

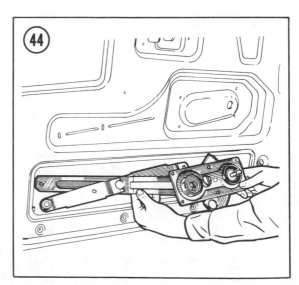

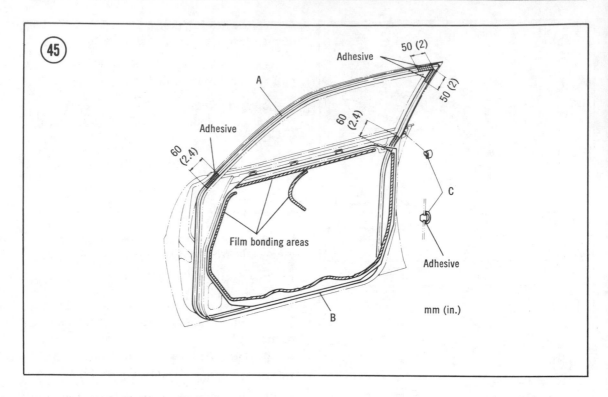

(45)

50 (2)

Adhesive

A

50 (2)

Adhesive

60
(2.4)

60
(2.4)

C

Film bonding areas

Adhesive

B

mm (in.)

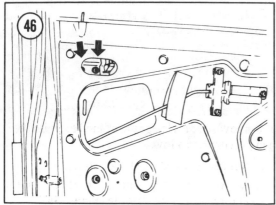

(46)

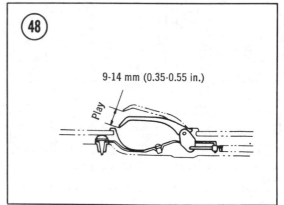

(48)

9-14 mm (0.35-0.55 in.)

Play

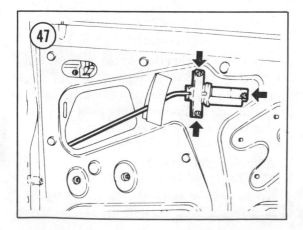

(47)

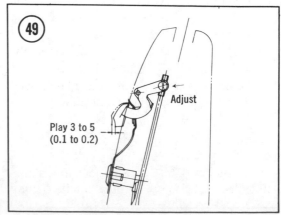

(49)

Adjust

Play 3 to 5
(0.1 to 0.2)

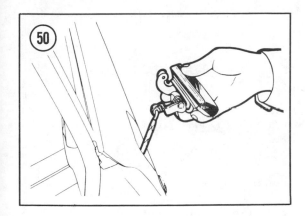

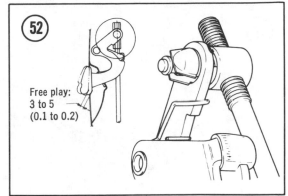

Free play:
3 to 5
(0.1 to 0.2)

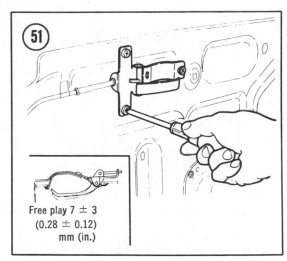

Free play 7 ± 3
(0.28 ± 0.12)
mm (in.)

Door Handle and Door Lock
(Removal/Installation, Coupe and Sedan)

1. Remove door glass as outlined in previous section and perform the following steps:

   a. Remove outer handle rod at handle side, and remove handle (**Figure 46**).

   b. Remove key cylinder lock rod at latch side, pull retainer off, and remove cylinder.

   c. Remove inside lock rod assembly attaching screws (**Figure 47**).

   d. Disconnect inside handle rod at latch side, then remote the inside handle and the lock assembly.

2. Check lock mechanism for damage or wear, and see if it operates smoothly.

3. To install, apply grease to lock operating parts, then check to see that the handle is connected to the rod linkage properly.

4. Install the inside handle and lock assembly, then see if it works properly. Adjust handle play as specified in **Figure 48**.

5. Be sure that when the inside lock is in the LOCK position, the door is not unlocked even if the door outer handle is operated (coupe and sedan).

6. Adjust outer handle play to 0.1-0.2 in. (3-5 mm) with the rod-side joint (**Figure 49**).

> NOTE: *Be sure that when the door outer handle is operated it has a specified play and the door latch always releases before the handle reaches the end of its stroke.*

Door Handle and Door Lock
(Removal/Installation, Station Wagon)

1. Remove door glass as outlined previously, then proceed as follows:

   a. Remove door inside lock rod.

   b. Disconnect outer handle rod at lock side, and remove outer handle (**Figure 50**).

   c. Disconnect cylinder lock rod from door lock, then remove cylinder lock.

   d. Remove door assembly.

2. Check lock mechanism for damage or wear. See if lock operates smoothly.

3. To install, apply grease to lock operating parts prior to installation. Check to be sure that the rod is connected properly and that the lock operates smoothly.

4. Adjust play of inside handle to 0.28 ± 0.12 in. (7 ± 3 mm), as shown in **Figure 51**.

5. Adjust play of outer handle to 0.1-0.2 in. (3-5 mm) at the latch joint (**Figure 52**).

13

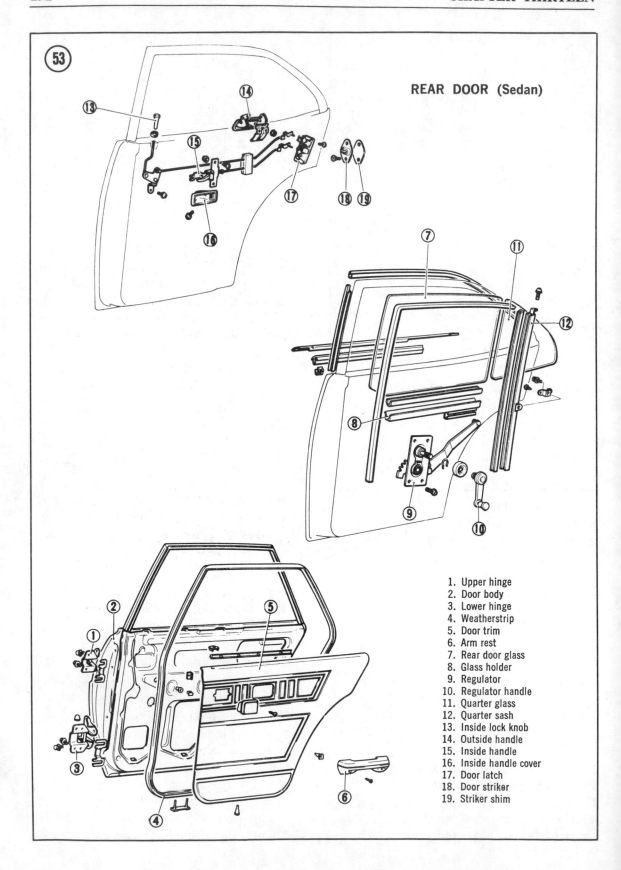

REAR DOOR (Sedan)

1. Upper hinge
2. Door body
3. Lower hinge
4. Weatherstrip
5. Door trim
6. Arm rest
7. Rear door glass
8. Glass holder
9. Regulator
10. Regulator handle
11. Quarter glass
12. Quarter sash
13. Inside lock knob
14. Outside handle
15. Inside handle
16. Inside handle cover
17. Door latch
18. Door striker
19. Striker shim

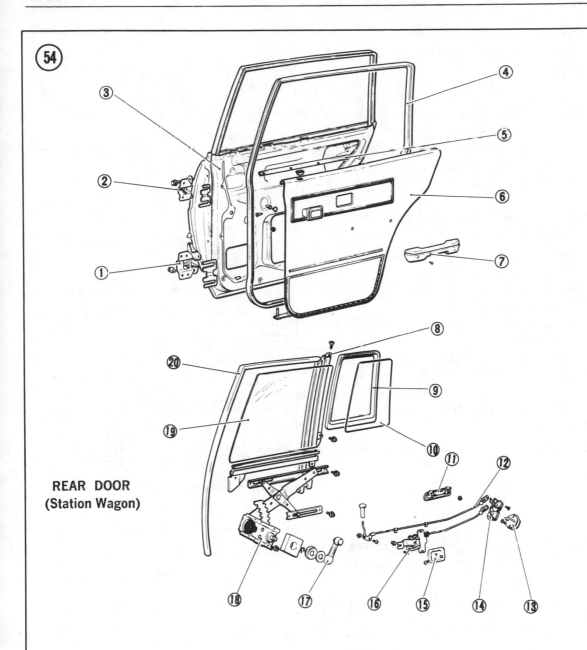

REAR DOOR
(Station Wagon)

1. Lower hinge
2. Upper hinge
3. Door body
4. Weatherstrip
5. Anti-rattler
6. Door trim
7. Arm rest
8. Run channel
9. Quarter window weatherstrip
10. Quarter window glass
11. Outside handle
12. Inside lock rod
13. Striker
14. Door latch
15. Inside handle cover
16. Inside handle
17. Regulator handle
18. Regulator
19. Window glass
20. Run channel

13

REAR DOORS

Refer to **Figures 53 and 54** for the following procedures.

Door Assembly and Door Hinges (Removal/Installation)

To remove and install door assembly and hinges, refer to the same section for the front doors, as outlined in previous section.

Door Glass and Winding Mechanism (Removal/Installation, Sedan)

1. Remove arm rest, winder handle and door inside lock knob.

2. Remove trim retainer with a screwdriver, then remove trim.

3. Remove door inside panel waterproof film from door body.

4. Disconnect inside handle rod at door lock side, then remove inside handle.

5. Lower glass, then loosen quarter sash attaching screws and remove glass and sash (**Figure 55**).

6. Tilt the glass, then disconnect it from winder arm roller and pull outward with glass rear edge first (**Figure 56**).

7. Remove winder attaching screws, then remove winder from lower part.

8. To install, apply a soapy solution to entire surface of quarter glass weatherstripping and sash.

9. Use adhesive to attach door waterproof films and weatherstripping (refer to **Figure 57** for sedan; **Figure 58** for station wagon). "A" in these illustrations refer to the door inside panel waterproof film; "B" to the corner weatherstripping; and "C" to the weatherstripping.

Door Glass and Winding Mechanism (Removal/Installation, Station Wagon)

Perform Steps 1-6 in preceding section, *Door Glass and Winding Mechanism, (Removal/Installation, Coupe)*, then perform the following steps:

1. Lower glass, loosen quarter sash attaching screws, then remove quarter glass and sash (**Figure 55**).

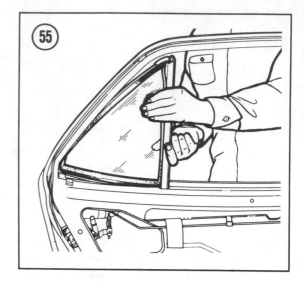

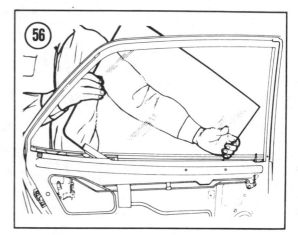

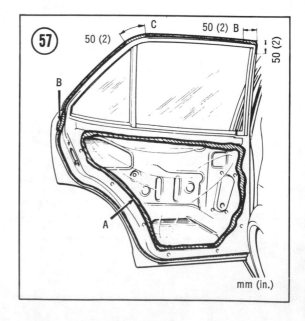

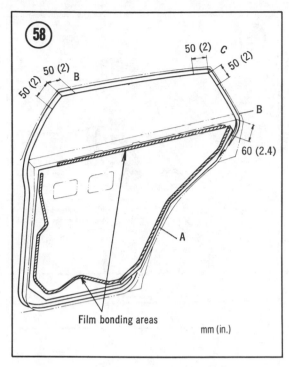

50 (2) *c*

50 (2)

50 (2)

B

50 (2)

B

B

60 (2.4)

A

Film bonding areas

mm (in.)

2. Proceed with Steps 8 and 9, preceding section, *Door Glass and Winding Mechanism, (Removal/Installation, Coupe)*.

Door Handle and Door Lock (Removal/Installation)

Perform same procedure for the front doors, given previously.

SIDE WINDOW (COUPE)

Removal/Installation

1. Pull off part of door opening trim. Refer to **Figure 59**.

2. Remove center pillar trim, then remove trim attaching link to body (coupe). See **Figure 60**.

3. Remove screws holding hinge to body, and the side window glass.

4. Remove link or bracket, and the hinge from side window glass.

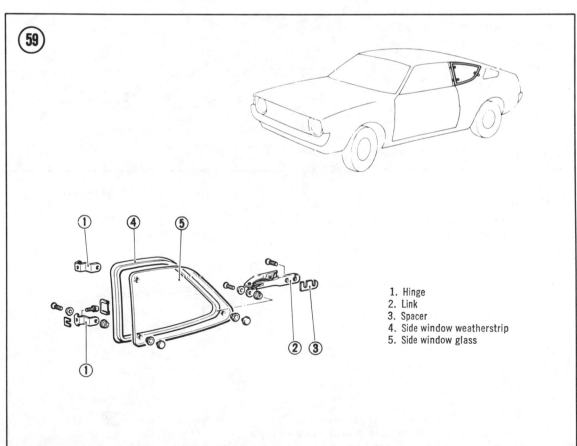

1. Hinge
2. Link
3. Spacer
4. Side window weatherstrip
5. Side window glass

13

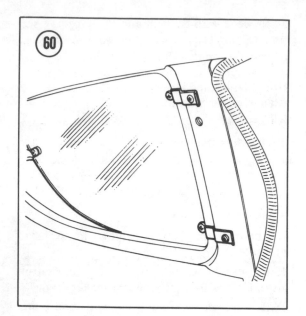

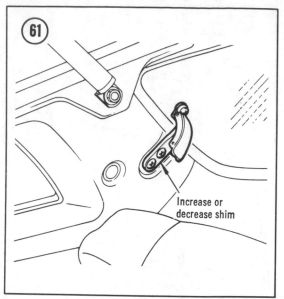

Increase or
decrease shim

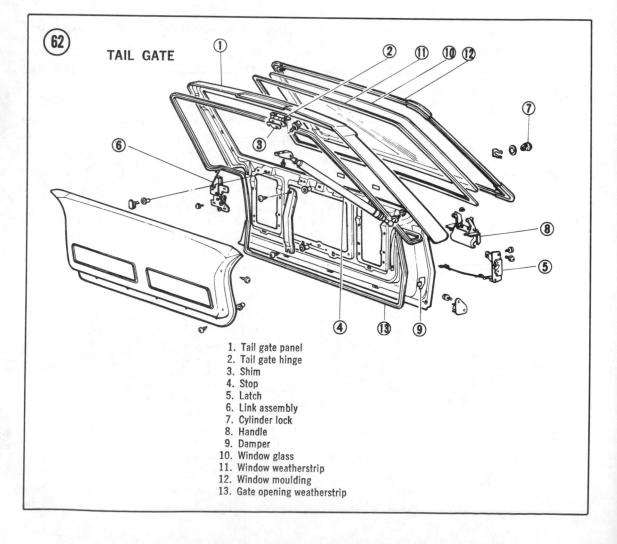

TAIL GATE

1. Tail gate panel
2. Tail gate hinge
3. Shim
4. Stop
5. Latch
6. Link assembly
7. Cylinder lock
8. Handle
9. Damper
10. Window glass
11. Window weatherstrip
12. Window moulding
13. Gate opening weatherstrip

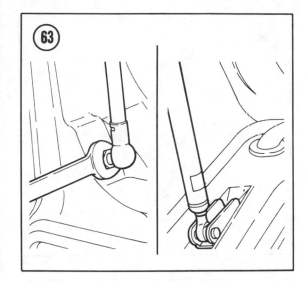

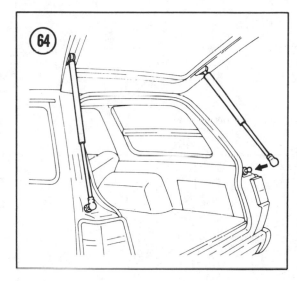

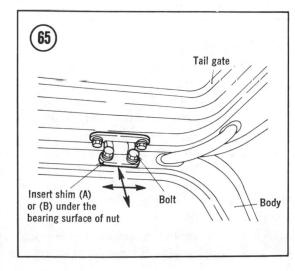

Tail gate

Insert shim (A)
or (B) under the
bearing surface of nut

Bolt

Body

5. Remove weatherstripping.

6. Installation is performed by reversing the preceding steps. In addition, check flange for deformation prior to installing the weatherstripping. Also, be sure that flange is clean.

Adjustment

To adjust the link operating pressure and glass-to-weatherstripping contact, increase or decrease the number of shims installed between the link and the quarter side trim upper (**Figure 61**).

TAIL GATE
(STATION WAGON)

Refer to **Figure 62** for the following procedure.

Tail Gate Assembly, Hinges and Stopper (Removal/Installation)

1. Remove head lining rear end clips and cargo light screws, then disconnect tailgate harness and washer nozzle.

2. Remove tailgate stop and hinges (**Figure 63**).

3. To install, reverse preceding steps, then grease or oil the hinges.

CAUTION
When installing tail gate stop assembly, connect it to the tail gate first, then to the ball-joints on the body. Great force is required to pull out the gas stop assembly from the ball-joint. To do so, disconnect ball stud from body (Figure 64).

WARNING
The tailgate stop is filled with high pressure gas. Do not disassemble the stop, or place it into a fire, or physical harm could result.

Adjustment

1. Adjust tailgate assembly position by loosening the retainer nuts on the body side (for vertical and horizontal positions). The longitudinal position can be adjusted by installing shim A or B (**Figure 65**) under the bearing surface of the retainer nut. Shim A is Colt part number MB020233, and is 1.2 in. (0.5 mm)

13

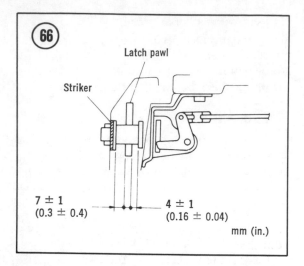

Striker
Latch pawl

7 ± 1
(0.3 ± 0.4)   4 ± 1
(0.16 ± 0.04)
mm (in.)

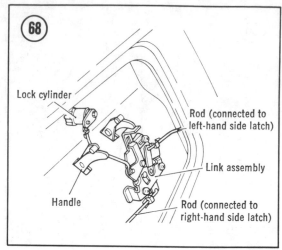

Lock cylinder
Rod (connected to left-hand side latch)
Link assembly
Handle
Rod (connected to right-hand side latch)

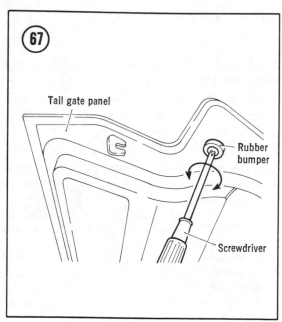

Tail gate panel
Rubber bumper
Screwdriver

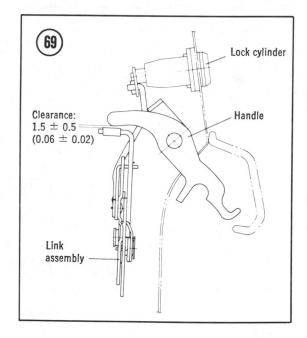

Lock cylinder
Clearance:
1.5 ± 0.5
(0.06 ± 0.02)
Handle
Link assembly

thick; Shim B is Colt part number MB020234, and is 2.3 in. (0.9 mm) thick.

2. Adjust latch-to-striker clearance with shims shown in **Figure 66**. Be sure that the clearances are the same on both the left-hand and right-hand sides.

3. To adjust the tailgate rubber bumper, turn the bumper bolt so that the body panel is flush with the tailgate panel (**Figure 67**).

Tailgate Lock (Removal/Installation)

1. Remove tailgate trim, then disconnect lock cylinder rod from key cylinder.

2. Pull off retainer and remove key cylinder.

3. Remove 2 rods connected to respective latches, then remove link assembly, tailgate handle, and right and left latches (**Figure 68**).

4. To install, reverse preceding steps, and apply grease to rotating and sliding parts of tailgate handle, link assembly, and latch.

5. Adjust tailgate handle-to-link assembly clearance to 0.6 ± 0.02 in. (1.5 ± 0.5 mm), as shown in **Figure 69**.

6. When installing link assembly, be sure that left-hand right-hand latches operate uniformly.

INDEX

14

NOTES

NOTES